T0336477

ADVANCED
Multi-Project Management
Achieving Outstanding Speed and Results with Predictability

Gerald I. Kendall, PMP
Kathleen M. Austin

ISBN-13: 978-1-60427-080-8

Printed and bound in the U.S.A. Printed on acid-free paper.

10 9 8 7 6 5 4 3 2 1

Library of Congress Cataloging-in-Publication Data

Kendall, Gerald I.
Advanced multi-project management : achieving outstanding speed and results with predictability / by Gerald I. Kendall and Kathleen M. Austin.
p. cm.
Includes bibliographical references and index.
ISBN 978-1-60427-080-8 (hbk. : alk. paper) 1. Project management. I. Austin, Kathleen M. II. Title.
HD69.P75K4577 2012
658.4′04—dc23
2012030918

Direct all inquiries to J. Ross Publishing, Inc., 300 S. Pine Island Rd., Suite 305, Plantation, FL 33324

Phone: (954) 727-9333
Fax: (561) 892-0700
Web: www.jrosspub.com

Table of Contents

Acknowledgments vii
Foreword xi
Preface xiii
Biography xvii
Web Added Value™ xix

PART I—WHY MULTI-PROJECT ENVIRONMENTS ARE SO MESSED UP 1
Chapter 1. Introduction—The Multi-Project Problem 3
Chapter 2. Resource Conflicts 17
Chapter 3. Poorly Defined Project Networks 25
Chapter 4. The Biggest Leverage Point for Improving 31

PART II—OVERVIEW OF THE PERMANENT MULTI-PROJECT SOLUTION 39
Chapter 5. Project Networks 41
Chapter 6. Strategic Buffering—Insulating Projects from Variability 49
Chapter 7. Controlled Project WIP—Aligning and Activating Multiple Projects 55
Chapter 8. Fast Execution, Single Priority System, Recovery 63
Chapter 9. Enterprise Resource Planning 73
Chapter 10. Multi-Project Software Requirements 81
Chapter 11. What Is It All Worth? 95

PART III—PROJECT PLANNING, NETWORKS, AND RISK AVOIDANCE 103
Chapter 12. Level of Detail—Not the Lowest Level 105
Chapter 13. Step 1: The Project's Measurable Goals, Tangible Scope, and Sponsor Criteria 111
Chapter 14. Step 2: The Backbone 119
Chapter 15. Step 3: The Skeleton 129

Chapter 16. Step 4: Additional Dependencies—First Risk Avoidance........ 137
Chapter 17. Step 5: Checking against Project Goals and Scope—Second Risk Avoidance........ 143
Chapter 18. Step 6: Resourcing........ 147
Chapter 19. Step 7: Expert Scrutiny—Third Risk Avoidance........ 155
Chapter 20. Step 8: Time Estimates—Fourth Risk Avoidance........ 159
Chapter 21. Step 9: Duration Reduction without Compromise........ 167
Chapter 22. Step 10: Final Project Risk Assessment—Fifth Risk Avoidance........ 175

PART IV—INSULATING PROJECTS FROM VARIABILITY 179
Chapter 23. Three Points of Network Insulation........ 181
Chapter 24. Operations versus Project Responsibility—Resource Insulation........ 191
Chapter 25. Project-to-Project Insulation........ 197
Chapter 26. Common Cause versus Special Cause Insulation........ 201

PART V—ALIGNING AND ACTIVATING MULTIPLE PROJECTS........ 205
Chapter 27. Setting Project Priorities........ 207
Chapter 28. Two Different Ways to Align Multiple Projects........ 211
Chapter 29. "What If" Analyses on Timelines and Resources........ 221
Chapter 30. Finalizing the Project Schedule and Activation........ 225

PART VI—MULTI-PROJECT EXECUTION 229
Chapter 31. Project Manager Execution Role........ 231
Chapter 32. Resource Manager Execution Role........ 243
Chapter 33. Senior Management Execution Role—Daily Fast-Track Meetings........ 253
Chapter 34. Senior Management Execution Role—Full-Kitting Projects........ 257
Chapter 35. Senior Management in Stage Gate—How to Avoid the Huge Damage........ 265
Chapter 36. Senior Management Execution Role—Portfolio Review Process........ 275

PART VII—ENTERPRISE PROJECT RESOURCE PLANNING 285
Chapter 37. Distinguishing between Temporary Bottlenecks and Need to Hire/Contract........ 287
Chapter 38. Supervisor and Management Loads........ 297

Chapter 39. Increasing Load on Operations from Project Completion......309
Chapter 40. Short-, Medium-, and Long-Term Challenges..........................317

PART VIII—MULTI-PROJECT SOFTWARE REQUIREMENTS............. 325
Chapter 41. Software Planning Requirements—Buffers, Global Resources, and Alignment..........327
Chapter 42. Software Execution Requirements—Buffer Penetration, Project, and Resource Trends..........337
Chapter 43. Role-Based Software Views..........347

PART IX—EXECUTIVE BUY-IN AND CONCLUSIONS.......................... 351
Chapter 44. Executive Buy-In and Simulations..........353
Chapter 45. Conclusions..........363

Appendix A: Strategy and Tactics Approach for Multi-Project Management..........367
Appendix B: Success Stories and Video References..........381
Appendix C: Sample Enterprise Resource Categories..........387
Appendix D: What about Agile?..........391
Appendix E: Complete Case Study on Project Planning..........395

Bibliography..........415
Index..........417

Acknowledgments

Since Steve Rollins and I wrote *Advanced Project Portfolio Management and the PMO* in 2002, I've had the chance to work with some great partners and fantastic clients. They pushed the envelope on how to systematically and permanently overcome the many problems of multi-project management and succeed. Without these experiences, this book would not exist.

So I thank, with all my heart, my clients who learned, endured, and implemented, with immense patience and excitement, the new multi-project practice. To Patrik Ernst, Managing Director, and Rudy Keller, Director of Rio Tinto Alesa; Pat Bennett, former CEO of Covad Communications and now President, CEO Strategies; Larry Dyck, President, and Stan Pauls, VP of Décor Cabinets; Shane Short, VP and General Manager, Royal Mouldings; Roger Cassell, President, Communications Electronics; and Lee Gopadze, President, Proxim Wireless—you were all willing to not only learn, but lead a radical change. You so deserve the success you have achieved.

There are five groups that I've partnered with over the past 20 years, who have all shared an incredible amount of practical, new knowledge:

- Realization Technologies recognized what a multi-project solution requires—much more than software, much more than web-based technology, and much more than a database. Sanjeev Gupta, CEO, is passionate about implementing a full solution, including processes, with focus to get results. Without Sanjeev and his fantastic people, many of the case studies and implementation processes would not exist today.
- Exepron—The collaborative project management solution. In particular, I single out John Thompson for his relentless pursuit to bring simplicity to project management. His effort to educate me on his fresh approach and his willingness to help with every request made the journey of creating this book easier.
- ProChain Solutions was my first partner, with new software and thinking brought to solve the problems of shipbuilding and repair. Rob Newbold, President, was instrumental in putting knowledge into the public do-

main through his books and bringing concepts to life through first-class training and implementations.

- Goldratt Consulting brought an integrated strategy and tactics in the format presented in this book to reality. The late Dr. Eli Goldratt invented and breathed life into many of the concepts presented.
- The Goldratt Institute has a well-developed framework, set of processes, and training to get results. For this, I'm indebted to Dee Jacob, Partner, and Suzan Bergland, President, North American Group.

To Denise Hart, CIO at Envision EMI, I am in debt for the detailed review of the book, comments provided, and insights into Agile. Everything you provided proved invaluable in adding clarity to the concepts.

This book would not have been possible without my talented coauthor, Kathy Austin. It is rare to work with someone who embodies the combination of fantastic work experience with writing skill. Kathy not only brings these attributes to this endeavor, but is prolific in her effort. Kathy—you are truly a pleasure to work with!

Drew Gierman, our beloved publisher, and all the folks at J. Ross Publishing have guided this effort from the beginning. Their support, flexibility, responsiveness, and professionalism are unparalleled with anyone else I've worked with in the publishing industry.

My wife, Jackie, who has partnered with me on so many implementations, probably has mixed feelings about my writing. She edits everything I write, and always has amazing insights in her responses. She challenges the clarity and conciseness. She makes sure that I don't exaggerate. I think she enjoys this work, but at the same time dreads the weekends and evenings lost to my obsession to get it down and get it out. Someday, maybe I'll get up the courage to ask her. In the meantime, thanks, Jackie!

Gerald I. Kendall, Smoky Mountains, Tennessee

I too have had the chance to work with some wonderful teachers, coaches, mentors, and colleagues; great partners; and fantastic clients. You all have caused me to use the Thinking Process tools to expand and break through the envelope on how to improve multi-project management, clarify and simplify the concepts, and quickly and easily implement to achieve order-of-magnitude results. Without these experiences, this book would not exist.

So I thank, first of all, Heavenly Father, from whom all good comes.

Thank you to my teachers, coaches, mentors, and colleagues on this journey: Eli Goldratt, Bill McClelland, Bruce Watson, Gordon Whitehead, Dee Jacob, Ted Hutchin, Oded Cohen, Jim Cox, Alan Leader, John Zahora, Suzan Bergland, Hugh Cole, Dale Houle, Eli Schragenheim, Alex Meshar, Vaughn Johnson, and Antoine van Gelder.

I've had the opportunity to work with great partner organizations whose dedicated people made me think outside the box to cross our communication and sometimes conceptual chasms. I've learned so much from all of you, but especially Sridhar and Ajai Kapoor at Realization; Carl Erickson and Patrick Bacon at Atomic Object; John Thompson, Danny Walsh, and Avraham Mordoch at Exepron; Mike Lawrence at Sciforma; and Rob Newbold and Dick Moore at ProChain.

Our clients—out there on the battlefront every day (literally and figuratively) Larry Dyck, Gary Mallaley, Jerry Guest, Joe Dale, Carl Dane, Mishawn Leadingham, John Leslie, Kirk Maples, Tony Hauser, Marty Payne, Jeff Madore, Ed Ludwig, and Mark Short—giving them the tools to achieve more success, even more quickly *is* the point!

I am so honored to be asked to coauthor this book with Gerry Kendall. His quiet competence, broad experience, and ability to distill even the most complex ideas down to their inherent simplicity made him a joy to learn from and work with. I can't count the number of times we had "just a philosophical question" for each other that always broke through the obstacles we were experiencing at the time. You always made everything I wrote better. Plus, this was just fun! Thank you.

My husband, Dick Peschke—thanks for all your help, support, encouragement, and just plain putting up with me! Other than these, I don't have words enough for all you've given me. For all you do, for all you are, for time and eternity.

Kathleen M. Austin, Wagner Lakes, Nebraska

Foreword

Have you ever felt as if most project portfolio management (PPM) advice just adds work and slows you down? *That's probably because it does.*

One of the most popular sayings in the world of PMOs is "project management is about doing things right. Portfolio management is about doing the right things." There is a bright line drawn between the two subjects that separates them and the roles that people play in each process. An individual who manages projects has very little to do with the projects that are selected. Someone who manages portfolios is viewed as a godlike gatekeeper who never soils their hands with the actual work.

With that same industry mindset, books on PPM often focus tightly on project selection, which is only a small part of the job. Most of those types of books guide you through ways that you can use PPM tools to define, report progress on, and prioritize projects. They don't even begin to help with getting things done effectively. It's simply assumed that getting things done is "project management," which feels like another discipline altogether.

This book is different. It's about making big things happen at your organization at the portfolio level. It gets you engaged in what is really going on at the project level in ways that make sense for you and every stakeholder you touch. It does that by giving you some fairly simple rules to follow that streamline your PMO work and give you more time to focus on what matters. It helps you break your efforts down into a simple process and shed all of the dead weight that's holding you back.

Think about the hidden challenges you face every day:

- Below the "which projects are we doing" decisions, you have conflicting resource priorities that slow down work across the board. *These seem beyond our control, but they're not.*
- Complex project planning approaches that add overhead and promote conflict. *The process offered by this book can help change that.*
- Team members are constantly juggling their "real jobs" with project tasks, multitasking their way to lower productivity. *This is having a greater impact than you think, but can be easily fixed.*

- "Flavor of the month" new projects are forever being added, as standing efforts face stiffer headwinds. *This can be managed in fairly simple ways, as you will see when you read on.*
- Project problems are identified too late to really do much about them. *Efficiently staying on top of projects on a daily basis can help a lot here.*

Kendall and Austin have done a tremendous amount of research and ultimately uncovered simple solutions that the rest of us might have come to intuitively, but never really had a solid approach to making it happen. Anyone can say, "If your project management process is too complex, simplify it," or "If you have too many decision makers addressing resource issues, designate one person to make those decisions." But at the end of the day, how do you do it? Most of us would give each problem some thought, then view any solutions that we come up with as impossible or impractical. The authors guide you through making each seemingly impossible change happen—revolutionizing your PPM efforts in a matter of months.

Reading this book got me excited from a career perspective. I picture many friends and colleagues introducing bold new approaches to managing multiple projects within their organizations and becoming true change agents, recognized as leaders who make a difference. My hope is that this book will have that kind of impact on you, so you can "be the change" in ways that may have seemed out of reach before.

Dave Garrett, CEO, projectmanagement.com (formerly gantthead.com)

Preface

This book will show you how to complete your projects at least 25% faster, without sacrificing scope or budget. Dozens of organizations that implemented the approach succeeded in doing exactly that (see Appendix B). But that is not all. They were able to increase the number of projects executed with the same resources by 70%, and in the process generated over 50% more throughput for their organizations. They represent some of the biggest, well-known names in the world—Boeing, Rio Tinto, ABB, Chrysler—organizations with dozens or hundreds of projects. The list also includes some very small organizations that were struggling to get a few projects completed per year.

These organizations are atypical. In our opinion, most multi-project management systems today behave like the U.S. air travel system—unpredictable at best, often taking much longer than planned with unpleasant surprises. Managers often point the finger at not having enough resources, or at *Murphy*—variation that they encountered. We can tell you definitively that looking to solve the multi-project challenges by getting more resources does not work. And the organizations mentioned above that succeeded beyond their wildest dreams haven't found a way to lock *Murphy* in the basement. Elimination of project variability is not a magic wand; managing variability differently is the key to success.

Six multi-project gears must be perfectly meshed to drive speed with predictability. If you only address one of the six, the organization will have invested time and money yet will still be grinding away in the world of grim statistics, with more than 50% of all projects delivering late, over budget, or not within scope. If you have five of the six gears synchronized well but ignore one, our last 15 years of experience screams that you will be leaving a major portion of the benefits on the table. The six gears provide:

1. Staggering of projects according to an organization's project capacity
2. Resource-based project networks that meet the organization's goals
3. Strategic buffers used to managing project *Murphy* or variation
4. A single priority system in execution
5. Fast, daily execution management
6. A consistent project recovery process

When just these *few* multi-project practices are changed, it is easy to quickly get results. Unfortunately, many people look to *sophisticated* estimating and accountability techniques as the Holy Grail. Project management maturity models, stage gate processes, and PMBOK best practices are imposed upon teams like the laws about drinking age are imposed on college students and have about the same effect—some marginal results, but the major problems persist. The current practice resembles fixing a broken toilet on the Titanic. What is counterintuitive is that the toilet is broken and really needs to be fixed. But there are much bigger problems that are not getting the proper management attention. Over the past 20 years, these approaches have not delivered the needed impact to achieve all projects on time, within budget and scope, simply because they address symptoms of problems and NOT underlying root causes.

Some techniques, such as capability maturity models and stage gate approaches, are valuable concepts. Yet they often encumber rather than facilitate project results through much too much bureaucracy. These complex processes are burdened with excessive data capture, reporting, and meetings. In our opinion, they are leading many organizations down the wrong road. The mountains of data and reports mask how little an organization often knows about its projects and whether or not they will yield the desired results.

Current popular practices leave multi-project organizations with horrible conflicts, which in turn create mistrust. For example:

- *Conflict 1:* Senior management is pressuring to activate a new project now, one that could mean big payoffs for the organization. But the program managers are already overwhelmed with project work, issues, and fights over resources, so they are pushing back on initiating anything new.
- *Conflict 2:* When people who manage project tasks do reviews only once a week, there is a disaster waiting to happen. It often takes a trend for managers to realize that a task has gone astray. This means that weeks can pass before anyone realizes there is a problem. If this happens on just a few critical tasks, the project *will* be late with almost no chance of recovery. However, even when project managers suspect there is a problem, they don't want to be accused of micromanaging, so they often find themselves in a conflict—call now for help or wait until the disaster is proven!

How should these types of conflicts be addressed? Project managers are tasked to deliver projects chosen by others with resources they do not totally control—resources who are stretched. They are frequently given aggressive deadlines, which senior leadership urgently needs in order to reach company goals. And they are given a scope that is typically not fully understood or bought into by all key stakeholders.

As if those obstacles aren't enough, a further major challenge comes from the fact that some critical resources, which are needed to successfully execute a project, are not even modeled in most project plans. For example, senior managers may be needed for decisions or a stage gate review. Other resources needed to support project tasks are used ad hoc (legal counsel, IT specialists, graphic arts, and sales support). It may be for a few minutes or an hour. Modeling such a task in a project is a waste of time. Yet, such people can hold up a project for days or weeks while team members wait for their availability or decisions.

When the help of these supporting resources is not available immediately, those people responsible for the task often make the decision to proceed with the task. And what happens? The overall design engineer makes a decision that results in specification changes, and some or many tasks must be reworked. The IT group finds ugly surprises in a vendor's promises, and scope must be scaled back. The legal counsel puts a roadblock in front of a risky approach, and scope is increased.

Within these challenges, we have implemented an approach that has dramatically altered the way that organizations plan and execute in a multi-project environment. Over the past 20 years, Gerry has worked with four other organizations, which have covered well over 200 such implementations, each time adding knowledge and process to increase the probability of success—success which is well documented in the public domain.[1] Kathy's implementation experience working with one of these partners over the past 20 years has proven that our approach works in every imaginable environment. Each partner that we have worked with had pieces of the puzzle, but they were still not happy.

If your car runs out of gas (or battery power) or has a flat tire, it will not get you to your desired destination, despite all the parts, electronics, and technology that work perfectly. Similarly, the powerful multi-project solutions we partnered on were missing key pieces. They were still wildly successful—beyond the norm, and the credit goes to those implementers who persisted and drove it. Sometimes the missing pieces were discovered after the fact. Sometimes they were found and driven by the individual implementing. Sometimes they were not recognized and the implementations left money on the table. Sometimes the implementers became too sophisticated and turned off prospective clients with their complexity.

The problem over the past 10 years is that so much of the *knowledge* needed to successfully implement a predictable, viable, sustainable multi-project solution did not exist in the public domain. Today, with this book, that has changed.

But do not rush to implement the solution yet unless you enjoy banging your head against a wall!

To succeed at change, you must have the full understanding of the problem before you start to implement. You must have a darn good reason to change what you are doing. That requires a very aggressive goal. You must have full buy-in to the strategy and the tactics needed to achieve that goal. All of this is covered in Part I of the text. You also need a comprehensive road map, which you will find in Appendix A.

Part II overviews the six major interdependent subsystems within any multi-project environment. They must be aligned to achieve success. Each of these subsystems is described in detail in Parts III through VIII.

If you are wondering where human behavior fits into all of this, we have included it within Part II, Chapter 8, and throughout Part VI on execution. The solution will not work without changes in behavior, from senior management through resource supervisors and project managers.

There is one question that we deal with in every encounter worldwide: "How do we get the executives to buy into this?" This topic is addressed in Part IX. We will not be so arrogant as to claim the solution will work simply based on its brilliance. Executive buy in is essential. In our combined 70+ years of experience, we've learned that failure to get executive buy in prevents the solution from being sustained. This section suggests two short simulations to enable executives to understand their role in driving multi-project results through less project work in process. This is a major paradigm shift—the simulations help them understand why "the sooner we start a project, the sooner it will finish" is not valid. Combined with the question addressed in Chapter 11, "What is it all worth?" Part IX provides a way to bring executives to be part of the solution and no longer remain part of the problem.

In our journey, we have been asked about *Agile* as a method for driving better project results. We believe there are vast differences in the approaches, with Agile originally designed for software development projects and our process generic to all types of projects. We have included a brief overview, provided by a CIO, in Appendix D.

For anyone who is willing to share their insights and feedback, we welcome it. Gerry's e-mail address is gerryikendall@tocinternational.com and Kathy's is kaustin@aptconcepts.com.

Endnote

1. See www.realization.com, www.goldratt.com, and www.toc-goldratt.com for examples of public domain success stories.

Biography

Gerald I. Kendall, PMP, Principal, TOC International, is a recognized world expert at implementing strategic planning, project portfolio management, and Theory of Constraints (TOC). His clients span the globe, including engagements in Malaysia, Bangladesh, Australia, Europe, the United States, and Canada. Clients include SAP, Telstra, Adidas, British American Tobacco, Alcan Aluminum, Rio Tinto, and Lockheed Martin, with a wide variety of small company clients. He has implemented solutions for manufacturing, distribution, projects, marketing, sales, people management, and strategy and tactics.

Gerald began his career with IBM as a systems engineer and became an IT Director. After expanding into international sales and marketing, with global executive responsibility, he broadened his experience in strategic planning, supply chain, and operations.

Gerald is the author of four books, including the top-selling book in the PMO and project portfolio management space, *Advanced Project Portfolio Management and the PMO*. His first book, *Securing the Future*, continues to be in demand in its 13th year of publication.

Gerald is a graduate and Silver Medal winner of McGill University. He can be contacted by e-mail at gerryikendall@tocinternational.com or at www.tocinternational.com.

Kathleen M. Austin, Principal, APT Concepts, is globally recognized for her work in TOC implementations, development, and facilitation. Her U.S. and international clients include both military and commercial, ranging from the shop floor to the boardroom.

Kathleen served over 12 years in the U.S. Air Force as an acquisition project manager and manufacturing manager for radar, missile, and aircraft programs. She has spent the last 20+ years working in TOC and integrated TOC Lean Six Sigma (TOC-LSS) implementations, instruction, development, coaching, and mentoring in the following areas: project/portfolio management, supply chain management, strategic planning, thinking processes, and management skills/organizational alignment. Most recently she has been applying these skills in software development.

Kathleen has a Master's Degree in Logistics Management from the Air Force Institute of Technology and a BSBA from the University of Nebraska at Omaha. She can be contacted by e-mail at kaustin@aptconcepts.com.

This book has free material available for download from the Web Added Value™ resource center at *www.jrosspub.com*

At J. Ross Publishing we are committed to providing today's professional with practical, hands-on tools that enhance the learning experience and give readers an opportunity to apply what they have learned. That is why we offer free ancillary materials available for download on this book and all participating Web Added Value™ publications. These online resources may include interactive versions of material that appears in the book or supplemental templates, worksheets, models, plans, case studies, proposals, spreadsheets and assessment tools, among other things. Whenever you see the WAV™ symbol in any of our publications, it means bonus materials accompany the book and are available from the Web Added Value Download Resource Center at www.jrosspub.com.

Downloads for *Advanced Multi-Project Management* include:

- An average improvement pdf: This file shows the improvement 59 organizations reported in reducing project duration, increasing the number of projects completed per year, and increased throughput following the approach described in the book.
- A critical path versus critical chain white paper: This article, written by Gerald Kendall, describes the differences between the traditional critical path methodology and the critical chain methodology.
- Multi-project management strategy and tactics: This file provides the complete strategy and tactics shown in Appendix A of the book. It has instructions that show a user how to navigate between the road map and the individual components of the strategy and tactics.
- A multitasking exercise: This document describes a simple exercise in multitasking that can be performed with colored sheets of paper and a stopwatch. It is easy to use with a group and demonstrates the effect of multitasking on time required to do a task and the impact on quality.
- A multi-project management multitasking bead game: These slides detail a game that demonstrates the effects of multitasking on project duration and is very effective with multiple teams doing the exercise.

- A multi-project flow simulation with a Mancala board: These slides are used to illustrate the effect of activating many versus a few, select projects. The simulation measures how many projects finish in a year and how much money is generated from these projects.

PART I

WHY MULTI-PROJECT ENVIRONMENTS ARE SO MESSED UP

There are many symptoms of problems: late projects, fights over resources, multitasking between project and operational responsibilities, scope changes, etc. There are thousands of books on project management, and even some really, really good ones. So why are project results still so unpredictable worldwide? Part I builds an understanding of the single, common root problem of all multi-project environments that continues to be ignored. Understanding the problem is halfway toward solving it. By the end of Part I, you will be ready to capitalize on the leverage points within multi-project management. Fortunately, there are only a few to master.

1. Introduction—The Multi-Project Problem

The Dilemma

For the first time in his long, successful career, Joe Turano felt like he was losing control. As director of European supply chain, he was next in line to take over from his boss as president–Europe for a major apparel company. Last month, Joe's boss, Kevin Vaughan, told him that the company's board of directors had approved a merger with a much larger company. Joe would have a new boss within a couple of months. But equally challenging, within six months, their supply chain would have to be fully integrated with the other company's logistics, IT, and financial/ERP systems. This was an urgent project, necessary to show the stock analysts how successful the new company was. Failure to do so would put Joe's position in jeopardy.

Joe's stomach lurched as he heard Kevin's voice call him from the corner office.

"Joe, where is that update you promised me on the status of the merger project? You know there's a board meeting next week and they're going to want to know that the project is back on track."

"Yes, I know, Kevin. I'll get it to you this afternoon. It's just that I've been dealing with the truckers' strike in France and trying to fend off retail's demands for more marketing programs."

"Joe, don't lose your focus. Hey, how are those extra people I got you from engineering doing? They must be making a significant difference for you by now."

"Um, sure," Joe said, but the truth was written on his face. Adding resources had not paid off as he had hoped.

Joe already had dozens of major improvement projects on the go, including finding 15 new Chinese, Vietnamese, and South Korean suppliers; fixing shortages within their distribution and retail channels; opening two new distribution centers; improving the forecasting system accuracy; and providing better

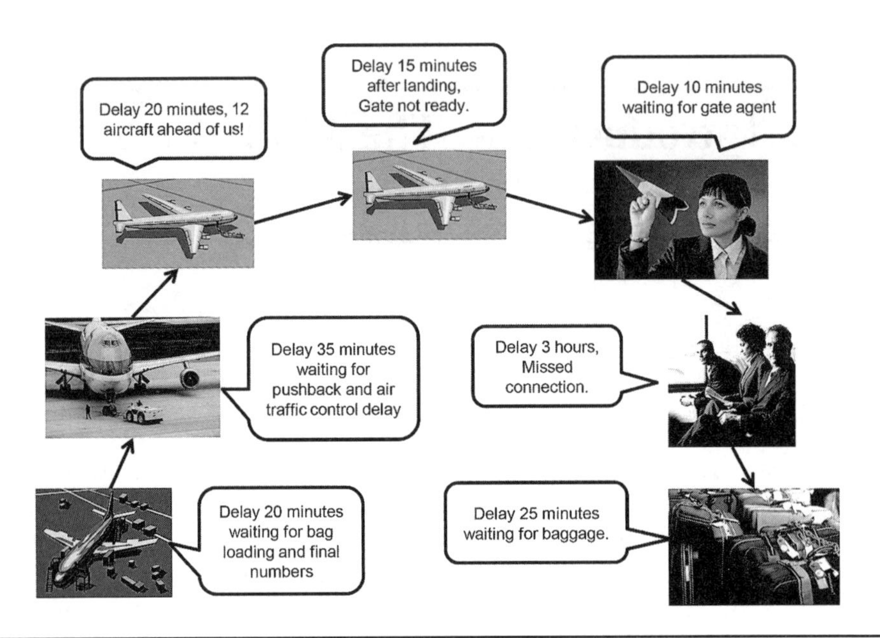

Figure 1.1 Today's multi-project performance is like the airlines—perfect mis-synchronization

information for sales and marketing. Even without those projects, his people were busy enough dealing with day-to-day operational challenges. In addition to the truckers' strike in France, his team had to overcome supplier schedules missed, new product introductions—the list went on and on.

Their most critical resources were already spread too thin between these existing projects and operational responsibilities. It was an enlightening example of misalignment between projects and resources (see Figure 1.1). How on earth was Joe going to find the time for himself and his people to integrate with another company?

Joe's dilemma is generic to every company in the world that has to manage multiple projects:

Assign resources to start urgent new projects now
OR
Keep resources only on existing projects

In the past, Joe's direct reports had often pushed back whenever Joe initiated a major new project. He had heard so often, "We can't do it—we need more resources—we don't have time." Sometimes he would back off, but mostly he pushed his people hard and it seemed to work. All of his key initiatives moved much too slowly, from his perspective, but at least there was progress. He left late many evenings, but was rarely the last person to leave the office. Occasionally, he wondered if there was too much on everyone's plate. Even he had trouble keeping track of dozens of major projects. Sometimes, he would get a resignation with the feedback that "this just isn't a fun place to work anymore."

But what could Joe do? He needed those projects to succeed in order to meet his annual goals. And now, he also needed to integrate with the newly acquired company at the peril of losing his job or, worse, keeping his job and stagnating for years. His people would just have to work harder over the next six months. If they couldn't do it, he would find others who would.

Why Can't We Get More Done with Existing Resources?

As Joe began to think about his available choices, he found none of them satisfactory. If he delayed new projects and tried to free up resources as they came off existing projects, he believed he would kill his chance of meeting the company's quarterly and annual goals. Plus, from past experience, he knew that the integration with the new company would be painful and require a lot of time from his best people.

A second choice was to freeze some existing work. Again, his assumption was that would hurt his company goals. In the past, whenever he went to the president with any hint of freezing initiatives, his boss exploded. "If we can't get ALL of these projects completed successfully," his boss exclaimed, "I'll end up missing year end targets. My job and yours will be down the drain!" he shouted.

Joe thought about hiring subcontractors, but by the time they would be available and brought up to speed, it would have about the same effect as the other choices or worse—it could drain his best people in supporting the contractors. In the short run, he would have to explain the added operating expense without the results to show for it. And he wasn't sure about the longer run—so often, subcontractors couldn't deliver the results, couldn't take the pressure, and often left just when they were turning productive, putting more pressure on his most experienced people to carry the dual load of doing the work and training new subcontractors.

Another choice was to simply add the new project to the existing load and let his people figure out a way to cope with it. Deep within his brain and his heart, he feared this one the most. His best people were already upset about what from their perspective was the constant overcommitting. From their perspective, this caused extensive overtime. Their overtime frustration was compounded by scope changes, rework, and missed deadlines, all blamed on the resources who were working the hardest. Several of his best people had told him that their families would not tolerate the extensive overtime much longer. No, there had to be a better way.

The Criteria for an Answer

If there was a possible way out of all of the daily conflicts that could be a win for everyone, it would have to meet some tough criteria. The solution must:

1. Get *more* project work done with the *same resources*, with *less overtime*
2. Get all projects completing *faster*
3. Make projects much more *predictable* in his world of constant surprises
4. Be *simple* (i.e., easy for his team to understand) and *fast to implement*

Joe had tried too many times over the past five years to solve these problems. One of his program managers had strongly recommended new multi-project software. Accepting this recommendation, Joe worked with IT for a full nine months to evaluate different multi-project software solutions, negotiate with a vendor, implement the new software, convert existing data, and train all project, program, and resource managers. The multi-project server approach made it easier to share project data between project and resource managers over the web, but didn't fundamentally change how the project tasks were managed. They squeezed about a 3% improvement in project execution out of that multimillion dollar effort—barely enough to make a dent in the problem and pay for the software and implementation costs despite IT's near perfect effort.

He tried increasing head count. His company had almost double the number of project managers as two years ago, which seemed to cause all projects to slow down. These additional project managers created a much higher demand for other resources. They were now hitting time-consuming bottlenecks because of holdups with legal counsel, users unable to absorb the change quickly enough, and demand on IT, administration staff, and other resources not even taken into account when the projects were planned. All of this increased exponentially over the past two years and held up project tasks for long durations. Sometimes it was an executive decision that delayed things. Sometimes it was a supplier delivering late. Sometimes it was a stage gate review.

In fact, Joe had also implemented complicated initiatives such as project management maturity models and certification programs for project managers. He had spent a lot of money on training project and resource managers, with minimal or no tangible impact on project durations. Projects were completing just over 50% on time, on budget, and within scope, which Joe was told was above average. Big deal!

Six Elements of a Solution

It would be incredible if Joe had been able to invent the full answer to these challenges within a few days, or even weeks. As it turned out, it took Joe a full year to put together the common pieces that at least correlated to high success. He researched the web, listened to over 50 videos presented by organizations that got major improvements in project management (see Appendix B), read 10 profound books (see Bibliography), attended conferences, and spoke with project management solution providers who focused on results rather than just process or software. He discovered that the answer had evolved over the prior 15 years. Joe noted that every organization which had documented tangible results had six common elements. These elements had to work in concert to meet all of the solution criteria he had previously identified, and so he pictured them like gears perfectly meshed (see Figure 1.2):

- *Gear to mesh the amount of project work in process.* When a system is so clogged with work that almost every task is waiting, drastic action is required to get fast results. In this case, the drastic action is to cut the amount of active project work significantly (e.g., often by 50%) and then

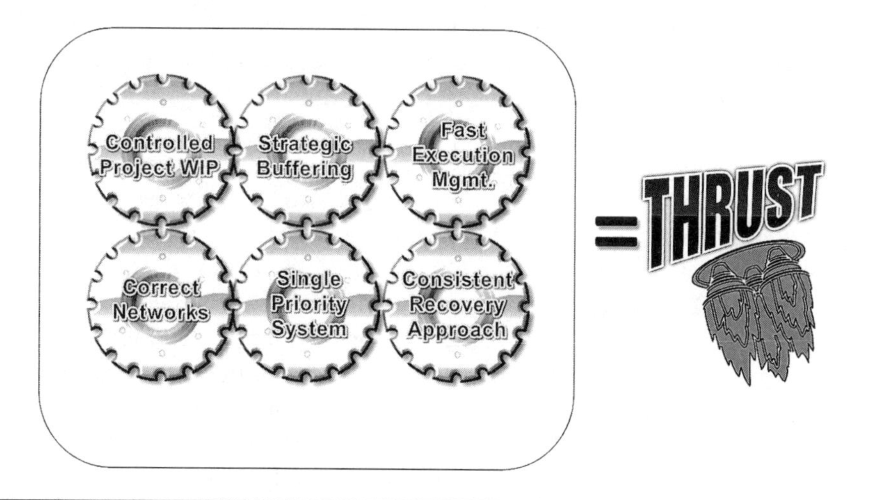

Figure 1.2 Six gears of multi-project management

stagger projects to match organization capacity: When a system behaves like our air transportation approach, it takes more than a few canceled flights to permanently remove the problem of overloading. Joe reasoned that he could have 30 active projects completing within the next year, with a 50% track record of on time, if he kept doing the same thing. However, by reducing the number of active projects in half, to 15, he knew he could meet one of his criteria to get more work done with the same resources and his second criterion of getting the work done faster. What Joe discovered was that his organization did not need to kill any of the remaining 15 projects. It only had to freeze them, and then all 30 projects would get done faster. To get the results, it also did not matter to the system which 15 started out as the active ones and which were frozen (he knew that choosing the projects to freeze would be done easily by using his company's overall project prioritization system). By controlling project work in progress (WIP), and getting about the same results as the 50 companies he researched, he projected that he could complete 10 projects per quarter, or 40 projects per year, with close to 100% on time, on budget, and within scope. New projects were not allowed to start until existing project phases finished, an approach referred to as *staggering* projects.

- *Gear meshing correct, resource-based, project plans or networks.*[1] Typically, most of an organization's project plans are sitting in someone's desk drawer gathering dust during execution. After his study, Joe realized why so many project plans are abandoned. He saw that several mistakes in networks drove poor project results:

    1. The use of resources is so poorly modeled in networks that it is doomed to cause projects to fail in execution. Project tasks are often held up waiting for a resource to finish work on another part of the project, not just waiting for a prior task to complete. For example, the electrical crew who is laying the cable on one floor of a building is the same crew installing and testing wireless devices on another floor of the same building. Since this crew has specialized skills, they are not interchangeable with general electrical contractors. Yet traditional project plans modeled using the critical path do not show these types of resource dependencies. Resources must be modeled by skill sets, and then the project network must show the critical path which also takes resource skill dependencies into account (this is referred to as the *critical chain* of a project).
    2. A second problem is that it is hard to define work that you haven't done before when you try to go into too much detail. It is impossible to predict every variation that a project task might run into.

When project managers try to define tasks at too great a level of detail, the plans require a lot of front-end effort and quickly become obsolete during execution.

3. A third major deficiency is the disconnect between the project network, the stakeholder needs, and the goals of the organization. When networks are complex and too detailed, stakeholders often do not review them to validate that accomplishing that project network will actually meet their goals. No wonder that major scope creep occurs, especially in the last third of a project.

Joe realized that when a team follows a simple, 10-step process and multiple people rigorously scrutinize the plan and the scope, many missing elements and mistakes in logic and resource dependencies are found and corrected before starting work. Meshing this network gear is 100% necessary to make projects more predictable.

- *Gear to buffer projects strategically.* Just like a car uses shock absorbers in strategic places, because roads are never perfect, so must projects use buffers in the right places to absorb variation in project task work as the project executes. Many tasks do not execute exactly as planned. One key for Joe's criteria of predictability is to have the right kind and strength of shock absorber (called a *buffer* throughout this book). The second key is to learn how to use task estimates and buffers during execution. He could see from the client presentations that buffers give an early warning to project managers when they are being consumed so quickly that they are in danger of running out before the end of the project.
- *Gear facilitating a single priority system.* Joe's organization, before implementing the change, was complex. He found at least four active priority systems in place:

1. The project manager's; whichever project manager screamed the loudest got the resources, regardless of whether their project was in trouble or not.
2. The resource manager's; based on their judgment of which task best suited a resource. This often did not match other people's perceptions of which task needed priority.
3. Joe's; as the senior executive responsible for all projects in his division.
4. Joe's boss; depending on which of his goals was jeopardized in the current quarter.

This resulted in constantly changing priorities and frequent reassignment of resources, even when they were in the middle of a task. The single priority system meets the need for a solution to be easy for the team to understand. When assigning tasks, priority must be given to those projects most in danger of finishing late. Acceptance of such a logical priority system by project and program managers, resource managers, and executives means that resources are not shifted by who is screaming the loudest.

- *Gear driving fast execution management.* Joe realized that in many of the 50 videos he listened to, executives talk about moving from lengthy weekly and biweekly reviews to quick daily reviews on all projects. The difference in the time it takes to discover issues and the speed of recovery has a major impact on the speed of project execution and mitigating risk. Many organizations complemented this with rapid recognition and response to blocking issues. Problems that used to wait a week or two to even be recognized, and then took days or weeks to resolve, were now recognized and dealt with within 24 hours. For sure, Joe understood that this is essential in order to get projects completing faster.
- *Gear driving a consistent, timely project recovery approach.* When the signal is given that a project is in danger, project and resource managers must know how they can work together in case recovery is needed. If options are not identified in advance, the typical approach is to escalate, which can result in overreaction and chaos. The organization must have sufficient capacity and skills to recover from typical project variation without calling 9-1-1. Joe realized that this engine makes it easier for the team and, by proactively dealing with danger, helps projects complete faster.

Experience over 15 years shows that these six engines can be implemented within three months, resulting in an average 22% reduction in project durations, and an increase of 33% in projects completed per year.

Joe's Big Question: How Could So Much Project Capacity Have Been Hidden?

After three months, Joe's organization was completing more project work faster than ever before, with no increase in resources and with much less overtime. What on earth had everyone been doing before the change? As Joe reflected, he realized that there were a few major differences in how work was done:

- Before, project work was not strategically insulated from uncertainty. As a result, a lot of the project and resource managers' time was spent in meetings fighting over priorities and robbing one project to help another. Now, strategically placed and monitored buffers, combined with new execution practices (see below) prevent fires and endless meetings. Buffers account for one third of a project's total duration, yet insulate projects and get them completed 25% faster than before. This required other changes in how tasks were estimated, which is detailed in Part III of this book. See Figure 1.3 for an example.

- Before, some people had spent a lot of time shifting often between tasks. Some of the time permanently lost was in the mental adjustment necessary when moving from one task to another. Some of the time was lost when a resource dropped task #1 to work on task #2 for a week, which meant task #1 and all tasks following that one on the project waited a week. Now, resources rarely multitask because a project resource is only allowed to be assigned to one task at a time. It seems totally counterintuitive—the less work assigned at a time, the more work gets done and the faster it gets done. This is true even when a person doing the task has to wait occasionally for some needed answers or input.
- Before, projects were activated without consideration to existing workload. Now, a new project is only activated when another finishes or when a phase of another finishes.
- Before, there was no single individual responsible for escalating issues and getting answers. Now, one executive, a member of the senior management team, spends 15 minutes each day fast-tracking issues through to resolution, preferably the same day. These meetings do not start out as 15-minute sessions. Initially, all participants go through resolving some crises that have built up for many projects over time. However, within

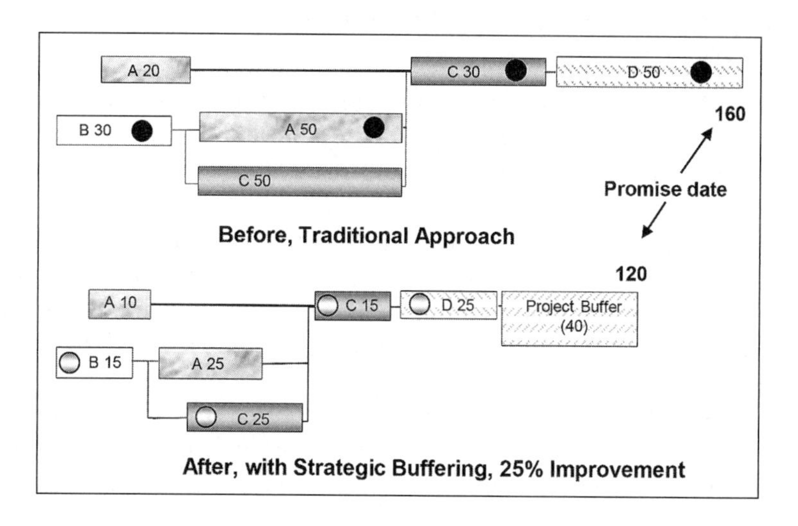

Figure 1.3 Strategic buffering

the first one to two months, as the new system works better and better, and behaviors are changed, a lot of issues are resolved, and this becomes a 15-minute meeting.

- Before, people assigned to project tasks also had operational responsibilities and frequent interruptions from work on prior projects. Now, for the most part, when any resource has project tasks assigned, other responsibilities are either delegated elsewhere or the interruptions are minimized. Real-life examples are provided in later sections of this book.
- Before, there was much more rework and unnecessary extra work on projects. Now, tasks are better prepared before handoff. Once tasks are handed off, the daily reviews catch mistakes or misinterpretations within one or two days, rather than weeks of wasted effort.
- Before, each project manager drew on their own experience to define the project plan and network of tasks to be accomplished, using whatever format with which they felt comfortable. Now, all project managers constructed a PERT (Program Evaluation Review Technique) network, using exactly the same process. Resources are always modeled correctly because all projects use a single, organizational, resource definition. Every task in a project is connected to stakeholder needs. The plan is reviewed to ensure that all stakeholder needs are met. Since this approach is done with a simple yet rigorous 10-step process, and not a magic wand, it leaves much less to discover during execution.
- Before, key phases of a project began without ensuring that all necessary, finalized decisions and material input were ready. With a new *full kit* process in place, projects were rarely delayed and rework was largely unnecessary.

So there it is—the answer in a few easy steps. But if that's all there is to it, why do some organizations fail in the implementation, whereas others take a year or longer to implement? The answer, from 20 years of experience, is that the current paradigms—the beliefs and the ways of planning and executing projects—are deeply embedded in organizations. Some of the performance measures that drive the behavior of project resources are simply wrong and must be changed. However, without deep understanding of why these metrics drive poor results, some team members may think the changes required are crazy. If this happens, they will ignore some of the golden nuggets.

This book provides the step-by-step approach for dramatically improving your multi-project performance. By concentrating on one step at a time, you have a rigorous, tested road map for change. Read this book from beginning to end. It will save you a lot of pain and rework.

Part I of this book briefly explains the underlying *root* problems of current multi-project environments. We can summarize all that we have said into three underlying root problems:

1. Project plans incorrectly account for variation (with poorly defined networks and without correct buffers).
2. Too much project work is active in execution (beyond the organization's capacity to flow it quickly).
3. Project tasks suffer poor execution (through excessive multitasking, conflicting priorities, and long wait times to resolve issues).

In Part II of this text, you will find a comprehensive overview of the entire solution.

Part III dives deeply into project networks and shares a 10-step process for building a plan that can be used throughout execution.

Part IV tells you how to plan buffers that will insulate your project from variability.

Part V shows you the two simple methods of synchronizing projects. You only need to choose one of these methods, and how to make that choice is described in detail.

Part VI explains the new metrics you will use during project execution and the other fail-safe mechanisms for ensuring better than 98% due date performance with faster execution than before.

Part VII shows the new approach to managing multi-project resources.

Part VIII discusses software. Yes, you do need software. The good news is, relative to the benefits obtained within the first year of implementation, any software expenses are typically recovered within weeks or months.

Part IX discusses the key that unlocks the door to success—executive buy-in.

The book also provides five valuable appendices. Appendix A contains the step-by-step comprehensive strategy and tactics *tree*, a PowerPoint road map document that you will use every day during your implementation. It not only tells you what to do; it provides the measurable result of each step and the assumptions behind the steps and results. Before this kind of format was available, the failure rate was much higher and the implementations took much longer.

Appendix B contains references to videos and the stories behind them.

Appendix C contains examples of how resource pools are defined in different types of organizations.

Appendix D provides a brief overview of the differences between Agile and our approach.

Appendix E contains a detailed case study on project planning and network building for use by professors, instructors, and readers who want to practice Part III of the text.

Conclusions

Many companies have tried to fix the problems of multi-project management by hiring more resources or getting better project managers. This approach often works for a short time, but rarely achieves sustained results, because this deals with the symptoms of the problem and does not recognize the real issues blocking project flow: poor project plans, too much active project work in execution, and poor task execution. The overemphasis on capability maturity models, stage gate processes, project management certifications, and other complicated efforts has not had the desired impact on performance, according to feedback we continuously receive worldwide.

The answer lies in successfully implementing a few key changes:

- Use a formal process for building project networks, tied closely to stakeholder needs.
- Buffer projects strategically to absorb unexpected delays.
- Activate a new project only when another project or phase finishes.
- Assign only one task to an individual at a time to eliminate multitasking.
- Remove other responsibilities, including operational responsibilities, from people doing project work.
- Review task progress daily.
- Implement a daily process, run by a senior executive, for fast-track issue resolution, to eliminate waiting for answers, materials, etc.

If you have lost patience with all of the jargon in traditional project management approaches and need results quickly, we believe you will be happy with the road map provided in this text.

Endnote

1. When referring to project plans or *networks*, we mean any of the many, diverse ways that people view the work that needs to be completed in order to claim that a project is finished. Some organizations use PERT diagrams, others use GANTT charts, and many use task lists.

Questions

1-1. Why do the authors claim that every organization has a conflict between starting urgent new projects and focusing on existing projects?

1-2. What happens when you hire more resources—do the multi-project problems go away?

1-3. What are five common challenges in managing a multi-project environment?

1-4. Explain the five elements of a solution.

1-5. When the same people are able to complete a third more work after a change, when the content of their work is the same, how do you explain what they were doing with their time before the change (assuming they were not sitting idle)?

1-6. Why do you think it took Joe three months to implement such a simple solution?

1-7. What were Joe's criteria for a good solution to his company's problems?

This book has free material available for download from the Web Added Value™ resource center at *www.jrosspub.com*

2. Resource Conflicts

The Premise

Resources are at the heart of the multi-project management problem. However, resources that perform tasks on projects, even the ones that are in high demand and short supply, are not typically the biggest issue blocking project flow. Getting more of those resources does not solve the underlying issue. That is because the actual time it takes for resources to perform project tasks does not account for the majority of the time it takes to complete a project. It is vital for you to understand this premise, so that you can examine the assumptions and choose either to agree or disagree. The direction for a solution that provides a breakthrough in multi-project management is based on the premise in this section.

Perspective—Resources Are NOT the Problem in Multi-Project Management

Universally today, companies are involved in exponentially more projects than they were 20 years ago. Today, with the dual challenges of global influences and reduced employee loyalty and longevity, top management juggles a lot of balls. But what is different now, compared to 20 years ago, is that top managers often lack the experienced middle managers who can catch those balls, address project issues quickly, and drive the change. Today, a lot of project tasks suffer from issues that take a long time for middle and senior managers to address.

With less experienced managers and workers on the scene, and shorter product life cycles, in a more complex environment, company managers spend more time firefighting and more time in meetings. The threat of not meeting quarterly expectations drives executives to initiate more and more new projects. Projects now spend more time waiting than being executed.

Other Reasons Why Resources Are Not the Underlying Problem

There was another interesting phenomenon. When the senior executive's pet project got into trouble, the senior executive jumped in and expedited project tasks. Of course, this had an impact. The top executives received reinforcement that if you pushed harder, their project progressed. What they didn't formally acknowledge was the damage to all the other projects whose wait times increased.

Gerry went to Australia and worked with a company rolling out new products every week to its communications market. New vendors waited months to get approved by top management, including legal counsel who had to make sure new vendor contracts met their criteria and that they weren't violating any other conditions. Then, the products were launched with a big hullabaloo and millions in advertising, only to have customers wait in stores that didn't have or had run out of stock of the new products.

Gerry also worked in Malaysia with a company putting in a new bar-coding system on its inventory. This corporate mandate was taking them a year to implement—ridiculous when you think that the actual project tasks were measured in a duration of just a few weeks and the technology was not new. But even worse, the benefit of the technology would not be realized until they changed current practices and cut inventory in half. They would not be doing this until the following year. Why? Management was too busy attending to other business issues.

We were not yet convinced that this was a general phenomenon until literally every client we worked with exhibited the same symptoms. Gerry developed strategy with a half billion dollar distributor. The CEO told Gerry that he needed help with his *strategic imperatives*. The Excel spreadsheet contained 75 projects he was monitoring, with a staff that spent the vast majority of their time managing a growing operation and fighting fires. With the minimal time the staff had left, they would have been challenged executing more than five projects at a time. Every week, his direct reports had the perfect excuse for not attacking the strategic imperative to which they were assigned. They were too busy dealing with operational emergencies. This had been going on for a full two years.

The last two manufacturers Gerry worked with, who had hundreds of shop floor employees, had dozens (one had over 150) of projects on the go, with a capacity to really focus on a few. Over the past five years, Gerry tested the assumption that the #1 issue in project success is management and support group attention. With occasional exceptions, hiring more project resources tended to make the situation worse—projects took longer to complete, operating expenses increased without significant benefit, and users felt more stressed and unsatisfied. In hindsight, this was just one symptom that the company management and support groups were already way over capacity in the projects they were trying to undertake.

In all of the above examples, even if projects were operating optimally with perfect resource loading, skill sets, planning, and execution, these bottlenecks would have doomed them! By taking the approach of reducing the amount of project work in progress, and bringing in a few processes to plan and monitor execution effectively, management finally had the time to focus on the few factors blocking projects. Resource managers were able to finally coach and mentor the resources doing the tasks. Users had the time to engage in projects and implement change.

Other groups needed by projects (legal counsel, senior management, etc.) could finally prioritize their work effectively and help drive projects faster. This ability to influence the behavior of non-project resources is a result of two key changes in the organization:

1. Reduced demands on their time, through reduced active project work in process. This means they have less juggling to do.
2. A mandate, driven from an understanding by all senior management, that every delay in completing a project also delays those benefits. The mandate is to have all groups who support projects behave like relay runners when a critical project task is at stake. The mandate is that supporting critical project tasks is the #1 priority. Exceptions require top management approval. Again, when there is much less project work active, this mandate becomes much easier for these other groups to support and achieve.

When these changes are made, these other groups typically do not need more resources in order to effectively support all currently active projects.

Management Attention—A Closer Look

Example 1: An Engineering Company (before the Change in Multi-Project Management)

This company's main business is engineering design for large conveyor systems that sell in the millions of dollars. The company has about 100 employees. Almost every dollar they earn is from doing projects. All of the manufacturing is subcontracted to other companies. The 25 mechanical engineers are waiting for work from another department—design engineering—which completes the front-end overall design work before giving the mechanical and electrical engineers the specifications needed for detailed drawings and other work.

The head of design engineering, a very senior manager in this organization, has a pile of overall design drawings waiting for him to review and approve, before letting the mechanical engineers do the detailed design. He also has a pile of decisions waiting for him on existing projects where specifications have changed or manufacturers do not have the exactly specified parts available. Where is he? He is not at his desk in Europe. He is in Dubai where a conveying system is being assembled on a customer site and has run into problems. It will be a week before he is back in the office and able to give approvals. In the meantime, the work waits. A week goes by. Is he back yet? No! He is in Quebec dealing with issues that the Montreal office has raised on another project.

In the same company, the head of mechanical engineering doesn't want his staff to be idle as a result of the delays in getting the above overall design drawings approved, so he gives the available mechanical engineers preliminary specifications on a new project, fearing that half of the work they will do will need to be redone. In fact, as a result of rework from previous projects, the manager of mechanical engineering now feels compelled to spend half his time doing drawings. He really should be developing the skills of his 23 people and coaching younger engineers to avoid mistakes and costly rework.

Note that the work of these two managers is not modeled in any project plan, but the projects are delayed or encounter rework because of their practices.

Example 2: A Manufacturing Company (before the Change in Multi-Project Management)

Unfortunately for this Canadian manufacturer, in 2008 they supplied about 80% of their product to the U.S. housing industry. Business had turned down, which resulted in more pressure to bring new products to market, improve their website including new facilities for automated order entry, put out new catalogs, open up new dealerships, and improve internal processes and product quality. Each one of these is a project, and not a trivial project at that. Each project involves their already overworked IT department. In addition to the dozen projects that are on the senior management team's radar and reviewed monthly, the manufacturing director has another 40 improvement projects in process in the plant.

When you look at just one project—putting out a new catalog for customers containing the new products and website instructions, it is labor-intensive. The specifications for the new products have to be perfect, with ordering instructions nailed down. The website changes have to be well tested, which is not easy in a company producing custom products with thousands of options. The project involves the VP of sales, the marketing department, customer service specialists, procurement, an outside graphics firm, outside web developers, and the IT department among others.

When you consider all the tasks and all the people involved, it easily takes two months to get a new catalog out with an average of six people involved at any point in time. Typically, in past experiences, such a project has required eight months or more of elapsed time to get it done.

On closer examination, here is what was consuming the six months of additional elapsed time. IT was backlogged, so every task they were involved with encountered about a four-week waiting period, even when planned in advance. The customer service representatives required to check the new catalog specifications and test the order entry system had other full-time responsibilities. Instead of taking two people out of customer service for a week and dedicating them to getting the work done, they allocated one person for two hours a day, which took a task with 35 hours of work content and extended it to eight weeks. When the VP of sales was needed for a decision, it typically took one to two weeks to get an answer. No, the VP of sales was not indecisive and the decisions were not difficult. It was simply his travel or work schedule that delayed these decisions.

Once again, we find that the time spent waiting for project work to get done far exceeds the actual task time.

Two Directions for a Solution

If project tasks spend an inordinate amount of time waiting to be worked on, the first question to ask is, "What are tasks waiting for the most?" If the answer suggests one type of resource that actually does project work (e.g., IT developers), the solution is not to immediately rush out and get more of this skill set. The first step is to get more out of what you have. In our experience, at least 25% of this resource's time is wasted either by multitasking the resource (not ensuring that they are given one and only one task at a time and left alone to work on it) or by involving that resource in less critical work (unnecessary meetings, interruptions, operational emergencies, etc.). When a critical resource is assigned a project task, all other work should be delegated, *even if their other work will be done less efficiently by others*. This is the time to address the issue of cross-training and delegation. After all, what would have happened if that resource had gotten hit by a bus, become ill, or quit the company? There should be no more excuses.

On the other hand, if the answer to "What are tasks waiting for the most?" is resources who are not modeled in the project plan (e.g., top management decisions, work of other groups who are used by project tasks, etc.), then the clear direction for a solution is to drastically reduce the project work in progress so that this work is driven to get done much faster. In our experience, when this is understood as the problem, and senior executives view the increase in project flow as having a direct impact on their goals, they find ways to easily address the delays. Further, by putting one of the senior management team in charge of addressing such delays daily, the damage caused by such delays becomes much better understood and is addressed almost immediately.

We are often asked, "Why not just add more resources—either resources that can do more project tasks or the resources for the other groups who support project tasks—legal counsel, administrative, etc.?" Sometimes, rarely, this is the correct action to take. More often than not, when you reduce the amount of project work, the organization discovers that it simply does not need more resources. It would have been a complete waste of money. But much worse than that, it would have taken a lot of time away from existing resources to train them, orient them to the organization, and get them working effectively with the existing team. So the correct action to take is to first reduce project work in process. Then hire additional resources if you need to, but not before you have a stable, predictable system. Do not bring new people into chaos.

Conclusions

Although resources seem to be at the core of managing multiple projects successfully, adding more resources typically does not solve the problem. The underlying root problem lies either with one critical resource skill set who impacts project durations more than any other skill set and whose capacity is at least 25% "wasted," or it is the management and support group resources whose time is typically not modeled in project plans. If the problem is the critical resource, don't immediately get more of it. Rather, reduce the multitasking and misuse of that resource. If the problem is the management and support group attention, cut active project work and put a senior manager in charge of daily, fast-track issue resolution.

Questions

2-1. If resources are at the heart of the multi-project management problem, why wouldn't simply hiring more resources improve the problem?

2-2. If the resource issue relates to one critical skill set, why do you think the authors claim that you shouldn't *immediately* hire more of that skill set?

2-3. What are the two different directions for a solution to the resource issue?

2-4. How would an organization know which of the two different directions for a solution it should pursue?

2-5. Provide two examples of how resources that are not modeled in projects can cause project tasks to wait for long durations.

2-6. Why do the authors claim that having project tasks wait for non-project resources is commonplace?

2-7. Why should you have a top manager review project blocking issues daily?

This book has free material available for download from the Web Added Value™ resource center at *www.jrosspub.com*

3. Poorly Defined Project Networks

The Premise—Why Focus on Project Networks?

To avoid confusion and arguments about what a project network is and how it should be represented, we will use the following definition. To us, a project network is a model of the major work needed to meet the stakeholder needs and drive some part of the organization's goals. Regardless of whether people are using Program Evaluation Review Technique (PERT) networks, lists, GANTT charts, or some other format, the network is the raw material of projects. In some form, it describes tasks, the correct sequence of the tasks (what must come before something else), the effort expected to complete the work, the resources, and other notes about the work that may not be understood from a simple diagram.

Some people distinguish between a network and a project plan. It is true that when you are using a particular software package or methodology, this terminology can represent two physically different things. For our generic purposes, it is sufficient to use the definition as stated above.

The project network impacts everything—the time and skill demands on the resource, the understanding of the work needed, the ability to monitor execution against a valid plan, the insulation against variability, and the ability to meet the organization's and sponsor's goals. Therefore, like resources, project networks are at the very heart of the multi-project management system.

There are so many legitimate areas in project planning and execution that can be improved. Therefore, why do we claim that project networks are worth more focus than elsewhere? To begin answering this question, consider that so many issues that you face today relate back to the project network. For example:

- *Poor task estimates.* Estimating tasks is part of the network building process. If the network is constructed properly with the right players scrutinizing the work, the estimate has a much higher chance of correctly reflecting the nature of the work. If a task is estimated with a much better understanding of the scope that is necessary to meet stakeholder needs, then there is less chance of scope creep. However, there are two other factors that must be taken into account. A project task time estimate, in our opinion, is never one number; it is two numbers. This is essential to capture the range of variability in the work. Secondly, any estimate is just that—an estimate. There is absolutely no statistical validity to having predictability in a single task time estimate. Statistics provide predictability, but only in aggregate, for the entire project and not on individual tasks. The poorly built network compounds this estimating problem after the fact, during execution. A good network properly addresses it.

- *The resource assigned does not have the best skill set.* In a multi-project environment, it is impossible to have the *best* skilled resources on every single project. For one thing, that best resource could have left the company, become ill, been promoted, and so on, just at the time they were needed to start a task. It is futile to count on always having the best resources available.

  We see so many organizations today that are in a straitjacket trying to schedule projects that require a particular resource skill set that only one or two people have. They attempt to assign specific, named resources to project tasks during a planning process, weeks or months in advance of when the task will actually be started. This embeds assumptions in the project network that are dangerous for the organization. The correct action in building the network is to recognize the issue up front and look for a way to address it permanently. In the past, with so much active project work, and with resource managers having so little time available to develop their people, the organization perhaps had no other option but to count on Mary, the systems architect, to be available from June 1 to July 20. Now, with the new paradigm, the approach should be to plan the network using a systems architect and to have two of that skill set to choose from come June 1.
- *Frequent scope creep.* This problem must be addressed in the network building process, which you will see in a later chapter. The project goals, tangible deliverables, and success criteria must be stated explicitly and clearly before even beginning to define tasks. Every task and the collection of tasks must be confirmed as both necessary and sufficient to meet the project objectives. During execution, scope can still change. Three parts of the process in this book help minimize the occurrence and/or effect of scope change:
  1. A scope change that could have, and should have, been caught at the outset must be prevented by having a robust network building

process to begin with. The process detailed in Chapter 5 is proven to have such an impact.

2. The faster a project is executed, the less chance there is for significant scope creep. With the pace of change in our world today, a project can become irrelevant if it takes too long to implement.
3. When a scope change is legitimately required, the buffering system outlined in Chapter 6 often still accommodates the change without rescheduling. If the scope change is so significant and is justified by the company goals, the alignment process outlined in Chapter 7 ensures that the newly scoped project is realigned to the organization's capacity to do all of the project work of the company.

Good networks are like good road maps. They allow you to chart a high-speed course. They provide warning signs for curves and bumps before you reach them. They clearly lay out the boundaries over which you are traveling, and they enable project managers to focus their energy on dealing with poor road conditions, detours, and construction, instead of charting the course as they go. They will have had a chance to preplan alternative courses should a roadblock be encountered. In this way, they help you get to your destination safely yet at high speed.

What Causes Poor Project Networks?

The two problems that we've seen universally in building project networks are:

1. No formal process is used. Just like doing preflight checks, network building requires a series of precise, well-executed steps. Miss one step and the project will crash.
2. Scrutiny of the network is missing. Pilots and copilots cross-check each other. No one person has all the information necessary to understand all of the work of a project. Without scrutiny, a project network is a fantasy on paper.

Direction for a Solution

It is much easier to define the content of a task if you know who is going to use the output of the task and what they need before they can start their task. In other words, it is the input needed by the next task that defines the predecessor task's work content. Therefore, it makes sense to construct a project network working from the end to the beginning.

However, once a network is constructed, what is the best way to scrutinize that series of tasks and milestones? For most people, the answer is in the sequence in which the work will be performed. Therefore, build the network from the end to the beginning, but check a network working from the beginning to the end.

One analogy is having an architect design a house. They start with the end in mind. How big will the house be, how many bedrooms, how many floors? Then, for each floor, how many rooms, which rooms must have windows, what view must the window have? Then for the windows, how big should they be, what insulation factor do you want, what type of material is needed? For the builder doing the construction, they work from Step 1 forward. They need to know that they must first clear the lot, then put in the footings, then lay the foundation.

Task estimates need to be done by people with expertise in the given collection of work. With an architect's design and with the help of a general contractor, an electrician can estimate how much work is involved and how long it will take to wire the house. The HVAC expert can estimate the number of units required and the work and cost to lay the ductwork to heat and air-condition the house. Just as one would expect a general contractor to rigorously check the estimates for building a house by validating with skilled tradespeople, we need a project manager in collaboration with subject matter experts to validate each collection of project work, by skill, for both correct content and estimated time and cost.

Another key issue in planning is determining how much and what types of uncertainty to account for. Since any individual estimate can be wrong, the people building the network must understand the amount of variation possible in the work. The problem is that at the time the network is being built, there are a lot of unknowns. However, when you remove the uncertainty about resource availability, caused by confusing priority systems and bad multitasking, you are able to focus much more on the task content. When you further remove the uncertainty of how long it will take to get help and decisions from management and other groups in the organization, it is easier to judge the unknowns.

It's also crucial to understand *where* the biggest variability is likely to occur—more toward the beginning or end of a project. If the biggest variability is toward the end of the project, we must have a healthy buffer of time left at that point in the project in order to account for and absorb that potential variability.

As an example, a web designer tells us that it will likely take five days to complete the design work we've asked for. After discussion (detailed in Chapter 19), we agree that it is possible to do all of the work in three days. If we check with the designer at the end of the first day, and they say "10 more days to go," we have the right and obligation to ask what happened. And if we are a skilled task manager, we can also offer to help in some way that will bring the time closer to the likely time. Has the content changed? Is the designer stuck waiting for a user decision? The original estimates framed the work in a way that we can now manage it effectively during execution.

Using the same example, if we are undertaking a project where the majority of the variability in changing a website is at the front end, then the fact that we have used up the majority of the buffer halfway through the project is not alarming; it is expected.

The mistake we often see in network building is putting in too much detail during the planning stage. A network plan of more than 200 tasks is almost useless to a project manager. It signifies that they are trying to plan and manage the work, rather than the project. The project may actually require thousands of tasks. If so, subnetworks can easily be added for those people managing portions of the project. However, in order to see where variability is likely to occur, in order to quickly spot scope problems, in order to identify missing chunks of work, the project network for scrutiny must be succinct. Therefore, after learning and using the process detailed in Parts II and III, make sure that a network of 200 tasks or less exists and is used for overall scrutiny and during execution by project, program, and senior managers.

Conclusions

Project networks are the building blocks to complete a project successfully. If you don't have enough building blocks and you have to get more during execution, the project likely fails to meet its time and cost projection. If the blocks are made of poor material (poor understanding of the work), they will crumble during execution. If we don't understand which blocks go where, and which blocks are needed before we can put the next ones in place, we'll have a lot of rework. From experience, it is worth the effort to have and use a formal process for both constructing and scrutinizing networks. It is also essential to have at least two estimates for every task within a project network, in order to understand the amount of variability and insulate effectively against risk. This chapter provided the overview of network building. Details are provided in Part II of this text.

Questions

3-1. Why are task estimates a logical part of a network building process?

3-2. When estimating time duration for tasks, should you assume the best resources will work on that task?

3-3. How does obtaining two estimates for every task help you better understand the work?

3-4. What are two causes of poor project networks?

3-5. Why should an organization focus more on its project networks than on other project management issues?

3-6. How does building a network from the end to the beginning help define tasks better than starting from the beginning and working toward the end?

3-7. If a project network requires 10 completely different skill sets, how many different people would be involved in scrutinizing the network and providing task estimates?

4. The Biggest Leverage Point for Improving

The Premise

A project task is ready to be worked on when all preceding tasks on which it is dependent are complete and all other elements that the task needs to begin are ready. Study how project tasks behave during execution of a project, and you will quickly see two common, underlying problems:

1. Most tasks, when ready, wait either to start being worked on or wait for significant periods of time while actively assigned to a resource.
2. Some of the time almost every task incurs is rework time, because the task was not defined clearly enough to begin with or because the resource made some mistakes in doing the task.

To explain the waiting, picture a typical work environment. A manager who wants to assign a project task to a resource faces several challenges:

- All the resources are currently busy on other projects, so the task must wait until a resource is available. This could be days or weeks.
- Urgent operational problems crop up, and the resource that was planned for a project task is now assigned to deal with operational emergencies.
- Decisions needed to complete the work definition or provide permission to proceed are not yet made.
- The user has not yet clarified the scope sufficiently.

Then, the task begins but the resource manager is very busy. We see many resource managers actually doing project tasks, trying to help overcome project delays. So a resource goes about doing a task, with minimal intervention. A week or two goes by before the manager has a chance to review. And sometimes, the review uncovers an issue that could have been easily discovered and corrected on day 1 or 2.

Another common problem is that the resource starts a task and hits a roadblock. Although some such blocking issues are legitimate and take some time to resolve, we have found that the vast majority can be resolved by a senior manager within 24 hours. However, without any process in place, issues linger. The resource either works on other tasks or goes to their manager, who assigns another task to keep the resource busy. The other task is not removed when the first task is again ready to be worked on. Now the resource has multiple open tasks on their desk and is actively multitasking between them.

But wait! The resource is diligently working on a task for one project when along comes another project manager, who demands to see progress on his/her project. This project manager works around the resource manager, going directly to pressure the resource to drop everything and work on the task on his/her project. Some resources resist the pressure. Some resources check with their manager first, who often complies with the pressure. The end result is more multitasking.

Management Attention Is the Root Cause

Take any project environment, in any industry, anywhere in the world, and freeze (reduce) the active project work by at least 25%. Most people can predict some of the results, but are surprised by the magnitude of all of the effects. Some of the results are completely counterintuitive.

Predictable results:

- All remaining project work moves (and completes) much faster than anticipated (until or unless the system is again overloaded with work).
- There are much fewer resource conflicts/conflicting priorities.
- Stress levels for resources and managers are reduced.
- There are fewer meetings.
- Multitasking of resources is reduced.

Counterintuitive results:

- Management and support groups provide *much* faster response to the fewer existing projects, reducing overall project delays by 38% on average. The part of this that is counterintuitive is the magnitude of accumulation of current delays. Today, management, and especially senior management, does not see themselves as part of the problem.
- On average, 70% more projects than originally planned are completed per year (depending on how organizations measure this).
- On-time delivery of ALL projects increases to over 90%.

- Organization throughput increases by over 50%.
- The projects which were frozen at the outset of this process, sometimes for weeks, finish earlier than originally anticipated.

If you doubt this is the case, consider the hundreds of cases now in the public domain, some of which are referenced in Appendix B in this book.

The root problem of poor multi-project results is insufficient management attention. An organization cannot improve until its management decides what it will STOP doing and frees up capacity to focus on projects. In projects, the first leverage point is to stop pushing new projects into the system, over the capacity of the organization to do project work. Note that we haven't yet explained how to decide which work to freeze and exactly how much to put on hold. That is covered in detail in Part II.

With far less project work active in the system, senior managers and support groups have much fewer project decisions and interactions. This allows them to respond much more quickly when needed. Resource managers have far fewer project tasks to manage, and thus are able to provide much better mentoring and help to their resources.

If an organization takes the further action of preventing resource managers from doing project tasks, project work progresses even faster, resource skills are developed more quickly, and mistakes are prevented. Also, if an organization puts the policy in place of assigning only one task to a resource, multitasking delays and mistakes are prevented.

The Rest of the Answer

After you freeze the project work, management must have a way to quickly identify when a project is in trouble. Many project management systems do not give the leading indicators until it is too late.

Before management can concentrate on the few projects that need help, the organization must have a predictable system—project plans that have a much better approximation of the work effort and are properly buffered against Murphy. (Note: Murphy means variation, which often occurs unexpectedly and at the worst possible time!) To get predictability, you must address a few other key issues:

1. *Project networks are unrealistic.* Part III of this book is devoted to the 10 steps to build a much better network. In every organization we've worked with, we found huge opportunity for improvement and major revelations as we used the process to really understand the work involved and the scope of the results needed.

2. *Project variability is not well understood and therefore not correctly addressed.* To be predictable, a final project plan must allow for all the variability that the project expects to encounter and even allow for recovery in situations where variability is greater than expected. Part of this issue is addressed with buffers in a few strategic places in the project plan. Even with these buffers, the project should finish much sooner than under the current planning approach. Otherwise, what's the point of changing? This speed of execution is not caused by the buffers, but rather facilitated by monitoring the consumption of buffers during execution. However, the buffers help to avoid the endless project crisis meetings, by not having to react to every bit of variability encountered. During execution, the monitoring of the buffers allows the project manager to know, at all times, where the project is relative to where it is expected to be and to recognize abnormal variability soon enough to be able to do something about it. Part IV of this book addresses this topic extensively. Part VI describes the execution processes that drive faster project completions.
3. *When new projects are released, they often create major conflicts with existing projects, especially over resources.* This issue is about knowing when you can release new projects without creating major negative effects. To know when to release new projects, Part V of this book provides a proven approach.

Once we have projects moving faster, in a very predictable manner, a few remaining management attention issues continue to block some of the huge potential to decrease project durations and get more project work done with the same resources. You only need to focus on these other opportunities one at a time, to continue to drive measurable improvements in project velocity. In sequence of typical impact on the organization, here are the problems:

1. *Blocking issues take too long to resolve.* Any issue that is blocking a critical task from moving forward is causing irreparable damage to the project and to the organization. The major damage in most projects is not in cost overruns. It is in delaying the benefits the project would have brought to the company—damage by not bringing new products to the market quickly enough, damage by not solving issues that hurt the company reputation, damage in investor confidence, and more. Chapter 33, on daily, fast-track issue resolution meetings, brings the correct approach to light.

2. *Resources are multitasked.* A resource juggling two balls moves both balls much slower than a resource dedicated to one task. This is the opposite of the current management belief. In fact, we often see recruitment ads where one of the key qualifications is being good at multitasking. Frankly, we personally would not have believed how much improvement is possible by significantly reducing multitasking. Organizations think it is much more efficient to give a person multiple tasks because many tasks encounter wait periods. However, instead of tolerating the wait, what would happen if we focus management on addressing the issue of waiting? With less project work active, most project tasks can move to completion with almost no waiting. Rampant multitasking across an organization breeds built-in delays in every task. When you put a stop to this, the impact is immediate and amazing. Chapter 32, which describes the resource manager's role in eliminating multitasking, addresses this topic.
3. *Problems are discovered too late.* Tasks are reviewed much too infrequently. We strongly claim that reviewing and updating active project tasks daily yields immense progress and saves a lot of time. Resource managers almost immediately reject this, claiming it is "micromanagement." Believe us, the authors are the last people in the world whom you would succeed in micromanaging, and we hate it when we see others being treated this way. We advocate daily task review because, done correctly, it makes work life much more enjoyable for resources and brings major improvement to the organization. Therefore, to reject a daily review process without even listening to why it is NOT micromanagement, how to do it effectively, and the impact it has on results is symptomatic of a much bigger problem in companies today. *Managers who are already overwhelmed with work are reluctant to try a different approach that appears risky. However, methodologies such as Agile have successfully adopted this approach.*
4. *Resources reach capacity without enough time to hire and train additional resources.* We have seen some skill categories where it takes years until a resource is at full productivity, for example, with certain engineering and IT skills. There are trend data for project resource loading, in combination with management prediction of what lies ahead, to do a much better job on resource capacity planning. When existing resources do not get sufficient management attention, their skills develop much more slowly. When new resources are brought on without sufficient manage-

ment attention, the time until they are fully productive is much longer. For this reason, we have devoted all of Part VII to this topic.

Continuing Improvement and Sustaining the Approach

Once you have a stable, predictable, fast-moving multi-project system, you can continue to improve results without devoting significant top management attention. The things that continue to cause projects to wait are opportunities for improvement—at least those things that can be influenced by ordinary humans!

By formulating a list of what projects wait for, and keeping count of how often project tasks are waiting for each item when tasks are significantly delayed, you have a basis for focusing on one—and only one—item for improvement. Chapter 42 covers this topic with examples.

Conclusions

Today, in most multi-project environments, projects progress slowly due to lack of management attention. Tasks spend inordinate amounts of time waiting to be worked on and being reworked. To get every project moving more quickly, an organization must cut the amount of project work in the system drastically. It is counterintuitive, but all projects complete more quickly this way. However, you must also plan and buffer projects correctly to have a stable, predictable, fast-moving system. In addition, once predictability is no longer an issue, several key processes reduce project durations even more. These include fast-tracking project blocking issues, reducing multitasking, daily task reviews and updates, and knowing how to discover problems early enough to recover. All of these topics are detailed much further in later parts of this book.

Questions

4-1. When you reduce the amount of project work, why are some results predictable whereas others are much less so?

4-2. How might you explain why projects which are frozen for several weeks would still finish earlier than originally expected?

4-3. Describe the three elements essential for predictability in multi-project environments.

4-4. Once you have a predictable multi-project environment, explain two other ways to speed up projects.

4-5. Do you think that it is difficult to do longer term resource capacity planning for all project resources or just for a few of them? Explain your answer.

4-6. The authors made a point that managers do not experiment when discussing daily task reviews. Why is this so important when trying to improve anything with a significant change?

4-7. The authors claim that multitasking is the cause of rampant delays in project task execution. Can you explain, through an example, why this might be true?

PART II

OVERVIEW OF THE PERMANENT MULTI-PROJECT SOLUTION

Most of the organizations that implement this solution achieve significant results within two to three months, some even faster. There are relatively few changes needed, but we warn you that the changes are profound and counterintuitive. A summary of the changes are:

- A 10-step process for project planning and networks
- A buffer system to insulate projects from variability
- A method for aligning and activating multiple projects
- A few key practices in multi-project execution
- A proactive approach to enterprise resource planning for projects
- Multi-project software

This section, Part II, is an overview. The details are in Parts III through VIII.

5. Project Networks

The Premise

Many project plans are not used once a project begins to execute. This means that either:

- They were created only to satisfy some policy of the organization or
- They are obsolete upon starting execution or
- They were not structured in a way to facilitate execution (e.g., dependencies incorrectly mapped, not organized in a fashion that aligns with how the work will be accomplished, and so forth)

If our experience is common, that over 75% of the value of a project plan only comes during execution, then no matter which above case is true, the effort to plan was almost a total waste of time.

To avoid this waste, the first thing to do is to not make the common mistakes. There are four such mistakes in building project plans and networks, which leave them difficult to use during execution:

1. *Assigning named resources (i.e., specific people) to tasks at planning time.* People leave companies. People get sick. People get tied up on other projects longer than expected. People get assigned to other projects. This approach simply does not work. Note that this does not absolve a manager from assigning a named resource or thinking about who can be assigned to a task as it comes ready to execute. The issue is about timing and predictability. Also, if there is only one resource in the organization who has a certain unique skill set, then the skill set and the resource are one and the same. This is a huge red flag to an organization about its vulnerability to project delays.
2. *Using the wrong level of detail to construct the plan.* A project manager must focus on the few important tasks that really govern the project outcome. It is a huge mistake for a project manager to try to manage many hundreds or thousands of tasks. Breaking work down during a planning

stage to its lowest level of detail or work breakdown structure is unnecessary and error-prone. At the same time, a single task that is estimated to take more than two weeks probably needs to be broken down further.

3. *Not rigorously checking every task and the collection of tasks against the key stakeholder's needs.* Some tasks may not be needed because they add no value to the key stakeholder. Others that are essential to meet the needs are missing. In many cases, the stakeholder's needs are simply not well understood until it is too late. The key stakeholder should have a project goal in mind that is tied to the company goals. Often, other stakeholders see the project as a way to get other needs met, and it becomes like members of Congress attaching pork to a bill intended for something totally different.
4. *Not rigorously checking for additional and/or missing dependencies.* A missed dependency can mean the entire schedule is wrong. For example, we have seen a product launch delayed for weeks because the legal department's due diligence was not included in the plan. Subject matter experts can catch most of these mistakes before they happen, but they often are not included in the advance scrutiny of project networks.

Why Use Project Networks at All?

Within any organization, there are at most a handful of people who love to build project networks. For most people, building project networks seems to be too complex and gives them a headache, literally. Therefore, it is tempting to not build project networks or to put in a token effort to be able to show a plan, even though it is not useful. Another common practice is to let the project network expert build the plan almost stand-alone, in a way that only this person understands. For this reason, it is also common practice that networks are not rigorously checked with key stakeholders.

We have personally witnessed organizations that consistently get more than 95% of their projects completed on time, on budget, and within scope. Every one of them will tell you they could not have done it without the use of networks during both planning and execution. Therefore, you must find those people in the organization who love building networks—who think of it as a hobby, like solving crossword puzzles—that is a lot of fun. They must be coached to construct a plan with terminology that is easily understood by other humans who are not into the lingo of project networks. They must also be coached to communicate their assumptions behind the network and its dependencies in simple language.

In our opinion, about 25% of the value of a project network is from planning. It is almost useless for predicting short-term resource loading, because projects never execute as planned. Some tasks are executed more quickly; others take much longer. However, the plan provides an up-front prediction of the approximate workload. It is a sanity check that the work required to deliver the project results makes sense when compared to the benefits the project will deliver to the organization.

But there is another key value to the plan itself. The project plan allows the organization to know when the project can be released and approximately when the benefits will start to accrue. See Part V for more details about this.

We believe that 75% of the value of the plan comes during execution. During execution, it is the yardstick against which progress is measured. If a plan contains strategic buffers (blocks of time placed at the end of a project equivalent to at least a third of the total time of the project), these buffers provide the real truth about how effectively the project is being executed.

When you compare how fast a buffer is being eaten away, relative to how fast the most critical tasks in the project are being completed, you have a compelling and proven story about the real-time status of execution. However, most organizations wait too long to act on this story. *The network buffer story is only valuable if it is analyzed and acted on daily.*

Therefore, we claim that it is impossible for any organization to have its projects under control (meeting its goals better than 95% of the time) without properly constructed project networks used frequently during project execution.

The 10-Step Process

To us, a process is a series of steps that can be repeated by different people and will generate essentially the same results. This is the intent of the process that we describe, but do not detail, below. The details and associated examples and diagrams are included in Part III of this text. These steps must be followed in sequence. None of the steps can be omitted. The steps embed five different ways to avoid risks in the project plan: risks of missing steps, risks of missing dependencies, risks of including unnecessary scope, risks of missing key stakeholder needs, and overall risks of the project. The steps are:

1. Define the project's measurable goals, tangible scope, and sponsor criteria.
2. Define the tasks required for the backbone of the project network (one main path), starting at the end of the project and working toward the beginning.

3. Add the tasks required to build the skeleton (other paths), working backward from the end, completing all other paths.
4. Read the network forward, from the beginning, rigorously looking for additional dependencies (first risk avoidance).
5. Check every task against project goals, scope, and sponsor criteria (second risk avoidance).
6. Determine resources (skill level and maximum number) that could be assigned to perform the task.
7. Scrutinize the network logic using subject matter and/or skill set experts (third risk avoidance).
8. Define time estimates, with range of variability (fourth risk avoidance).
9. Seek ways to reduce overall project duration without compromise.
10. Complete a final, overall project assessment (fifth risk avoidance).

When the organization has such a rigorous process, and every project network is built using the process, two excellent results are achieved:

1. Templates that describe a type of project (e.g., new product development, IT service implementation or upgrade) can be developed and reused, saving a lot of time in understanding the tasks involved in constructing a new project plan in the future.
2. Projects become more predictable, with the consistency of rigor and validity across all projects.

Each of these steps is described in detail in Part III of this text. Since this is an overview, there are only three more topics to understand about project network building.

Who Should Be Involved?

The key stakeholders, sponsor, and project manager must participate in Step 1, defining the goals, scope, and sponsor criteria. If a customer is involved, then the customer must be part of this process. The key caution here is DO NOT PRODUCE A 20-PAGE DOCUMENT! We have seen project charters of this magnitude, and due to their size, they are virtually useless (or perhaps more accurately described as "not used"). The goals, scope, and measurable outcomes are one to two pages and used as a checklist in Step 8 of the network building process.

Steps 2 through 5 involve building the first pass network. This is where you want the leadership of the person who thinks network building is *fun*! In addition, include the project manager and one or two other team members. The team members should be people who understand the overall requirements, how the organization works, and all resource skill sets in general. If the organization has a project management office, then someone from this office would be involved. These team members will remain for all following steps.

In Step 6, bring in the experts for each section of the network. For example, there may be a section related to product design and another section related to product development. There may be a relatively self-contained section related to web support, with another section for marketing and yet another for sales. Step 6 is intended to find missing pieces of the network, by having experts in specific sections review their relevant parts of the network for deficiencies or missing elements. Don't bring in all such resources at once, since this will be a gross waste of time when reviewing sections not relevant to specific experts. This would also definitely deter those experts from wanting to collaborate again in network building.

In Step 7, you want the resources with the skills (either a resource with the skill set or a manager of that resource group) to provide estimates, including the kind of variability you will likely encounter in executing those tasks. As above, have those resources only look at their relevant sections of the overall network.

By the time you reach Step 8, you expect to have all of the tasks identified that are needed to complete the project. The original team members from Steps 2 to 5 check these tasks against the project goals. They may call back in one or more of the key stakeholders if they are not sure about specific tasks and meeting the key stakeholder needs.

Step 9 uses the same team, who now thoroughly understands the total network logic and seeks ways to reduce overall time duration. One key difference from traditional practice is that this is *not* done by reducing time estimates provided in an earlier step.

Step 10, final risk mitigation, should be done with the original team, the sponsor, and the key stakeholders. The conclusion could be (and hopefully is) that the project network, as built, is sufficient. However, if anyone on this team sees significant risk, the time to address it is before the project is formally scheduled and activated.

What about Buffering?

Since our approach to strategically buffering a project plan does not impact the task dependencies, the actual tasks that are defined, the skill sets needed to do the tasks, or the ability of the tasks to meet the stakeholder needs, we look at buffering as a process that happens after a network is built using the 10-step process. The topic of buffering is overviewed in the next chapter.

How Long Does It Take to Build a Network?

Personally, we have spent up to two days working on a network. There was no preestablished template to use, and the company had not done formal project plans before. Much of the time was spent discussing scope and not adding tasks to the network. We have heard of cases where it took a week or more to finalize a project template for a very complex project. However, the next time a similar project came up, it typically would require between an hour and a day to customize an existing template.

Remember, even in the most complex of projects, where there may be thousands upon thousands of actual tasks performed, you are looking for ONLY the 200 tasks on which the project manager must focus. For example, in building a large ship, there are hundreds of rooms that must be finished, involving different skilled contractors—painters, plumbers, electricians, drywallers, etc. The project manager does not need to know when Joe, the painter, will be painting room 127. In the project plan, he/she needs to know that the first 30 rooms are scheduled to be painted over a period of one week. Before the painters arrive, the project manager must make sure the plumbing and electrical work is complete, and the drywall has had time to dry.

Do not be disheartened if you already have a project plan, and you rebuild it using this process and find it requires a longer duration. All this means is that the original plan was destined not to work because it was missing pieces.

Conclusions

We have not heard of a single case of any organization getting predictable results from projects without having a rigorous project plan, constructed using a disciplined and consistent process. This implies that the process cannot be left up to each individual project manager to determine from their own experiences. This chapter overviewed a 10-step network building process that included five risk avoidance techniques. Details for each of these steps are found in Part III of this text. To end up with a good end product, you must not only follow the process, but also have the right people involved in the network building process, as described within this chapter.

Questions

5-1. Why should project networks be developed working backward from the end to the beginning?

5-2. In Step 9, when looking for ways to reduce overall project duration, is it effective to simply cut task time estimates? Why or why not?

5-3. What is a project template, and how can it be used to save time in network building?

5-4. If you already have a project template, what steps in the network building process would you not need to go through?

5-5. Why does an organization need project networks at all?

5-6. Many organizations have small projects (e.g., implementing an income tax change in a set of tables) requiring only a few days. Should these projects go through the rigor of building a project network?

5-7. What is the maximum number of tasks you would expect to see in a project plan built using this process (at the project manager level)?

6. Strategic Buffering—Insulating Projects from Variability

The Premise

"This year's [2009] results show a marked decrease in project success rates, with 32% of all projects succeeding which are delivered on time, on budget, with required features and functions," says Jim Johnson, chairman of The Standish Group. This means that out of the thousands of projects surveyed, most did not succeed to insulate themselves against variability, resulting in failure to deliver on time, on budget, and within scope. It also implies that within the thousands of project management books available, most do not appear to have the desired impact. Why not? It is our opinion that a few common practices held precious by many in the project management world are simply wrong. For example:

- One common practice is to try to insulate each task from variability, by either improving estimating accuracy or adding some level of protection to each task. Our experience with improving estimating is that it is close to futile. After several years, assuming that your project resources and the nature of the tasks stay almost identical, you *might* get a 5–10% improvement. These two premises (same people, same tasks) are simply not true most of the time. However, the second reason this practice doesn't work is that the same task performed by the same person on another project encounters different variability every time. For example, the same person going to lay 1,000 feet of cable runs into these challenges on two different jobs:
  - Normally, the cable is on-site in 100-foot spools, which are heavy, but movable by one person. On one site, the cable was ordered by a different purchasing agent and arrived as single spools of 400 feet, weighing several hundred pounds. The resource had to wait 90 minutes until a forklift driver was available, four times during the day.
  - One morning, one of the lead resources had a bad fight with his wife. His productivity that day was about half of his norm.

- It is physically impossible in a project environment to reduce variability to zero.
- Some organizations have a poor project change control process. A good project change control process involves much more than paperwork and approvals!
- Projects take too long to execute. Before the project is complete, the market changes or some other factors change, which seriously diminishes the value of the project. At that point, the only choices are to either kill the project (if the value is so low in finishing it) or to incur a major scope change and redefinition.

Given these premises, there are two categories of action necessary to insulate a project from variability:

1. *Planning.* Projects must be planned to execute much faster than current practices permit, and protection must be pooled where it can work, statistically and strategically, to protect a project overall (i.e., we abandon the practice of trying to protect each task, and instead work to protect the overall project from the effects of variability).
2. *Execution.* A pool of protection works like an insurance pool. Consider insuring houses, for example. If most or even many houses burned down, fire insurance would cost almost as much as the house itself. (In fact, people who live on a hurricane-prone coastline see this effect.) With pooling of protection, we count on not using the insurance for the majority of the pool. With project tasks, we must take some steps to ensure that we have similar (not identical) effects.

To insulate projects in planning:

1. *Pool protection for the entire project in one place—at the end of the project.* This protection is termed *a project buffer.* It typically equates to one third of the length of the project duration, as determined by the longest chain of dependent tasks. Note that tasks have dependencies either because:
   - There is a preceding task which must be mostly or entirely completed before another task can start or
   - There is a preceding task, scheduled by the same resource, which must be complete before the next task on a different path can start.

Aside from the inherent statistics favoring this buffer sizing, buffering this way has been proven in hundreds of cases to be sufficient to insulate against all kinds of variability.

2. *Use protection for non-critical paths in the project only where variability is either high or unpredictable.* For example, in a new house, we must have all kitchen and bathroom cabinets delivered and kitchen and bathroom tile complete (non-critical paths) before installing cabinets. We schedule the cabinets to be delivered and the tile to be complete one week before our cabinet installers (critical task) are scheduled to arrive on the scene. Our past experience tells us that one week is sufficient time to deal with almost any variability in this area.
3. *Put as many of each resource as practical on the project, even if resource efficiency suffers slightly.* In most instances, you have much more to gain by increasing the speed of execution of the project (decreasing total duration) than you have to lose from some small inefficiencies by having more people work within a given skill set. Anyone who has read Frederick Brooks's incredibly good book *The Mythical Man-Month* understands that there is a law of diminishing returns when it comes to adding resources to a project task. The extra time required for communication and explanation of tasks and the risk of misunderstanding increase as the number of resources increases. However, most project environments today suffer from the opposite—resources are spread too thin. Further, Brooks wrote his original book in the 1970s when projects did not have the benefit of some of the practices and software outlined in this book: daily task management, proper task definition with entrance and exit criteria, fast-track issue resolution, etc.
4. *Stagger the project in a manner that recognizes the capacity of the organization to do project work.* Activating too many projects at the same time is a self-fulfilling prophecy—competition for resources will create chaos, constantly changing priorities, and multitasking, robbing the company of capacity. It is like being an insurer and only insuring houses in a fire-prone or hurricane-prone area.

To insulate projects in execution:

1. *Use daily task management to minimize the impact of variability due to late discovery or lack of coaching.* By checking task status daily (a one-minute conversation, unless there is a problem or someone needs coaching), we avoid the syndrome of discovering a week or two later that a task is out of control.
2. *Use fast-track issue resolution meetings run by top management to unblock issues within 24 hours.* A senior executive can resolve issues in 15 minutes per day that would otherwise wait days or weeks to get his/her

attention. This reflects NOT on how easy or difficult the issue is to resolve. Rather, it reflects on the acceptance by all senior managers that projects must not be delayed and that most (not all) decisions are just as good when made within 24 hours as with longer deliberation. When all projects benefit every day from this speed of execution, it brings projects to completion much sooner. This provides value well in excess of the time invested by senior management. In reality, it takes senior management less time to resolve issues this way, because the issues do not have a chance to fester and create bigger problems.

3. *Use buffer management to determine when a recovery plan is needed and when the recovery plan is activated.* Projects sometimes hit brick walls, where the variability makes a series of tasks take much longer than planned. If the buffer is not big enough to absorb the variability and gets used to a point where the project is in danger of failing, the project and resource manager(s) formulate a recovery plan. Within their authority, they may be able to subcontract some of the work, put some resources on overtime, expedite production and/or shipping of critical materials, put more resources on the project, etc. A plan must be made before the situation becomes critical. If the situation changes to critical, the plan is activated.

For all of the companies with which we have worked in implementing the above approach, these insulation processes have succeeded with more than 95% of all projects when followed rigorously.

Two Different Approaches to Dealing with Variability in Projects

The common approach that we observe universally is to try to reduce variability everywhere within project tasks. To do so, organizations try implementing the entire PMBOK and certifying all project managers, but variability still persists. There are entire books written about reducing variability in projects, through improving estimating, forbidding changes in scope, detailing work to very low levels, etc. These techniques simply either do not work or yield such minimal improvement that they are hardly worth the effort. Within these approaches, the literature is laden with the assumption that past history on project tasks is a good predictor of the future. It is not.

The other management approach—the one we use—assumes that variability exists and will continue to exist on every project. Although we may choose to work on one of the top 30 causes of variability as part of a process of ongoing improvement, we choose to accept and deal with variability as a fact of life. We assume it will never be zero. Therefore, the sooner we recognize and overcome it, the faster the project will proceed and the less the impact of variability on the project outcomes.

Common Cause versus Special Cause Variation in Projects

When you implement a daily task review, you want intervention ONLY when something out of the ordinary is occurring. If management intervenes every time a task is projected to take longer than estimated, the task manager will drive his/her resources crazy! Therefore, a task manager must be able to distinguish between *common cause* and *special cause* variation. These terms, coined by Dr. Edwards Deming almost a century ago, referred originally to manufacturing processes. This great scientist further explained that when managers intervene in a situation of common cause variation, they actually do worse than drive their people nuts. They *create* chaos. Things would have been better if the manager had done nothing.

Common cause variation is expected in a process. The problem with project work is that most of it, by definition, includes tasks of a nature such that we haven't done exactly the same work content before or have done it infrequently. So when doing a task review, how does a task manager know when to intervene and when to leave things alone?

We suggest that it is difficult, if not impossible, to know what is normal or expected variation without having some kind of range of variability on a task. For example, if you send your 15-year-old son to the store to buy milk and ask him to come right home afterward, you might figure a range of variability in your head. It's a 10-minute walk to the store. He might meet a friend on the way or daydream in another section of the store, so the variability might be between 20 and 45 minutes. In this case, some past history of behavior might have been useful a year ago, but now you know he has a girlfriend, so his sense of promptness has changed for the worse. However, if he's not back within 45 minutes, you are worried. After an hour, you are calling his cell phone. If you don't get an answer, you're starting an active search.

When you have a range of variability for each task, at least there is an expectation. It is perfectly normal for some (or many) tasks to have a range of variability that doubles their optimistic time or even triples it. For example, in research environments where there are many unknowns, and some tasks may go through a variable number of iterations before progressing, the range of expectation can be huge.

Deming suggested that work should complete according to its goal without intervention about 95% or more of the time in order to call a process *under control.* We use the same guideline in project tasks. However, the guideline we use for tasks is the outer range of variability given to us by someone familiar with the work content.

Conclusions

In projects, it is proven that companies that accept variation as a fact of life and learn how to manage it achieve much better results than those organizations that try to eliminate variation. In order to insulate against variability, a project plan must contain a pool of protective time (a project buffer) and the resources to achieve the plan quickly. In execution, the project must only be activated when the organization has the capacity to get the work done quickly. The work must be monitored in a way that recognizes special variation quickly and overcomes it. This approach is proven to ensure that over 95% of all projects finish on time, on budget, and within scope.

Questions

6-1. What are some reasons why traditional project management practices do not deal effectively with variation?

6-2. What must a project plan contain in order to protect a project from variability?

6-3. What practices must be implemented in executing a project to ensure the project meets all of its goals in spite of variability?

6-4. Describe two different approaches to dealing with variability in projects. Why do the authors claim that one of the approaches is not effective?

6-5. What is the difference between common cause and special cause variation, according to W. Edwards Deming? Give some examples of each in a project environment.

6-6. Why would it be worth 15 minutes per day of an executive's time to facilitate a fast-track issue resolution process for projects? Give one example from the private sector and one example from a government or not-for-profit organization.

6-7. How would a task manager performing daily reviews with his/her resources avoid micromanaging those resources?

7. Controlled Project WIP—Aligning and Activating Multiple Projects

The Premise

Every organization has a limited capacity to execute projects. When an organization activates too much project work, the ultimate negative effect is that project execution is delayed, resulting in the project benefits being significantly (i.e., 25% of the project total duration time) delayed, reduced, and/or eliminated. There are several reasons why this happens, including:

- People are multitasked. Precious resource time is wasted in the time it takes to start and stop tasks multiple times and to recover from multiple interruptions.
- Management and support group attention is harder to get, causing tasks that require it to be delayed. Every project demands some degree of management and support group attention. When too many projects are active, tasks spend too much time waiting for approvals, for IT and other service support, for lawyers to review documents, and so on.
- With too many balls in the air, resource/task managers take longer to discover problems, wasting precious resource time until intervention occurs.
- Resource/task managers are very busy and do not take the time to clarify tasks before assigning them to people or making sure that the task is really in the proper shape to assign it (i.e., all necessary entrance criteria are met, has clear definition, etc.).

If you have any doubt that this is happening in your organization, simply look at the tasks within a recently completed project. If those tasks were assigned the maximum practical number of resources, and the resources were able to execute the tasks working with totally dedicated time, without any execution delays, how long would the project have taken to execute? Do not accept, at face value, that it would have been impossible to execute that way.

Project work in progress or WIP refers to all of the project tasks that are active at any point in time. Each task contains a workload beyond just the resource doing the task. The resource's manager must manage the task. Senior management has to sometimes make decisions relative to the work content or other project questions. Support groups are often involved in supporting project tasks. Too much project WIP implies that many project tasks spend more time waiting to be worked on than actually being worked on.

For most organizations, the value of reducing project WIP by changing how they stagger projects according to the organization's capacity ranges from 15 to 50% of the organization's project portfolio value (see www.realization.com or www.prochain.com for many such examples).

Organizations must overcome two challenges relative to having the right amount of project work in process:

1. *Get out of a huge hole to begin with.* As the saying goes, when you find yourself in a hole, the first action is to stop digging. In this case, a hole means that the organization has far too much project work currently active. If you try to slowly climb out of a deep hole, our experience shows that it is like trying to climb a 5,000-foot cliff without a ladder—it will take a long, long time and be very painful. And if the only benefit comes when you are on top of that cliff, many people will get impatient long before you reach the top. The way to get out of such a hole quickly is to freeze a lot of currently active project work and release frozen work rigorously. In our experience, other approaches, such as outsourcing, rarely work because the issues of support and task monitoring are not addressed. Outsourced tasks require even more attention. See the discussion below.
2. *Stay out of the hole.* A formal mechanism is essential to prevent the same syndrome (too much project WIP) from occurring again. Two options are discussed next.

Two Ways to Stagger Projects

Staggering projects means that the activation of projects is controlled, much like air traffic control on runways. For example, in Knoxville, Tennessee, there is one runway. If an airplane taking off or landing is compared to a project, the capacity of the airport is to have a maximum of one active *project* at a time. Note that other airplanes can be en route, but if they arrive much too early, they end up queuing for a long time, wasting fuel and passenger time. If they arrive too late, the crew can *time out* and have a domino effect on future flights.

Project staggering has similar considerations. Its goal is to have projects activated not too early and not too late. There are two different methods of staggering projects according to an organization's capacity:

1. *Strategic or critical resource (skill set).* Pick a skill set that is multitasked the most or that projects wait for the longest (see Figure 7.1 below for an example). Stagger projects according to that resource's capacity to do the work, and schedule the work so that it is done in a short time. If you have two or more contenders for which resource skill set qualifies, pick any one of the contenders and schedule accordingly. It will become apparent within a few weeks if you picked the right one or not. In case you picked the one that was not the most heavily multitasked, you will still experience long waits for the other one. However, no damage would have been done because you still would have reduced the amount of project work in process by staggering work according to the first choice resource's capacity. In the example in Figure 7.1, the IT Services group is used as the staggering mechanism. In this case, assume that it is a small group where all of the IT Services resources were used on the first project. When finished with that project, the loading of the resources allowed work on two other projects.

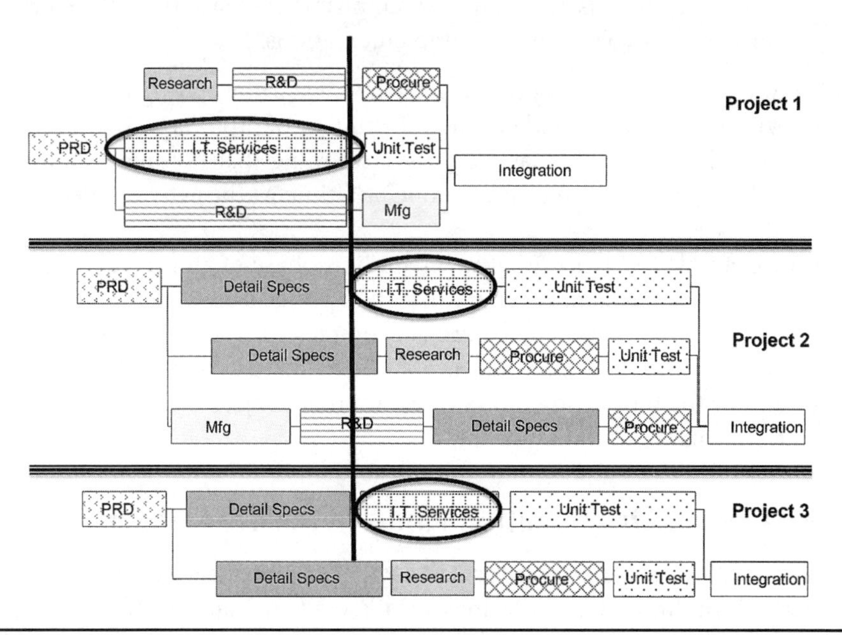

Figure 7.1 Staggering example, assuming that IT Services is the strategic resource skill set

Note that preparatory work on the second and third projects can be initiated and aligned to be ready when IT Services is planned to be available to do that work.

2. *Management and/or support group attention.* When you observe tasks during execution, you notice long gaps of time during which active tasks are waiting—not being worked on. They may be waiting for the resource assigned to execute the task, who is busy either on another project task, undertaking operational responsibilities, on a training program, or ill. In some cases, the resource would have been ready and able to work on the task, but could not because the resource was waiting for something before he/she could proceed. They might be waiting for a manager to approve something related to the task. They might be waiting for some information or support from inside the company. If hours or days go by and tasks often remain in this wait mode, these gaps in execution provide a great opportunity to stagger projects to dramatically increase management/other support resource availability. Take a glance at Appendix B to see actual figures of improvements achieved using this approach. Although we cannot attribute the portion of these improvements directly to reduced wait times for management and other support resources, there is a great deal of empirical evidence from the stories of the people involved in these implementations.

Typically, organizations using this approach will start by cutting the amount of active project work in half and cutting the number of projects active in the chosen phase in half. Projects that are *frozen*, meaning that no one is allowed to work on those projects, are unfrozen one at a time as the active projects complete that phase.

In the example in Figure 7.2, the integration phase of all projects is used as the staggering mechanism. No more than two projects are allowed to be active in integration at a time. When one project completes this phase, another project is allowed to enter this phase. Projects are scheduled so as to be (approximately) ready to enter the integration phase when another project is scheduled to complete integration.

How Does an Organization Know What Its Capacity Is?

The first time an organization formally staggers projects according to one of the methods outlined above, it is making a guess at its capacity. If resources are still multitasking, or there are still significant gaps within or between project tasks waiting for support groups, waiting for decisions, or waiting for the next resource to perform the next task, then these are all signals that there is still too

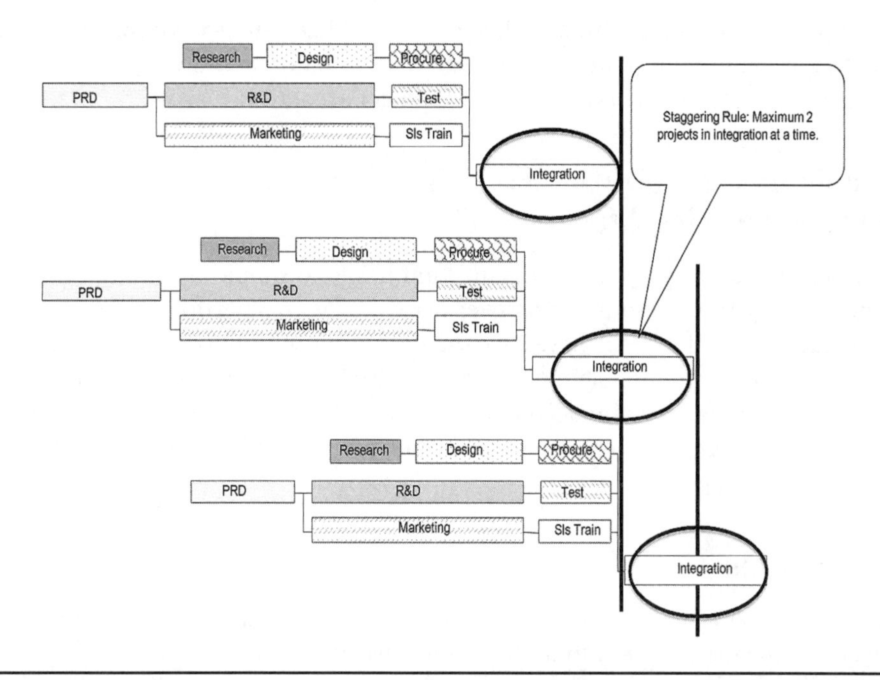

Figure 7.2 Staggering example, assuming that integration is the phase used for management attention

much active project work. Here, the buffers provide a good signal. The signal occurs when projects are consuming buffers to the extent that projects are in the red zone more than 10% of the time, and the reason for being in the red zone is waiting. In that case, reduce the amount of active project work further.

If, on the other hand, there are no significant delays and resources who could be doing projects are idle, this is possibly an indication that the organization can handle more. *Be careful to not interpret occasional lulls in project work as equivalent to having real capacity to do more projects. By its nature, project work has ups and downs in load on different resources.*

Before activating more project work, the resource managers should determine if any available resources could be used to speed up existing project tasks. This requires looking at the nature of project work through a different lens. Typically, tasks were assigned to resources in the past. In the new paradigm, resources are assigned to tasks. If by adding a resource we can speed up the delivery of the project, and by so doing speed up the benefits received by the organization, then resource managers need to find new ways of getting more people working on tasks without destroying their productivity. In this paradigm, we are not seeking the optimum work efficiency. Rather, we are seeking faster workflow, with minimal degradation in productivity. But some degradation in individual productivity is acceptable to accomplish speed of project execution.

Could an Organization Have More than One Staggering Mechanism?

The short answer is yes. If an organization has two completely separate project portfolios, with no resource crossover between the two portfolios, it is possible that each portfolio might have its own staggering mechanism. The reason we use the words "it is possible" is because it is also possible that both portfolios are suffering from lack of management attention. In that case, there should still be only one staggering mechanism—one that ensures sufficient management attention to both portfolios.

Conclusions

There are two ways to align and activate multiple projects, according to the capacity of the organization to do the project work quickly. One way is to stagger projects according to the capacity of a single resource pool or skill set. The chosen resource pool is the one that is either multitasked the most or which causes projects to wait the longest. How much project work can this group of people do without multitasking? How much project work can this group of people do when we assign as many of these people as we can to individual tasks? The organization follows this process, according to these rules, and everyone in the organization, including top management, obeys the rules.

The second way is to choose a phase of a project (e.g., integration) and to allow a maximum number of projects active in this phase at a time. This might be the phase that demands the most management or support group attention, or it might be the longest, most labor-intensive phase of a project. By limiting the number of projects active in this phase, project tasks are no longer kept waiting for management help or decisions, resource manager help or proper work in preparing tasks for execution, or support group attention. The number of projects that can be active is not determined scientifically or by any formal measurement. Usually, an organization starts with half of the current number of active projects and adjusts from there if necessary.

Questions

7-1. Explain two different ways of staggering projects.

7-2. Why would every project finish faster when staggered using either one of the two mechanisms?

7-3. Why would any organization have capacity to do more project work overall by staggering projects according to either one of the two mechanisms?

7-4. Describe an organization that might benefit from two, rather than one, staggering mechanisms.

7-5. Why is it often so difficult to convince senior management to adopt and not interfere with a staggering mechanism?

7-6. How would you decide which one of the two different mechanisms might be best for an organization?

7-7. When using the strategic resource pool/skill set as the staggering mechanism, how do you determine how much project work to freeze?

8. Fast Execution, Single Priority System, Recovery

The Premise

The purpose of multi-project execution is to have all planned projects finish on time, on budget, and within original scope as quickly as possible.

Assuming that we have a good understanding of the real work needed to accomplish the project (through the network building process) and that the organization has the capacity to quickly execute projects (through controlling the amount of project work in progress), the stage has been properly set for fast, effective execution. You now have about a 25% chance of succeeding. The remainder of your challenge now lies in how you execute the collection of projects.

Variability in project execution exists. Murphy (unexpected, nasty events) will occur, guaranteed. Effective multi-project execution is not about eliminating variation. It is about daily management of variation to minimize its effects. Here is what to expect in reality:

- Some task estimates will be way off (actual task time will be 150% or more of estimated time).
- Some resources will not be available when planned.
- Some suppliers will disappoint the project.
- Management/customer decisions will not be forthcoming.
- Support groups (IT, legal, finance, marketing, etc.) will be bogged down with other work.
- Unexpected operations and other emergencies will monopolize resources that we had planned to use for projects.

Our project must succeed in spite of all of this variation.

A Simple Example of How Buffers Determine Priority

Following the approach in this book, assume that we have two projects, 1 and 2, both of which are expected to complete 108 days after starting the project. Each project has critical and non-critical tasks as illustrated in Figure 8.1. Each project has a buffer of one third of the total project duration—one third of 108 is 36 days.

In this case, in Project 1, the first critical task, B25, has completed. It was estimated to require 25 days and actually took 26 days to complete. This means that it *ate* or consumed 1 day of the allotted 36-day buffer (see project buffer at the end of the project diagram).

On the other hand, Project 2 had a 15-day task at the beginning of that project, task B15, which actually took 35 days to complete. Therefore, it consumed 20 days of the allotted 36-day buffer.

Each project's buffer is divided into thirds to determine what zone the project is in: green for the first 12 days of buffer consumption, yellow if between 13 and 24 days of the buffer are consumed, and red if more than 24 days are consumed. By this definition, Project 1 is in the green zone, and Project 2 is in the yellow zone.

For each project, the next resource is a type A resource. If the resource manager sees that there is only enough type A resource to satisfy one project task,

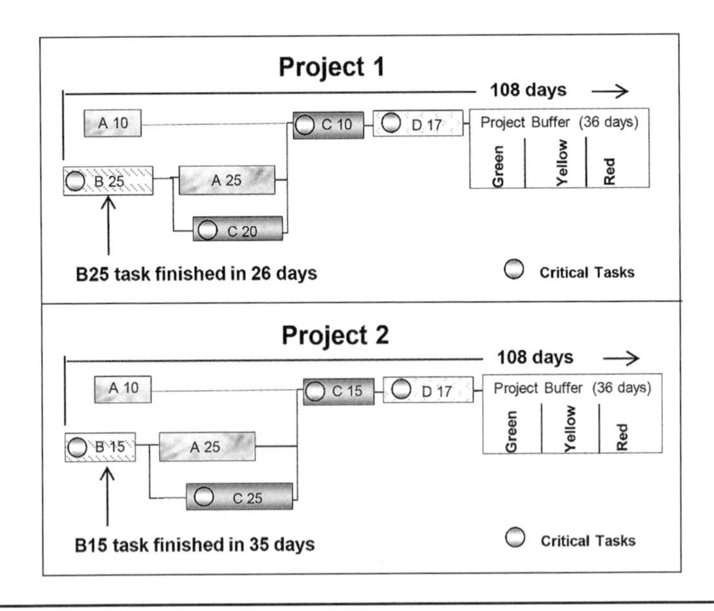

Figure 8.1 Which project's task should get priority?

which task should get priority? In this case, Project 2 clearly gets priority because that project is in the yellow zone versus Project 1 which is in the green zone.

Ensuring Fast Project Execution

By using the following processes and practices within the following roles, organizations succeed in moving projects much faster, within 100% (or very close) predictability.

Task manager. Assigns a maximum of one project task to resource(s). This person prepares each task to ensure that there are clear entrance and exit criteria (objective: no rework and only the necessary work to meet specifications). They ensure that the task has all necessary preparations, decisions, and materials in order to complete the task without stopping. The task manager is the subject matter expert on the work and follows up daily, asking the resource how many days are left to complete the task and whether the resource has any issues stopping them from making progress. They have the necessary expertise to know when the resource needs help, but the vast majority of the time have the necessary empowerment skills to leave the resource alone to do the work without unnecessary interference. If this person cannot resolve an issue quickly (within the day), they escalate the issue to a fast-track issue resolution daily process meeting.

Resource manager. Looks at all upcoming, available tasks and determines priority of task assignment based on buffer penetration (how much risk there is of a project deadline being missed). This is the person who determines which resource(s) will be assigned to the highest priority available tasks. They decide who the task manager will be for each task. The resource manager looks for the maximum number of resources available and capable of assigning to a task, with the objective of minimizing task durations. They work with project managers in case there is a need to expedite (take emergency action to recover buffer) projects.

Project manager. Ensures project progress, unblocks issues, attends daily fast-track issue resolution meetings to ensure that blocking issues are raised and overcome, continues to work with sponsor and customers (internal and external) to clarify scope, prevent rework, and ensure the project delivers according to the goals of the organization. The project manager works with resource and other managers to plan recovery actions when a project is tracking to fail (yellow or warning zone or negative trend) and executes the recovery plan when the normal efforts to reverse a bad trend do not work (red zone). The project manager must STOP EXPEDITING RESOURCES directly. The system will do it automatically according to buffer penetration into a red zone. The project manager's new responsibility is to plan and execute project recovery actions, but only when a project reaches a commonly understood negative state.

Daily fast-track issue resolution. This process, normally run by a member of the senior management team, is a daily meeting with project managers to identify and resolve blocking issues (see Chapter 33 for details). The manager of this process is expected to resolve all blocking issues within 24 hours or else freeze the project. With senior management buy-in into this process, our experience is that this is achievable.

Buffer management driving a single task priority system. Note that in the following discussion, this priority system is for tasks, not projects. Overall project priority determines when a project should be released or activated, based usually on the benefits it brings to the organization. Once projects are released, the single task priority system is designed to bring ALL projects in on time. Since it is perfectly normal for any individual task to take much longer than estimated, there must be a process to identify when a project is in real trouble. A single time buffer for an entire project provides protection against schedule variation, and a single monetary buffer provides protection against budget variation. During project execution, such buffers are consumed when tasks take longer than expected or consume more money than expected. Similarly, such buffers are increased when tasks take less time than estimated or cost less than budgeted. The buffers are there to be consumed as part of a project plan. However, when buffers are being consumed faster than critical work is being completed, there is a risk of using up all of the buffers and not finishing the project according to expectations. Although there are different methods of monitoring this, the one that has been consistently successful is shared in much more depth in Part IV of this text.

The less buffer a project has left, relative to the amount of critical work left to complete, the greater the danger of the project not completing on time. A single task priority system, based on the degree of project risk, must clearly show which task (if any) must be given priority in order to reduce the risk of the project finishing late. If no projects are in trouble, then resources can be assigned to the next available task in the queue.

Senior management. Agrees to abide by the rules of the system and by a single priority system. Every member of the senior management team must stop trying to push their new projects into the system and must stop expediting tasks related to their projects. The above system is designed to work without management intervention, except when the system indicates you are in the red zone in a project. This will happen infrequently (i.e., less than 15% of the time). If senior management chooses to ignore the system and instead expedites, they are guaranteed to create chaos.

Consistent recovery approach. When leading indicators show that a project is getting into trouble, the project manager must develop a recovery plan. The challenge that we see in most organizations is that the recovery plan is often *seat of the pants.* It includes such elements as *push the resources harder, scream at the resource manager, go to the project sponsor to apply pressure,* and *cut scope.* These approaches can work, but often at the expense of causing problems for other projects or creating ill will with resources or stakeholders. A consistent recovery approach requires examining a set of alternatives that would allow the project to meet original scope, budget, and timeline, and if those standard alternatives are not workable to then work together with other managers to define a practical recovery approach. A recovery plan is made when a project is heading into trouble and only executed when the project is actually in trouble. Remember that the next task being worked on might finish much more quickly than expected, precluding the need to implement the recovery plan. Standard recovery approaches include such elements as subcontracting, reviewing scope to ensure that there was no unintended scope creep, overtime of critical resources, adding resources to get remaining work done faster, providing highly skilled coaching for remaining tasks, changing out resources, and figuring out ways to do future tasks in parallel. Note that a standard recovery approach does NOT include cutting scope, since this implies reducing benefits to the organization. Cutting scope implies that these processes have failed.

Getting Started with Project Execution

Changing the way an organization executes projects does not require a long, extended effort. Typically, a team tasked with this mandate can do all required preparations within a few weeks (two to six weeks per portfolio of projects, depending on the level of complexity of the organization). The key pieces are:

1. *Organization:* Defining the roles and responsibilities per the above definitions, and assigning people to and training them in these roles just before going live.
2. *Technical:* Building good project networks, defining good resource pools (see Chapter 9), and having easy-to-use software to manage daily updates and provide information.

Once the organization has completed the above preparations, it *goes live* with this new approach and begins the daily task managing, updating, and reporting.

You can assume that some people within each of the above roles will return or stick to old habits. Therefore, the team responsible for implementing these changes must be prepared to monitor for a few weeks, correcting behaviors and solving implementation issues, until the new system is working smoothly and delivering desired results.

Role of the Project Sponsor

During project execution, the project sponsor may be called on to answer questions, make decisions, and referee or facilitate any requests for scope changes. Their job is to respond as quickly as possible to questions/issues/decisions with the objective of never holding up project tasks or progress. They also have a responsibility to limit or eliminate scope creep and stick to the minimum requirements of the project to meet originally planned company goals.

Recently, we experienced an infrastructure project, which involved the relocation of several functional groups. The objective was to improve the productivity of an R&D group by providing a better facility for them to work in. At the same time, the relocation of marketing resources who had been scattered physically had the objective of improving communication within this group. It was an infrastructure project with no tangible, identified cost savings or revenue increases, but was considered an absolute, necessary condition of the business.

No sooner did the project surface when managers of all functional groups started lobbying for additional changes. "Since we are already planning this move, why don't we also build offices for some of my people?" one manager pressured. Another said, "We only have a unisex bathroom—why don't we build men's and ladies' bathrooms?"

The requests were endless. Each one of them made sense. But what they would have done was add more time and money to the project without any tangible benefit to the organization. This is common with any project.

The project sponsor must be deliberate, yet practical about managing scope. Using a healthy measure of common sense, he/she might ask, "How do I make sure that no other infrastructure work will be absolutely necessary over the next year, so that we can really focus our time and attention as a company on the things that will deliver our profit goals?" By asking such a question, the project sponsor can minimize the duration and cost, while avoiding near-term rework or having contractors constantly doing construction work on-site during the coming year, disrupting productivity.

Role of the Master Project Schedule

The master project schedule shows when each project is planned to be activated (started). It is typically overseen by an executive steering committee.

When a project report shows that its final task has been done, this does not mean that the project is complete and a new project can start. Sometimes (and in some organizations often), the last task of a project results in many other tasks being initiated. This is because the project did not achieve its objectives, and that realization only became clear at the end of the project schedule. For new product rollout, it often means that intended markets are not buying the product yet or in the expected quantity, and either more product development work is needed or some additional marketing is necessary. It might also mean that corrections must be made to product design and further tested. For an internal change, often there are unexpected consequences. For example, the new computer system or equipment doesn't work as specified.

In such cases, a huge conflict can occur between freeing up the project resources to begin the next project, leaving the problems for operations people to sort out, or leaving the project resources to finish the project according to its original goals. However, in the system we have described in the preceding chapters, these conflicts almost always disappear because:

- The project scope was carefully defined using the network building process, thus providing greater assurance that there are no surprises at the end of the project.
- The project buffer allows for additional, unexpected work to be done and still complete the project on time.
- Senior management's involvement through the processes of full-kitting projects and daily fast-track meetings raises these types of issues earlier and gets senior management's attention on them earlier than under the traditional approach.

In the rare case where a conflict still exists, we highly recommend NOT releasing project resources and NOT starting a new project until the first project is complete. Otherwise, the organization will be back once again into bad multitasking and all the other negative effects. The pressure should be on finishing the project properly or killing it!

The steering committee, which controls the master project schedule, is responsible for activating new projects and communicating this to all concerned. This team must ensure that they only activate new projects according to the rules. One of the rules is related to other projects being complete, meaning there is no additional project work being done by existing resources. Therefore, they must get sign-off either by the project sponsor or the senior management team that a project is, in fact, complete. The CEO or one of the senior managers may need to referee this process, to mitigate projects that otherwise would drag on indefinitely, and with the authority to kill such projects and move on, after a reasonable effort has been made in a relatively short time frame to properly finish the project.

Their other role is to perform *what if* analysis to understand the impact of different possibilities for activating new projects. Once the owner of the multi-project portfolio (typically a very senior functional manager or steering committee) has decided the project commitments, they must assess the implications and ensure that resource managers understand the implications for their area of responsibility.

In some organizations, there is a more technical resource who is very knowledgeable about the software (see Chapter 10 for a discussion of software requirements and references to specific solutions) and who undertakes responsibility for training users, producing and distributing reports after daily updates, and performing the *what if* analysis described above.

Conclusions

Seventy-five percent of the benefit of multi-project process changes comes from a new way of managing multi-projects during execution. Key roles must be defined and rolled out to the organization. These roles include task manager, resource manager, project manager (but with modified responsibilities), fast-track issue resolution manager, and the multi-project master scheduler. The roles of senior management and project sponsors also change, as described within this chapter. Unlike before, the system is now designed to move projects to completion much faster, but without constant management intervention and reaction to who is screaming the loudest. Allow a team two to six weeks to prepare for this new environment, and give them some time within the first few weeks of implementing these changes to adjust and reinforce the right behaviors as described within this chapter.

Questions

8-1. Briefly describe the two types of work necessary to implement the new way of multi-project execution.

8-2. What are the key roles and responsibilities in multi-project execution?

8-3. Why should a project sponsor be concerned about scope creep and try to prevent or eliminate it?

8-4. How might you convince a project manager to stop constantly expediting resources to their project?

8-5. When the last task of a project is finished, the authors suggest that the project is not necessarily finished. Provide an example outside of those shared in the chapter, and describe the actions that the master project scheduler should take to address such a situation, assuming no one else in the organization has such responsibility.

8-6. According to the authors, which approach is recommended—to try to eliminate all variability that might affect a project or to assume that some variability will exist and find a way to manage it? Why?

8-7. Think of a case where you might want to reduce a specific type of project variability. Provide an example and how such an effort would be worthwhile.

This book has free material available for download from the Web Added Value™ resource center at *www.jrosspub.com*

9. Enterprise Resource Planning

The Premise

Although we do not consider enterprise resource planning as one of the six big leverage points for improving multi-project management, we believe that a lot of time is currently wasted on it. Organizations waste time trying to come up with plans that predict, perfectly, how much work a resource will expend on each task and then balancing the workload plans across projects. This does not work and will never work because projects do not execute as planned! Furthermore, we are in the midst of historical changes, which have implications for the way we plan and manage project resources at an enterprise level.

Many of the organizations that we visit tell us a similar story: the workforce is aging and they have major challenges in recruiting, training, and motivating new people coming in. While we saw the first wave of this challenge appearing 10 years ago with technical and trade skills, it is continuing with many of the skill sets used in project work. The challenge lies in replacing the skills of an aging workforce quickly enough to sustain and even improve project performance.

In order to address these major challenges, managers must stop doing the wrong things. For example, it is futile to attempt to balance the workload for all project resources because:

1. Tasks rarely land on someone's desk on a planned start date that was determined weeks or months in advance. Therefore, resource loading based on project plans is only a rough guide to the volume of project work. A projected overload on a resource based on a project plan will rarely occur on the day or even within the week projected.
2. Although any single resource doing a critical project task can cause a delay, very few resources actually govern the success of a multi-project system. By concentrating on one resource pool or skill set, rather than all of them, an organization makes far greater progress.
3. Often, the work that most determines project delivery is done by a resource that is not even modeled in the project plan. These resources can

be groups that support projects (such as legal counsel, finance, marketing or IT), they can be senior or functional management, or they can be external resources (customers, suppliers, and so forth). The constrained resource may not even be a person—it could be a lab, access to a production facility for prototyping, a crane needed for new construction, and such.

4. With the buffering system described in Chapter 6, and the overall system of controlling project work in process to avoid constant overload, any temporary resource overloads that do occur are *easily* dealt with (more easily than recruiting, hiring, and training new people!).

Therefore, the proven way to do enterprise resource planning is:

- Plan by project resource skill set, NOT BY NAMED INDIVIDUALS.
- Look at utilization *trends*, not just utilization *figures*.
- Capture and examine statistics about what resource skill set you are waiting for when a project goes into a red zone. Remember that the resource skill set you are waiting for may be a resource that is NOT modeled in the project plan.
- Focus management to increase productivity in one pool—the one with the biggest impact on project durations.
- Appoint a capacity elevation team, with responsibility for identifying and overcoming longer term resource capacity issues.

Plan by Project Resource Skill Set (Resource Pools)

To enable real control over enterprise project resources, start by planning projects using resource skill sets, not named individuals. It's not helpful for overall resource planning to know that three months from now, Joe looks like he's going to be overloaded. Joe may not even be working for the company then.

When skill sets are used for planning (e.g., IT architect, mechanical engineer, marketing subject matter expert), the project resource loading shows on the skill sets. Instead of looking at dozens, hundreds, or even thousands of individuals, you are looking at typically 20–40 types of project skills.

With visibility to the medium- to long-term demand for specific skill sets (e.g., over the next two to six months), a senior resource manager responsible for capacity of those resources can make hiring/contracting decisions in time to meet future project requirements. Such visibility is provided by software tools and is a by-product of the project information, *as long as you do the planning by skill set and not by named individual.* See Table 9.1 for an example.

Table 9.1 Example of a resource pool

RESOURCE POOL	QTY	CURRENT OWNER	% UTILIZATION AND TREND
IT Design	12	IT Director	120 ↑
IT Development	56	IT Director	97 ↑
Financial Analysis	2	VP Finance	76 →
Clerical—Finance and Admin.	10	VP Finance	43 ↓
Engineering Design—Electrical	3	Engineering Director	61 ↑
Engineering Design—Mechanical	1	Engineering Director	72 ↓
Engineering Drawings	3	Engineering Director	78 ↑
Industrial Engineers	2	Plant Manager	55 →
Production Processes	2	Plant Manager	46 →
Production Management	5	Plant Manager	34 ↑
Purchasing	1	Purchasing Manager	29 ↓
Operations Analysis	3	VP Operations	83 →
Marketing	4	VP Marketing	70 ↑
Sales	3	VP Sales	80 ↑

Look at Utilization Trends, Not Just Utilization Figures

Table 9.1 provides an example of the kind of report that is actionable in a multi-project world. Pay particular attention to the last column, which suggests the need for further investigation and possible action. Note that the utilization figures are only describing project utilization. Some utilization figures appear to be very low, but note that it does not mean those resources are idle the rest of the time. They typically have other significant non-project responsibilities.

In looking for the areas needing management attention, consider, for example, the IT Design skill set. It is already overloaded, and the trend is rising. We know this is a problem, but how long is it projected to last? Which projects will it impact? To answer these questions, we need to review other information.

For example, histograms can show utilization by week, but only for as long as the planning horizon for projects. In other words, if the only projects reflected in a histogram are for the next six months, then you may need other investigation of future planned projects to fully understand the need for action. In the above example, a multi-project management system should be able to show where IT Design tasks are on a critical path or critical chain and whether or not they are currently delaying projects. Senior IT management should have an idea of future project requirements for this skill set that are not yet reflected in the system's planned projects.

Another interesting example from Table 9.1 is Engineering Design—Electrical. On the surface, this one looks like it's *not* urgent, since we're only currently using 61% of the capacity of that resource pool. But it is trending up. The key question is, how quickly?

Although different project environments call for different guidelines, generally when the utilization of a resource pool is over 50% and trending up, it should be reviewed in more detail. Remember that 50% does not include non-project responsibilities and does not include the buffer. For example, this engineering design group may be trending up so quickly that within a few weeks we'll be out of capacity, or there may be a major new project that is not yet documented in the system, which will put a huge demand on certain resource pools.

Also, note that in project companies (organizations that earn their revenue by doing projects), employees do not want to report idle time. If the organization penalizes resources who are not 100% billable (e.g., by laying them off or scolding them), and does not provide alternatives, employees will always record their time against project tasks, even when they did not productively work on those tasks. When this practice exists, we find many distortions in reported data. For example, in one such company, we discovered that a third of the time reported was to projects that were no longer active. The company had simply neglected to close those projects out of the system! Since we have not found a generic answer to this issue, but have always found an answer, suffice it to say that the organization must find a way to eliminate such distortions. Please e-mail us if you wish to discuss this further.

In other words, these kinds of reports, although extremely useful, trigger investigation and not necessarily action. Multi-project environments still interact with the real world, and not everything is documented or reflected in a report or in software.

Capture Red Zone Statistics

When a project enters a red zone (by whatever criteria an organization uses to define *red*), it is in danger of failing. It is important that every time a project enters a red zone, we capture a simple piece of information: What are we waiting for? This capability must either exist within the software used by the organization or be captured manually through a simple process.

The things we wait for in projects are numerous. Therefore, the value of the statistics is to focus our energy on the thing we wait for the most when a project is not faring well. In the case of a resource skill set, this tells us that if we put our energy into correcting the underlying problem(s), this will have an impact on the duration of future projects. Going forward, by correcting the underlying problem, we should rarely be waiting for this resource when a project is in the red zone.

In other words, with limited management time to overcome systemic problems, this approach focuses management time on the areas where the organization stands to gain the largest benefits. It is vital for managers to understand why a certain resource shows up so often in a red zone. Root cause analysis may be necessary to fully understand the problem.

Also, note that the resource will not necessarily be one of the resources modeled in the project management software. It could be senior management, for example, or customers or suppliers. Enterprise resource management should not focus solely on project resources, since the goal is to dramatically speed up project execution, regardless of which resources are holding up project flow.

Focus Management to Increase Productivity in One Resource Pool (at a Time)

Some examples best illustrate the principle. In working with an engineering firm that designs and commissions ship unloading and conveying systems (in a range of $15–50 million projects), the key resource turned out to be mechanical engineering. It takes several years to develop the skill sets of these engineers to be able to produce sophisticated drawings without significant coaching. The number of projects that this company could undertake in any given year depends on the capacity of their mechanical engineering.

This company faced two challenges with the productivity of this resource pool. First, out of the 25 mechanical engineers, several lacked the desired experience. However, the manager of these people was so busy correcting mistakes, reviewing drawings, traveling to client sites, sitting in meetings, and doing project tasks that he had little to no time left to develop and coach his people. When this was recognized, all of his project tasks were removed, and he was able to devote much more time to coach his people. By doing this, the company was able to leverage all of the mechanical engineers and do much more than compensate for the tasks on which the manager no longer worked.

To accomplish this change, the company's general manager had to set the new policy in place that resource managers no longer were allowed to work on project tasks. As a general policy, this increased the productivity of all project resources.

Another example comes from the world of two smaller companies (one a $5 million and the other $40 million). In both cases, the resource most holding back project progress was senior management. Projects stagnated for weeks or months, begging for management attention. In that case, we brought the focus from dozens of active projects to only one major project and one to two minor projects.

When senior management has only one project to focus on, they stop multi-tasking. Their attention is given to needed decisions. The projects move much faster. In fact, the VP of sales of one company commented that they had never produced a catalog so quickly in their 30-year history. Even though the catalog was a single, small part of a much larger project to increase sales, the productivity of their entire company and external marketing people had an impact on every one of their 130 customers' productivity, as well as their own people's effectiveness.

We have such examples from every single one of the dozens of clients with whom we've worked. The lesson is to stop trying to improve project resource effectiveness everywhere and focus on only one place.

Capacity Elevation Team

There are common issues involved in understanding a multi-project management environment, especially as it involves resources. Having one team, who broadly understands this entire system, deal with the resource capacity issues adds value to the organization by reducing unnecessary expenditures and getting the most out of the resources. Note that for smaller companies, this newly defined task is typically assigned to one person or to one of the senior managers.

The challenge is beyond a typical resource manager's view of the organization, because multi-project environments contain multiple subsystems. There are projects, resources, multiple functional areas, project execution data, customers, vendors, and other parts all interacting. One resource manager can see their resources and their part of a project.

The idea of a capacity elevation team is to have a small group of people who think cross-functionally, think systemically, and broadly understand the multi-project cause-and-effect relationships. They only need to meet for one to two hours, once or twice per month, to assess the current situation and decide if investigation and/or action is required.

Remember that their focus will typically be only on one or two resource pools. Their mission is to prevent chaos in enterprise resource management, by anticipating project resource demand (according to data available). Their task is then to get all necessary approvals for hiring/contracting/procurement in place beforehand, and then to trigger the action in time to prevent disruption of project flow and results.

Having such a team builds useful intuition about anticipating resource constraints and ensures that the organization will continue to meet its goals year after year, implementing the necessary organization changes and new capabilities on time, on budget, and within scope.

Conclusions

Many organizations waste a lot of time trying to do the impossible: to balance the workload of all their project resources based on project plan data. Project plan resource data are based on task time estimates, which by definition will not occur as planned in real-life execution. A much more effective way to manage enterprise resources is by:

- Tracking utilization and trends by skill set
- Focusing on the one or two resource skill sets that are most affecting project durations
- Having a capacity elevation team in place to investigate and take action before project chaos results
- Recognizing that the resources which most impact project durations may not even be modeled in project plans (e.g., top management, legal, support groups, customers)

Resource loading data provided by project management software, usually displayed as histograms, are useful but only provide a partial picture. Such data can trigger investigation of resource issues. However, most project software does not reflect everything that people are doing in an organization, nor project ideas that could become active projects within the planning horizon.

By combining good enterprise resource data with proactive, cross-functional communication about project plans, and focusing on one resource pool at a time, enterprise resource management becomes practical. This approach is proven to achieve rapid improvement in both individual productivity and project productivity (accomplishing more projects with the same resources).

Questions

9-1. What is wrong with putting individuals' names, rather than skill sets, into a project plan?

9-2. What two pieces of information are vital for determining whether or not action is needed for a given resource skill set?

9-3. What is the role of a capacity elevation team in enterprise resource management? What skill sets would you want in such a team?

9-4. What is the difference(s) between resource management of a single resource pool (group of people with similar skills) and enterprise resource management?

9-5. Why do the authors claim that it is better to focus on one resource pool at a time to improve productivity, rather than try to improve productivity everywhere?

9-6. What information from *red zone* statistics might be useful in managing resources? Explain how you would use the information to make resource decisions.

9-7. What role does a functional manager play in enterprise project resource management?

This book has free material available for download from the Web Added Value™ resource center at *www.jrosspub.com*

10. Multi-Project Software Requirements

The Premise

Although we believe that software, by itself, is not a leverage point for improving multi-project management, for most organizations it is a necessary element. The problem is that most organizations choose age-old software that is complex and difficult to use and does not bring the necessary transparency and benefits to the organization. Note that we do not advocate a specific software package. Rather, we use this chapter to state generic multi-project software requirements, and at the end of this chapter indicate a few different solutions that have most of these capabilities.

Software (or making a software change) is justified only when it removes a significant limitation that an organization is experiencing, which is blocking the organization from achieving its goals. What is the biggest limitation of a project? Is it the cost of the project, or is it the time it takes to complete the project?[1]

Since an organization undertakes *most* projects in order to gain the benefits that those projects provide, the benefits must, by definition, exceed the cost. Yes, you can note the exceptions where a project is done strictly to meet government or other legal requirements, where cost might be a bigger factor. But by far, it is still the return on investment, the years of positive cash flows from all the projects, which justify those projects. What most limits the organization from achieving the full potential of all the cash flows or benefits from the entire collection of projects?

For the set of projects that senior management chooses, the longer each project requires to deliver the benefits, the bigger the limitation is. Therefore, any multi-project software must help dramatically reduce project durations in order for it to be useful. If the top management of the organization does not clearly see how such a bottom-line impact will be achieved by implementing the software, then it's better to do nothing—at least you won't have the negative effects of increased software operating expense and investment.

What about resources? If you want to do projects more quickly, don't resources become the overriding limitation? The answer to this question is totally counterintuitive. If you want to get projects done more quickly, have fewer projects activated at a time. Stop the multitasking of resources. When these two major paradigm shifts are done, the end result is that resources are almost NEVER a limitation, and projects move much more quickly. In fact, the organization is able to complete much more project work with the same resources. Therefore, only a simple software approach to resource management is needed.

To overcome the limitation of current project durations, multi-project software must facilitate new rules/practices/policies of the organization as follows:

1. Activation/staggering of new projects according to a strict governance mechanism (critical resource or project phase). Note that this must include easy-to-use *what if* analysis, with ability to stagger projects based on the demand on highly utilized critical resource skills. Often, the governance mechanism is a senior management policy and not inherent in a software package. However, the software must have the ability to hold planned, but not released, projects within the system.
2. Ability to freeze projects in the event too much work is activated or one or more projects hit an unrecoverable snag.
3. Transparency of status. The ability to report project and task status according to their relationship to a holistic project buffer in real time. See Figure 10.1 for an example.
4. Provide super-easy task updating, viewing, and tracking for all levels and functions, including senior management. See Figure 10.2 for an example.
5. Ability to operate according to a single priority system for all projects and tasks within a portfolio. The logical priority system is based on which project is most in danger of missing its schedule or budget goal. See Figure 10.3 for an example.

Project Name	PB Status	Project Status	Recommended Start Date	Last Modified	Project Due Date	Early Warning	Critical Chain Remaining	Project Manager	Start / Freeze Project	View/ Update Task	E-Mail	Print	Plan/ Schedule
building a house II	100 %	Started		Mar 4, 2012	Jun 25, 2012		100%	Gerry Kendall					
22 Task Test	31 %	Pipeline	May 15, 2012	May 15, 2012	Oct 19, 2012			Gerry Kendall					
PMG1	28 %	Pipeline	May 15, 2012	May 15, 2012	Oct 26, 2012			Gerry Kendall					
Build a House	0 %	Pipeline	Mar 9, 2012	Mar 4, 2012	Jun 28, 2012			Gerry Kendall					
Task Name 21	0 %	Pipeline	Mar 5, 2012	Mar 4, 2012	Aug 24, 2012			Gerry Kendall					

First Previous 1 Next Last

Figure 10.1 Transparent view of all projects, by project manager. Thanks to Exepron Software for the screen shot (www.exepron.com).

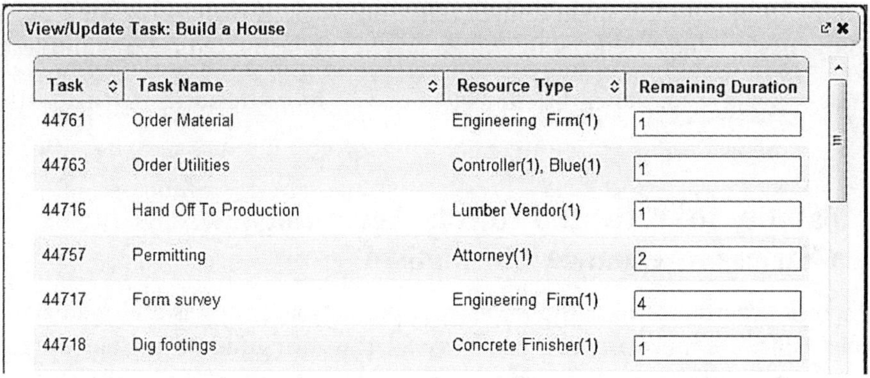

View/Update Task: Build a House

Task	Task Name	Resource Type	Remaining Duration
44761	Order Material	Engineering Firm(1)	1
44763	Order Utilities	Controller(1), Blue(1)	1
44716	Hand Off To Production	Lumber Vendor(1)	1
44757	Permitting	Attorney(1)	2
44717	Form survey	Engineering Firm(1)	4
44718	Dig footings	Concrete Finisher(1)	1

Figure 10.2 Super-easy task updating. Thanks to Exepron Software for the screen shot (www.exepron.com).

Name	Resource Names	Projected Start	% Buffer Impact	Remaining Duration
Catalogue Printing	Outsourced	Wed 7/22/09	87	10 days
Door Builder	Mars Hill	Wed 7/22/09	77	2 days
Thank-yous	Marketing[2]	Wed 7/22/09	77	1 day
Prototyping and finalize material choices	Production[3]	Fri 7/24/09	77	1 day
2020 – new catalogue version	Marketing	Thu 7/23/09	61	12.5 days
Create Training Package for Catalogue	Marketing[2]	Wed 7/22/09	60	5 days
Drive consumers/dealers to website	Marketing	Wed 7/29/09	33	2.5 days

Figure 10.3 Single priority system according to buffer impact

The above conditions are essential. In today's world, the capabilities below are secondary, but are increasingly important the larger the organization:

1. Allow resource planning views by skill sets, across time and project horizons.
2. Contain a level of security by role/responsibility for both data access and transaction capability.
3. Data accessible anywhere, anytime, and backed up frequently (e.g., hourly).
4. Allow people who are not physically in the same place to work together on a project plan.

5. Allow a project management office or program manager to view cross-project dependencies and potential resource constraints across projects.

These topics are discussed briefly below and in more detail in Part III of this text.

Capability to Activate Projects According to a Strict Governance Mechanism

Whereas governance over the *number* of projects activated is an organization policy, software must provide the ability for staggering (activating and spreading the start) of projects according to the policy in order to manage capacity. Some software forces you to do this manually, deciding when to start a project and how to line up future projects. Although annoying and time-consuming to have to do so manually, this, by itself would not negate using a specific software package. Some software tries to do this by resource leveling across projects, a totally futile and ultimately destructive mechanism. The reasons for this were described in earlier chapters on managing resources.

Ideally, software has:

1. The capability to stagger projects according to either one most heavily loaded resource skill set or according to project phases. See the examples in Chapter 7, Figures 7.1 and 7.2.
2. The ability to do *what if* scenarios on non-activated projects that are ready to be released, to see the implications on future resource loading and future cash flow impacts.

This is described more fully in Part III of this text.

Ability to Freeze Projects

When an organization has too many active projects, you can witness various symptoms of chaos. Priorities frequently change. People are moved frequently from one project to another. People are multitasked. Projects get further and further behind, without the ability to recover.

When these symptoms happen and the team responsible for multi-project management decides that they cannot recover with any other action plans, then the time has come to freeze some projects. Software must provide the ability to do this and in turn free up the resources on the frozen projects to instead work on projects in trouble.

Before reactivating any of the frozen projects, the software must provide the ability to do *what if* analysis, to determine whether or not these projects must be rescheduled or new due dates have to be set. Before unfreezing any projects, the team must determine that the multi-project system is once again under control. This means that *most* projects and tasks are not in a red zone, and project goals can be achieved without excessive expediting.

Operating According to a Single Priority System

In order for a software system to understand the sequence in which to stagger projects, the software must be able to capture and use the unique project priority. When you have, for example, 10 projects in a queue, ready for activation, the software must look at the #1 priority and activate that project before any others. If you want to activate 2 projects out of the 10, the software must activate the #1 priority project first, stagger it according to the organization's policy, and then determine when the second project can start, based on the staggering rules. See the examples in Chapter 7.

By far, the biggest software consideration is the ability to sequence tasks, by resource manager, according to a single priority system. The priority used for scheduling tasks is according to the degree of danger of missing the project deadline. The resource manager must be able to see:

1. Which tasks, of all tasks that are currently active, are most endangering a project. This tells the resource manager where their coaching or other type of help is most urgently needed.
2. Which tasks that are available for assignment but not yet assigned are most urgent.
3. Which tasks that are not available for assignment (because prior dependent tasks are still being worked on) are likely to endanger the project because they should have already been available. This allows the resource manager to anticipate problems.

For all levels of functional management and for project managers, the single priority system provides transparency as to which tasks are urgent and why resources are assigned as they are. The transparency allows anyone with permitted access to project data to ask questions about anomalies. For example:

Project manager: "Why did you assign Roger to the electrical engineering task on Project 1, when the system shows that Project 2's electrical engineering task is higher priority?"

Resource manager: "You are right—Project 2's task is higher priority. However, that task cannot begin until we get a clarification on the specifications from the customer. That is being worked on today, and we expect to have it tomorrow. By tomorrow, I'll have Joe available to assign to this task."

When the transparency is there, and people can explain their actions logically, according to the guidance of a single priority system, we have the basis for all projects being completed on time and fast, without constant chaos and changes.

Report Project and Task Status According to Holistic Buffers

If you accept the assumption that it is impossible to predict every place where variation might occur on a project, and the assumption that people often do not fully understand the requirements of their task until they really get into it, then the following software requirements for buffer status will make sense to you:

1. Software must be capable of assigning a significant portion of project duration to a single project buffer during the planning stage of a project. In the critical chain methodology, for example, the buffer size is typically one third of the overall project duration. Software must not allocate such a buffer to individual tasks, given the first assumption above.
2. Software must be capable of monitoring the consumption or use of the buffer during execution.
3. Software must be able to compare critical work completed against the amount of buffer consumed, in order to gauge whether a project status is red, yellow, or green (in danger of missing a due date, in a situation requiring investigation, or in a normal situation requiring no intervention).
4. Based on project status, the software must be able to look at the tasks that are not yet complete and assign a red, yellow, or green status to each task in every project in the system, based on whether or not it is the task currently causing the buffer condition.
5. The software must be able to show each role (project manager, resource manager, senior manager, project sponsor, etc.) the status of their project(s) in a meaningful way.

The software is considered holistic if and only if it provides a single, common basis for decision making and allocation of resources across all projects.

Super-Easy Task Updating, Viewing, and Tracking

When senior management is able to ask questions triggered by meaningful software views of projects, this drives behavior within the organization. For example, when the president of a small manufacturing company reviewed the new project management status, the first week after implementation, the most important project of the company was already in the red zone. He knew within minutes of the task updates, because he was able to see a simple report on buffer status for the project.

The arrowheads at the left in Figure 10.4 show that the buffer was 100% consumed after five days and none of the critical tasks were complete. When the president investigated, the project manager was able to tell him immediately which task was causing the buffer consumption.

This software did not tell him why the task was so far from its estimated time that it consumed the entire buffer of a four-month project. We're not sure that any software package would reveal the truth. In this case, it turned out to be significant scope creep. The president corrected the scope creep, not just this one time, but several times during the project.

The point of this story is that without an easy way for resource managers to complete daily (or at least frequent) task updates, the president would not have even heard about the problem until it was too late. Without the president having a view of project status easy enough to understand, he would never have asked the

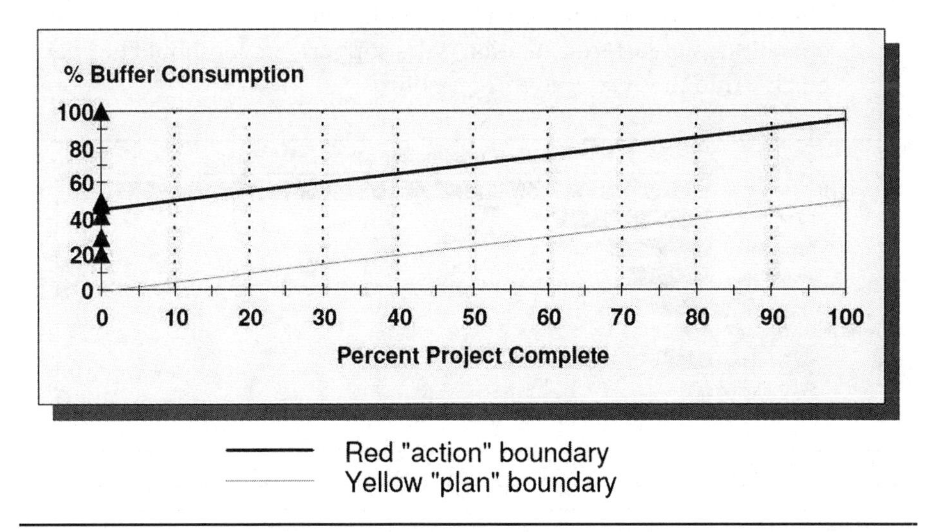

Figure 10.4 Real-time view of project status

right questions. Without easy views and tracking for the project manager, it would have taken them longer to track down which task was causing the problem.

Many of the project management software packages we have seen are horribly complex to learn and use. For most of the people involved in projects, their job is not project management—it is something else (i.e., resource managers, resources, functional managers, senior managers, sponsors, or support groups). Software that takes more than an hour to learn sufficiently to begin to benefit a non-project manager is already dangerously complex. The danger is that the person won't use it, and either the data developed in planning won't be used in execution or the data will not be updated frequently enough to be meaningful.

The software should be easy enough that a task manager can update the status of any task in seconds and easily add relevant notes to describe unusual situations. For anyone other than project managers, the individual should be able to find and understand relevant data with minimal training (e.g., an hour or less).

Resource Views

A manager of a resource skill (e.g., IT system architects) needs to know the following information from a project management software package:

1. How often are my resources not available when needed and when a project is in the red zone? See Figure 10.5 for an example.
2. What percentage of my resources are allocated to projects? This is important because typically my resources have other responsibilities (e.g., operations support, consultation, sales support, etc.). I should be able to quickly find the answer to this question.

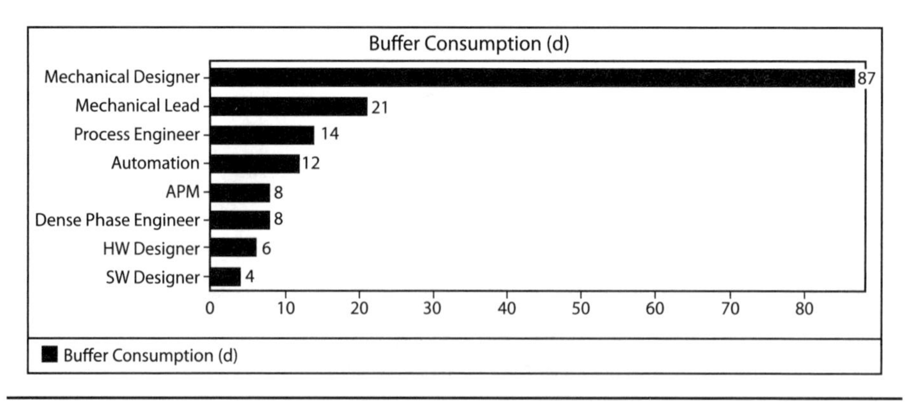

Figure 10.5 How often are my resources holding up a project?

3. In the short term (e.g., over the next four to six weeks), do the project requirements across all projects show any overloading of the resources I am responsible for? How much overloading is there (i.e., are they loaded to 125%, 150%)?
4. In the medium to long term, what are the loads and what are the trends for the resources I am responsible for? Typically, software will show this by week. It is also important to be able to see this by projects that are planned but not yet activated. This can trigger hiring decisions at the appropriate time, considering lead times for both hiring and training resources.
5. In the medium to long term, what are the loads and trends for other resource skill sets? This can be extremely important because my resources do not operate in a vacuum. For example, in one mechanical engineering department we have worked with, their workload depended entirely on completion of overall design work by another department. When the overall design department was overloaded, either specifications slowed down for mechanical engineering or specifications were so crudely provided that they resulted in a lot of rework for mechanical engineering. Since the manager of mechanical engineering is part of a team of resources trying to fulfill customer requirements, this was vital information to help him bring issues to his team of peers.

No doubt, resource managers who interact frequently with project management systems would have a lot of other requirements. However, without negating the value of other software features, the above are the critical moneymakers. These few pieces facilitate a proactive resource management organization, which increases project flow both short term and long term.

Data and Transaction Access Security by Role/Responsibility

When we go through an airport, we often think there is such a thing as too much security and security in the wrong place. However, for the user of a system, including airports, the key word above is *access*—security is secondary to making money from your company's projects.

We want only one manager to have responsibility to update their resources' project tasks. We want only one person in the organization to have responsibility for activating and freezing projects. A project manager should be able to view their project data, including tasks and resources assigned, but should not be able to change priorities or assign individuals to tasks. Project sponsors and senior management must be able to view all projects under their purview.

The person managing this security and access for the entire multi-project environment should be capable of adding access in seconds by simple check marks or fill-in-the-blank forms. Ideally, a non-IT person should be capable of administering such security in a matter of minutes with minimal training.

Data Accessibility Anytime, Anywhere with Frequent Automatic Backups

The heading says it all. With current technology, the most accommodating environment is something called *cloud computing* or Software as a Service (SaaS).[2] This is, for example, what Amazon uses for all of its data and makes available to thousands of other companies for use. Backups are automatic and frequent (e.g., half-hourly). Data can be accessed worldwide, as long as you have the web available. The data are stored in the external (to the company) server that is providing the cloud capability and is typically as or more secure than any internal computing environment. This is the kind of computing that is used by Apple, for example, with its current technologies.

We are not technicians, and we are not saying that there is no other way to provide 24-hour-per-day worldwide access to project management data. What we can say is that we have seen the cost of enterprise project management come down from up-front expenditures of hundreds of thousands of dollars to less than $200 per month (e.g., 50 users, dozens to hundreds of projects). At the same time, we have seen the capabilities and ease of use on a par with or much better than the more expensive systems.

The cloud computing capability has democratized project management, and is bringing its simplicity and availability to the masses.[3] However, a cloud solution must also include the kind of backup and protection that server-based software typically includes. We have heard a complaint about losing data updates when Internet connections are lost, which requires either a software capability (e.g., automatic updates every X minutes) or a heightened user awareness.

Software Solutions (in Alphabetical Order) with Our Comments

Exepron (see www.exepron.com). This is the newest of the solutions. It is cloud-based, with no software needed to be installed on a PC or device. It is intuitive, easy to use, and offers the ability for multiple users to collaborate simultaneously together over the web in developing and updating project plans. Its monthly fee makes it attractive. As a relatively new yet proven product, it needs more reporting capability, and its resource management screen views need young eyes! However, it has all the major capabilities needed to drive results.

Microsoft Project Server (see http://www.microsoft.com/project/en-us/project-management.aspx). With millions of users, Microsoft cannot be ignored. It integrates very nicely with SharePoint, bringing some additional functionality in the staggering of projects. However, it lacks some of the necessary elements as described above. As one of the first project management software products, and given its early user base, most people we engage with find it complex, burdensome, and frustrating to use. With the add-on of ProChain (see below), it has most of the capabilities we outlined above. It would be great to see Microsoft completely redesign this product for the 21st century as a more user-friendly web- and personal device-oriented product.

ProChain Solutions with Microsoft (see www.prochain.com). This add-on to Microsoft Project was developed in the 1990s and provides a robust solution, including most of the capabilities outlined above. It is proven and effective, especially to those organizations that already have Microsoft Project in use for their projects. This organization continues to invest in meeting user needs and getting results. Rob Newbold and his team have also contributed greatly to the literature.[4]

Realization (see www.realization.com). Realization tackled the multi-project challenges and got major results, starting in the late 1990s. They contributed significantly to the processes needed to drive results, including task management, full kitting, and different mechanisms for staggering projects. Their website is full of videos of clients providing insights to and testimonies of their results and implementation challenges. Realization uses a database to provide necessary data manipulation and coherency and ease of use in the user interfaces. Microsoft Project is used for data entry and can also be used for project views, but a great deal of the user interface is provided within Realization's screens and reporting.

Sciforma (see www.sciforma.com). Sciforma (previously Scitor) has been dedicated to project management for over 20 years. Their products are perceived to be easier to learn and use than Microsoft, with their own proprietary database. They have an enterprise approach, with a fully integrated multi-project management software. Their newest release offers a cloud-based approach, although much of their experience is on enterprise servers.

Conclusions

This chapter explains why the #1 focus of project management software must be to reduce project durations. In order to accomplish this, the software must facilitate:

- More productive, faster projects, through governing the activation of new projects according to the organization's capacity to do project work
- A single priority system, to avoid needless and frequent priority changes and shuffling of resources
- Project buffer management, a holistic way of knowing how projects are faring and when management needs to intervene to make course corrections

When the software and, more importantly, the people who control the multi-project environment focus on the above, resource issues disappear and projects flow much more quickly. Projects are the way that organizations accomplish change. Yet much project management software has been slow to keep up with organization needs. Today, a lot of collaboration is needed to keep projects moving quickly. Software should facilitate this collaboration by making project data transparent and accessible anywhere, anytime, and easily used by non-project managers.

Endnotes

1. The issue of strategically choosing the right projects is a different topic, fully discussed in G. I. Kendall and S. C. Rollins's text, *Advanced Project Portfolio Management and the PMO* (Boca Raton, FL: J. Ross Publishing, 2003).
2. See http://en.wikipedia.org/wiki/Software_as_a_service for more information about SaaS and clouds.
3. Although we do not endorse or recommend any specific software, as an example of cloud-based software, see www.exepron.com.
4. See Rob Newbold, *Project Management in the Fast Lane* (Boca Raton, FL: CRC Press, 1998); *Billion Dollar Solution* (Lake Ridge, VA: ProChain Solutions, Inc., 2008); and Andreas Scherer, *Be Fast or Be Gone* (Lake Ridge, VA: ProChain Solutions, Inc., 2001).

Questions

10-1. What is the limitation of an organization that projects must address? Explain.

10-2. Describe five essential capabilities in any project management software.

10-3. Pick one of the three secondary software considerations and explain why it is secondary.

10-4. Define *staggering* and why it is essential to govern the release/activation of new projects. What would software have to be able to do in order to provide a *staggering* capability?

10-5. What size of organization needs multi-project management software? Explain the rationale for your answer.

10-6. Older generation project management software typically relied on weekly or monthly batched reporting for many roles (e.g., senior management, sponsors, and resource managers). Provide two examples of why this style of reporting would not remove the limitation that multi-project management software must overcome.

10-7. Why should security of access to project management data be administered by the owner of the portfolios of projects and not by IT?

11. What Is It All Worth?

The Premise

Over the past six years, over 60 organizations publicly reported results using some of the methodology described in this book. See Appendix B for the details. These reports are in the public domain and include small, medium, and large organizations from many industries. The well-known organization names include Boeing, Siemens, Tata Steel, U.S. Air Force, Erickson, Proctor & Gamble, ABB, Rio Tinto Alcan, and many more. Here are the average improvements they reported:

- Project duration reduction of 38.8%, with a range of 13.3% (worst case) to 77.8% (best case)
- Number of projects completed per time period increased by 70%, with a range of 15% (worst case) to 222% (best case)
- Throughput increased by 52.9%, with a range of 14–150%

Some frequently asked questions about the measurements include:

1. How can you measure a reduction in project duration if you didn't perform the identical project twice? One way that this was measured is by the expected duration according to traditional planning techniques and the new duration when replanned using the approach in this book. Some companies that complete a large number of projects used average durations for all projects before and after the changes. Yet other organizations tracked cycle times in different project phases before and after.
2. How can an organization claim that it completed more projects on average? Certainly, a valid disclaimer on the results is "If each project is unique, and therefore has a unique duration, perhaps the organizations simply had much shorter projects in the post-implementation period." Not all organizations reported on this statistic. However, the ones that did were very sensitive to this metric, because it typically tied to the overall organization success. For example, in the U.S. Air Force, aircraft

readiness is a key metric. The number of maintenance/overhaul projects completed per month ties directly to this metric. In other organizations, for example companies that receive almost all of their revenue from projects, like Rio Tinto Alcan Alesa Engineering, the number of projects completed through the mechanical engineering phase per quarter ties closely to their revenues and profitability. In the pharmaceutical industry, companies like Dr. Reddy's Laboratories look at how many new products are launching or getting ready for trials each quarter. The number of new products per quarter became a key metric.

3. How does an organization know that all of its throughput increase came as a direct result of better project management? In many industries where projects are used for new product development (e.g., pharmaceutical), reduced cycle time translates directly to speed to market, which also translates directly to much more revenue for the same product. In project companies, being able to reduce cycle times means being able to do more projects with the same resources. This directly impacts throughput. Is it possible that some of the throughput increase came from producing better products or other improvements? Of course. However, those increases typically occur in much smaller increments—less than 5%. Therefore, none of the companies reporting these results had any reservations about most of the throughput increase coming from the new way of managing their multi-project environments.

One of the biggest wastes of time and money comes from investing in software and training without having a strategy for and tracking the return on investment, that is, having no expectation of a measurable, tangible, bottom-line result. This is very common today. The amount of money spent on project management software and certifications is huge—in the billions of dollars worldwide. Many certification organizations and training companies claim results, yet you hear very little from their clients who are making the investments.

Too often, projects are measured by their expected return or benefits and not based on what they actually achieved. The problem with project metrics today is that, for many projects, it takes too long to find out if the project actually provided the return. For example, for a new pharmaceutical product going into trials, it will be years before we have a known dollar impact. For any product development effort, the same can be true. That is why the metrics of project duration (sometimes called *project cycle time*), number of projects completed, and throughput are a better *leading* indication of future ROI/profits/cost savings. This does not preclude also having the lagging metrics.

Setting Up Before and After Metrics

Remember that not all of these measurements are appropriate for every organization. Pick two or three key ones out of the following, and the value of your next investment in multi-project management will become much clearer. Often, current measurement reports do not exist on the items below. Therefore, many organizations have to look closely at their data to derive the *before* situation.

Number of projects completed. There are three key elements of this metric:

1. One element is the time period you wish to measure. For organizations that have only a few projects with long time durations, a quarterly or semiannual time period works best. Other organizations have monthly measurements.
2. Another key element is whether you measure a phase (section) of a project or an entire project. For example, in Rio Tinto Alcan Alesa, projects could go for more than a year, with a lot of client and other contractor dependencies. However, the part they had full control over was the mechanical engineering. Therefore, the number of projects completed through the mechanical engineering phase was key to their company performance.
3. A third potential element is the project backlog. In some organizations, when the backlog of projects waiting to be activated is growing, or is not decreasing, it is potentially a symptom of existing projects completing too slowly. We use the term *potential symptom* because it is always possible that you will see a spurt of new projects identified in a short time period, with no relationship to the speed of existing project execution. However, as a statistic, it is a good red flag to warn the organization of potential problems.

Average project duration reduction. If you are applying a new project planning approach, use the current duration in elapsed time (days) and the new duration in days for each project. Of course, this result is only meaningful if your due date performance or scope is not sacrificed to meet a reduced project duration metric. In all of the cases from the above 60 companies, they reported reduced duration while increasing on-time performance, and in some cases with increased scope. Since you are only executing the project once (not twice with old and new methodology), it would be impossible to compare actual times. If project on-time performance improves with the new approach, you can predict that the disparity between actual times would be even greater than with planned times. Therefore, planned time duration reduction is a conservative measure of success.

On-time (on budget and within scope) performance. The faster you complete projects, the more likely you will also have a positive impact on budget and scope. You are welcome to measure all three separately. However, the percentage of projects completed on time, when challenged with a reduced project duration and identical scope and budget, is a real sign of improvement. The measurement should be generally according to the original planned time, not project deadlines that get revised after starting a project. Once again, the *before* picture is often not clear, either because it is not tracked at all or because it is tracked according to revised times. There is a more important aspect of this metric. It is not just about the increase in predictability within shorter planned durations. It is also about when a project is late, how late is it? In most organizations that we've worked with, consider projects that average three months in duration under a new system versus, for example, four months in duration before. We'd rather have a 95% on-time performance within three months, with the other 5% of projects finishing within a week of the target date, than 100% on time with projects finishing within four months on average. Speed has value. Being a little late on a small percentage of projects, in most environments, does no damage.

Throughput. This measure has been used in for-profit and not-for-profit project environments. It applies where completing more projects faster has a direct and immediate impact on tangible organization goals. For example, in the U.S. Air Force maintenance centers, if the maintenance work can be completed in half the time, there are more aircraft returned to bases and available either for training or missions. For that organization, this is tangible throughput. In a company using the methodology to speed up periodic major plant maintenance shutdowns, gaining a week on a three-week shutdown means millions of dollars in throughput. In a shipyard, delivering a large ship weeks earlier than scheduled had no value to the owner who commissioned the ship. However, for the shipbuilder, being able to produce more ships per year with the same resources had a huge impact on throughput, as measured by the gross margin value of projects completed per quarter. Since this company actually has three dry docks (small, medium, and large), the quarterly measurement is valid, since they increase project flow on all sizes of projects. Another company, Amdocs, which does hundreds of projects per quarter in customized software development, used a variation on this measurement: revenue per man-month.

Other metrics. Another example of a metric that senior management considered important was the number of projects in crisis. When senior management is devoting too much of their time to firefighting sick projects, this metric can be key. The goal was zero, and the organization achieved this with the new methodology. For some projects, finishing early has huge value, so the number of projects finishing early and how early became metrics. For other companies that subcontract a lot of their work, the reduction in subcontracted hours became a productivity measure of project success. There are several documented cases where a company or division went from a loss to a profit, due to changing how they managed projects. In one case, the VP of the division described how they went from being considered a "dog" by the parent company, losing money every quarter, to having paid every cent of operating expense for the entire year by April of that year and having every dollar of net revenue (revenue minus cost of materials) from customers drop to the bottom line for the rest of the year.

Implementing Metrics versus Operational Data

Understanding and reporting what the solution is worth is vital. An organization usually does best with two to three metrics at most: one primary and one or two secondary measurements. The rest of what an organization tracks makes for good operational data—useful for everyone to understand what is going on. Be careful what you call a metric—make sure it is holistic in nature (i.e., causing the people/parts within the multi-project system to do what is good for the organization as a whole).

There are some important data worth tracking that we would not call *metrics*. Nonetheless, these data help the organization get more value from the solution. For example:

- *How full is your pipeline of projects?* This question applies to projects not yet active but ready to be worked on. In a project company, this is a sign of how healthy the next few quarters will be—how much backlog of work exists. For a manufacturing or products company, this indicates how many new products or improvement projects are waiting to be worked on. We have seen several cases where there were actually not enough new products in the pipeline, indicating a pending disaster if ignored.
- *How many projects are in a red zone?* A system with more than 10% of projects in a red zone implies a system out of control. You can predict deteriorating throughput, project completions, and all the other negative effects.
- *How often are tasks being started earlier than planned?* This is symptomatic of anarchy—people are reverting to bad multitasking habits. If an upward trend is not reversed, you can predict all the same negative effects as before you started implementation.
- *Priority violations/changes*. Following the basic rules of a single priority system ensures that all or almost all projects get completed on time. Once

again, violations are predictive of the multi-project system losing control and soon losing value.

- *Number of project tasks completed per week.* Within certain skill sets, this is a great measure of overall productivity and a predictor of more projects being completed in the near future. The trend is the key. If the trend turns negative, it signifies an immediate need for intervention or help required to continue driving tangible value.

Conclusions

In most multi-project environments, it is worth the intense focus of senior management on a strategy to get at least 10% more on the bottom line from the project investment portfolio. A strategy as outlined in this text, combined with the right measurements, has proven successful much more often than not. Here are the right measurements:

- Average project duration—seek percentage reduction, quarter over quarter.
- Number of projects completed with the same resources—seek to increase per time period.
- Percentage projects on time (on budget, within scope)—time is the key factor, especially when combined with reducing project durations.
- Throughput—if you can tie project completions to revenue or other organization goal units, then seek a dramatic increase in throughput as you implement the new project management methodology.

Too often, organizations ignore metrics and supporting project operational data. Although sometimes difficult to measure, project success is key to continually improving an organization's bottom-line performance. Hundreds of case studies are now in the public domain, so there are no good excuses left for not measuring ROI on project management investment.

Questions

11-1. Explain each of the key metrics that could be used to track ROI on improving multi-project management. For any one of the suggested metrics, explain why it might be difficult to obtain current performance data from an existing project management system.

11-2. Which metrics are useful in combination? Why?

11-3. What is the difference between a metric and supporting data?

11-4. What do you think the damage might be from having more than two or three metrics?

11-5. How is it possible for an organization, with the same resources, to generate 50% more throughput or to reduce project cycle time (duration) by more than 20%? Review case studies at www.realization.com, www.prochain.com, or www.goldratt.com and provide three examples.

11-6. If you begin to measure the number of project tasks completed each week, and a task that you measured as complete last week now needs rework, how should this be counted in a data report? What behavior are you trying to encourage by these data, for resources and for the people managing the resources and tasks?

11-7. An increase in throughput could be a result of many different things in an organization, other than project management improvement. Is it worthwhile trying to distinguish between the throughput increase that comes from other sources and that which comes from multi-project management improvement?

PART III

PROJECT PLANNING, NETWORKS, AND RISK AVOIDANCE

For years, in our opinion, project networks have failed in most organizations to drive correct behaviors among program and project managers, executives, and resource managers. Many people involved in projects do not like to use networks because they are so cumbersome and often obsolete soon after execution begins. You will find Part III useful if you are:

- Someone who uses project networks but still has difficulty getting projects done on time, on budget, and within scope. You will discover how to build a resource-based project plan with less detail and with a much higher probability of meeting all the project goals.
- Someone who has built networks but found them too difficult to deal with or only useful for planning and not for execution. Part III will show you a more robust approach with a simpler outcome that is useful for execution.
- Someone who has never built a network before. This section provides a step-by-step, easy-to-follow approach with examples that make the process clear, even for beginners.

This section, Part III, is devoted to correcting the decades-old problem of useless project networks.

12. Level of Detail—Not the Lowest Level

The Premise

There are two extremes we can describe in how organizations plan projects. One extreme is a *seat-of-the-pants* methodology. To our surprise, we have worked with multibillion dollar organizations, undertaking multimillion dollar projects, without any documentation of the project plan. The other extreme is finding hundreds to thousands of tasks, at a level of detail that makes it very difficult to manage or distinguish what is important. The correct answer is not a compromise, but to know when enough is enough. This chapter, and the ones that follow in Part III, provide the necessary knowledge.

Level of Detail in a Project Network

What a dilemma planning a project can be! Expectations for project plans usually include many of the following:

- Usable for costing the project
- Structure to track while executing the project
- Doing resource loading
- Calculating earned value
- Detailing exactly what every task should be and/or should include
- Providing information about inputs for the task
- Defining each task's exit criteria
- Describing any specific notes or details about each and every task
- Enabling managers to know who are the primary performing resources (people, equipment, facilities) and who are supporting resources (those not used for the entire time of the task, but required to achieve the task's exit criteria, etc.)

Don't forget, the project plan must also include all of the work required to meet the stakeholders' consensus of project scope. Oh yes, a project plan should also be easy to manage!

Figure 12.1 The unavoidable conflict in building project networks

It is easy to see the conflict for project planners. On one hand, in order to assure project success, the project plan must be manageable, which means there's pressure to not have a very detailed project plan (because otherwise it would not be manageable—the focus would be diluted on too many tasks). On the other hand, in order to assure project success, the project plan must provide all the data needed during project execution (to manage resources, work, costs, timelines, estimates to complete, etc.), which means there's pressure to have a very detailed project plan. It sure sounds like a project plan is being used for more than planning, scheduling, executing, and managing a project—it's also required to be the entire project database! Is that reasonable?

Project organizations have tried to provide a way out of the conflict for project planners: no more than 350 tasks, no task is longer than 80 hours, and plan at a very low level of detail, but manage at a much higher level. One of the common standards for detail is the work breakdown structure (WBS),[1] which calls for detailing ALL of the work required to achieve objectives and sufficient for costing and labor hour reporting. Have these approaches been effective for all projects? Our answer is "definitely not."

In our opinion, there is a huge problem with using the WBS as the project plan. These structures do not represent the interdependencies of work required to meet stakeholder needs. When there is so much detail, you lose focus on these interdependencies.

We acknowledge that the less detail/more detail conflict exists for project planning and approach project planning from this perspective: *Start planning at a high level, then "explode" the plan into more detail only when and where needed.*

This section on project planning defines the 10 steps to get to the right level of detail for your project with the correct scope to meet stakeholder needs. We'll also discuss how each of the steps helps to mitigate project risks (technical, schedule, and financial).

We do project planning by creating a project network—an interdependent relationship of tasks (boxes) and flow of work (arrows) that are required in order to achieve the goals, scope, and sponsor criteria of the project.

The 10-Step Process

The 10 steps, detailed in the following 10 chapters, to build a robust network at the right level of detail to meet stakeholder needs with minimum risk are:

1. Define the project's measurable goals, tangible scope, and sponsor criteria.
2. Define the backbone of the network.
3. Expand the skeleton of the network.
4. Define additional dependencies.
5. Check the network against project goals, scope, and deliverables.
6. Resource the project tasks.
7. Scrutinize with subject matter experts.
8. Estimate time durations.
9. Reduce durations without compromise.
10. Perform a final risk assessment.

Creating and Using Templates to Speed Up the Process

Many times an organization performs similar types of projects. In these cases, templates can be used to speed up project planning, typically to a half day or less after understanding the project's scope. We do not recommend creating templates from scratch; our recommendation is to create actual project networks for the various similar types of projects first and then turn these into templates.

Creating a template from an existing project network:

- For any task in the template, there will likely be both standard and project-specific attributes. Remove the project-specific elements and you have a template!
- There are some task times that will remain the same for all future projects. For example, a testing process that requires a piece of equipment to run continuously for 100 hours will remain 100 hours for all projects; other

test tasks will be different, depending on project requirements. Our experience is that all other task times should be removed from the template; otherwise there is too great a temptation to use the *template task time* instead of estimating the task time for the specific project being planned. A similar case exists for resources.

- Ensure the template is kept up-to-date and available for future project planning.
- When using the template, add the project-specific elements using the steps below.

Using a template to speed up project planning. The 10-step process for building a project network is modified as follows when using a template:

1. Unchanged: Define the project's measurable goals, tangible scope, and sponsor criteria.
2. Review the appropriate template in terms of the project's goals, scope, and sponsor criteria. Make any required modifications to the template, saving it as this project's plan. Do not forget to modify the task notes as required.
3. Skipped.
4. Skipped.
5. Skipped.
6. Check the network against project goals, scope, and deliverables.
7. Scrutinize with subject matter experts.
8. Resource the project tasks for any required project-specific resources.
9. Estimate time durations as required.
10. Perform a final risk assessment.

Conclusions

There are two commonly used approaches to project planning, both of which do not work well. One is *seat of the pants*, where projects are run without a formal, written, scrutinized plan. The other is a plan worked to the lowest level of detail. Such a plan is so detailed that the underlying problems are masked and the plan is difficult to scrutinize. In the 10-step process outlined in this chapter and defined in the following 10 chapters, detail is only advocated where absolutely necessary because there are task interdependencies or other crucial elements of scope. It is our assumption that excessive detail does not help control a project—in fact, the outcome is often the opposite. The assumption is backed up by years of experience with organizations that have used this assumption with much greater than average success with projects.

Endnotes

1. See http://en.wikipedia.org/wiki/Work_breakdown_structure for a detailed description of the WBS.

Questions

12-1. What is the purpose of a project plan?

12-2. What are the compelling arguments for planning a project at a very detailed level?

12-3. What are the compelling arguments for planning a project at a higher level (less detailed)?

12-4. What are examples of each of the kinds of project risk (technical, schedule, financial)?

12-5. What is the difference between the project's WBS and the project's plan?

12-6. What are other examples of the conflicts project planners face?

12-7. Provide other examples of the ways organizations *help* project planners out of the conflict between *more detail* and *less detail* in project plans.

13. Step 1: The Project's Measurable Goals, Tangible Scope, and Sponsor Criteria

The Premise

We frequently hear user complaints about project outcomes. Scope creep is one of the most voiced issues in project management. No wonder. In the vital *giving birth* stage of a project, once again we witness two extremes. Either we see a 20+ page document, sometimes called a *project charter*, which has so much detail in it that it is almost guaranteed to put you to sleep and, further, to not be very useful in gauging whether or not the project will meet all of the key stakeholder needs. The other extreme is brief project scope and/or objectives statements that are so vague as to be proclaimed an open invitation for scope creep within days of project initiation.

Figure 13.1 Step 1 provides the blueprint for the project plan

This step is analogous to having a blueprint for building a house. Before you start building, you must have a pretty good idea of how big the house will be and its dimensions, or you will not know where to put the footers or how strong the footers must be. Everything else flows from this key front-end definition of stakeholder needs. Do not skip this step or any of the elements described below! There are too many anecdotes about a project's budget and timeline being almost totally gone when the project team finds out that what's being produced is not what the stakeholders expect.

What is the desired result of Step 1? The project planners and all stakeholders understand and agree upon the goals, scope, sponsor criteria, functional criteria, and boundary conditions for the project.

There are two parts to this step:

1. Preparing yourself for the project stakeholders' meeting
2. Holding the project stakeholders' meeting

Preparing for the Project Stakeholders' Meeting

Meeting attendees. First identify the project stakeholders and other key people who should be invited to the meeting. If you're not sure, these questions may help in developing a checklist of meeting invitees for this and future projects:

- Who does the project manager report to for this project?
- Who is sponsoring this project?
- Are there customers for the project? Please note that a project's customers may be internal or external to your organization; at times there can be both internal and external customers.
- Who is providing funding for the project?
- Who provides resources for the project (human, equipment, facilities)? Again, these resources may be internal or external. Who represents each of their interests? Do unions represent any of the resources?
- Are there key functional areas that should be represented (engineering [and those subsets], production, marketing, sales, contracting, legal, safety, product development, technical documentation, distribution, and so on)?
- Are there additional people (internal or external) that require project progress reports?

Meeting logistics. After determining who should attend the meeting, determine when and where the meeting will take place. It may also be important to set up video-conferencing for some attendees.

Meeting self-preparation. This is not so that you can provide all the answers at the meeting! It is intended for you to begin to understand what you are going to hear from the attendees as well as giving you the *big picture*. This preparation will also help you ensure nothing is left out at the meeting.

- Gather and study any existing project documentation, including any planning documents, trade studies, etc.
- Ensure you understand how each of the customers plans to use the output of the project—similarities and differences.
- What the scope of this project is. How many, what is involved, which locations? Is the scope the same for each customer?
- What are the tangible deliverables and what functional requirements must they meet?
- What is the project's output—an analysis, a prototype, a production-ready unit, a quantity of product delivered to multiple distribution warehouses with technical support fully staffed and ready to answer questions, a new product available at all locations with full advertising campaign and fully trained sales staff?
- What impact this project has on your organization: What is the predicted bottom-line positive garnered from delivering the project on time, within budget, and with full scope? When does the organization expect to begin seeing those bottom-line impacts? If there is not a bottom-line positive impact, why is the project being done? There must be a benefit statement of some kind; expect it to be measurable, even if it is qualitative rather than quantitative.
- What is the budget(s) allocated to the project (remember, a financial budget is not the only type of budget)?
- What are the risks to the project's success? Include known technical, schedule, and budget risks. Will the major items that the project needs (e.g., equipment, prototypes, software, long-lead-time items) be available when promised? Will these items likely be according to required specifications?

Now that you have done your homework, you're ready to conduct the meeting. Gather data from the experts in the room in a manner that fully accomplishes the meeting goals without wasting time and money.

Final thoughts. Consider whether your prework will be similar for all projects. In many cases, it makes sense to follow a checklist in preparing for every project meeting (see Table 13.1).

Project Stakeholders' Meeting

Ensure that the person whose role is to facilitate the project stakeholders' meeting uses this standard approach. Remember, in a multi-project environment, if

Table 13.1 Pre-stakeholders' meeting sample checklist topics

Project Name
Meeting Attendees? List required and optional
Project Access, Information, Considerations, Security, Sensitivities?
Project Due Date(s)? What is required on this date/each date?
Project Customers (internal and external)?
Project Documentation Required? Specify both internal and external requirements
Project Reviews? Specify type, quantity, and dates, if already scheduled
Customer-Furnished Data, Drawings, Materials, Specifications, etc.?
Required Tests? Specify types, locations, requirements, attendees
Minimum or Maximum Intervals between Tests?
Test Data? Sent to whom? In what form and format?
Required Permits or Certifications? Specify types and sources
External Resources or Facilities? Specify
Long-Lead Items?
Public Affairs/Legislative Constraints?
Marketing/Sales/Legal Constraints?
Global Manufacturing Constraints?
Government Involvement/Constraints? Specify level, agency, involvement/constraint

some project networks and scope are defined poorly, this will create chaos for ALL of the projects during execution.

Use multiple whiteboards or chart paper that you can stick on the walls. Since this will be a multipage outcome, using a computer is only practical if you are able to print what you capture for all attendees as you go. All the attendees need to be able to see what's written in its entirety. The facilitator's prework is to get in the right mindset to listen and gather data, not to tell the attendees what he/she thinks the project should be! Follow the meeting outline.

- Present this meeting's goal: "The project planners and all stakeholders understand and agree upon the goals, scope, sponsor criteria, functional criteria, and measurable outcomes for this project."
- Identify the scope and goal(s) of the project. What IS this project? There may be one or multiple statements of scope elements. Identify whose goal (perspective) it is as you go, since different stakeholders/key people may state the same goal in different ways, or it may sound the same but have a very different meaning to some attendees. This also helps determine whether there are conflicting goals (or whether they are just stated from

a different perspective). The facilitator is the *clearinghouse*—making sure everyone understands what's been said and that terms have the same meaning for all.

- Make sure that the goals are expressly and measurably related to the goals of the organization. How much new revenue will be generated? How much will operating expense be reduced? How much will this add to the organization's profits? How much faster will patients get through an emergency room? How many more aircraft will be ready for missions and testing? How much shorter will customer lead times be?
- Ensure all customers/types of customers are listed, including what needs this meets or issues this resolves for each of the customer types. Reminder: Customers may be internal, external, or both.
- Define the tangible deliverables—the project's output(s). How many, in what form, delivered to which customer, delivered where (to the loading dock, delivered to a distribution facility, etc.)? Are there any interim outputs that must be provided? Are any of the interim outputs date sensitive? Are the outputs products, drawings, an analysis, a prototype, a production-ready unit, a fully ramped-up production line, and so on? What must accompany the output? Ensure the functional requirements or specifications of the project's output(s) are defined as well.
- Are there any major items needed for this project (e.g., equipment, software)? When will they arrive? From whom? What are the specifications required for those items?
- When does your organization start making money (gaining bottom-line benefit) from this project? Do the goal and scope statements reflect that? For example, is the project to construct a new production facility or is the project to be at full productive capacity in the new production facility? There is a significant difference between those two project scopes! The goal and scope should always be stated in a way that reflects when your organization realizes bottom-line positive value.
- Are any customers imposing mandatory reviews? Are there contractual milestones?
- What are your budgets to accomplish this project? Budgets can be financial, facilities, head count, or a combination.
- Describe the technical, schedule, and budget risks to the project.
- Define any sponsor criteria that have not yet been defined.

When you have achieved the meeting's objectives, summarize and close the meeting. After the meeting, review what's been gathered. Do a final check to make sure all statements and documentation are clear. Ensure all attendees receive a copy of what's been documented (see Table 13.2).

Table 13.2 Template for stakeholder meeting results

Scope/Goal(s):
•
Customer(s):
•
Tangible Deliverables/Functional Requirements of Output(s):
•
Major Items/Specifications Needed as Project Inputs:
•
Bottom-Line Impact to Organization:
•
Budget:
•
Risks:
•
Sponsor Criteria:
•

Case Study

Appendix E contains a complete, detailed case study for the entire planning process covered in Part III of this text. The case study is intended for:

- Professors
- Instructors
- Business readers who wish to practice the planning process on an example and who are not enrolled in a course or workshop using this text

Answers to the case study questions and actual documentation and network examples are available to the above readers upon request. Answers are not available to students enrolled in a course or workshop using this text.

Conclusions

To avoid scope creep and its ultimate consequences—project delivered late, over budget, and/or not within scope, a careful process is needed. The process includes people who must be invited to a meeting to define the project, topics to be covered, and documentation of the outcomes. This documentation forms the basis of checking every task in a project plan, to see if it is needed and if it, in fact, helps the project meet these stakeholder criteria. Furthermore, this documentation allows the team to check that all criteria are met, once the network is finished. To be useful, such documentation must be organized, succinct, and directly related to the goals of the organization. Chapter 14 includes an example of such documentation.

Questions

13-1. What is the desired result of Step 1?

13-2. What are the two parts to Step 1?

13-3. What is the harm of not preparing for a stakeholders' meeting, using all the steps?

13-4. Describe five mandatory elements of preparation for a stakeholders' meeting.

13-5. Give three examples of goals of a project, according to the authors' recommendations.

13-6. What is the maximum number of pages you would expect to require to document the results of a stakeholders' meeting? Why is this important?

13-7. What action should you take if there are no identified bottom-line impacts of the project?

14. Step 2: The Backbone

The Premise

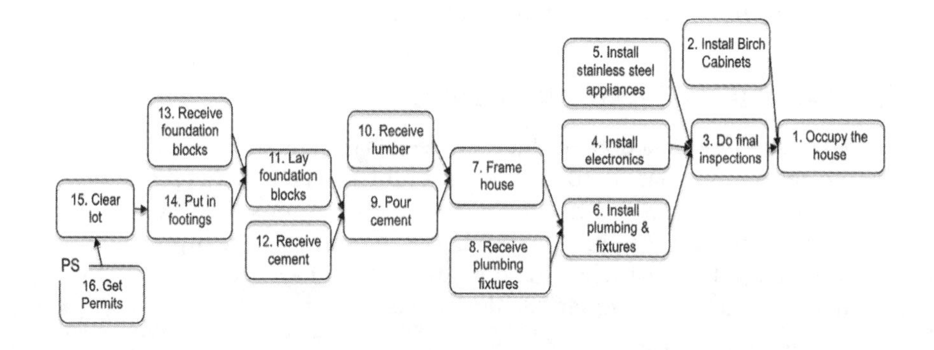

Figure 14.1 Example of a network spine or backbone

Network building begins only after Step 1, the stakeholder needs, are clearly documented and understood! Every project network has some long strings of tasks with many other tasks *feeding into* these strings. For example, consider the string of tasks in building a house (see Figure 14.1). After the house is framed, other strings of tasks would be performed before the builder would arrange final inspections (e.g., electrical, plumbing, drywalling, painting, etc.). But to start building the network, we only consider one of these strings, and we'll use the example of Figure 14.1 as a sample starting point.

Step 2 defines the tasks required for the backbone (or spine) of the project network, starting at the end of the project and working toward the beginning. This is where the leadership of the person who thinks network building is "fun" is crucial! In addition, include the project manager and one or two other team members. The team members should be people who understand the overall requirements, how the organization works, and all resource skill sets in general. If the organization has a project management office, then someone from this office would be involved. These team members will remain for all following steps.

Network Building Tips

- Use sticky notes (Post-It®[1] type notes or pieces of paper and Post-It® glue sticks) large enough to write on and large sheets of paper to begin network building.
- We strongly recommend that you do NOT build your project network on the computer; build it on large paper so that you and your team can see the interconnections and add to them. Put the network into the computer only when you are ready to print or plot it.

First Box on the Network Diagram

> **2.1.** Using the stakeholders' meeting results from Step 1, pick a tangible deliverable that is produced later in the project. At this point, do not worry about the other tangible deliverables; they will be built into the network in subsequent steps. Using the example for this chapter from Table 14.1, we select the item of scope to have the house available to occupy by October 15. The verb is:
>
> "Occupy the house."
>
> Write the selected starting point on a Post-It® and place it on the far right of a large sheet of paper. The tangible deliverable should be written as a sentence minus the subject, starting with an action verb.

Some ask why should we build a network backward, starting from the end, rather than forward, starting from the beginning? Working backward, we include ONLY those tasks that are absolutely necessary as input to the next step. By working this way, we find that much less detail is required, yet the end result still meets all stakeholder needs.

For example, assume we have a wedding project. If you try planning this from the beginning, you can probably think of dozens of tasks that need to be done, all muddled together in the brain. However, working from the end, the last task is for the clergy to marry the couple. What must we have immediately before we accomplish this task? We must have the couple in place, the guests seated, the clergy ready, and the wedding music playing. We can continue working backward on any one of these streams and will find that there are typically only one or two items at a time that we need to identify immediately before each task.

Table 14.1 Output of a stakeholders' meeting

Scope/Goal(s):
• Ready to occupy 3000-sq-ft lakefront, ranch-style, 3-bedroom, brick home with attached 3-car garage no later than Oct. 15th
Customer(s):
• Mr. and Mrs. John Doe (no children, no pets)
Tangible Deliverables/Functional Requirements of Output(s):
• Hardwood floors in all but kitchen and bathrooms • Ceramic floors in kitchen, bathrooms, mudroom • All granite countertops • Stainless steel appliances • Custom Birch Cabinets and finishes • Frame house • Lakeside: floor to ceiling windows, French doors • Full house electronics (TV, games, intercom) • Summer kitchen on extended lakeside deck • Full formal landscaping including path to dock and boathouse
Major Items/Specifications Needed as Project Inputs:
• Hot tub on lakeside deck
Bottom-Line Impact to Organization:
• $ 50,000 net profit
Budget:
• $450,000
Risks:
• Permitting and inspection processes • Weather • Tile contractor • Electronics installer
Sponsor Criteria:
•

The network is constructed in a logical, orderly way and we only identify those elements that we must have to meet the end goals.

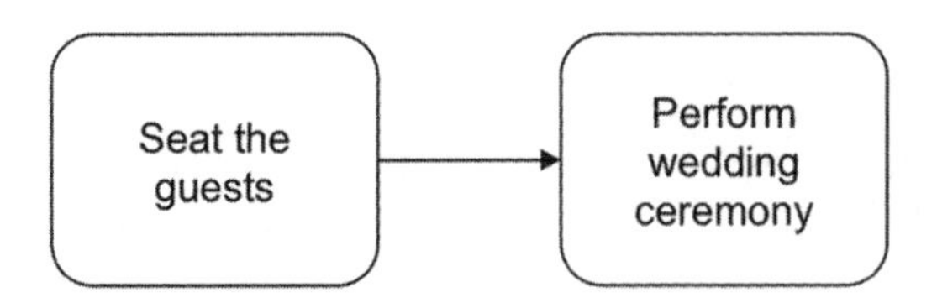

Figure 14.2 Meaning of boxes and arrows

Boxes and Arrows

A project network consists of boxes and arrows. The boxes are where the work of the project occurs and will have resources and time estimates identified in later steps. The arrows are used to indicate handoffs of work between boxes.

An arrow implies that a box on the right of an arrow **must have** the input from the boxes to the left of the arrow before it can start work. Output from the left is input to the right.[2] For example, in Figure 14.2, we must have the guests seated before performing the wedding ceremony. There are actually two types of *must have*, which are discussed further in Chapter 21 on ways to reduce project duration.

Building the Backbone

Building the backbone requires knowing the first box you will use on the network diagram and understanding how boxes (tasks) and arrows are used. We have that information so it's time to understand the process for building the backbone.

> **2.2.** Ask, "What must be completed (or finished) immediately before <u>the task on the right</u> can start?" For example, "What must be completed immediately before '<u>Occupying the house</u>' can start?"

Tip: Asking out loud helps you to listen/think about the question more closely. Fill in the underlined words with the actual wording of the task on the right—the task at the tip of the arrow.

Another way of asking the question is, "What input is required before Mr. and Mrs. Doe can begin occupying the house?" The answer should be written on a Post-It® in task format (starting with the action verb) and placed immediately to the left of the task. Check the logic by saying, "In order to start (<u>the task on the right</u>), we must first have completed (<u>the task on the left</u>)." If the team agrees, write the arrow connecting the two tasks. Note that sometimes "ing" must be added to the verbs to make the building and checking sentences flow. See Figure 14.3.

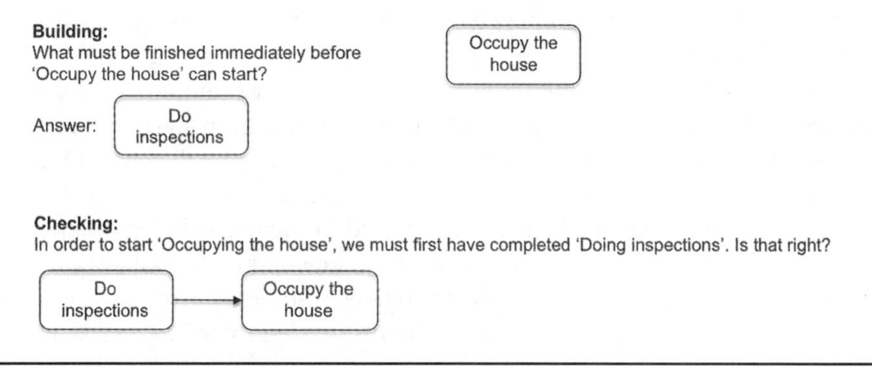

Figure 14.3 Building and checking a task interdependency

2.3. Ask, "Is there anything else that must be completed immediately before (the task on the right) can start?" Or "Is any other input required to be able to start (the task on the right)?" Use a Post-It® to capture that task, ensuring it is written in the correct format (starting with an action verb, no subject, sentence that describes what must have been completed). Check the logic by saying, "In order to start (the task on the right), we must first have completed (the task on the left)." If the team agrees, draw the arrow connecting the two tasks (tail of arrow at predecessor, tip of arrow at successor). Repeat this until all tasks that must be completed immediately before the starting task have been identified. Don't forget to build and check every dependency using the wording above. This is also a good time to start uniquely numbering each task for identification purposes. This will make it much easier for people who have a comment or question on one of the many boxes to describe to which box they are referring. See Figure 14.4.

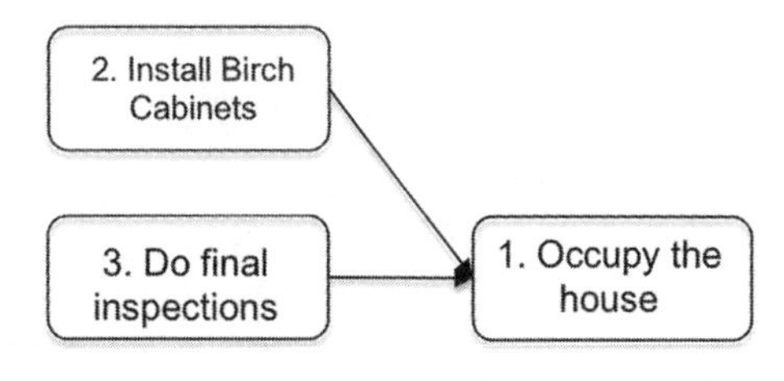

Figure 14.4 Results of Steps 2.2 and 2.3

Sometimes there can be disagreement among the team members about whether or not a task belongs immediately before the task on its right (whether its output is required as an input to the next task or whether it is needed earlier in time).

If this occurs, leave the task where it is for now; if it truly is needed earlier, the process will identify that and the task can be moved earlier at that time.

This process can seem counterintuitive to some. For example, "Install Birch Cabinets" must be complete before "Occupy the house" can start, and the next step for many is to look for what must be completed immediately before "Install birch cabinets"—what we would call looking for the linear flow. Do not fall into this trap! Identify *all* the tasks required immediately before the task on the right—that is the best way to ensure all the inputs that the task on the right needs to begin will be available. There is no fixed number of arrows required for a task. Remember to identify ONLY the inputs needed to begin the task on the right.

2.4. In order to continue building the backbone of the network, examine each of the tasks to the left that you just inserted. Based on the team's understanding of those tasks, which one requires the most work to be done? That will be the task from which to build the rest of the backbone. Repeat Steps 2.2 and 2.3 to identify first one task to the left of your newly selected "right" task and check it and then identify all other required tasks to the left. See Figure 14.5.

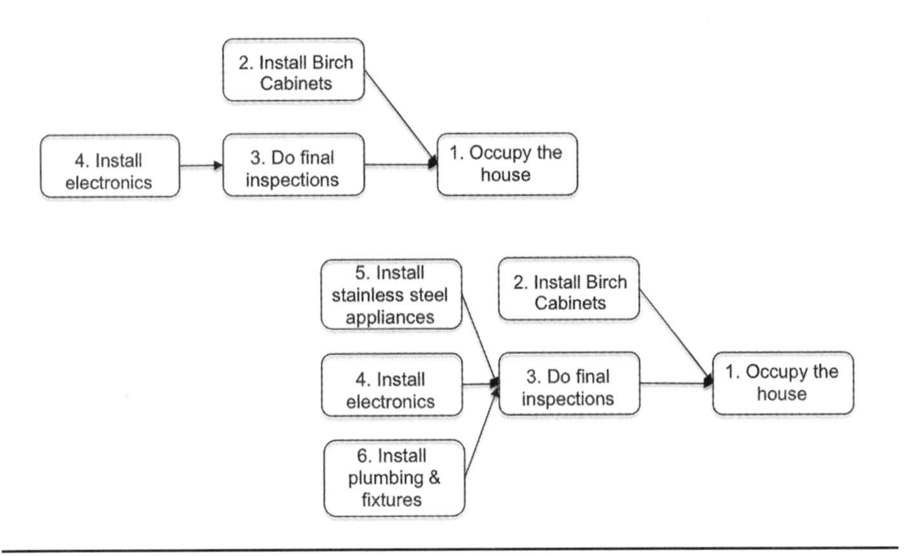

Figure 14.5 Result of Step 2.4

2.5. Repeat Step 2.4 until you have reached a task that could be started today if the project go-ahead was given. That task is called a path start or an entry point and should be designated as such. Typi-

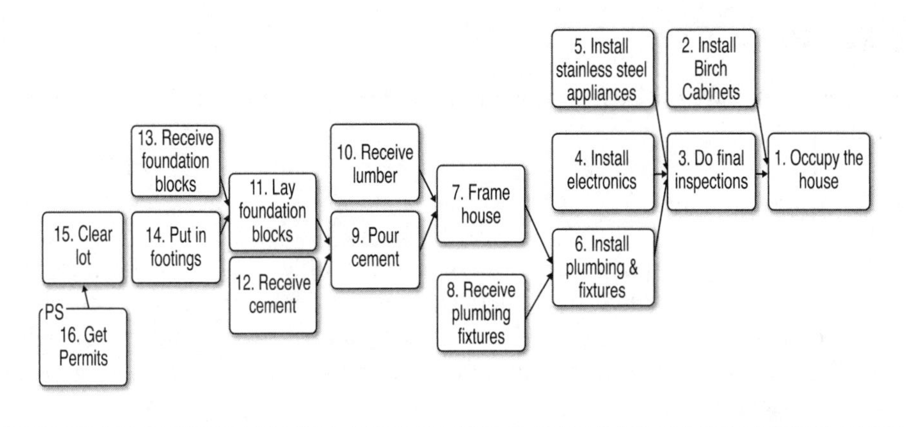

Figure 14.6 Result of Step 2.5

cal conventions are to put "PS" or "EP" on the task. Congratulations! Your team has completed the backbone! See Figure 14.6.

Note that we have only worked back to the beginning on one path. So even though other tasks have no tasks to the left of them (e.g., task 13, receive foundation blocks), we have not yet determined that this is, in fact, a path start task. Further steps in the process will complete the network.

Some organizations require the project network to look like a football (American style)—that is, one starting point and one ending point. Although we agree on having one ending point, there is not a requirement for a single starting point. Check to make sure that a single starting point isn't really an administrative or overhead task—these should not be in the project network. Only tasks that are necessary to create or produce the tangible deliverables of the project should be in the project network.

As the backbone emerges, it becomes tempting to begin adding tasks that *you know* must be in the final network for the project. Do not do that—yet. It is very important to keep network building at a high level, breaking down into more detail only when and as required. Too often, network builders get too detailed, too early; this makes for networks that are very difficult to manage and can significantly lengthen the time it takes to build a project network. It really doesn't matter what you *know* must be in the network, right now. The required level of detail will make itself known through the process of network building, which does have multiple steps and multiple risk avoidances/risk mitigations built in. This is the beginning of the first pass! Staying at a less detailed level can be difficult for experienced project planners and managers. This can be hard to *un-learn*! Please be patient and let the network develop over the required steps.

Case Study

See Appendix E for the next section of the case study, relating to Step 2 of project planning.

Conclusions

Network building must begin only when the stakeholder needs have been clearly identified and documented from Step 1 of this process. Once this is complete, the following steps are performed by a small team of two to four people who know both the overall project goals and the organization very well. The steps to build the backbone are:

> Step 2. Define the tasks required for the backbone of the project network (one main path), starting at the end of the project and working toward the beginning.
>
> **2.1.** Using the stakeholders' meeting results from Step 1, pick a tangible deliverable that is produced later in the project.
>
> **2.2.** Ask, "What must be completed (or finished) immediately before (the task on the right) can start?"
>
> **2.3.** Ask, "Is there anything else that must be completed immediately before (the task on the right) can start?" Or "Is any other input required to be able to start (the task on the right)?"
>
> **2.4.** In order to continue building the backbone of the network, examine each of the tasks to the left that you just inserted. Based on the team's understanding of those tasks, which one requires the most work to be done? That will be the task from which to build the rest of the backbone. Repeat Steps 2.2 and 2.3 to identify first one task to the left of your newly selected "right" task and check it and then identify all other required tasks to the left.
>
> **2.5.** Repeat Step 2.4 until you have reached a task that could be started today, if the project go-ahead was given. This task is called a path start or entry point and should be designated as such. Typical conventions are to put "PS" or "EP" on the task.

Endnotes

1. Post-It® is a trademark of 3M.

2. For those readers who are familiar with the jargon of project networks, this means the only arrows used in the project network are *finish to start* arrows.

Questions

14-1. What is a task?

14-2. What do project network arrows signify?

14-3. Why is it important to use specific wording when building and checking parts of a network?

14-4. Why build the project network from the end to the beginning?

14-5. When is a project network complete?

14-6. Why build the task interdependency diagram on large sheets of paper instead of putting it directly into the computer?

14-7. Why stop building the backbone when a path start task is reached?

15. Step 3: The Skeleton

The Premise

The spine or backbone of the network was completed in the prior step. Continuing the process, every task or collection of tasks that you add must now be somehow connected to this spine. All of Step 2, the backbone, must be complete before starting this step. The analogy is that in building a house, you must have the footings and foundation before you start putting up walls. The backbone of a project network is the foundation.

Figure 15.1 The skeleton of a house

Building the Walls of the House

Building the skeleton means adding the additional required tasks and paths of the project, following a structured, disciplined process. Remember to stick to a high level of task definition—you are not putting all the finishing touches on the house. Don't worry about choosing carpets, light fixtures, paint colors, etc. Just make sure that this skeleton matches the blueprint definition of Step 1. In this step (Step 3), the same process steps are repeated until the entire project skeleton is complete, meaning the project network has been completed.

3.1. Using the project backbone already completed, go to the far right of the backbone and pick one of the latest occurring tasks. Continuing the example from Chapter 14, there is only one option, task 2, since we have already built the backbone from task 3. See Figure 15.2.

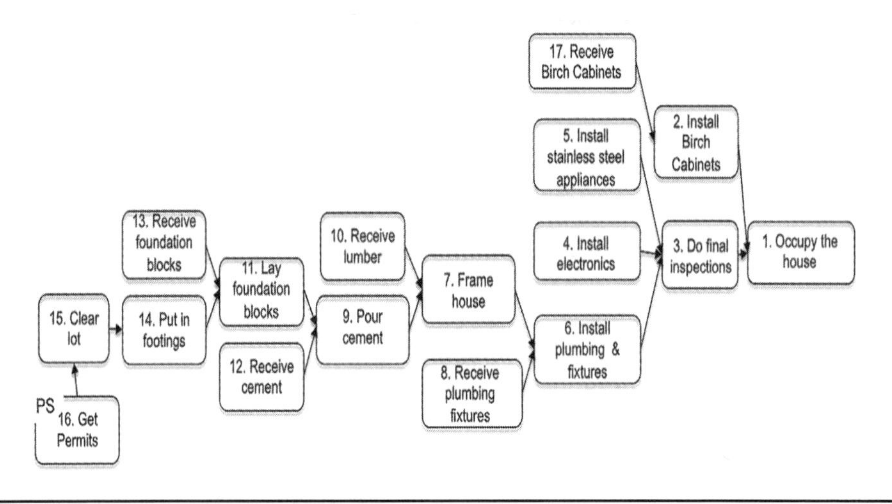

Figure 15.2 Choosing a skeleton starting point

3.2. Ask, "What must be completed (or finished) immediately before the task selected in Step 3.1 can start?" Asking out loud helps you to listen/think about the question more closely. Always read the entire task. Another way of asking the question is to ask, "What input is required before we can begin (the task selected in Step 3.1)?" The answer should be written on a Post-It® in task format (starting with the action verb) and placed immediately to the left of the task on the right. Check the logic by saying, "In order to start (the task selected in Step 3.1), we must first have completed (the task on the left)." If the team agrees, write the arrow connecting the two tasks.

What must be completed (or finished) immediately before "Install Birch Cabinets" can start? The answer is the new task, 17, "Receive Birch Cabinets." In order to "Install Birch Cabinets" we must first have completed "Receive Birch Cabinets" (see Figure 15.3).

3.3. Ask, "Is there anything else that must be completed immediately before 'Install Birch Cabinets' can start?" Or "Is any other input required to be able to start 'Install Birch Cabinets?'" In this case the answer is no, so no additional tasks are added to the left of task 2. If the answer had been yes, you would have identified each of the required tasks to the left, using the building and checking wording.

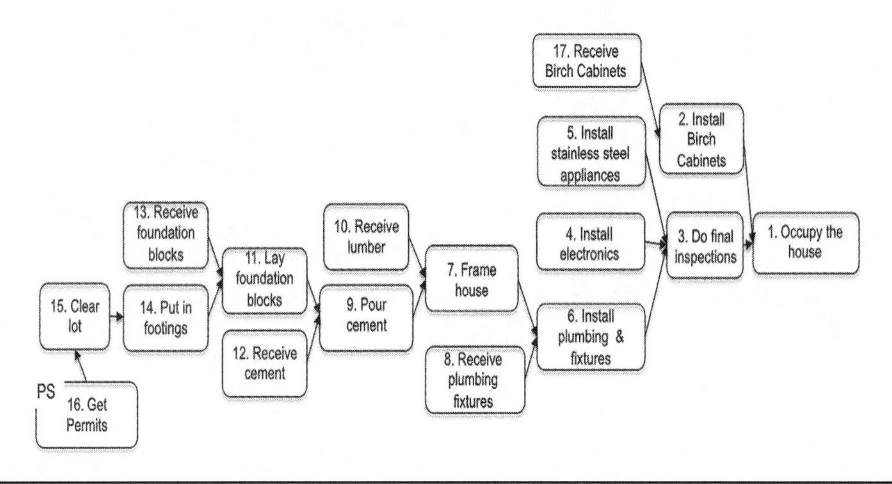

Figure 15.3 Result of Step 3.2

Warning: There is a trap that is very easy to fall into. Many begin adding tasks that describe the steps involved in accomplishing the task on the right, in effect decomposing or detailing what is needed to accomplish the task on the right. What we are looking for are the tasks that must be completed immediately before beginning the task on the right, not how we are going to accomplish the task on the right. For example, for the task "Install Birch Cabinets," it is tempting to detail that task by adding tasks such as "Remove Birch Cabinets cartons" and "Assemble Birch Cabinets." This is the trap we are referring to, which is describing the subtasks of installing Birch Cabinets rather than what tasks must precede it.

3.4. In order to continue building the project network, we next examine task 17 and repeat Steps 3.2 and 3.3 to identify first one task to the left of task 17, check it, and then identify all other required inputs to task 17.

What must be completed (or finished) immediately before "Receive Birch Cabinets" can start? The answer in this case is task 18, "Purchase Birch Cabinets." In order to start "Receive Birch Cabinets" we must first have completed "Purchase Birch Cabinets." Is there anything else that must be completed immediately before "Receive Birch Cabinets" can start? No. See Figure 15.4.

3.5. Repeat Step 3.4 until you have reached a task that could be started today, if the project go-ahead was given. That path start task should be designated with "PS." See Figure 15.5.

3.6. Follow Steps 3.1 through 3.5 until all tasks with no arrows leading to them have been properly designated as PS tasks.

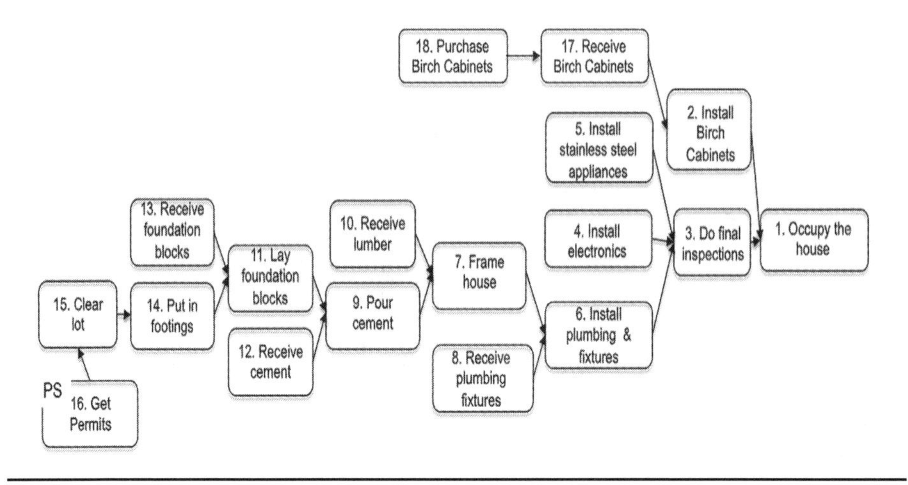

Figure 15.4 Result of Step 3.4

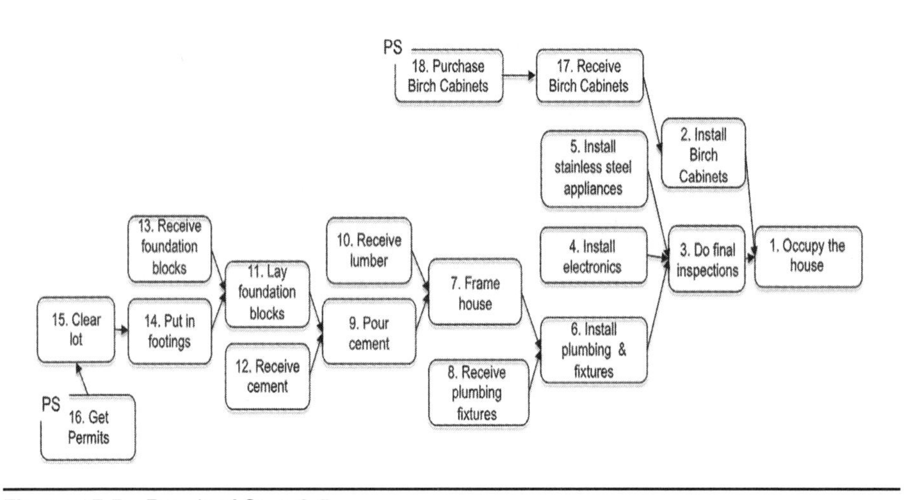

Figure 15.5 Result of Step 3.5

Continuing our example, now that task 18 has been designated a path start task, go back to the far right of the project network to look for the next task from which to build backward. The two options are tasks 4 and 5, since tasks 1, 2, 3, 6, and 17 have already been addressed. We recommend choosing the task you believe has the most work preceding it. For our example, we'll choose task 4, using the same building and checking questions. See Figure 15.6, where tasks 18 and 19 have been added. Note that we are staying at a high level, "electronics," rather than breaking the tasks into the specific electronic elements (TV, games, intercom) that are in the stakeholders' meeting results. Why? There has been no

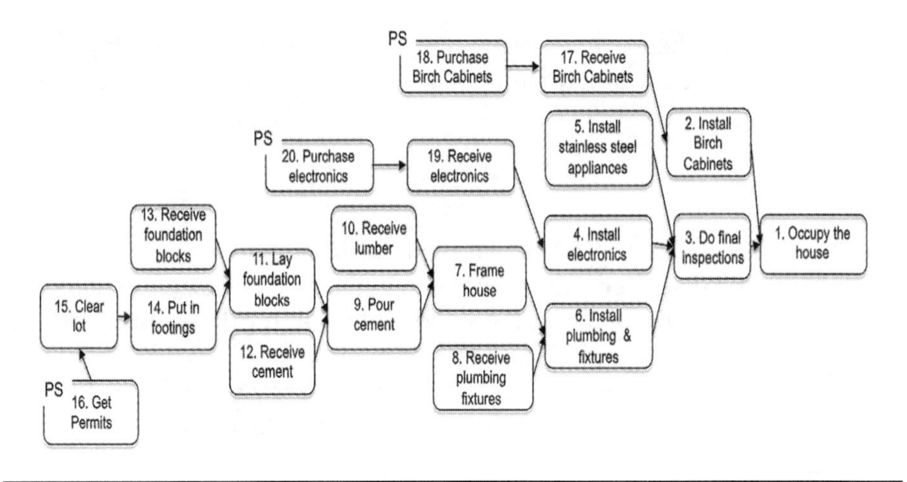

Figure 15.6 Step 3.4, building from task 4

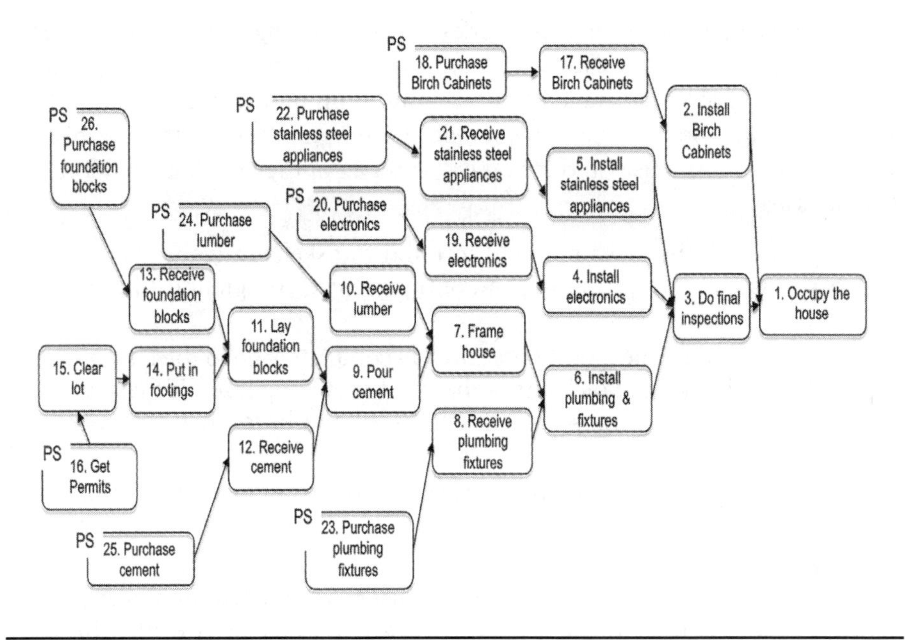

Figure 15.7 Result of Step 3.6

compelling reason to do so. The process steps will let us know when and where we need more detail in the project network.

Since task 20 is a path start task, we go back to the next option for building backward, task 5. Next will be task 8, then 10, then 12, and finally 13 (see Figure 15.7).

As a reminder, there is not a requirement to have one single starting task in a project; in a few cases it may naturally work out that way, but do not strive to achieve it.

Tips

- Ensure each task begins with an action verb.
- Each task should be descriptive enough that the completion criteria are clear. If there is not enough room to capture all the details necessary, include those additional details in a task note.
- There should *not* be a subject (i.e., name of a resource skill) for the task. The subject (resource or resources) will be added in a later step.

Conclusions

Building a skeleton of a project network is like continuing to build a house, once the foundation and footings are in place. It is vital to remember to keep this effort at a high, not very detailed level. You are framing the house—not putting up drywall, not choosing paint colors, not putting in all the detailed, finishing touches. The frame tells you that you will meet all of the key stakeholder needs. The steps are:

> Step 3. Add the tasks required to build the skeleton (other paths), working backward from the end of the project, completing all other paths.
>
> **3.1.** Using the project backbone already completed, go to the far right of the backbone and pick one of the latest occurring tasks. If there are multiple options, choose the one that seems to have the most work required to accomplish it.
>
> **3.2.** Ask, "What must be completed (or finished) immediately before the task identified in Step 3.1 can start?" Use the building and checking wording.
>
> **3.3.** Ask, "Is there anything else that must be completed immediately before the task identified in Step 3.1 can start?" Or "Is any other input required to be able to start the task identified in Step 3.1?" In this case the answer is no, so no additional tasks are added to the left of task 2. If it is yes, identify each of the required tasks to the left of the task identified in Step 3.1, using the building and checking wording. If the answer is no, go to Step 3.4.
>
> **3.4.** Examine the task selected in Step 3.1 and repeat Steps 3.2 and 3.3 to identify first one task to the left, check it, and then identify all

other required inputs to the task selected in Step 3.1.

3.5. Repeat Step 3.4 until you have reached a task that could be started today, if the project go-ahead was given. That path start task should be designated with "PS."

3.6. Follow Steps 3.1 through 3.5 until all tasks with no arrows leading to them have been properly designated as PS tasks.

Questions

15-1. What does it mean to "build the skeleton"?

15-2. Why is it important to start each task with an action?

15-3. Why are details important when writing the task description?

15-4. When building or checking the box-arrow-box relationship, what are we really looking for?

15-5. How is a task that could be started today, if the project has the go-ahead, identified?

15-6. Ensure each task begins with a/an ___________________.

15-7. What is the purpose of completing the backward pass in building a project network?

This book has free material available for download from the Web Added Value™ resource center at *www.jrosspub.com*

16. Step 4: Additional Dependencies—First Risk Avoidance

The Premise

One type of chaos that occurs when executing projects is to assign a resource to a task, only to discover after starting the task that some prior task's output was needed and is not ready. The resource manager had scheduled to use that resource in order to ensure that the project continues progressing. Now, the resource manager has two problems to overcome: first, what to do with this resource, and secondly, when will he/she actually be able to assign this task and what impact will this have on the project? If this happens once a month, everyone can live with it. But if project network teams do not follow Step 4 in the network building process, this type of chaos could well become a daily occurrence. Step 4 significantly reduces this risk.

Finding Additional Task Dependencies

Step 4 is the forward pass of building the project network. Specifically, it is reading the network forward, from the beginning, rigorously looking for missed additional task dependencies. In our analogy to home building, it is like saying, "This wall must be built before the fireplace goes in upstairs because it is a load-bearing wall for the fireplace. But we never noted before that this is also a load-bearing wall for the indoor hot tub. We better make sure that this wall is complete before we move in the hot tub!" This is the first risk avoidance in that we are ensuring that no tasks will be started, during project execution, with missed dependencies.

Before beginning this step, ensure all previous steps have been completed; the tasks, dependencies, and all required notes have been entered into the computer; and a fresh plot/printout of the network diagram is available.

Pick one path start task (denoted by PS). You will see that it is already connected to one or more following tasks. Ask, "Is the output of (this task) needed to begin any other task (for which we have not shown the arrow or dependency)?" An alternative wording would be "What other task cannot start without the output of this task?"

The two keys to this step are to identify any missing inputs and to ensure no incorrect inputs are added. See Figure 16.1 for an example of an incorrect input. There already is a pathway from task 25 through task 12 to task 9. Adding an arrow from task 25 directly to task 9 is incorrect because the output of task 25 (Purchase cement) is not the *immediate* input for task 9; the cement must be received (task 12) before it can be poured (task 9). The key is to show the correct flow of work as it is passed along the arrow!

Continue along this pathway, using the checking wording above and a colored pencil to help identify the pathways completed, until you reach the last task on the right of the project. Continue the process, going back to an unchecked path start task, until the forward pass has been accomplished for the entire project network.

As the forward pass is being accomplished, there are two typical modifications that are made to the project network:

1. Adding an additional arrow going to another task on the right from an existing task on the left. This means that the output of the task on the left is required as an input to an additional task not previously identified.

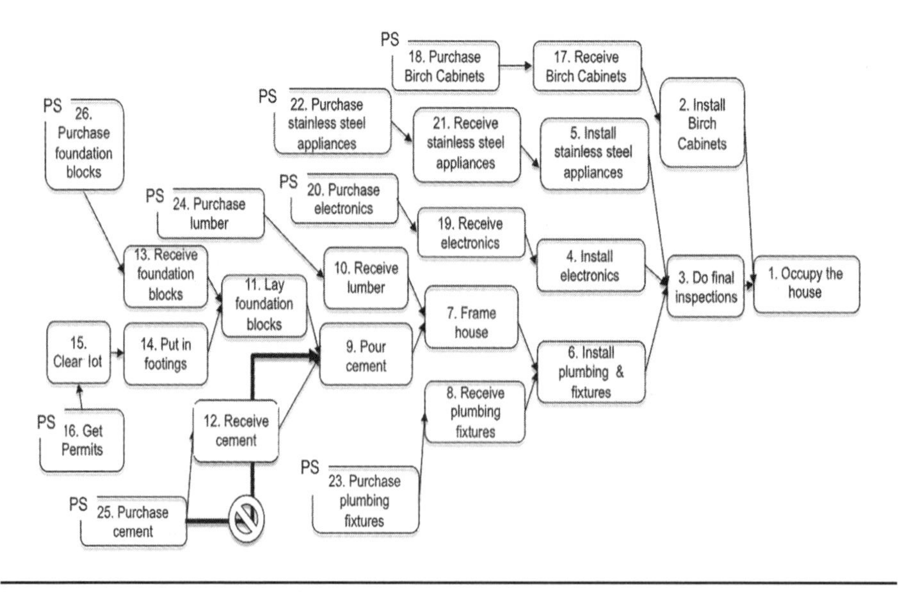

Figure 16.1 Forward pass, incorrect arrow, 25 → 9

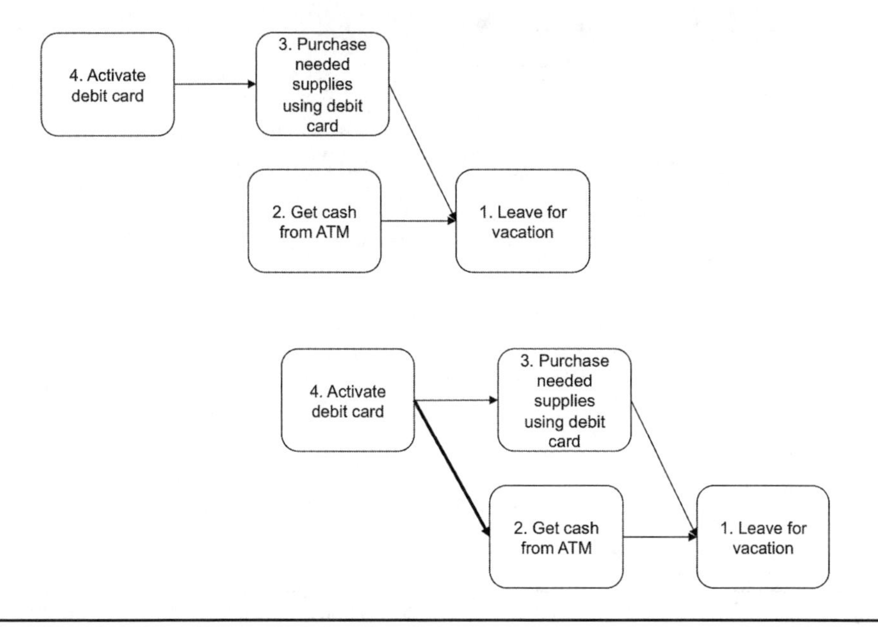

Figure 16.2 Forward pass, adding an arrow

For example, the output of task 4 in Figure 16.2 is an activated debit card. An activated debit card is needed to purchase supplies (task 3), as shown by the existing arrow in the upper part of Figure 16.2. An activated debit card is also needed in order to withdraw cash from the ATM (task 2), so the new arrow is drawn from task 4 also to task 2.

2. When it looks like there should be an arrow from one task to another (see Figure 16.3, from task 4 to task 2), but the output of one is not the *immediately* required input of the other, it is likely that there is a task missing between the two. It seems that "Reserve the church" must be an input to "Seat the guests." Otherwise where would you seat the guests for the wedding ceremony? But the church reservation (output of task 4) is not what is required in order to begin seating the guests. However, reserving the church is an input to decorating the church (task 5), and decorating the church is an input to seating the guests (task 2). So in this example, the forward reading of the network has helped identify the missing task and arrows, as shown in Figure 16.3.

Step 4 is not complete until all pathways have had the forward pass performed.

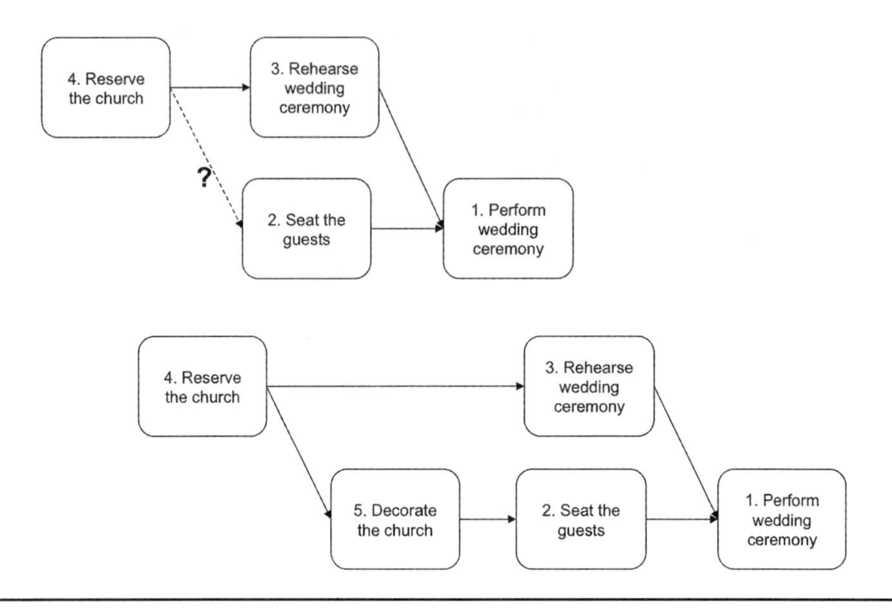

Figure 16.3 Forward pass, adding an arrow and discovering a missing task in between

Tips

- Do not add extra, incorrect pathways. If tempted, ask yourself if the output of the task on the left is needed in the exact same form/format as an input for the candidate task on the right.
- Colored pencils can be useful for indicating where you have and have not done the forward pass on your plot. They can also help highlight when you've accidently created an extra incorrect pathway.
- This is not a step used to dive into deeper detail in the network. This step's only purpose is to identify missing dependencies.

Conclusions

Every project encounters some surprises during execution. The fewer the surprises, the more likely all projects will complete on time, on budget, and within scope. Although some surprises are unavoidable, this chapter helps eliminate or at least drastically reduce the surprises from missed task dependencies. This is the kind of surprise where a resource starts a task, only to find that they needed the output of another task in order to progress on the current task. This could mean that they encounter a wait period, forcing them to multitask on some other task, or they have rework on the current task. Further, the completion of the task is delayed and this forces resource managers to waste precious time rescheduling. Step 4 of the network building process avoids this risk by having the team read the network from beginning to end, rigorously looking for these missing task dependencies.

Questions

16-1. Why is it important to finish the backward pass (completing the skeleton) before beginning the forward pass (finding missing dependencies)?

16-2. Why must you always do a forward pass?

16-3. What is the key to Step 4?

16-4. When doing a forward pass, when do you move to the next path start?

16.5. Why might you use a colored pencil/pen when doing Step 4?

16-6. When is Step 4 complete?

16-7. How can you determine whether an arrow is an extra, incorrect one or not?

17. Step 5: Checking against Project Goals and Scope—Second Risk Avoidance

The Premise

This step provides three types of risk avoidance. First, it avoids the risk of missed scope, by ensuring that all the tasks required to meet the project's scope and goals are included in the task interdependency diagram. Second, this step avoids the risk of wasting resources, by ensuring that no extra tasks are included that exceed the project's scope and goals! Third, this step prevents some risk of scope creep, by ensuring that the tasks are sufficient to meet goals and deliverables that were discussed during the initial team meeting. Specifically, Step 5 checks every task against the project goals, scope, and sponsor criteria identified in Step 1 (project stakeholders' meeting). One way to think about this step is that it ensures that what the stakeholders require has been translated into work specifics for the project's resources and managers.

Ensuring that the Project Meets All Stakeholder Needs

Do not begin this task until all previous steps have been fully completed. Gather the documentation created during and after the project stakeholders' meeting. Make sure there is a clean plot/printout of the task interdependency diagram as well as all task notes available.

Carefully check the project stakeholders' meeting result's template against the project planning done so far (see Figure 17.1). Did we remember to include tasks to put electrical outlets in the kitchen island? Do we have a task for ordering the microwave? Does the task have the correct microwave specifications? Some items from Step 1 will be explicitly shown (the tangible deliverables), whereas others are implied by the work that will be accomplished. Where criteria have been specified, ensure that is documented in the task description or

Figure 17.1 Check network against scope

task notes so that proper exit criteria for a task or pathway reflect those criteria.

If items of scope or tangible deliverables are missing, add those tasks and build in the required dependencies using the established processes for building and checking. Ensure both a forward and backward pass are done to mitigate the risk of missing any required dependencies.

When tasks are in the network diagram that are not needed to meet the project scope defined in Step 1, delete them. Use the standard building and checking processes to ensure correct relationships with the remaining tasks.

Conclusions

Any multi-project environment deteriorates quickly when project after project yields unpleasant surprises. No one expects a project network to be perfect, but when every network is full of holes, the results are predictable: many projects will finish late, over budget, and not within scope. Step 5 plugs the hole caused by missing key stakeholder criteria. It also avoids doing unnecessary work by checking every defined task in the network against the definition of project scope from Step 1. The result is a far more robust network with a much higher probability of meeting stakeholder expectations without big surprises.

Questions

17-1. This step ensures that all tasks required to meet the project's __________ and ________ are included in the network.

17-2. According to the chapter, what is one way to think about Step 5?

17-3. Do not begin Step 5 until _______?

17-4. What do you do if you find out items of scope or tangible deliverables are missing?

17-5. What should be carefully checked against the project planning done so far?

17-6. What do you do with tasks in the dependency diagram that are not needed?

17-7. Using the outputs from Steps 1 and 4, check the case study task interdependency network against the results of the stakeholders' meeting. Make any required adjustments and check appropriately.

18. Step 6: Resourcing

The Premise

The high-level network diagram of the *work* of the project has been completed and checked. The next step (Step 6) is to determine resources (skill level and quantity) that could be assigned to perform the tasks. As pointed out in Chapter 5, this step does not assign named resources (specific people) to perform tasks. Instead this step identifies the number and type of resource skill(s) capable of performing to the required level of quality and task completion criteria.

In keeping with the desire to increase the speed of executing the project, we will assign as many resources as practical to each task in this step. The more resources we can assign to a task, without causing unmanageable waste in executing the task, the fewer tasks we will have active. The fewer the number of active tasks, the more management and support group attention can be given to active tasks, and therefore the shorter each task will wait for decisions and actions by any other group in the organization. Also, if proper consideration is given to the number of resources we can assign to work on a task, the faster the task will complete.

Some Basic Facts about Resources

Although people are the most common type of resources that perform task work, they are not the only project resources. Other resources can include equipment (ovens, cutters, test equipment, etc.) and facilities (laboratories, chambers, buildings, ranges, etc.). Not every resource needed to perform a task is identified. Critical resources, meaning those that the task would wait for, must be included. For example, in a research project, assume there is a task to "Review test results." While five people are involved in the review, it is three days of a senior engineer's time for which this task will wait. Much of this person's time is spent overseeing the review and approving the results before proceeding to a next step. But, because there is technical information presented during the review that is good for other resources to hear, other resource skill levels believe they must also be listed for the task. Be very clear and specific as to what is required for the task; if it is a task for which only a few resources are actually required, the other resources can be listed in the task notes as "nice-to-have" resources. A deciding factor as to whether a resource is critical or "nice to have" is to ask if the task would wait/be delayed if the resource skill level was not available. If yes (would delay), the resource skill is critical; if no (no delay), the resource is only listed in a task note and not modeled in a project plan.

We need to ensure that the identified critical resources are not multitasked (asked to perform more than one project task at a time). Typically, critical resources are required for the entire length of a task. In Step 6, we are still in a planning, not execution, stage. Typically, all software available today has the capability, during planning, to prevent a resource from doing two project tasks at once, by following a process called *resource leveling*. However, what the software does not know is that a resource may have non-project responsibilities that require one day per week, for example.

Since it has been proven time and time again that multitasking delays projects and causes rework, it is important in the planning stage that resource and functional managers recognize the bad multitasking caused by frequent interruptions of project task work and consider ways of facilitating more dedicated resource time. Sometimes, this can be accomplished by simply doing a temporary assignment of all other responsibilities of the resource to another individual. This is important at the planning stage, because multitasking dramatically impacts the time required to complete a task.

Critical Resource Skill Levels and Quantities

When determining the critical resource skill levels for project planning, do not use organization charts or phone lists; they will steer you to include all resources, whether critical or not. We have found that identifying the critical resource skills on the first projects planned using these steps is the best way to identify not only the resources that are truly critical, but also the "master" critical resource list (see Appendix C for a generic example).

Resource Pools

Typically, an organization is more than one deep in a resource skill. Resources of similar skills and levels are grouped into a *pool*. Resource pools can have multiple levels, such as a junior or apprentice level and a senior or master level. Do not have too many levels in your pools! Remember, the purpose is to identify critical resources whose absence would delay the start of project tasks, not a human resources classification of all the resources in the organization!

Keep track of the resource pool definitions. Many times, identifying a resource pool also includes additional resources and equipment that would normally accompany the resource. As an example, a *software training developer* is assumed to have access to a computer with the software loaded as well as the current software training materials. This assumption may not be correct for subcontractors, for example.

There is often a question as to how many pools there should be. We've covered the people resource pools, but have not yet discussed facilities and equipment. Typically, critical equipment is considered to be large, expensive pieces of equipment, such as a water jet cutter or 3D modeler—resources that are used a lot and are difficult to schedule; a copy machine or scale would not be considered critical equipment. Including facilities and equipment, we typically find that a range of 30–50 resource categories is sufficient to model a portfolio of projects. We have implemented with less than 20 and achieved outstanding results.

Resource Continuity

In some types of projects, the specific resource that performs an early task in one part of a project (one path) can save time and improve quality later if brought back to work in the same path. This is called *resource continuity* (RC). The thinking is that another resource from the same skill pool would take too long to get up to speed for task/project knowledge and quality if it's not the same resource that worked earlier in the path. In these few cases, note within the project plan that this task has a need for RC in the task notes, along with the resource skill type, if there's more than one resource skill level identified for the task. For example, the task note could read, "Resource continuity desired—software engineer."

Identifying Critical Resource Skill Levels and Quantities per Task

6.1. Identify which portions of the network will most likely be performed by which resource pools (color-coding is often useful). Identify which subject matter experts (functional managers, resource managers, etc.) are the best to assign resource skills and quantities to tasks. The preference is to start at the beginning of the project and work left to right. Bring these subject matter experts in one at a time and orient them to the project network before beginning Step 6.2.

6.2. Begin at the left side of the project network. Pick a path start task. For that task, determine what resources are critical for accomplishing the task; that is, the task cannot start without those resources being available. Note that there may be more than one resource skill level.

Let's use "Update Software Training Materials" as an example (see Figure 18.1). There is a pool called *software training developer*. Are any other resources required for the task? Making a list of the steps or activities required to meet the task completion criteria helps to identify any other critical resources. The subject matter experts also often provide task notes that will be useful during task execution—not only to understand what must be accomplished in greater detail, but also to assist in providing estimates of time remaining to accomplish all of those steps. For example, draft training materials must be put together for the software testing. Since the software training developer creates the draft training materials, it sounds like creating the draft training materials is a step in accomplishing this task—we would make that a task note. (Since the software training developer would hand off the draft training materials to himself/herself, we consider this one task; if there was a handoff to another resource, it may be a reason to break this task into more than one task.

Update Software
Training Materials

Resource: Software Training Developer

Steps:
1. Understand New Software Release
2. Determine "What, Where, How" For Each Training Module
3. Determine And Create Exercise(s) For Each Training Module
4. Create Draft Training Materials (Overview, Planning, Execution For Leadership, Execution For Users, Task Updating)
5. Review Results Of Usability Verification Testing For Any Required Changes To Materials
6. Create Final Version Of Software Training Materials

Figure 18.1 Resourcing

Examining the steps in this task, Step 5 is performed after the usability verification testing, which is another task, performed by another resource. This is a justifiable reason for breaking this task into more detail: there is another task, performed by another resource, embedded inside it. Fixing this situation looks like Figure 18.2.

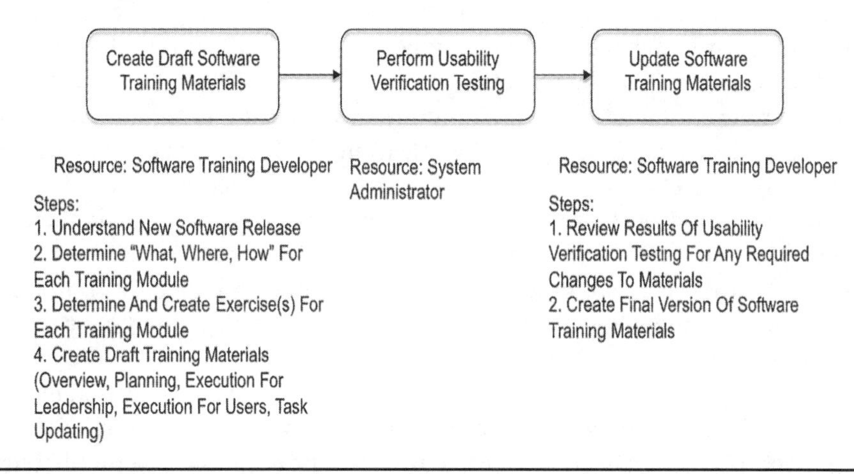

Figure 18.2 Breaking a task into more than one task. Justification: Resource hands off some task work to another resource.

During the initial planning, identify the lowest critical resource skill level capable of performing the job. The rationale is that later, before execution, if there is a need to further compress the schedule, we can identify the best places to put higher skilled resources as a way to do that, rather than counting on scarcer resources unnecessarily. The philosophy is to plan initially with the lowest skill level capable of meeting the required task completion criteria, and then add higher skilled resources only where and when necessary (see Chapter 21, Step 9: Duration reduction without compromise). Assign the largest quantity of resources of that skill set as practical.

6.3. After the resource skill level(s) and quantities are identified for the first task on a path, follow the same process for the successor tasks on the path, noting any RC issues in the task notes.

6.4. Repeat for all pathways in the project.

Special Types of Tasks

Many times while identifying the correct resource skill levels and quantities for tasks, we find that there is no resource that is required for the entire time the task is going to be worked. Consider the situation when a long-lead part must be ordered (see Figure 18.3). Actually, doing the ordering requires a customer service clerk; however, looking at the task notes we find that what is really meant by the task is ordering and receiving a specified long-lead item. In this case, we would actually have two tasks: "Order the __________ long-lead item" (fill in blank with the specific item), which is done by the customer service clerk, and "Wait or delay for the __________ long-lead item." This task is performed by what we would call a *dummy* or *vendor* resource (so called because it is not a resource we would necessarily track, but is not the same resource as the customer service clerk); in some software, there is no need to list a resource for the "Delay . . ." task. There are other delays and/or wait tasks that exist in projects. We recommend modeling them similar to long-lead tasks, changing the task description appropriately.

In other cases, someone (external to your organization) has promised to provide you with an item on a specified date. We refer to this item as a *receivable* to the project. The receivable is a required input to a project task. The unreliability

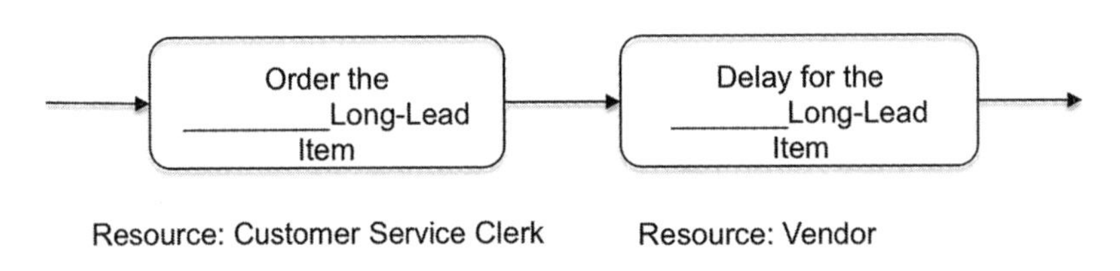

Figure 18.3 Modeling ordering and receiving a long-lead-time item

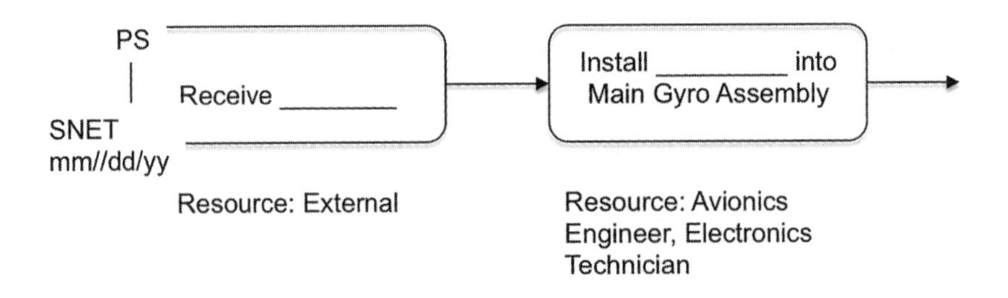

Figure 18.4 Modeling a "received" item

of the provider should not be measured within the task time itself; the task cannot start until the part arrives! Any project management software allows you to create a "start no earlier than (SNET)" task with that date and the amount of variability expected. By making that task precede the task that needs to use the part, this SNET task becomes a placeholder, modeling the expected arrival time. The predecessor, SNET task, is a path start (see Figure 18.4).

Conclusions

In most current paradigms, tasks are like hot potatoes. Resource managers assign tasks to resources at the planning stage. Every resource has multiple tasks to do, including non-project work such as operational responsibilities, ongoing improvement tasks, etc. In this new paradigm, instead, the resource manager plans to assign as many resources as practical to critical tasks, to drive projects faster to completion. The resource manager looks to have only one task assigned to a resource at a time and therefore considers, at this planning stage, how their resources can be freed from other responsibilities during the performance of a project task, so their time can be dedicated (not multitasked). The formal parts of Step 6 are:

> Step 6. Determine resources (skill level and quantity) that could be assigned to perform the task.
>
> **6.1.** Identify which portions of the network will most likely be performed by which resource pools (color-coding is often useful). Identify which subject matter experts (functional managers, resource managers, etc.) are the best to assign resource skills and quantities to tasks. The preference is to start at the beginning of the project and work left to right. Bring these subject matter experts in one at a time and orient them to the project network before beginning Step 6.2.
>
> **6.2.** Begin at the left side of the project network. Pick a path start task. For that task, determine what resources are critical for accomplishing the task; that is, the task cannot start without those resources being available. Note that there may be more than one resource skill level.
>
> **6.3.** After the resource skill level(s) and quantities are identified for the first task on a path, follow the same process for the successor tasks on the path, noting any RC issues in the task notes.
>
> **6.4.** Repeat for all pathways in the project.

Questions

18-1. Step 6 adds what to the task sentence?

18-2. Why don't we identify all resources, facilities, tools, and pieces of equipment needed for each task?

18-3. What type of resource must be included in Step 6?

18-4. What makes a critical resource critical?

18-5. What is resource continuity?

18-6. During initial planning, what skill level should be identified for a task?

18-7. Why is it important to plan for the largest quantity of a resource skill as practical for a task?

19. Step 7: Expert Scrutiny—Third Risk Avoidance

The Premise

Until now, we have used a small team of very knowledgeable people to build the project network. We have used people with good overall knowledge of the company, of projects, and of the network building approach. We have made many assumptions along the way, both with regard to the tasks that need to be accomplished to meet the stakeholder needs and in terms of resources who can do the work. Step 7 is intended to find missing pieces of the network, by having experts in specific sections review their relevant parts of the network for deficiencies or missing elements. We want to ensure that we have not missed any tasks, not misstated any of the necessary interdependencies, and appropriately identified the critical resource levels and quantities. In other words, we want to make sure that we have the *work* and *critical workers* of the project correct before we start gathering task estimates.

Identifying and Using Expert Scrutiny

By now it's likely that themes have developed in the network. There may be a section that involves the start-up of the project, followed by multiple paths of work branching off from the start (e.g., hardware, software, documentation, integrated testing); likely there is some final section of the project (which may include system test, packaging, shipping to distribution centers, and so forth). These themes help indicate whose expertise is needed to do the scrutiny and when.

Consider having smaller groups of experts in for scrutiny of their specific theme area. Recognize there may be overlapping areas of expertise and plan the scrutiny accordingly. Warning! Do not bring in all the experts at the same time and plan to go over the entire network diagram. Bring the appropriate experts in only to review their specific sections! Otherwise, you will waste a lot of the experts' time listening to reviews of areas in which they have no interest or expertise to share. This will cause them to resist future efforts to enlist their help.

Ensure you provide a broad overview of the project to the experts before going to scrutiny of a particular section. As an example, "This project is to accomplish the upgrade of Absolutely Essential software at GENEXCO." Give them enough depth on the stakeholder needs and deliverables so that they can scrutinize their section within a context of the needed results.

Referencing the clean network diagram before them, and starting from the left, show them the different sections before going to their section under scrutiny. This gives them an understanding of what work is done before getting to their part(s) of the project. It's useful to have a computer to display the task notes (and to add any additional notes that the experts recommend).

The experts should have experience in their theme area as well as knowledge about the skill levels of the organization. The experts may be the resource managers for the thematic areas or senior experienced resources. It's not unusual for management team members with previous expertise in the thematic area to be called as scrutinizers.

Make any recommended changes at the end of each scrutiny session and reprint a fresh network diagram before starting another scrutiny session. Remember that any additional tasks are subject to the Step 5 scrutiny—make sure that you are not adding tasks that are not required to meet the scope of the project.

Conclusions

Expert scrutiny gives the team constructing the project network a chance to have the most knowledgeable, experienced people in the organization review the tasks defined within their subject area. The project plan is broken down into themes according to subject matter categories. Subject matter experts are brought in, separately, for each theme area. With an overview of the project objectives, scope, and sections of work that precede their subject area, they can quickly review the tasks defined and advise if changes are necessary. The result of Step 7 is an almost finished project network. The work definition should not change extensively in Steps 8 through 10. With this work definition reasonably complete, the team is now ready to obtain time estimates.

Questions

19-1. What is Step 7 intended to find?

19-2. Why is it important to have experts scrutinize the project network at this point?

19-3. Before gathering task estimates, make sure you have what correct?

19-4. What should you provide before scrutinizing a specific section of the network?

19-5. Why is it useful to have a computer display task notes during scrutiny?

19-6. What must be done after a scrutiny session before starting the next session?

19-7. What project risks does this expert scrutiny mitigate?

20. Step 8: Time Estimates—Fourth Risk Avoidance

The Premise

In the new world you are embarking into, do not put a lot of credence in individual task time estimates. The entire solution provides a multi-project environment where work will be completed faster than ever before. Remember that this effort is not mainly about creating good project networks. We are:

- Dramatically cutting project work in progress, thus giving senior management, other resource groups that support projects, and resource managers a much faster response time to resource issues and better coaching of resources
- Eliminating multitasking of project work
- Providing mechanisms such as a fast-track issue resolution process, daily task updates, and full kits, to remove blocking issues quickly and prevent rework
- Much more carefully defining the project plan so that work that is needed before a task is started is more likely to be available, with a much clearer definition of the work to be done
- Changing to a single priority system, preventing the constant juggling of resources

You cannot expect people who are providing the time estimates to understand or even believe that all of the above changes will be in place when their tasks execute. Therefore, this process needs to be accomplished in a way that does not confront the people providing the estimates, but at the same time arrives at much more ambitious task estimates than typical of the past.

Approach to Gathering Time Estimates for Each Task

In Step 8, it's important to have two time estimates for each task: an ambitious time (if not too much difficulty is encountered accomplishing the task completion criteria) and a standard time, which includes the variability one might experience if there is more difficulty than expected achieving the task completion criteria.

Variability exists in almost every task of a project. We don't expect the same type of variability in every project or even every task. Some projects have more variability in the beginning, some at the end, others in the middle, and some experience different levels of variability throughout the entire project. Having an understanding of the potential variability in a task gives a context for understanding task updates during execution; that is, is the task proceeding as expected, better than expected, or are problems occurring which need more time to achieve the task completion criteria? This is crucial information for project and resource managers to know.

In project organizations, the same *types* of tasks are performed repeatedly by similar resource pools. It is tempting to scour the historical records of similar tasks to identify actual task durations and use those (or averages or weighted averages, etc.) for task estimates. We strongly recommend against that practice. Having the historical records are important for evaluating trends to uncover potential improvement areas; however, even when executing similar tasks a second time, we find that history does not repeat itself. The person doing the task may be different. It may be the same person but in a completely different frame of mind. The computer might work perfectly this time, where last time it broke down.

Most organizations that we have worked with did not capture task variability when planning a project. They typically solicit one estimate for each task. But what are the upside and downside characteristics of most tasks? Project tasks do not behave like repetitive, production-type tasks where the downside and upside are about the same. This production type of variability is captured in statistics as a *normal* (symmetrical) curve (see Figure 20.1), meaning an equal chance of achieving an outcome below the average or above the average, with the same level of variation possible in either case.

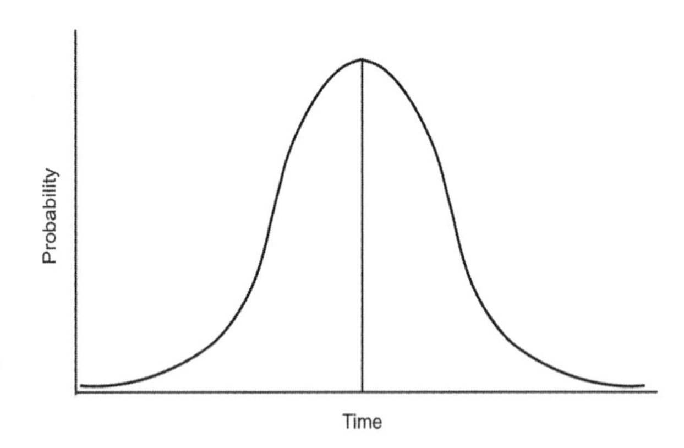

Figure 20.1 Normal distribution

However, when thinking about variability in project task times, the normal curve rarely applies. A project task time typically behaves more like estimating how long it will take to get to work in Los Angeles or, worse, Bangalore, India. People who live in big, busy cities may find that, on average, it takes 45 minutes to get to work. They can recall times when they arrived in just under 30 minutes (minus 15 minutes from the average). But is the worst case plus 15 minutes from the average? No! These people can tell you about the time it took them three hours to travel exactly the same distance. In other words, in project tasks, the downside is much worse than the upside. And since people are often held accountable to their estimates, no wonder they tend to estimate much higher than an average time to complete a task.

Every project task has some minimum amount of time that it takes to accomplish the steps required to achieve the task completion criteria—that means there is a definite lower limit to the curve which is greater than zero. Depending on the amount of variability that is estimated to accomplish the task completion criteria—the inherent task variability only—the right tail of the curve can go on for a long time (see Figure 20.2). A task estimated to take five days might easily require plus five days, but it will never finish in minus five days, or zero time.

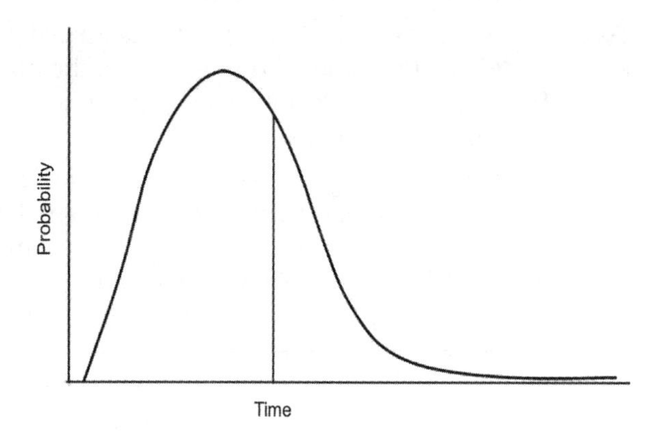

Figure 20.2 Skewed task time distribution

What we need for the time estimate is an understanding of both a more ambitious time and a standard time expected for the task. The standard time is according to how tasks are typically estimated today, without all the benefits of the solution described above. In gathering the task times from people with experience both in the amount and type of work required to reach the task completion criteria and also the skills of the resource(s) identified, start at the left of the project network for that skill set (ideally, start with a resource skill set that is a path start).

8.1. Work with only the experienced people for that resource skill set or sets and that type of work for a specific section of the project (again, we are not looking for a large group tied up for a significant amount of time; multiple small groups should be used so as not to waste people's time).

8.2. Ensure you have presented an overview of the project work so they have a context.

8.3. Present the task description and the resource skills and quantities that are assigned to the task.

8.4. Go over all the task notes for the task being estimated to ensure they have an understanding of the work involved and the task completion criteria; if they suggest additions or modifications—especially to the steps or activities to ensure the resources are clear what work to perform, be sure to include them in the task notes.

8.5. Explain that we want to capture the range of time, from ambitious to standard, so we will be asking for two task estimates, based on the resource skills and quantities identified.

8.5.1. Ask first for the time that is typically estimated for this task—this is considered the standard or right side of the variability range. Remember that people are not likely to give a task estimate that they have a high chance to miss.

8.5.2. Next ask for an ambitious time—how long it would take to accomplish the task completion criteria if no unusual problems occur. This time gives us the left side of our range for planning and scheduling purposes. We are not looking for the minimum time estimate. This is a time with *less* safety in it because fewer problems (variability) are expected and because most problems that do occur will be recognized and addressed much faster than before.

8.5.3. The two task times are written as (ambitious, standard) with the time descriptor (d for days or h for hours) added. For example, if the standard time is eight days and the ambitious time is six days, it would be written as (6d, 8d).

8.6. Repeat for all tasks with the appropriate subject matter experts.

Calendars

When gathering the task time estimates, we are interested in the working calendar only. If the resources work eight hours a day, five days a week, the example above represents a week and a day for the ambitious time and a week and three days for the high-end time.

When multiple resources work on a task and work different schedules, you must accommodate this. This does make it more complex to determine overall estimated task duration times; it is not only the resource(s) that are estimated to need the most time, but also how the resource(s) spread their task work over their available calendars.

Long-Lead (Delay) Variability

When ordering long-lead items, the vendor provides the lead-time estimate. Use that estimate as the ambitious time. Use your experience with the accuracy of the estimate to determine the standard time. For example, if the vendor states a lead time of one month (typically 20 working days) and your experience is that they deliver in that time, use (20d, 20d) as the lead-time task estimate. However, if they estimate one month and your experience with them is that they are more likely to deliver within six weeks (30 days), use (20d, 30d) for the lead-time task estimate.

Receiving Task Variability

Receiving tasks have a SNET (start no earlier than) date attribute that represents the date the supplier has committed to providing the item to you (at your location). There is a chance they will deliver on time and the ambitious time reflects that—use 0.1h (typically that is as close to zero time as your software will allow). For the standard time, use your experience with the provider. If they are typically two weeks late, the task would be estimated at (0.1h, 10d).

Iteration Variability

Iteration variability occurs when a series of tasks have to be repeated in order to reach the last task's completion criteria. This can happen when a test is at the end of a group of tasks; if the test is not passed, the work of preceding tasks must be repeated.

Not every project has iteration variability. It must be accommodated and accounted for when it is part of the project environment. Note: Ignoring or denying that it exists on paper does not cause it to go away!

In Figure 20.3, if the spindle prototype does not pass inspection the first time, the machining, polishing, and inspection must be repeated. There can be variability in the number of times the tasks must be repeated before the task

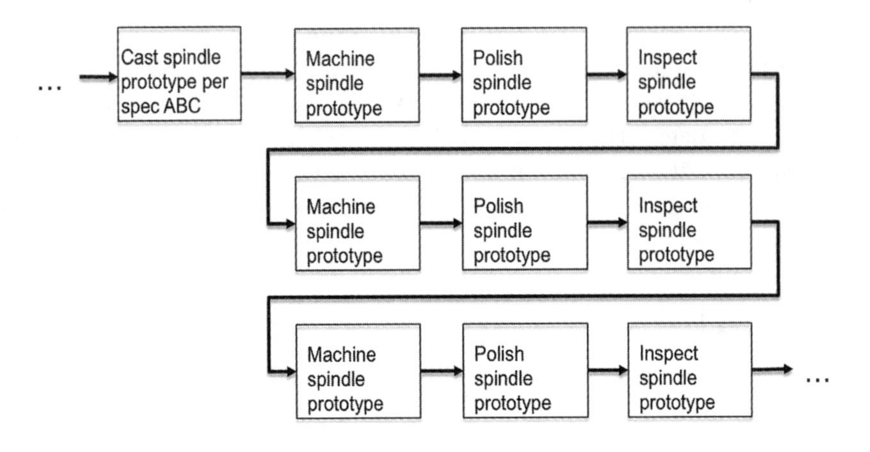

Figure 20.3 Iteration variability example

completion criteria are met. Therefore, the process for identifying the quantity of iterations is similar to the process for identifying task times:

1. Identify the tasks likely to be iterated (in Figure 20.3, they are the machining, polishing, and inspecting tasks).
2. Determine the standard number of iterations (in Figure 20.3, the standard number of iterations is 3).
3. Determine the ambitious number of iterations (in Figure 20.3, the ambitious number of iterations is 1).
4. Determine whether or not the task times for iterations 2 and 3 are the same as for iteration 1. Depending on the work being done, the task times can remain the same, be shorter, or be longer. Ensure you understand and document the estimated task times for EACH iteration in the task notes.

Figure 20.4 shows how the network diagram indicates ambitious and standard iterations when the task times are estimated to be identical for each iteration. The tasks put into the network are the ambitious number of iterations. For example, if the ambitious and standard number of iterations for our example were (2, 3) the tasks would be shown in the network as in Figure 20.5.

When task times are different for each iteration, the network diagram would be as shown in Figure 20.3 with the task times indicated per task.

Important note: There is often confusion about what iteration variability means. It is NOT the number of times work must be repeated within a single task to reach the task completion criteria; that would be reflected in the task's ambitious and standard times. Iteration variability occurs specifically when

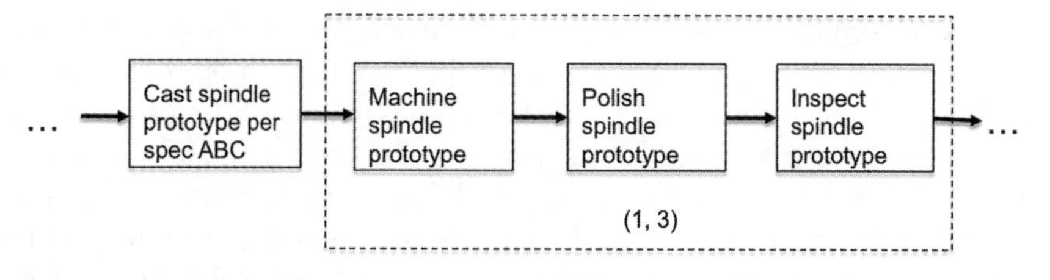

Figure 20.4 Identifying the variation in the number of iterations between 1 (ambitiously) and 3 (standard)

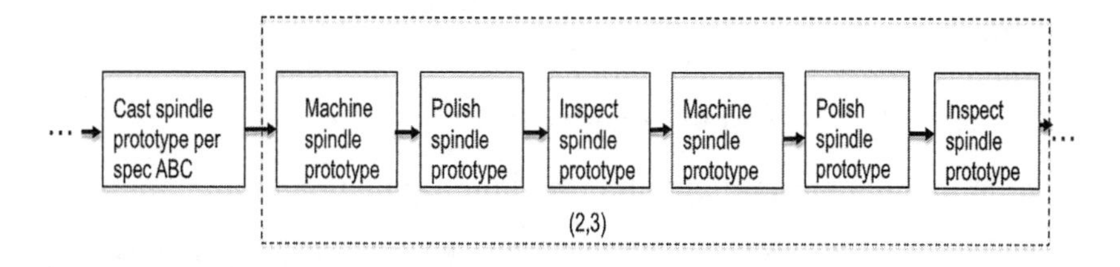

Figure 20.5 Identifying the variation in the number of iterations between 2 (ambitiously) and 3 (standard)

multiple sequential tasks must be repeated in order to achieve the completion criteria of the last task in the series.

Task Time Estimate Final Check

Step 8 is not complete until you've reviewed all of the task times. Whenever there is an ambitious estimate of more than two weeks, that task should be broken into multiple tasks. Why? It's another perspective on risk mitigation, this time in planning for execution. During execution, task updates will be done in the context of remaining duration. It is very difficult to really provide a realistic estimate of remaining duration when a task is planned to be more than 10 days long.

Conclusions

In much of the project management literature and in many project management improvement efforts, a great deal of fuss is made over task time estimates. The world would have been much further ahead if the same effort had instead been put into helping people get tasks done more quickly. Estimates are just that—educated guesses, based on past experience, of how long it will take to do a piece of work several weeks or months in the future. In our opinion, it is a waste of time to focus on accuracy of estimates as a means to improving multi-project results. Instead, in Step 8, we quickly gather two estimates for each task to capture the variability of task time possibilities: one estimate is if things go as normal (a standard estimate) and the other estimate is if almost no problems and delays are encountered (an ambitious estimate). With this range of variability, we are ready to put these estimates into the plan and see what the total project duration is likely to be.

Questions

20-1. Why is it important to gather two task times?

20-2. Why not gather the minimum and maximum task times?

20-3. Explain the importance of detailed task notes and assumptions.

20-4. How does gathering task times reduce project risk?

20-5. Why should you gather the *standard* task time first?

20-6. Why not use historical averages and cut them in half?

20-7. What is the impact of ignoring iteration variability when planning a project?

This book has free material available for download from the Web Added Value™ resource center at *www.jrosspub.com*

21. Step 9: Duration Reduction without Compromise

The Premise

The project planning team now thoroughly understands the total network logic (tasks, interdependencies, resources, and time estimates that enable the accomplishment of the project scope, objectives, and tangible deliverables). It's time to determine the duration of the project to see where to focus to reduce overall project lead time. For most projects, when the time estimates that you've obtained in Step 8 are plugged into the network, the software provides a duration that is longer (often much longer) than the executives and other stakeholders find acceptable. Therefore, the premise of this chapter is that the network building team must be prepared to go through some iterations to reduce project duration, without having to shove unrealistic estimates down people's throats and without adding additional risk to the project.

Finding the Tasks That Will Govern Duration

There are two commonly used approaches for determining how long a project is likely to take, in elapsed time. The critical path process was developed in the late 1950s and defines the longest chain of task dependencies within a project. There are several assumptions about critical path, based on statistics, that proved useful until around 20 years ago. There are many good books written about critical path, and Wikipedia[1] has a very good explanation of the approach.

Beginning in the 1990s, as the number of projects activated in organizations exploded, many tasks found themselves waiting not on another task, but on a resource that was already working on another part of the same project. This syndrome of the project duration depending not just on task dependencies but also on resource dependencies was verbalized in a book called *Critical Chain* by Eli Goldratt. Wikipedia also provides an excellent overview of this approach.[2]

In our opinion, critical chain is a more conservative and realistic approach since resource constraints in the multi-project environment are pervasive. Therefore, we will devote a portion of this chapter to explain it further. From our experience, this focus yields excellent results in reducing project duration. The project's critical chain is the longest chain of dependent tasks through the project, where the dependency could be based on either:

- One task depending on another task finishing before it can start because it needs the result of that task in order to start or
- One task depending on a resource who must finish another task on another path of the same project

Software makes identifying the critical chain an easy task. Regardless of whether you decide to use critical chain or critical path, you will have the best chance of reducing a project's elapsed time duration by focusing on that subset of all the project tasks that most likely will drive it.

Overall Project Duration Reduction

When looking to reduce duration, it is necessary to do it without adding any risk to the project. That means we cannot arbitrarily begin reducing either ambitious or standard times. The steps below offer a useful process for reducing duration, without increasing the risk to the task completion criteria. There's an old saying that changing the estimates on paper does not change reality. Do not fall into that trap. Remember during this process that it is possible to go too far—additional resources and more experienced resources are key recovery options during execution; the more you've used those to reduce durations, the fewer options you'll have if recovery is required.

9.1. Focus on the critical chain or critical path tasks first, since they are the primary determiners of project length. Since we do not know which of these approaches you are using, we will simply refer to these tasks as *critical.* Examine the critical tasks looking first at the longest ambitious times. Note: Being able to sort the tasks by ambitious times (highest to lowest) is very useful.

9.1.1. Take a hard look at the ambitious and standard times. Given the team's thorough understanding of the project, do they have a gut feel that any of the task estimates are overstated? This can result from a lack of understanding of the tasks when they are estimated. Often things are caught when looking at the big picture that are missed when looking at tasks or paths in isolation. Perform a detailed review of those tasks and pencil in the new estimates. In the software, make the changes and save a copy of the project file under a different name (e.g., project name_reduction_version 1). Document the changes and validate the new assumptions with the appropriate experts. Rerun the software to identify the critical chain or critical path; it may be different!

9.1.2. Examine the resulting critical chain or critical path tasks. Can any significant ambitious and/or standard task estimates be shortened by changing from the minimum skilled resource to a higher skilled resource? Does such a resource exist? Looking at the potential added cost of a higher skilled resource versus the benefit to the organization of bringing in the project earlier, does the benefit justify the cost (if any)? Note that in many cases, there is no added real monetary cost when the higher skilled resource already works for the organization; that is, you are not paying them a higher salary to work on this project! However, cost allocations by project accounting systems can drive some extremely poor decisions.

9.1.3. Would the ambitious and/or standard task estimates be shortened if additional resources were added to the task? Note that this does not always reduce task estimates—nine women cannot have a baby in one month! If additional resources do make a difference, do those resources exist? See the discussion above on project cost versus benefit considerations.

9.1.4. Repeat the process on all significant ambitious critical chain or critical path task estimates.

9.1.5. When finished, rerun the process of identifying the critical chain or critical path. Check to see if Steps 9.1.1–9.1.5 should be repeated.

9.2. Examine long feeding paths. All tasks that are not on the critical chain or critical path are considered to be on a feeding path. Every project has only one critical chain or critical path, but has multiple feeding paths. Any path that feeds into or merges with the critical chain or critical path is considered a feeding path. For very long (a rule of thumb is two thirds the length of the critical chain/critical path) feeding paths, follow Steps 9.1.1–9.1.3 on these paths.

9.3. When you are finished reducing durations, rerun identifying the critical chain or critical path a final time.

9.4. As a final step, ensure the experts you've used for resourcing (Step 6) and time estimates (Step 8) validate the changes made. A double-check by people serving as senior resource manager(s) and senior project manager is also recommended.

Important note: Scheduling is not complete. Identifying the critical chain or critical path is part of scheduling but is not all of the scheduling process. You will learn much more in subsequent chapters; scheduling the project will not be complete in a multi-project environment until Chapter 30.

How Many Resources on a Task?

There is one school of thought which teaches that all resources in a resource pool should be put on a task when planning and scheduling in order to complete the task in the shortest possible time, whereas another school of thought teaches to put the minimum number of resources required to reach a task's completion criteria on a task in order to save project budget costs. Which is correct? We believe there is no hard and fast rule; it depends! What is important is to know what it depends on so that you can properly evaluate the situation.

For example, assume that a project requires completion of 500 engineering drawings. If that work represents one or several long critical tasks, it will make sense to put as many qualified resources on it as possible in order to reduce time. However, if the project task is to wire and install measuring devices between bulkheads 234 and 246, there may be only two resources that can physically fit in the space. Yes, these are two extreme examples!

Consider also that resources will not be multitasking while working a project task: once a resource begins work on a task, he/she/it will work on that task until task completion criteria are met. However, resources are assigned to tasks, not entire projects. Plus, by not multitasking, resources are not needed as long for the same task work. These are examples of key considerations when determining how many of a resource pool should be planned for a task to reduce overall project duration.

For those projects with budget constraints, experience shows (both ours and also from public presentations by organizations using this kind of approach that also have to meet budgets) that the shorter the project duration (driven by not multitasking and quick issue identification and resolution and full-kitting projects), the less rework, the less resource time consumed, and the less waste. That is, there is both a correlation and cause-effect between shorter duration and less money spent.

Other Considerations for Reducing Task Duration

1. One of the most common mistakes in building networks is the assumption that ALL task dependencies are, for the most part, correct. Is it

possible that nowhere near all of task A must be finished before even starting task B, even though we modeled it as a 100% dependency between the two tasks in the network? In almost all cases, we find a few such instances where the model was ultraconservative, and in fact most of task A can be done in parallel with task B. When you change these assumptions, by removing these dependencies, the typical result is a shorter duration.

2. Where significant amounts of time are used up by outside dependencies (e.g., vendors), determine what the value is of expediting delivery for critical items. For example, a project in Bangladesh was delayed for months waiting for high-end generators from an outside supplier. The value of the project was several million dollars per year and was very tangible. The return on investment was less than one year. Each generator was selling for approximately $150,000. If you figure the traditional way that a vendor values the sale, they usually expect a product gross profit contribution of 40–50%. That means that about $75,000 is their profit margin. If you were to offer them a $25,000 bonus for delivering early, that increases their profit margin by a third. This is one way to expedite with vendors. If you simply ask them if they can possibly deliver earlier, the answer is automatically "no." But offer them a significant premium and the answer can change quickly. In this case, the added cost was trivial in comparison to the value of getting early delivery from this vendor.
3. Re-examine the tasks against the scope and stakeholder needs. In many cases, we find liberal assumptions about tasks being required. When checking back with the stakeholder, we often hear responses such as, "Yes, that would be nice to have, but what I'm really after is . . ." You are *not* cutting scope if these kinds of tasks are trimmed before the project is even started. The key stakeholders are often the strongest supporters if it means that they can get the most important benefits much sooner without the nice to haves.
4. Re-example the major chunks of project logic. Sometimes, we find mistakes in how the project was modeled. For example, in one product development effort with a California high-tech company, there was a 15-day testing period during which no other development work could be done. Ninety-five percent of the time, the result of the testing is that the product solution is proven to work and is ready for beta testing with clients. However, being ultraconservative, they modeled the testing under a marketing resource heading, because they did not want marketing to

proceed until the product was proven. In fact, there were several time-consuming and critical marketing tasks that could proceed in parallel with the testing. When this was modeled to reflect those changes, 15 days were cut from the project duration.

5. Double-check the arrows along the critical chain/critical path. Is the task to the left really required to be complete before the task to the right can begin? In reality, most *must have* dependencies are one of two types:
    - The task to the left absolutely has to be complete before the task on the right can begin; this type is the most common.
    - The task to the left does not *have* to be completed before the task on the right can begin, but completing it first reduces the chances for rework or delay. Think of an expensive long-lead part. The engineering drawing for that part does not have to receive final approval before ordering the part, but if the part is ordered before final engineering drawing approval and a change is made to the drawing after it's ordered, the project can experience a very expensive delay (a double whammy!).

Conclusions

In seeking ways to reduce project duration, it is vital to not arbitrarily cut people's time estimates. This usually proves disastrous in execution. The first focus should be on those tasks that are critical to the projects (i.e., critical chain or critical path tasks), since those tasks more than any other are likely to determine how long the entire project will take. The typical options to examine are time estimates that do not reflect the intuition of the team about how long they should take, the opportunity to add more resources to a task to get it done more quickly, and the opportunity to put more highly skilled resources on some tasks to reduce duration.

When finished scrutinizing the critical tasks, look at long non-critical paths with the same scrutiny.

If the project duration is still much longer than acceptable to stakeholders, then look for invalid assumptions about the network logic and dependencies, and review long vendor lead times as avenues for reduction.

Endnotes

1. See the Wikipedia definition of critical path at http://en.wikipedia.org/wiki/Critical_path_method.

2. See the Wikipedia definition of critical chain at http://en.wikipedia.org/wiki/Critical_chain_project_management.

Questions

21-1. Why is there a need to look at reducing task durations?

21-2. Why not determine how long a critical path/critical chain needs to be to meet the sponsor's requirements and reduce all the tasks proportionally?

21-3. Describe the structured process for reducing project duration.

21-4. What is the value in focusing on both task and resource dependencies when determining what will drive project length?

21-5. Think about gaps of time along the critical chain/critical path. If the gaps are removed, won't that reduce the project duration without adding risk? Why or why not?

21-6. If adding additional resources will reduce the project's duration, why focus on resource quantities at the task level?

21-7. Why not offer a premium for early delivery to all vendors as a way to reduce overall project duration?

This book has free material available for download from the Web Added Value™ resource center at *www.jrosspub.com*

22. Step 10: Final Project Risk Assessment—Fifth Risk Avoidance

The Premise

You now have the final perspective of all work required to accomplish the project's scope, goals, objectives, and deliverables, with task notes detailing activities within the tasks, significant assumptions about each task, and specific task completion criteria for each task. You have identified the risks to each task individually through the task notes and task time variability estimates. Durations have been adjusted/corrected where appropriate without compromising on completion criteria, budget, or timeline.

Given the overall understanding of the project stakeholder needs, the goals the project is intended to meet, and the work outlined in the project plan, the project team is now prepared to take one final step. Are there other significant risks posed by this project that would endanger meeting its goals, in spite of all of the preceding work in building a robust plan?

Holistic Risk Mitigation

It is time to look at the project as a whole in terms of risk mitigation. The final project risk mitigation should be done with the original planning team, sponsor(s), key stakeholders, and experts who have provided resource skills and quantities, expert scrutiny, and task time estimates.

This review should go over, in detail, all of the project details and open discussions as to missed risk mitigation. If any significant risks at the task level have been missed, that information should be added appropriately and documented in the task notes.

There are also risks that can occur during the project, but cannot be assigned to a specific task or series of tasks. Examples are:

- Some series of tasks are performed by external resources who do not always reliably deliver. You do not know in advance which external resources this will happen with, but experience has shown that in projects like this, it's likely to happen at least twice. When it does happen, delays of at least 10 days occur. Make a note that a project-level risk adjustment (upward or longer in time) needs to be considered; the specific technique to make the adjustment will be shown in Chapter 23.

- Some of the equipment being used on the project has significant scheduled maintenance downtime every 500 hours. That scheduled maintenance will happen sometime during the project, but there is no way to know when or the number of times it will occur. Document the number of times and the estimated downtime as another project-level risk adjustment (upward or longer in time) that must be considered.

If there is iteration variability present in the project, look at the number of times it is estimated to occur. Typically, if there are one or two opportunities for iteration variability, no project-level adjustment needs to be made; however, if there are more than two opportunities for iterations, consider whether the project is being *overprotected.* If so, document and note that a project-level risk adjustment (downward or shorter in time) must be considered.

Organizations have typically experienced so much project failure and underachievement that they are prone to overlook one of the biggest generic risks of a project: the risk of success beyond expectations. In the 1990s, when AOL launched its Internet service with massive advertising, it lost tens of thousands of customers almost immediately after launch. These customers tried to dial up the free AOL telephone numbers to connect and experienced busy signals for hours on end. (Yes, we understand we may be describing something that sounds like horse-drawn milk trucks and wagon trains to the younger generation!) Similarly, we've seen many cases of product launches where the stock needed to satisfy initial customer requests was grossly underestimated, and the lead time to manufacture more was long. Customers waited months, by which time competitors had caught up and offered their own products. In these situations, it's not just that the organization lost some sales—they made their customers so mad that they lost customers for life.

Another type of risk is what some insurance companies labeled the *front page* risk. This is the risk that a project results in customer complaints that are so severe that the story ends up as a feature on the news.

The final conclusion of the group should be that all significant task- and project-level risks have been addressed: the network as planned is sufficient (but not oversufficient) to deliver the full scope of the project, at or below the budget, on or before the due date.

Conclusions

The final risk mitigation step is intended as a last, holistic look at the project, to mitigate or prevent any other previously unidentified risks from being realized. With the full team of stakeholders, network builders, and other key players present, the project can be examined to determine if other tasks are needed for final risk avoidance. Most often, the outcome of this step is to proceed with the plan as is or with very slight modifications. However, in the rare case where a major risk requires rework of the entire plan, it is much better to find out before execution starts.

Questions

22-1. Why have all the recommended people performed this review?

22-2. What is the difference between task-level and project-level risk?

22-3. How do you define *significant* risk? Is it the same for every project?

22-4. Why is it important to document these risk assessments?

22-5. What other project-level-type risk examples (that increase project length) can you identify?

22-6. Are there other project-level *overprotections* that should be reasons to decrease the project length?

22-7. How is this risk assessment different from a technical risk assessment?

PART IV

INSULATING PROJECTS FROM VARIABILITY

Projects will encounter variability—guaranteed! Many organizations have implemented straightjackets for everyone involved in projects—hundreds of pages of procedures and countless control mechanisms, to prevent variation from occurring. You can't argue very effectively with any single element. However, holistically, what this level of process does is slow down execution to a crawl. And still variation occurs! We advocate for a totally different approach. A summary of the key points is:

- Variation will occur, just like bumps in a road; there are two places where you need strategic shock absorbers within a project plan
- How to insulate projects from operations and other demands on resources
- How to insulate projects from each other
- Distinguishing between *normal* project variation (common cause) versus variation that requires some serious management intervention (special cause)

This section, Part IV, kills the fantasy that variation can be totally eliminated from a project world and provides a method to deal with it effectively.

23. Three Points of Network Insulation

The Premise

When we talk about insulation in project terms, we mean strategically protecting the work of the project network in order to enable delivery of the project on or before the due date, at or below budget, and with full project scope.

There are three points in any project network that are logical places to insulate a project against variability. The first is the project due date. The second is any point that feeds into the project's critical chain or critical path. The third (which does not exist in all projects) is any point that represents a critical milestone date to the project.

Over the past 20 years, we have found the most effective method of insulating projects is with a few buffers of time. This chapter shows the details behind the buffer calculations and placement. The software referenced in Chapter 10 helps to model buffers and reduce the amount of manual effort required. You do need to understand the underlying reasoning behind the buffer calculations.

The Example

As we saw in Chapter 21, the critical tasks within a project represent the longest pathway of task and resource dependencies in the project network.

In the project network shown in Figure 23.1, each box is a task, task names are the letters inside the box, and the resources are represented by the patterns in the boxes. The ambitious and standard time estimates are shown below each task. There is one of each resource type available. The critical tasks, tasks H, J, B, C, D, E, F, G, O, P, and Q, are shown with a bold outline. This example uses the critical chain approach for identifying the most critical tasks within the project. For more information on this approach, see the books listed in the Bibliography. If you are not familiar with this approach, you may use a similar approach with the critical path methodology. If you are not familiar with either methodology, you may simply assume that these tasks were identified as the ones most likely to determine the duration of the project.

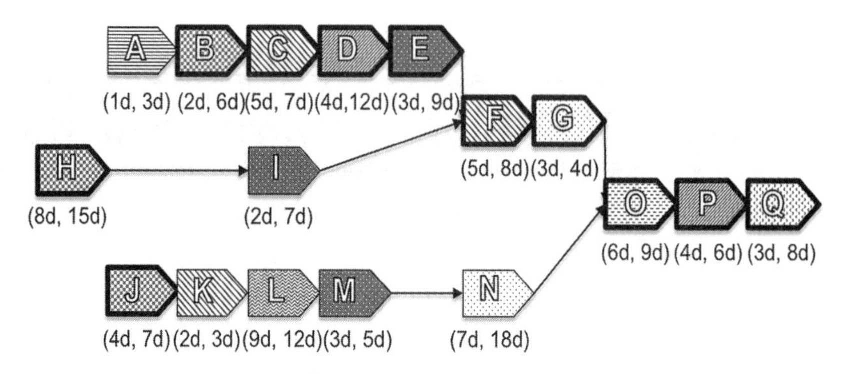

Figure 23.1 Project network with task names (letters), resources (patterns), time estimates (ambitious, standard), and critical tasks identified (bold task outline: H, J, B, C, D, E, F, G, O, P, Q)

The critical tasks are determined using the ambitious task times for each of the tasks in the project; this does not consider the inherent variability of each task. Ignoring variability on paper does not make it non-existent in a project, a fact unfortunately learned and relearned by many project managers. What we need is a way to understand and accommodate variability while planning and scheduling a project; during execution we need a way to understand when and where it occurs, as well as its impact on project completion. The variability we're talking about is the difference between the standard and ambitious task times. For future reference, we'll call this difference in task times the *variability factor*.

The problem with using only standard time estimates for planning, scheduling, and project execution is that each task attempts to account for variability individually. This is comparable to an insurance company trying to protect only one house, with a small premium. If the house burns down, the single premium will not have a hope to cover the losses. It only makes sense to protect against losses through aggregation—insuring a lot of houses where the loss is likely to occur only in a small percentage.

This same principle is used with these task time estimates. The variability factor is removed from the task time, leaving each task with an ambitious time estimate (a small premium). The variability factor is then cut in half, and the remaining half is aggregated into time buffers that insulate the network (protecting against *losses* or variability that will occur in some, not all, tasks).

Some organizations advocate for more sophisticated approaches to determining the size of project buffers. In our experience, 90% of all organizations will gain sufficient benefit from the inherently simple approach described above. Furthermore, once the organization has buffers and is monitoring these buffers during execution, it often finds that there are other much more important leverage points to further improve multi-project management.

We primarily use two types of time buffers to provide the needed network insulation:

1. The project buffer protects the project's due date from variability within and along the critical tasks. There is one project buffer per project.
2. Feeding buffers protect critical tasks from being delayed by variability along and within the non-critical feeding pathways.

Why and how are these two insulation points different and important? Traditionally, variability is embedded in each task and is not visible or managed in a project (typically one task time estimate is used—the equivalent to standard).

In addition, having the variability embedded motivates the wrong behavior in both leadership and resources during execution. Many times during project execution it seems that the task estimates somehow become deterministic numbers, translated into *due dates* for each task. Task due date compliance then appears to be a valid measure of not only project progress, but also employee *goodness.* What happens if the resource performing the task does not run into a lot of problems and actually is able to achieve the task completion criteria at the more ambitious time or even sooner? Is there any motivation to announce completion early? On the contrary! There are more reasons to NOT announce early completion:

- Many people doing project tasks fear that similar task estimates will be cut in the future, increasing their personal risk of not meeting the task due date compliance measurement.
- Others see holding on to the task as a way to have time (or budget) to accomplish other necessary project or non-project work.
- Sometimes there is a view that the work quality is not good if the resource takes less time than allocated. Also, knowing they are being evaluated according to task due date compliance, resources willingly allow work to *expand* to fill the time available (known as *Parkinson's law*).

The result of these motivations: almost no tasks are turned in by resources earlier than the standard task estimate and many finish later. Since actual project lead time is made up of the critical task time completions, it doesn't take many late finishes to equal a late project.

There is a better way to plan and schedule a project that enables successful project execution and management! The *best process* we've found for understanding and accommodating task variability is to gather two task time estimates (as was shown in Chapter 20) and use the understanding gained to protect or insulate the project strategically in the schedule and for execution. Then during execution, monitor and manage the use of the insulation. These concepts will be discussed further in upcoming chapters.

Project Buffer

A project has only one project buffer (shown in diagrams below as PB). Sometimes, a project has critical milestones. In this case, a portion of the buffer can be used for monitoring these milestones. Further explanation is provided below. The project buffer is placed between the last critical task and the project's due date (see Figure 23.2).

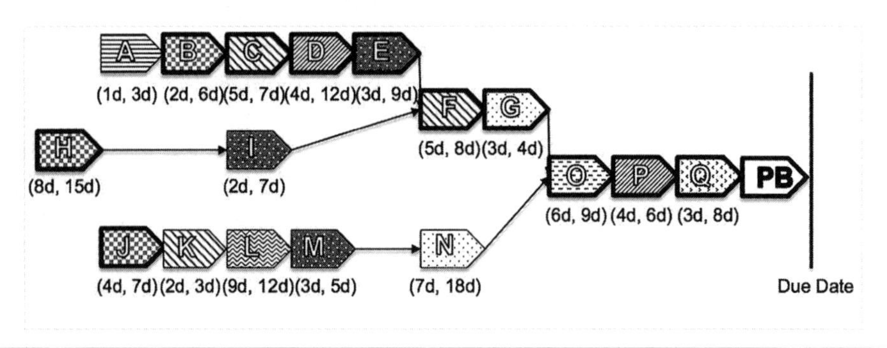

Figure 23.2 Placement of project buffer (PB)

The two important criteria for any project buffer are ensuring proper placement and proper sizing:

- *Placement.* The right side of any buffer is always placed directly before whatever it is protecting: for the project buffer, that is the project's due date. The placement is viewed as strategic for the project because the project buffer acts both as a *shock absorber* and a *time bank account* protecting the due date from variability in and along the critical tasks.
- *Sizing.* Ensuring the project buffer is properly sized allows it to act effectively as a shock absorber and time bank account. However, the project buffer is a unique type of shock absorber, since it can grow in size when critical tasks finish earlier than planned. In its traditional role, negative task variabilities are cushioned and protect the due date; a time bank account in that deposits (positive task variabilities) and withdrawals (negative task variabilities) can be made without negatively impacting the due

date—assuming the project buffer is being properly managed during project execution.

- At the end of the project, if the bank account has a positive balance, it means that the project finished earlier than planned. Sometimes, the organization can take advantage of this by releasing the final project output to the customer earlier than the promised due date. Sometimes this is not possible. However, even in the latter case, there is still a major positive impact of finishing earlier—all of the resources are freed up sooner to work on the next project.
  - Proper sizing of the project buffer starts with evaluating the variability of the critical tasks arithmetically. The typical rule-of-thumb arithmetic starting point for the project buffer is identifying the variability factor of each task time (standard minus ambitious), summing it up for the critical tasks, and then dividing by 2. In some environments, we recommend then adjusting (almost always upward) for specific, documented risks. Since readers of this text come from many different environments, we do not know whether there is a need to adjust the buffer and if so by how much.
  - In Table 23.1, you will see the calculation for the project buffer as 22 days, using the simple formula described above. Having now used this variability information for the critical tasks, you will see in Figure 23.3 that we are now showing only the ambitious times,

Table 23.1 Project buffer calculation

Task	Ambitious	Standard	Variable Factor VF = S – A
H	8	15	7
J	4	7	3
B	2	6	4
C	5	7	2
D	4	12	8
E	3	9	6
F	5	8	3
G	3	4	1
O	6	9	3
P	4	6	2
Q	3	8	5
			Total = 44
			½ VF = 22

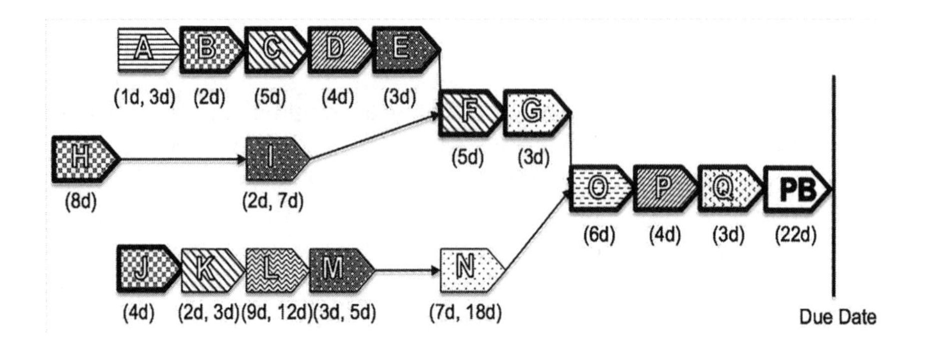

Figure 23.3 Properly sized and placed project buffer (only ambitious times are shown for critical tasks)

which are the times we will monitor as we execute the project. Since we have not yet calculated buffers for non-critical tasks, those tasks still show both the ambitious and standard times.

Feeding Buffers

Wherever tasks feed into the critical tasks, there is a danger that the feeding path will be completed late, causing an interruption in the critical tasks. To insulate against this variability, a time buffer called a *feeding buffer* is used. Each feeding buffer is placed with the origin (right side) up against whatever critical point it is feeding.

In Figure 23.4, there is:

- A feeding buffer between non-critical task A and critical task B
- A feeding buffer between non-critical task I and critical task F
- A feeding buffer between non-critical task N and critical task O

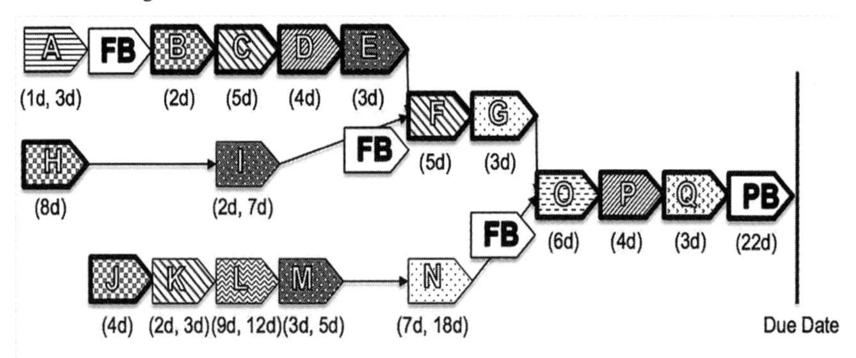

Figure 23.4 Properly placed feeding buffers

Table 23.2 Feeding buffer calculations

Feeding Buffer Projects	Feeding Chain Tasks	Ambitious	Standard	Variable Factor (VF) VF = S – A	Feeding Buffer Size (VF/2)
B	A	1	3	2	1
F	I	2	7	5	2.5
O	K	2	3	1	8.5
	L	9	12	3	
	M	3	5	2	
	N	7	18	11	

Sizing feeding buffers follows the same formula as the project buffer (see Table 23.2). Think of the feeding buffer as being the first line of defense against variability for non-critical tasks. Their second line of defense, although not preferred, is the project buffer. Figure 23.5 shows the entire project plan with ambitious times.

Iteration Variability and Buffer Sizing

As discussed in Chapter 20, iteration variability can occur along both the critical chain/critical path and along non-critical paths. When sizing either the project buffer or feeding buffers, iteration variability (where it exists) must be included in the original calculations. The ambitious number of iterations is already included in the pathway's buffer calculations (since the ambitious number of iterations is shown in the pathway). See Figure 23.6.

What remains is accommodating the variability of the potential additional iteration(s). Assuming the task times remain the same in all iterations, the buffer

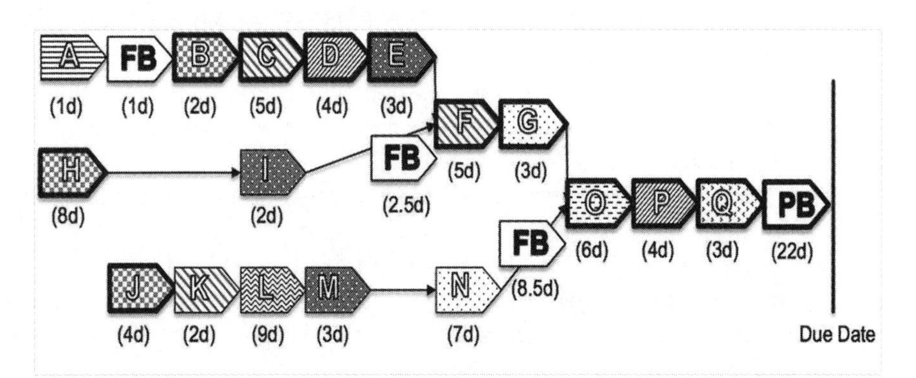

Figure 23.5 Properly sized and placed feeding buffers (only ambitious times are shown for all tasks)

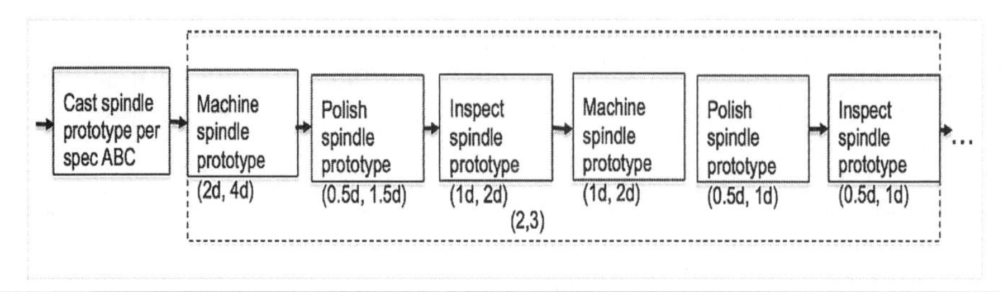

Figure 23.6 Iteration variability: ambitious 2 iterations, standard 3 iterations (2, 3)

adjustment is calculated by taking one half of the sum of the variability factor times the number of additional iterations. For example, if all the tasks within an iteration accounted for 10 days ambitious, and 22 days standard, then each additional iteration has 12 days of variability. Half of that, or six days, would be added to the appropriate buffer for each possible additional iteration.

Additional Network Insulation Point

There are a few cases where an additional network insulation point is needed within a project; it is referred to as a *contractual* or *critical milestone* (CMS); there are two types that can exist. Please note that CMS use should be avoided as much as possible; it often increases a project's lead time.

- *CMS type 1.* Portions of project work must be accomplished by a specific date, where a review (sometimes a *stage gate* or *milestone review*) must occur. All work stops until the review has been completed and approval is given (often via funding) to proceed with the project. The CMS date is protected by a time buffer called a *CMS buffer.* The CMS can occur along a critical path or a non-critical path.
  - *Modeling the CMS.* The task is a milestone (duration 0, 0) in the network but has a start date attribute associated with it—the date the review starts.
  - *Placing the CMS buffer.* The CMS buffer (time buffer) is placed between the last task dependency and the CMS.
  - *Sizing the CMS buffer.* The tasks that must be included for sizing this buffer are the longest string of task dependencies leading to the milestone. These task dependencies can include both critical and non-critical tasks.

    - *Impact on other buffers.* This type of CMS buffer actually *un-aggregates* the safety for the feeding or project buffer with which it is associated. When this type of CMS buffer is used, the associated feeding or project buffer must be adjusted.
- *CMS type 2.* Some projects require interim deliverables tied to a specific date. For example, a prototype must be delivered on or before a certain date. That date must be protected by a CMS buffer, but this type of CMS does not involve stopping project work to wait for approval/go-ahead; for this type of CMS, the tasks after the CMS can begin as soon as the tasks before the CMS are completed.
    - *Modeling the CMS.* The task is a milestone (duration 0, 0) in the network but has a start date attribute associated with it—the date the review starts. However, this CMS is not placed in-line. Typically, it is shown above the line of tasks, as its associated date is *external* to the remaining work of the project.
    - *Placing the CMS buffer.* The CMS buffer (time buffer) is placed between the last task dependency and the CMS, in this case not pushing the next project task.
    - *Sizing the CMS buffer.* The tasks that must be included for sizing this buffer are the longest string of task dependencies leading to the milestone. These task dependencies can include both critical and noncritical tasks. Remember: we are sizing this buffer to protect the CMS date.
    - *Impact on other buffers.* This type of CMS buffer does not *un-aggregate* the safety for the feeding or project buffer with which it is associated. The associated buffer does not need to be recalculated.

Conclusions

When projects are strategically protected with buffers of time at three points, they become much better able to achieve their outcomes. The problem in most environments is that protection is left at an individual task level, which almost guarantees failure. By removing the protection against variability that is inherent in most task time estimates, and moving it to aggregated buffers, the protection is in three places where it makes sense and can be carefully monitored as the project executes. This chapter provides the details behind how to calculate the three types of buffers and where to place them.

Questions

23-1. What are the primary two points in a project network that must be insulated?

23-2. What is the primary determinant of how long a project will take?

23-3. A variability factor is aggregated into what type of buffer?

23-4. What does the project buffer protect?

23-5. How many project buffers can a project have? Why?

23-6. A properly sized project buffer allows it to effectively do what?

23-7. What do you do with iteration variability when sizing buffers?

23-8. Why should you try to avoid CMS buffers?

24. Operations versus Project Responsibility—Resource Insulation

The Premise

The last chapter talked about insulating projects from variability. You may be asking yourself, "What is 'resource insulation' and why is it important?" Resources, whether people, facilities, or capital equipment, are available in limited quantities. In many organizations, the same resources that perform project tasks also have non-project work responsibilities. This non-project work is crucial for the organization's operational (day-to-day) success. This is another, often major conflict for project and resource managers as well as operational managers! This chapter uncovers some successful approaches for us to protect or insulate our resources so that all the required work can be accomplished.

Negative Effects of Multitasking

A common practice in many organizations is to interrupt resources assigned to a project task to go work either another project task or perform operational work, as priorities change. What happens, in terms of task duration, when task work is interrupted before it is completed? The clock keeps ticking on the task duration, but no work is being performed—the task is *suspended.* When task durations are extended because of *suspend* time, project durations are as well.

Task times are unlikely to be adequate when resources are interrupted frequently from doing project work or are often busy doing other work. If the task times are not adequate, project scope, budget, and due date are quickly threatened.

When a resource working on a project task is interrupted, it often requires substantial time to pick up where they left off. Time is needed to get set up again and/or review what is needed and what has been done already to know where to start. The result is that the task times are extended again, not because of task variability (which is how the task times were estimated), but because of the multitasking. According to *Harvard Business Review*[1] and the *New York Times*,[2] "when you switch away from a primary task to do something else, you are increasing the time it takes to finish that task by an average of 25 percent."

Our experience shows that the amount of damage from multitasking varies, depending on the nature of the task. Tasks that require a great deal of concentration, such as some engineering or IT architecture or debugging tasks, suffer much more than the 25% time damage. They also suffer from mistakes and rework.

You will have major gains in task durations and project predictability by fully stopping the multitasking of resources on project tasks. We are not saying that resources should be assigned to a project and not asked to do anything else for the duration of the project. We are recommending that when a resource has started a project task, there be no switching work until that project task is finished (another good reason why clear and precise task definition is crucial!).

Buy-in to this concept (no multitasking on project tasks) can be difficult, sometimes more difficult for the resources than for management. There are some resources that seem to like the security of having several tasks open for them to do. Some will say they need variety for when they are stuck. We have found that training and clear task definitions as well as management commitment will permanently resolve this issue. The positive results to project and non-project work are immediate. Multitasking is by far one of the biggest wastes of limited, available capacity in most multi-project environments today!

Planned versus Actual Resource Loading

During planning and scheduling, remember that you have used ambitious times for the tasks modeled with resources identified. The rest of the time allocation (a third of the total time) went into buffers and was not directly associated with a specific resource skill set. Since most tasks will not complete in the ambitious time or less, it requires a different perspective when evaluating resource loading. We expect some tasks to take longer than the ambitious time and some to take less; some tasks may even exceed their standard time. The planned time use of the resources with only ambitious times means that *fully loaded* must be viewed as much less than 100%.

Resource histograms (see Figure 24.1), when using ambitious times, will also be very sensitive to workday calendars. If resources are expected to be *at work* for eight hours per day, does that really mean they are expected to perform project work for the entire eight hours? What portion of their day is tied up with meetings, phone calls, e-mails, and administrative tasks? In some organizations, the available project work time can be four hours or less per day per resource.

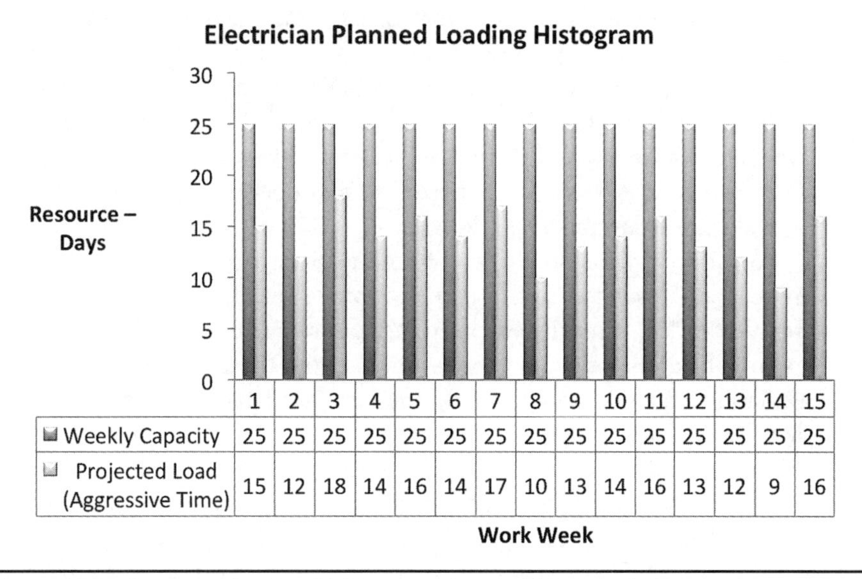

Figure 24.1 Resource loading histogram using ambitious task times

Consider carefully and document fully so that anyone using a resource loading histogram understands what they are looking at before making any resourcing decisions.

Let's say a resource is planned to be available for project task work four hours a day. If the task they are assigned to work is estimated to be (2d, 5d), does that mean they will spend at least two four-hour days working the task or was the task estimated with an eight-hour day? If the task was estimated based on an eight-hour day and the resource does four hours of project work per day, expect the resource to be tied up for at least four days (16 hours). Is the resource fully loaded at four hours a day for project work? Calendars and histograms need to be fully understood to have proper resource insulation!

Supporting Projects and Operations with the Same Resources

Depending on the organization's environment, these techniques work effectively, along with no multitasking, when the same resources are needed to support both projects and operations:

- Determine a way to prioritize the operations work and the project task work in the same system. At the beginning of each workday, assign

available resources in priority work order. At the end of each day, ensure task and operations updates are done so that the priority list is ready for the next day, as well as the list of available resources. If either operations work or a project task completes before the end of the day, assign the available resource(s) to the next highest priority work.
  - *Positive(s):* All work is prioritized so that operations as well as project tasks are accomplished.
  - *Negative(s):* It can be difficult to merge priority systems.
- Allocate the resources so that some people primarily work operations and the remainder primarily work project tasks. Typically, this is done on a rotation basis. For example, the resources work three months of dedicated availability for operational work, then are available for three months of dedicated project tasks.
  - *Positive(s):* The resources can focus fully on building operational skills; when required for overload situations on projects, these resources can be made available on a dedicated basis for a short time.
  - *Negative(s):* There are times when there is only one of a resource skill, so the resource must work both; there are no other options.
- Dedicate a portion of the workday to operations work and another portion of the workday to a project task.
  - *Positive(s):* Both are being accomplished.
  - *Negative(s):* Both will take longer since the daily work calendar for both operations and project work has been shortened.

Guaranteeing Subcontractor Availability

We have seen organizations use a contractual agreement (with financial compensation) for an external resource to guarantee its availability when needed to perform critical tasks. The project manager must give updates to the resource as the time nears for that work to begin. As an example, on a road construction project, a two-lane paving machine is required for a specific critical task. It does take time to move the paver from one location to another, and the project manager does not want to delay critical work waiting for it to arrive and be set up. In this case, part of the contract for the resource included a negotiated additional fee guaranteeing the paver would be available to work based on the previous task's completion updates. Note that the paver did not agree to be available on a certain date in advance; rather, there was a window of time that it was likely to be needed and then, based on task updates while the predecessor task was executing, a countdown was given to the paver. Warnings:

- Use contractually guaranteed resourcing only when the benefits outweigh the additional costs.
- Do not enter into a contractual agreement with resources that are not capable of fulfilling their part of the deal!

Conclusions

The conventional way of dealing with people who have both operational and project responsibility is to accept the conflict between the two as a fact of life. This chapter describes the proven damage caused by such acceptance and shows different ways to permanently mitigate it. One way is to dedicate an operational resource to a project for the entire duration of a single project task, delegating their operational responsibilities for this duration to someone else. Another approach is to allocate a portion of a day to operations and a portion to projects, thus at least minimizing the amount of damage caused by interruptions. A third way is to allocate a portion of a resource pool to operations while dedicating the remainder to projects. No matter which way is chosen, it is vital to get out of the mindset that it is OK to continually multitask.

Endnotes

1. Tony Schwartz, "The Magic of Doing One Thing at a Time," *Harvard Business Review*, March 14, 2012. Retrieved from http://blogs.hbr.org/schwartz/2012/03/the-magic-of-doing-one-thing-a.html.
2. Steve Lohr, "Slow Down, Brave Multitasker, and Don't Read This in Traffic," *New York Times*, March 23, 2007. Retrieved from http://www.nytimes.com/2007/03/25/business/25multi.html?_r=1&pagewanted/%20all=&pagewanted=print.

Questions

24-1. What is resource insulation?

24-2. What can happen to project duration when tasks are *suspended*?

24-3. Are project and feeding buffers sized to accommodate resource non-availability?

24-4. When a resource comes back to a project task, can it just pick up where it left off?

24-5. Multitasking wastes what?

24-6. Buy-in to the concept of monotasking (instead of multitasking) on project tasks can be more difficult for whom?

24-7. Why should contractually guaranteed resourcing be used sparingly?

25. Project-to-Project Insulation

The Premise

Chapter 7 introduced the topic of aligning multiple projects. Chapter 28 describes the specifics of aligning projects in a way that protects the organization's capacity to do projects. The analogy is like trying to evacuate a crowded auditorium with one exit door in a panic situation. If a thousand people rush to the one exit door and all try to get out at once, they jam themselves in the doorway. It takes a long time for everyone to get through. If the doorway has sufficient width to allow five people to exit at the same time, without interfering with each other, then this is the maximum number of people allowed through at once. What took an hour before to empty the auditorium is now done in 15 minutes.

In a multi-project situation, projects must be insulated from each other, or they will be constantly either trying to rob each other's resources or waiting on each other for long periods of time. The objective is to have the insulation contain the same properties as physical insulation does in a building—it is typically invisible, yet keeps out too much heat or cold. This chapter provides perspective on the overall system and how it works, somewhat invisibly, to keep projects insulated from each other.

Why Is Project-to-Project Insulation Important?

We have discussed in detail the impact of task and resource variability in a project. However, a multi-project environment means there are many projects executing at the same time, all fighting for the same, limited quantity, shared resources and management attention. In a project, what happens when a resource takes longer than the ambitious time? There is a project-level buffer to absorb the variability and still protect that project's due date.

When other projects are waiting for the same resource to finish, those projects are forced to absorb a delay until the resource finishes the project task it is currently working. We need a way to insulate for project-to-project variability without dealing with the impossible complexity of trying to balance resources across all projects and programs. But variability is not the only reason for insulating projects from each other.

Managers face a dilemma about how many projects to release for execution at any point in time. On one hand, managers need to complete the projects they've already committed to, so they feel pressure to not release any new projects. At the same time, knowing how long it currently takes to deliver projects, they feel pressure to release projects as soon as the customer commits to them—the thinking is often similar to "the sooner I start, the longer I'll have to catch up." The most common way out of the dilemma is to release all projects as soon as they are available and push the resources to multitask—thus appearing to show progress on all projects. Additionally, with all of the multitasking going on, it becomes very difficult to know what the real capacity of the organization is to perform projects—so much time is spent unproductively! When more than one project is seriously delayed by this multitasking behavior, it also becomes difficult to know on which projects and tasks to focus the *catch-up* effort.

There are other common coping mechanisms we often see in traditional multi-project environments. For example:

- Project priorities frequently change, frustrating managers and resources alike. As variability occurs in the project tasks that resources are assigned to, the impact of the delays to the other projects becomes unbearable. How do organizations cope? By instituting even more important (and changing) priority lists (e.g., the *Top 5*, the *Hot Projects*, the *Top 3*). The result: Resources are interrupted even more frequently, so the impacts of multitasking grow in magnitude. Plus, what about the projects that never make the changing priority lists (such as the number 6 project)? They get later and later.
- Many organizations try to prevent these delays and battle for the limited, shared resources by staggering projects to remove all resource conflicts for all resources across all of the projects. Unfortunately, although this looks good on paper, it doesn't change the reality that variability exists. This plan is usually obsolete before it has been distributed!

How Do We Provide Effective Project-to-Project Insulation?

We insulate projects from each other by:

- Aligning the number of projects in execution with the organization's capacity to effectively perform project work. This process provides project-to-project insulation from the negative effects of variability in one project impacting other projects. It also limits the amount of work in process, further reducing the potential for major cross-project resource conflicts.

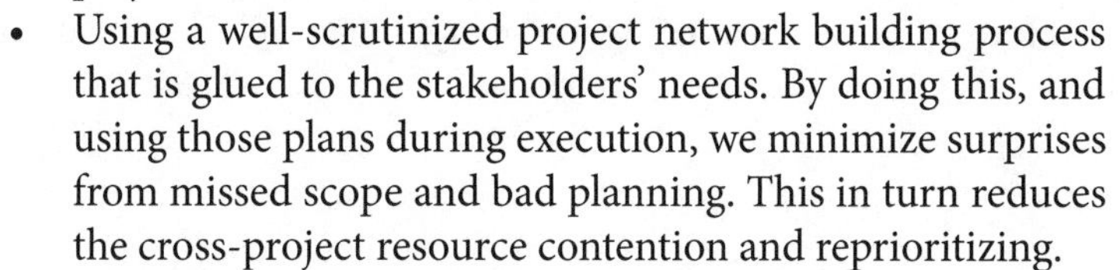

- Using a well-scrutinized project network building process that is glued to the stakeholders' needs. By doing this, and using those plans during execution, we minimize surprises from missed scope and bad planning. This in turn reduces the cross-project resource contention and reprioritizing.

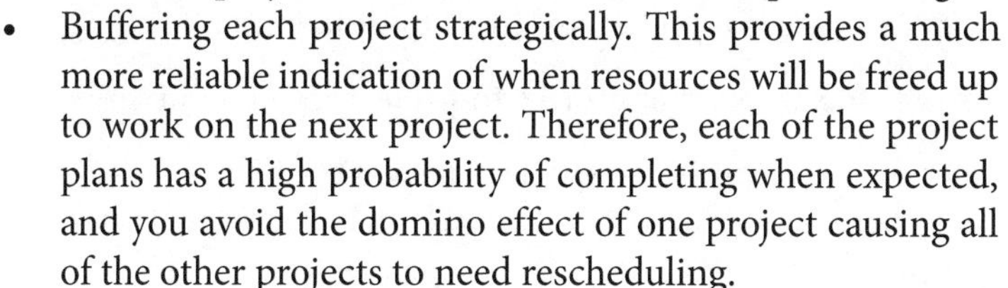

- Buffering each project strategically. This provides a much more reliable indication of when resources will be freed up to work on the next project. Therefore, each of the project plans has a high probability of completing when expected, and you avoid the domino effect of one project causing all of the other projects to need rescheduling.
- Having execution processes that discover and address issues quickly. This avoids having issues come up toward the end of a project that delay the project and tie up resources, holding up all other projects that were depending on those resources. Furthermore, the execution processes raise awareness of common issues that could affect all projects; for example, a shortage of IT support people, bottlenecks with legal counsel, etc. Whenever there is not enough insulation to protect projects from impacting each other or from multiple projects all being impacted by the same issue, the execution processes quickly uncover the problem and fix the insulation.
- Using a single priority system so that every project has the best chance of finishing on time. The fights over resources and the frequent recovery meetings from poor planning and poor execution are virtually eliminated.
- Forcing the use of a proactive recovery system. By doing this, we avoid having a project get into such deep trouble that it leaves management no other choice but to delay other projects in order to recover from a disastrous project.

Conclusion

In a multi-project environment, effective project-to-project insulation is a *must have*. Unfortunately, traditional methods have not been effective, and in many cases have actually caused even more problems. All six gears used in our multi-project management system provide necessary components of insulation to prevent projects from hurting each other. We'll introduce a process in Chapter 28 that provides effective project-to-project alignment by synchronizing the release of projects into execution according to the organization's capacity to perform that work.

Questions

25-1. Why is there a need for project-to-project insulation?

25-2. What are the indicators that project-to-project insulation is effective?

25-3. How does effective project-to-project insulation help all projects deliver on or before the due date, at or below budget, and with the full scope?

25-4. List the traditional ways organizations try to insulate projects and why they aren't as effective as expected.

26. Common Cause versus Special Cause Insulation

The Premise

The last several chapters have covered different ways of insulating tasks, resources, individual projects, and multi-projects from risk and variability. These risks and variabilities have been common causes. Common cause variation is those hiccups that occur often in projects, should be expected, and the project methodology should be able to accommodate that variation without management lifting a finger. These variations are primarily internal to the project and account for 80–90% of the variability we expect to observe during project execution. Examples are:

- A task taking twice as long to complete as estimated
- Some additional tasks being needed to complete the project
- A stakeholder requesting some changes

Special causes are primarily externally generated.[1] By *externally*, we mean that there are events or actions coming from outside the actual project task execution which have a significant impact on the project. The source of these events could be inside or outside the organization.

Although special causes cannot be predicted in most cases, there is one special cause of risk and variability in single- and multi-project execution environments that can be predicted and prevented: management intervening in the project incorrectly. Correct interventions will be detailed in Chapter 33. This chapter explains how the system we have described so far helps management to distinguish between common and special cause variation and therefore to know when to intervene.

Knowing When to Intervene

It's very tempting for managers of projects to *tinker* with the plan during project execution. However, incorrect intervention (tinkering) can have devastating consequences not only on one project, but also on all of the projects currently in execution. The most common types of incorrect intervention (creating special cause risks and variabilities) are:

- *Intervening when no action is required.* As you'll learn in Chapter 31, there are specific times when management intervention is required; for example, when a project buffer is almost used up and the project's critical tasks are only 10% complete. We expect tasks to have variability—during planning we get an understanding of the range of variability by gathering two time estimates for each task (ambitious and standard). The project buffer is sized to be the shock absorber between the variability of the critical tasks and the project's due date—we do expect to use all of it during project execution. As long as the project buffer usage is in line with the rate of completion of critical tasks, there is no need to intervene.

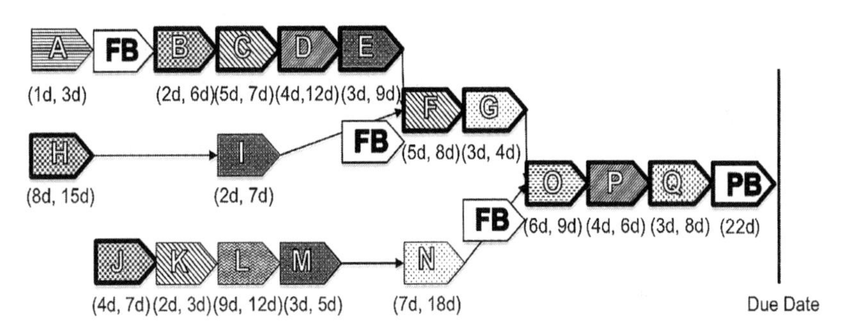

Figure 26.1 Project 1 example

In Figure 26.1, Project 1's project buffer is 22 days. Let's say that task H has completed in 10 days, two days longer than its ambitious time, and task J completed in seven days, three days longer than its ambitious time. What is the impact on the project due date? There is no impact because the buffer absorbed this variation. Five days of the 22-day project buffer have been used. The five days represent 23% of the project buffer that we have consumed so far. At the same time, we have completed 12 days out of the 47 days of critical work represented by the tasks in bold, or more than 25% of the critical work. Another way of describing this is that we are actually completing critical work faster than we are consuming buffer. *There is no need for the project manager to intervene.* Yet, it is very hard for the project manager not to do something—the first two critical tasks have taken longer than their ambitious time estimates!!! The sky is not falling!

To avoid creating even more problems, the project manager must not intervene when the rules clearly state that no action is required.

- *Not intervening when action is required.* Staying with the Project 1 example, let's say that more time has passed and the latest task updates indicate that 16 of the 22 days of the project buffer, or about 73%, has been used. However, the resources working on the project have only completed tasks B, J, and H of all the critical tasks, 12 out of 47 days of estimated work, or less than 30%. Our intervention signal is there. However, the project manager arbitrarily, on her own, decides that no action is necessary. Without a compelling rationale for this non-action, the project manager's non-intervention increases the risk to the due date. By waiting and intervening even later, the options to recover sufficiently to meet the due date are significantly reduced. Furthermore, not recovering this project soon enough jeopardizes all of the other projects in execution.
- *Taking the wrong action.* The intervention signal has been given (consuming project buffer at a much faster rate than completing critical work, to the point that more than two thirds of the buffer is consumed, with a much lower percentage of critical work complete). The source of the penetration is higher than expected variability on the critical tasks (now completed through task F). The project manager has decided to authorize overtime for the resources working task N. This is the wrong action because task N is not a critical task (the source of penetration). The correct action would be to reverse the penetration into the project buffer; only taking action on the remaining critical tasks can cause that change. Taking action on the feeding path will not help this project, will cause resources not to be available to work other projects, and will waste the resource budget.

Summary

Common cause insulation is provided by:

- Understanding the full scope, objectives, and tangible deliverables before beginning network building
- Continuous focus on each task's completion criteria during network building
- Backward and forward passes during network building
- Expert scrutiny of the network
- Gathering two task time estimates from experts with experience in and intuition for the work involved and the skill level of the resources identified for the tasks

- Documenting assumptions and potential risks for each of the tasks
- Identifying and accommodating potential iteration variabilities
- Strategically placing and sizing time buffers to protect the project due date
- Documenting project-level risks and adjusting the appropriate buffers to accommodate them
- Not multitasking resources between operations and projects (or even within or across projects)
- Providing effective project-to-project insulation

Special cause insulation is provided by ensuring management does not do the following:

- Intervene when *no* action is required
- Not intervene when action *is* required
- Take the wrong action

Conclusions

A multi-project management system must be set up to succeed in spite of common cause variation. Having project, resource, and senior managers who understand the two types of variation, the signals, and when to intervene and not intervene is mandatory to drive projects to completion quickly and predictably. Taking the right action on the right tasks is also part of an excellent intervention system.

Endnotes

1. Dr. Richard E. Peschke, MGMT 380 Operations Management lectures, Minnesota State University Moorhead, Moorhead, MN, April 10, 2003.

Questions

26-1. In most cases, can special causes be predicted?

26-2. List the three types of incorrect intervention.

26-3. The project buffer is sized and placed to protect what?

26-4. Do you expect to use all of the project buffer during project execution?

26-5. What is the *intervention signal*?

26-6. Where do the options for project buffer recovery come from in a multi-project environment?

PART V

ALIGNING AND ACTIVATING MULTIPLE PROJECTS

A multi-project system does not work if there is too much work in process within the system. The organization must learn how to reduce existing project work to the point that project flow dramatically improves. Then, the organization must have a strictly obeyed mechanism, fully supported by senior management, to release new projects into the system in a way that maintains a quick pace. A summary of the key points are:

- Overall project priorities must be in place in order to release projects according to top management needs. A single task priority system is essential to ensure all released projects complete on time.
- There are two different ways to align projects according to the capacity of the organization to do project work.
- Once the system is designed to be continually stable, then *what if* analyses allow experimentation with different scenarios to get better results.
- With all prior pieces in place, activating new projects according to a firmly scheduled set of start dates and committed finish date is mundane.

Part V provides further details on controlled project WIP.

27. Setting Project Priorities

The Premise

There is a great deal of confusion when you talk about *project priorities* in a multi-project organization. There are two types of priorities that often are not distinguished from each other and, in fact, must be managed totally differently:

1. Overall project priority, as viewed by the executives of the organization
2. Project task priority, often expressed by resources or resource managers with the question "Which project task has the highest priority?" or "Which project task is the most important one for me to work on next?"

This chapter explains these two different priority requirements and how to handle them to effectively meet the goals of the organization and all of the projects.

The First Type of Project Priority

The overall project priority is based on the importance of the projects to the organization's bottom line, now and in the future. Projects must be force ranked in priority (i.e., only one #1, one #2, one #3). The higher the priority, the sooner the project will be released for execution.

Some organizations' projects are primarily for external customers or clients. In those cases, the considerations for establishing a project's priority could include, for example:

- Profit the organization expects to receive when the project is delivered on or before the due date, at or below budget, and with full scope
- Potential bonuses or awards
- Market share
- Opportunities for future business
- First to market
- Client or customer needs
- Potential goodwill

Note that *avoiding penalties* is not on the list for setting project priorities. When organizations are delivering projects on or before the due date, with full scope, and at or below budget, there is no need to make penalties a part of the discussion!

Other organizations focus solely on completing projects internally; the organization itself is the customer. Considerations for establishing a project's priority for internal projects include:

- Potential increases in sales
- Potential decreases in operating expenses
- Potential decreases in inventory and investment expenses
- Potential decreases in raw materials and purchased parts expenses

Finally, there are many organizations that perform both external and internal projects. We strongly recommend prioritizing across both internal and external projects rather than having separate priority rankings. Whenever there is more than one project priority list for shared resources, confusion ensues!

The approaches to overall project prioritization, including forms and evaluation criteria, are discussed extensively in a book by Kendall and Rollins on project portfolio management.[1]

The Second Type of Project Priority

The first type of overall project priority is NOT used during project execution. When you are trying to determine during execution what project task to work on next, the answer depends on how much danger the project is in of missing its committed due date or budget. During project execution, task priorities for all released projects in a portfolio are provided by buffer status (see Chapters 31–33). In other words, although the purpose of the overall project priority is to release the most important projects first, once the projects are released, the goal of the priority system is to have all released projects finish on time, on budget, and within scope. To accomplish this second goal, a single task priority system is used.

It is important for managers and resources to understand that both priority systems exist and are never in conflict with each other. Too often we've seen project execution focus only on overall project priority for accomplishing tasks, which may help the top two or three projects, but greatly damages the chances of completing all other projects as promised.

Conclusions

Overall project priorities are used to determine when to release a project into the system, based on which project is most important to the organization's leaders. Task priorities are used during execution of all projects to determine which task on which project to work on, based on which task most endangers a project due date commitment. Once this is understood, and the systems are in place to use these priorities, organization goals and project goals have a much higher chance of being met with much less management intervention.

Endnotes

1. Gerald I. Kendall and Steven C. Rollins, *Advanced Project Portfolio Management and the PMO.* Boca Raton, FL: J. Ross Publishing, 2003.

Questions

27-1. Who sets an organization's project priorities?

27-2. Project priorities are set based on what?

27-3. True or false? *Avoiding penalties* is a consideration for establishing project priorities.

27-4. True or false? An organization that does only internal projects has no customer.

27-5. If an organization does both internal and external projects, how many priority lists should there be?

27-6. Are project priorities used during project execution?

27-7. What priorities are used during project execution?

28. Two Different Ways to Align Multiple Projects

The Premise

As introduced in Chapter 7, there are two different ways to align multiple projects: by strategic or critical resource (meaning by a skill set) or by a type or phase of project work. Before getting into the details and specifics of each, it is vital to understand why we absolutely must align multiple projects.

Every organization that is managing more than one active project at a time is caught in a tough dilemma—a short-term, long-term conflict. These organizations have current projects under way that they are working diligently to provide all of the scope and tangible deliverables on or before the due date and at or below budget. At the same time, since they continually endure new pressure on the organization, or their executives constantly find major new opportunities, they are pressured to activate new projects.

When new projects are awarded/approved, there is pressure to get started on them right away—that's what customers expect. But starting on the new projects dilutes the resources and management attention from the existing projects; finishing the existing projects before starting the new ones invites customer dissatisfaction. What seems to be an acceptable compromise for many organizations is to release the new projects as they come in, while continuing to work on the existing projects. The result? Pressure to multitask resources, frequently changing priorities, tasks and projects taking longer than expected, more rework than expected, missed due dates, due dates made but with budget overruns, due dates and budgets met but project scopes diminished, frustrated customers, frustrated managers and resources, decreased profits, and spiraling costs.

The premise of this chapter is that the compromise is not only totally unacceptable, it is completely unnecessary! To satisfy the needs of existing projects and still achieve much better execution and customer satisfaction, the organization *must* align the release of projects with the capacity of the organization to do projects!

What to Do about Current Project WIP

We operate on the assumption that, at the outset of implementing this new approach, there are too many projects currently competing for the limited resources available. Before proceeding:

- Determine what projects are currently executing, their priority to the organization, and their resource loads.
- Determine which projects to freeze (cease all activities on). Typically, we expect to freeze the lowest priority projects that are responsible for about 25% of the current project load.
- Implement and sustain the project freeze until after synchronization. Resources that had been assigned to the frozen projects are now available to speed up completion of the remaining projects.
- If not already accomplished, implement and sustain a no-multitasking policy on all project tasks.

Synchronization Concepts

Before introducing the processes for each of the two synchronization processes, here are some terms and concepts that make the processes easier to understand.

Synchronization

Project synchronization is staggering (spreading) the release of project work according to the capacity of the organization to do that project work. From vast experience, we offer two very simple choices to approximate the project capacity of the organization:

1. According to the capacity of a heavily loaded resource skill set that is used in most or all projects or
2. According to the number of projects that the organization can flow quickly, as defined within one phase or type of work

We present a further discussion on capacity below. We want to avoid overloading the project resources, which slows down all project work. Projects are synchronized around ONE synchronizer (resource skill or type of work). *Proper* synchronization means that we have resolved all of the conflicts for the ONE synchronizer during planning. By focusing the synchronizer on the biggest factor driving project capacity of the organization, we minimize the conflicts for all of the other resources. This does not mean that we will never experience demand for the same resource to work on two projects at the same time. In fact, we guarantee that these conflicts will happen because there is variability in the execution of project tasks. However, buffers take care of conflicts arising from variability during execution.

Synchronizer

The synchronizer is either a heavily loaded critical resource or a type of work/phase of a project that we use to perform the synchronization of projects to the organization's capacity. What we are looking for is a more heavily loaded resource or type of work that will give us the stagger between projects that we need.

- *Heavily loaded critical resource.* One way to determine which critical resources are heavily loaded is to perform load to capacity analyses (some software will do this for you, or you can easily set up a spreadsheet). Resources analyzed should be ones that are shared across all of the projects. Another way to identify candidates is to ask experienced managers and leadership about the projects: Are there resources that are in short supply or that you always need more of? Which resources do you end up waiting on the most when trying to schedule tasks? Note that when we're talking about a heavily loaded critical resource, the emphasis is on *a* heavily loaded resource skill, not *the* most heavily loaded, named individual resource.
- *Type of work/phase of a project.* An example of a type of work/phase of a project is system test tasks that may require many resources to work on an as-needed basis depending on what is found during testing. If that is a typical scenario when that type of work is occurring, we cannot expect those resources to be available to work uninterrupted on other project tasks at the same time. The power of synchronizing this way is based on the assumption behind using this type of synchronization mechanism. The assumption is that the organization's performance is based on how many projects can quickly move through this phase at a time. Another way of expressing this is to ask how many projects, in this phase, the organization's different resources, managers, and support resources can facilitate without unduly delaying the projects. Using this approach, a $40 million manufacturer with 350 employees discovered they could support only one major project and one minor project. This was because their executives were involved in a major way with the types of projects they were undertaking. In a $70 million engineering firm with 100 employees, they

found they had to cut the number of active projects from 13 to 6, in order to be responsive to project needs.

Synchronization Buffer

The synchronization buffer is a time buffer at the organizational level. An analogy would be the spacing of airplanes between takeoffs and landings. Imagine a busy airport with zero buffer between airplanes landing. Airplane A, a small regional jet, lands at 3:15 p.m. At 3:16 p.m., a jumbo jet lands. Oops—the regional jet has not yet cleared the runway. The jumbo jet touches down, sees the regional jet in its way, and manages to take off before a crash, but now it has to circle around. Unfortunately, it can't get back into the queue because there are 60 airplanes scheduled every minute for the next hour. This is likely to happen not once, but several times an hour because each airplane has some variation in both the time it is available to land and how long it requires to clear the runway.

The synchronization buffer provides insulation between projects in the same way that airplanes are buffered between landings. This time buffer prevents the variability of the synchronizer in one project from negatively impacting the synchronizer in other projects. Every project's internal buffers can adequately protect the project due date from other sources of variability.

Synchronization Process

Assumptions:

- Projects have been properly planned.
- Organizational priorities are known for all frozen and yet-to-be-released projects (if internal projects as well as projects for external customers are being synchronized, there is an integrated [one] priority system in place).
- The synchronizer has been established.
- Senior management is making the synchronization decisions.
  1. Take the highest priority project waiting for synchronization. Looking only at the first use of the synchronizer (whether resource or type of work), align this project so that the synchronizer appears immediately after where the synchronizer finishes work on the prior project. When there are multiple units of the synchronizer, choose the next highest priority project and synchronize it in the same manner. Figures 28.1 and 28.2 show a before and after example of resolving synchronizer conflicts on a critical resource. Since there is only one resource, Project 2 must be pushed to the right, but only enough to resolve the contention for the synchronizer resource. In Figure 28.2, we've highlighted

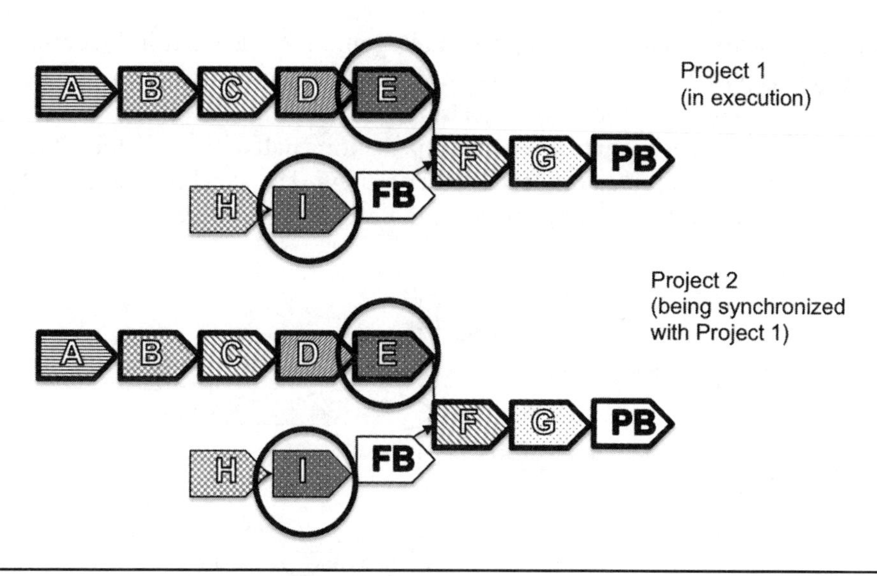

Figure 28.1 Projects 1 and 2 with synchronizer conflict before synchronizing

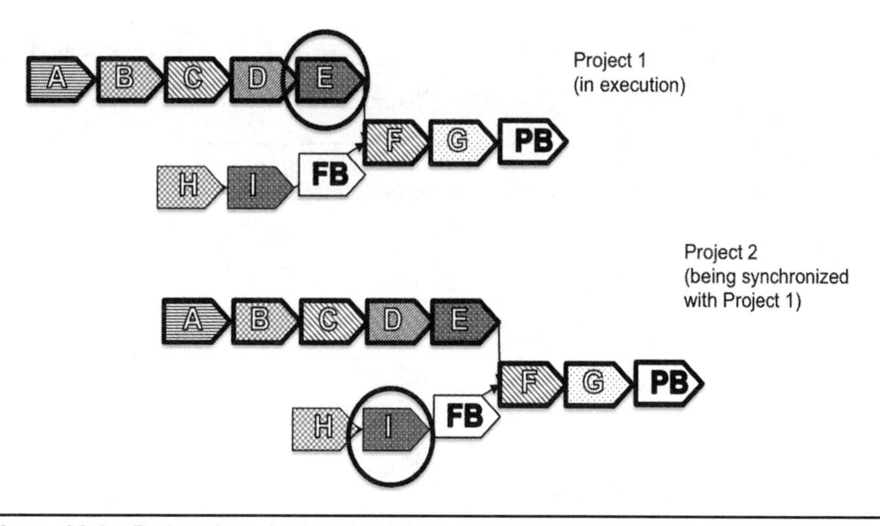

Figure 28.2 Project 2 pushed to the right to resolve synchronizer conflict

the last use of the synchronizer on Project 1 (task E) and the first use of the synchronizer resource on Project 2 (task I).

Figures 28.3 and 28.4 show a before and after example of synchronizing on a type of work/phase of the project (integration). In this example, the organization has the capacity to have two projects in integration. Notice that in Figure 28.4, Project C is pushed to the right only until integration is complete on Project A, not until it is complete for both projects.

2. Add a synchronization buffer representing half of the variability factor, exactly as calculated for all other buffers. The synchronization buffer is placed between projects—at the organizational level. In effect, it is

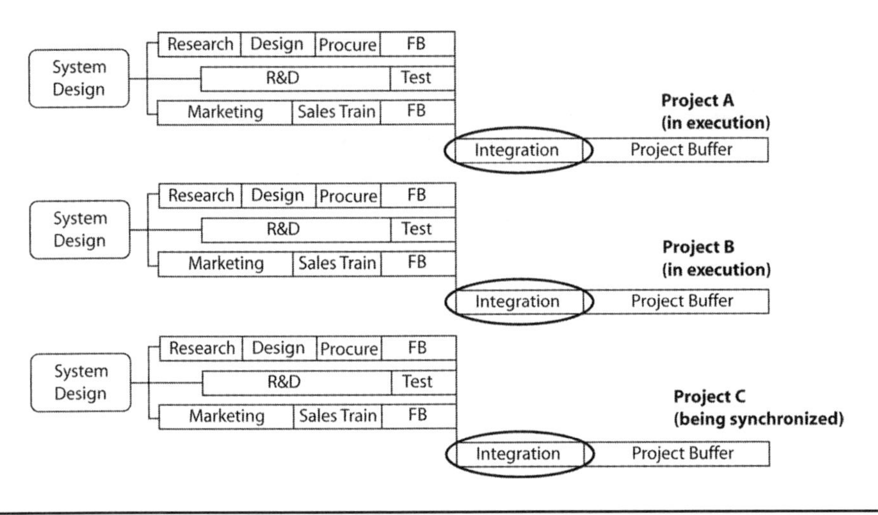

Figure 28.3 Projects A, B, and C with synchronizer (integration phase) conflict for Project C (using rule of maximum of two projects in integration)

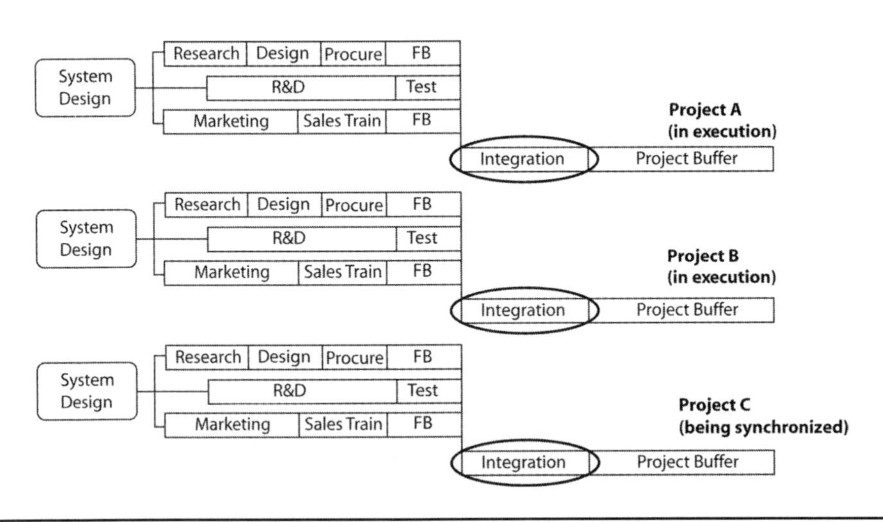

Figure 28.4 Project C pushed to the right to resolve synchronizer conflict

placed immediately after the last use on the earlier project and the first use of the synchronizer on the next project.

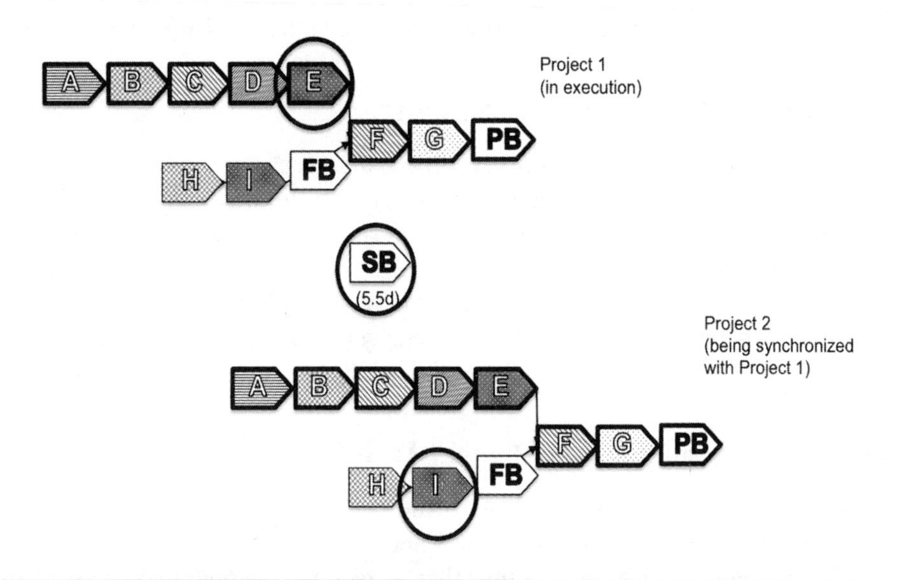

Figure 28.5 Adding the synchronization buffer between Projects 1 and 2

In Figure 28.5, Project 2 is pushed an additional 5.5 days to the right based on inserting a synchronization buffer of 5.5 days between the last use of the synchronizer resource on Project 1 (task E) and the first task of the synchronizer resource on Project 2 (task I). A similar process is used when synchronizing on a phase of work—the synchronization buffer is placed between the end of integration on Project A and the beginning of integration on Project C.

3. Check to ensure proper synchronization. This is a two-part step:
    - Ensure there are no conflicts across the projects planned and released for the use of the synchronizer (whether resource or type of work).
    - Ensure conflicts for other resources have been reduced to the point where the individual project's buffers can absorb the conflicts. This is an important check—do not skip it! Many times, when the most heavily loaded resource has been selected as synchronizer, we find that it does not sufficiently reduce the contention for other resources—that means either finding a different synchronizing resource or changing the synchronizer to a type or phase of work.

4. Repeat Steps 1–3 for the next highest priority project. Continue for all projects available to be synchronized. Note that this covers both new projects as well as those that were *frozen* earlier.
5. Release projects for execution according to the synchronized schedule.

Does the Synchronizer Ever Change?

As noted above, the synchronizer stays the same each time synchronization is done. However, over time, a changing business environment may cause the organization to find it is focusing on different critical resources or types of work. For example, an aviation electronics organization may find its focus changing from radar projects to anticollision projects over time. Periodically (every 12 to 18 months), it can be useful to analyze the staggering mechanisms and organizational capacity as well as review the types of projects to determine these trends.

Additional Thoughts on Project Due Dates

Many organizations find themselves in the situation where every project has a due date request of ASAP. Consider whether the customer really needs the project *as soon as possible* or whether they've given you *ASAP* because of your history as a supplier who has unreliably met due dates in the past. As your organization becomes consistently reliable at delivering on or before the due date, at or below budget, and with full scope, customer perceptions will change. We've seen cases where the customer requested ASAP, the supplier delivered it ASAP according to the methods in this book, and the customer ended up unhappy because the project was delivered too early and there was no place to store it! As organizations see results, recognize that policies and procedures that worked *before* (when you were not so reliable) likely will need to be changed to reflect your new operating reality. Communication with all project customers (internal and external) about what is changing, about how you plan, schedule, and manage projects, is definitely recommended!

Conclusions

Synchronization of all projects is a way to ensure that projects flow quickly to completion and do not constantly interfere with each other. The process involves spreading project work in a way that aligns with the organization's capacity to do the work. This chapter shows two different methods of synchronizing projects. One method uses a strategic or critical resource, usually the most heavily loaded skill set. Another method staggers project by phase or type of work and usually has a maximum number of projects active within that phase. Both methods have been used successfully to deliver more projects more quickly.

Questions

28-1. What are the two ways to align multiple projects?

28-2. There is a need to align the release of projects to what?

28-3. True or false? Synchronization means resolving all conflicts for all resources across all projects.

28-4. Is synchronization performed across all alignment portfolios?

28-5. Where is the synchronization buffer placed? Why?

28-6. What are the checks for effective synchronization?

28-7. Why do we need two checks? What if a project only passes one of the checks?

29. "What If" Analyses on Timelines and Resources

The Premise

Even if you had only a few projects with a couple of hundred tasks each, it would be almost impossible for you to understand the impact of activating a new project or shuffling projects around to determine possible practical finish dates. Project networks have many relationships between tasks, between resources, between paths of a project, between subprojects, and more. This is where software is needed and can be used to try different scenarios and help executives make decisions.

What if analyses can be performed on the synchronization mechanism, on the assumptions around how many projects can be active in a phase at one time, on the impact of adding or losing resources within a pool, and even on changing some of the logic in a project network and seeing the impact on that project and other projects. This chapter provides a brief introduction to this topic.

Manual and Software-Based What If Analyses

There are times that synchronization does not result in due dates that are acceptable to the customer (internal or external). When that happens, there are several courses of action to try:

1. Go back to project planning Step 9 (Chapter 21). Can further task duration reductions be made without adding risk to the project? Consider adding additional resources strategically and/or using higher skilled resources strategically; weigh the impact of the additional costs of these resources against the benefits of providing the project when the customer needs it. With software, these options can be tried in a version of the project network, and the impact can be seen immediately. Remember, though, that using these options can significantly reduce

your opportunities to recover time during project execution, if that is required. Don't forget to document all changes from the original baseline, whenever you make task time estimate or resourcing changes to the project plan.

2. Look at the project's buffers (Chapter 23). Can any in-line contractual milestones be negotiated away?
3. A third option is to perform synchronization *what ifs*. This requires software. What this involves is making changes to the overall project priorities for synchronization to see if there is another alignment strategy that allows all projects to be properly aligned (passing the checks for effective synchronization) and still meet the overall organization goals with the due dates projected by the software.

Other Types of What If Analyses

What if we were able to recruit another five IT specialists within three months? With good, resource-based project management software, this is easily modeled.

What if we were to only activate five projects in the mechanical engineering phase instead of seven? How much faster would each project get done? Could we put all of our resources on the five projects? How much sooner would we be able to start the next project?

What if we won all three major proposals we have made rather than two? How could we schedule these to meet all customer commitments? What additional resources would we need?

These are just examples of the kinds of analyses that are possible when you have achieved a predictable multi-project environment, where 95% or more of all projects are finishing on time, on budget, and within scope.

Conclusions

Many times, proper synchronization does not meet the customers' due date requirements. In those cases, three options that can be used individually or together are available to meet the customers' requirements without adding risk to any of the projects. These options, which are much easier with supporting software, are highly recommended. We do not recommend reducing/removing the synchronization buffer and/or project buffer. There are a few opportunities for reducing the size of feeding buffers without adding project risk, but they must be used carefully and documented fully. Other types of powerful *what if* analyses are discussed in this chapter. The key for all of this analysis is to have a stable, predictable multi-project system and the software to support it. Otherwise, all such analysis is pure fantasy!

Questions

29-1. What project planning step do you return to when synchronization does not support a customer's due date?

29-2. When considering adding additional resources and/or higher skilled resources, you must weigh the impact of this on what three things?

29-3. When making changes to the planned project, don't forget to:

   a. Remove buffers, re-resolve resource contention, re-identify the critical chain/critical path
   b. Make required buffer adjustments
   c. Leave buffer sizes and placements as is
   d. All of the above
   e. Only a and b above

29-4. True or false? Do not modify contractual milestones.

29-5. What types of *what if* analysis would be useful to executives? Explain with examples.

29-6. Why not just remove a feeding buffer and add that time to the project buffer?

29-7. Arbitrarily reducing the size of feeding buffer(s) and/or the project buffer in order to reduce the project duration is not recommended. Why not?

30. Finalizing the Project Schedule and Activation

The Premise

Projects are activated only after all of the previously discussed steps have been performed. It is only by doing so that the stage is set for success. This final step sets the commitments that the organization must live up to.

Setting Start and End Dates and Project Activation

Finally! The project is planned and scheduled to deliver the required scope on or below budget, at or earlier than the projected timeline. Risks have been considered, addressed, and documented. The individual project has been properly insulated from variability. The individual project has been aligned with and insulated from variability from all of the other projects that share critical resources in the organization. It is time to put scheduled dates to the project and activate accordingly.

- *Project due date.* The date determined from synchronization and its associated *what ifs*.
- *Critical chain or critical path start date.* Using the calendar, work backward (earlier in time) considering the project buffer, critical tasks, and any other gaps expected in execution.
- *Non-critical chain or non-critical path start dates (for each path).* Using the calendar, work backward (earlier in time) considering the project buffer, any critical tasks before the integration point, feeding buffer, non-critical tasks, and any gaps along the way.

Note in Figure 30.1 that the only tasks that have a *start date* are path start tasks. Once a pathway starts, as soon as the first task is finished, the next task is ready to start. Every project resource should now be operating in a *relay-runner* work ethic. When a task finishes earlier than planned, the project can capitalize on

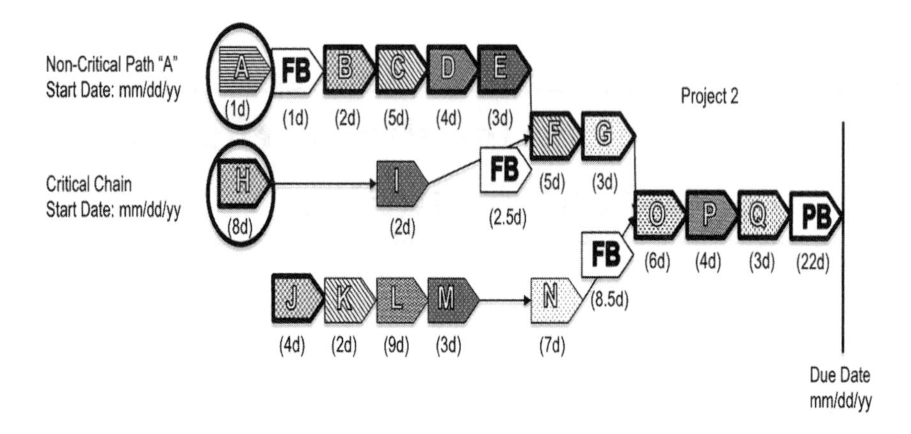

Figure 30.1 Putting dates to the synchronized project's timeline

this by immediately starting the next task in the sequence. In fact, this is why no tasks have scheduled finished dates. Just as relay runners are never told that it's OK to finish the race in the estimated two minutes, project resources must be encouraged to turn over their work as soon as it is ready.

Why does task J not have a path start date? It is the second task on the critical chain! It should start as soon as the resource working on task H finishes that task. Then this same resource is available to start task J.

Project activation is a key event that should be publicized to all stakeholders and affected managers in the organization. It takes place on the earliest path start date for a project. Projects are not started earlier, even if the resource for the first task is available earlier, because that would decrease the amount of synchronization buffer available, which would lead to additional, unnecessary resource conflicts, pressure to multitask those conflicting resources, and increase the chances of problems and variabilities in one project cascading into other projects. There are always possible exceptions to the rule of not starting projects earlier, but those would only be made if the people who run the multi-project environment fully understand all of the cause-and-effect implications of doing so.

Conclusions

If all of the work prior to project activation has been done, this step is really straightforward. Press the button on your computer, and the multi-project software provides the starting date for the project critical and non-critical paths and the project commitment date. All that is required of the organization is to obey these dates.

Questions

30-1. What three things do project stakeholders expect of every project?

30-2. What insulates a project from variability?

30-3. What insulates multiple projects from variability?

30-4. The date determined from alignment and its associated *what ifs* is called what?

30-5. True or false? All tasks have scheduled start and finish dates.

30-6. In Figure 30.1, what is the scheduled start date for task J?

30-7. When does project activation take place?

PART VI

MULTI-PROJECT EXECUTION

Twenty-five percent of the challenge in multi-project systems is planning; 75% of the challenge, and therefore of the potential for benefits, lies in execution. The way to have a huge impact on execution within three months is to concentrate on project flow and remove those horrible big rocks in the river that block flow. A summary of the key points are:

- Stop multitasking resources.
- Review daily, escalate issues daily, and resolve within 24 hours maximum.
- Full-kit one or two critical stages of projects.
- Eliminate delays from burdensome processes, such as stage gate, without losing the benefits.

Part VI is not optional; it is one of the most important elements of the overall solution, and the one that has the biggest paradigm shifts in behaviors. Therefore, this is where we must overcome huge resistance to change.

31. Project Manager Execution Role

The Premise

We've mentioned previously that overall project priorities are used only during synchronization, just prior to activating and executing projects. During execution, the project buffer drives project task priorities. This chapter explains what project managers are expected to do to make this system work and how to use simple, easily understood signals to drive their actions. It explains when they are expected to plan actions, when to take actions, and also when not to take actions. By managing the execution of projects according to these signals, all projects complete on or before their due date with full, expected scope and at or below the product budget.

Managing Buffers

Let's start with understanding how to manage time buffers (and which time buffers to manage)—that is the foundation for good project execution management. We manage only project buffers and contractual milestone buffers (if any) during project execution. (That means feeding buffers and synchronization buffers are not managed; we will get indications if they are not performing as expected.)

Figure 31.1 shows the reference project for this chapter. Before project execution begins, the critical tasks, using ambitious estimates, total 78 days. The project buffer calculations are shown in Table 31.1. The buffer is 45.5 days, giving an overall project lead time of 131.5 days. Another way of stating this is that we need a properly managed buffer size of 45.5 days to provide sufficient protection (insulation) for the expected variability along this specific critical chain or critical path.

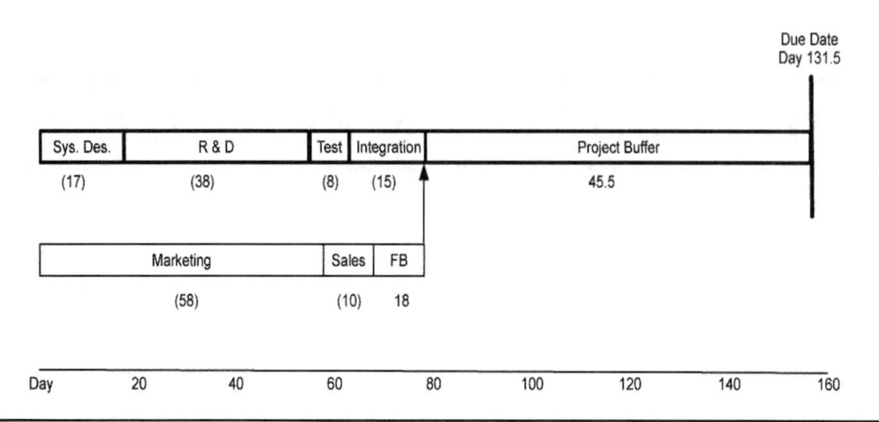

Figure 31.1 Chapter 31 reference project

Table 31.1 Buffer calculations (VF = variability factor)

Critical Chain Task	Ambitious	Standard	VF = S – A	VF/2	Buffer Size
System Design	17	35	18	9	45.5
R&D	38	72	34	17	
Test	8	42	34	17	
Integration	15	20	5	2.5	
Non-critical Chain Task	**Ambitious**	**Standard**	**VF = S – A**	**VF/2**	**Buffer Size**
Marketing	58	92	34	17	18
Sales Train	10	12	2	1	

There are some generally accepted rules for managing project buffers (whenever you see "project buffer" for the remainder of this chapter, assume we mean both project buffer and contractual milestone buffers).

1. *Assume task variability exists.* Some tasks will take less than their ambitious times, and some will take much more. At the same time, if we gain buy-in from team members to turn over tasks early when they meet exit requirements (something that is much easier to accomplish with daily task reviews), this will add to buffers. That means we should expect buffers to grow and shrink as the project progresses. This also means that one task's variability is not necessarily the same as the next task's variability.
2. *We expect buffer penetration.* If the first critical task completes in two days longer than its ambitious time, then two days of the 45.5-day

project buffer have been used; the amount of buffer penetration is the percentage represented by 2 days divided by 45.5 days or 4%.

3. *Buffer penetration can be in two directions.* For example, if the first critical task completes in two days less than its ambitious time, that task has made a two-day *deposit* into the project buffer; buffer status is 47.5 days/45.5 days or 104%.
4. *Time buffers have three regions:* green, yellow, and red. Later in this chapter, we describe how the colors drive behavior. Typically, each region is one third of the buffer length, with the red region or zone placed up against what it is protecting (due date or contractual milestone date). See Figure 31.2. Important note: We have simplified the example in this chapter to provide the concept of driving actions simply according to how much of the buffer has been consumed. In reality, there are often three other elements that drive a color and these are further discussed after the example.
    - *How fast the buffer is being consumed (usually shown by trend over time).*
    - *How much of the buffer is consumed versus how much of the critical work has been completed.*
    - *How much of the buffer is left versus how much variability we expect in remaining tasks.*
        - Green region is up to 33% penetration.
        - Yellow region is up to 67% penetration.
        - Red region is greater than 67% penetration.

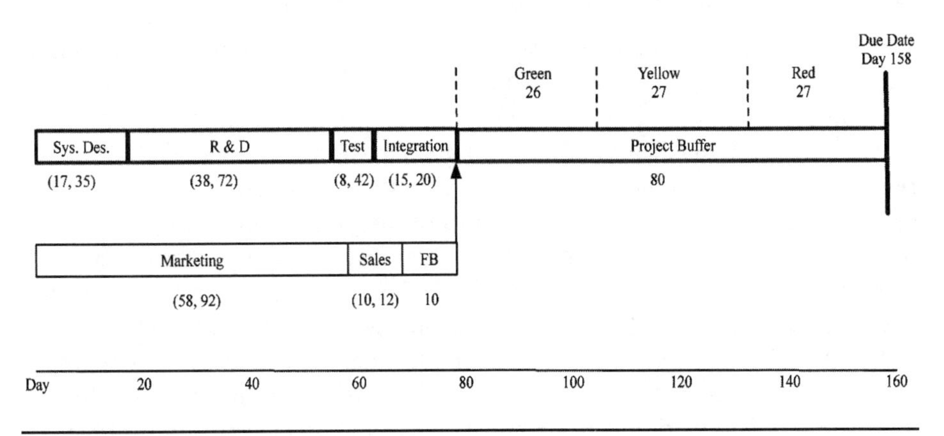

Figure 31.2 Project buffer regions

Notice in Figure 31.2 that the project buffer regions have been designated as 15 days for green, 15 days for yellow (cumulative 30 days), and 15.5 days for red (cumulative 45.5 days). Note that when the project buffer cannot be divided into three equal regions, the larger regions are red first and then yellow.

5. *Project managers are responsible for managing the time buffers appropriately.*
6. *Each region provides data and triggers specific actions* for project managers and resource managers.
   - Project managers:
     - Green: Expected variability; continue to monitor. *Do not intervene* (see Chapter 26).
     - Yellow: Expected variability but heading toward danger; proactively evaluate recovery options with appropriate resource managers, vendors, support groups, and senior managers to recover buffer time if penetration reaches the red region. *Do not intervene* (see Chapter 26).
     - Red: Time for action. Reevaluate buffer recovery plan and update if necessary. Implement recovery plan and monitor to ensure it is working (penetration should move back out of the red).
   - Resource managers: Buffer penetration provides task priority information for resource assignment to tasks and task activation. See Chapter 32 for more information.

Buffer Management During Project Execution

We'll simulate the Chapter 31 project in execution to get a better understanding of what intervention and non-intervention signals are available, as well as what intervention actions are appropriate. Proper task updating is taking place (covered in detail in Chapter 32). Although, using our recommended approach, resource managers would be updating the system information with daily task updates, we only show periodic *snapshots* of the project and its status. The actual problems shown below would have been discovered and addressed much sooner under the daily updating approach. However, to show this, we would have needed a chapter at least 10 times as long, without significant added value.

Day 1: The resources for the marketing tasks are assigned to work that task without multitasking. Before they begin, they are given an understanding of what the task completion criteria are, as well as all pertinent notes, drawings, etc. No task starts until all required critical resources are available to do the required work and all inputs are available; if any required critical resources are not available, the task is not started, and the delay is documented as well as an estimate of when all required critical resources will be available. For our simulation, we'll assume that all required resources were available and that the marketing task started right away on day 1 of the project timeline.

Day 8: All of the critical required resources are available, so the system design task begins right after the resources are provided with all available information about the task.

Day 30: Project status as of the end of day 30 (see Figure 31.3) shows that 22 days of work have been completed on system design and the task completion criteria have just been met; that task is now complete. System design did take 5 days longer than its ambitious time of 17 days. Since system design is a critical task, 5 days of project buffer have been used, leaving 10 days remaining in the green region of the buffer and a total of 40.5 days overall remaining in the buffer. Project buffer penetration is 5/45.5 or 11%. The 17 days planned for the critical chain have been completed, so the critical chain is 17/78 or 22% complete. Since project buffer penetration is in the green region, the proper action for the project manager is to continue to monitor buffer status as tasks are updated. No special meetings or interventions are required.

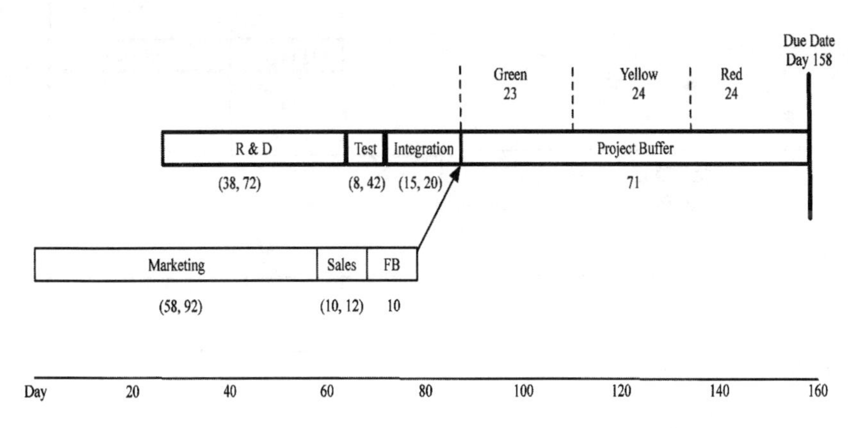

Figure 31.3 Day 30, end of system design

The marketing task has completed 30 days of work and is estimating 30 days remaining to achieve task completion criteria. This estimate means the marketing task is projected to take 60 days or 2 days longer than its ambitious time; the projected impact to the feeding buffer is 2 days out of the 18-day buffer or 11%. Also note that because the system design task took a little longer to complete, we do not need the marketing task until five days later than planned. This provides additional insulation to the critical chain from the feeding chain.

Although day 30 marks the end of system design, it also marks the beginning of the R&D task (remember, once a path starts, the next tasks begin as soon as the exit criteria for the earlier task[s] are complete and the required critical resources are available). The required resources are available, so R&D begins and the marketing task continues.

Day 49: Our next execution snapshot is partway through the R&D task (see Figure 31.4). As of the end of day 49, the R&D task has been in process for 19 days and is estimating 34 workdays remaining to reach the task completion criteria. Adding together the days completed and days remaining for R&D means the task is estimated to have an overall duration of 53 days, which is 15 days longer than the ambitious estimate. This means the R&D task is currently predicted to use 15 days of the project buffer. Cumulative project buffer penetration is now predicted to be 20 days (15 days from R&D along with 5 days from system design). The project buffer is yellow, 20/45.5 or 44% penetrated.

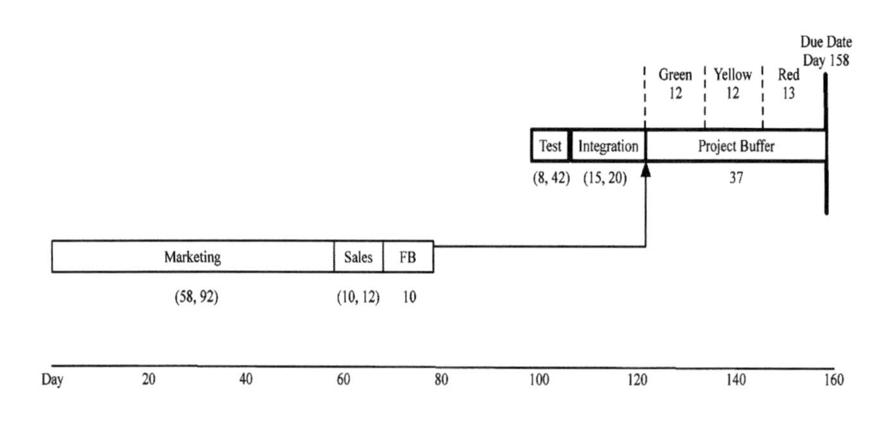

Figure 31.4 Day 49, during R&D

The project buffer has provided the yellow signal:

> "Yellow: Expected variability but heading toward the danger zone; proactively evaluate options with appropriate resource managers to recover buffer time if penetration reaches the red region. Do not intervene" (see Chapter 26).

To proactively evaluate the buffer recovery options:

1. *Determine how many days need to be recovered.* Note that you will not implement any recovery action unless and until buffer penetration reaches the red region, meaning you won't implement your plan until there are 15.5 or fewer days remaining in the project buffer. How many days should you try to recover? Although it would be nice to have a full buffer (back to the 45.5 days), getting to at least half the green (back to 38 days) should be the minimum. You'll need to plan to recover around 25 days.
2. *Determine the correct tasks to focus your recovery planning efforts.* The remaining portion of R&D, test, and integration—the remaining critical tasks—are the only candidates to evaluate. (If you were to evaluate the options with the marketing and sales path, there would be no impact on the project buffer. We want to ensure we don't waste time or money evaluating the wrong tasks!)
3. *Meet with the resource managers from R&D, test, and integration to determine the options for buffer recovery.* Some examples to consider include overtime, the impact of adding additional resources including subcontracting, and the impact of using a higher skilled resource. (Note that these are the same kinds of things considered when reducing the duration during the planning phase!) Consider not only the cost and impact of the recovery options to this project, but also the impact of these resources not being available for the other executing projects.
4. *Finalize the plan and get the required senior management approvals to implement the plan only when and if the red region is penetrated.*
5. *Do nothing further!* This is one of the hardest things for a project manager to do.

Let's discuss the feeding chain before leaving Day 49. The marketing task has been in process for 49 days and estimates 15 more days remain to achieve its task completion criteria, for a total of 64 days, 6 days longer than its ambitious time. This means 6 of the 18 days of the feeding buffer or 33% is being used. Given the delay in completing the R&D critical task, this delay on the marketing task is of no concern whatsoever.

Day 83: The R&D task is complete. The actual (cumulative) project buffer impact of 20 days has been realized. Project buffer penetration remains at 44% (20/45.5). Critical chain completion is (17 + 38)/78 or 71% (see Figure 31.5). The recovery plan does not need to be implemented since the project buffer is still yellow.

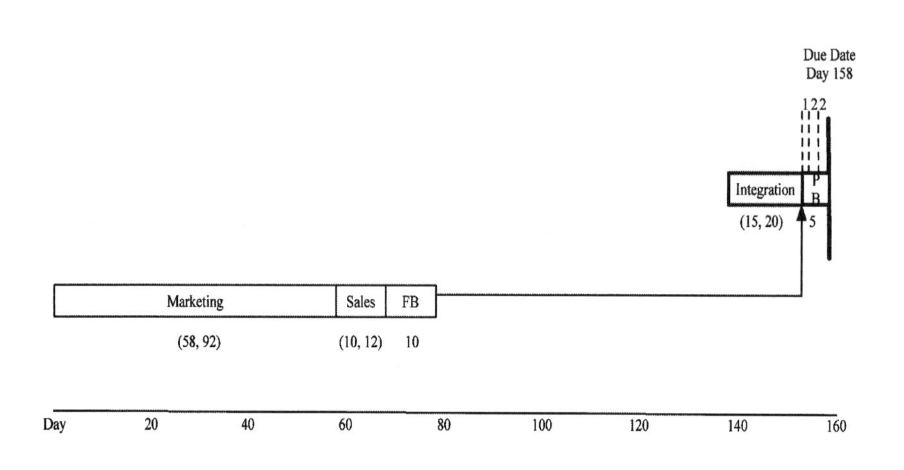

Figure 31.5 Day 83, end of R&D

On the non-critical pathway, the marketing task completed on day 64. Sales-required critical resources were available to start work immediately and that task has also completed, with a total duration of 19 days. In terms of feeding buffer penetration, the marketing task used 6 days and sales used 9, leaving 3 of the original 18-day feeding path buffer. That is of no concern to the overall project. This is one of the reasons we do not manage feeding buffers the way we do project and contractual milestone buffers.

Action on a feeding chain is only required when the feeding chain variability is so large that it is causing the most penetration into the project buffer. In this case, the project manager would implement a recovery plan so that focus can be restored, once again, to the critical tasks.

Day 93: As of the end of day 93, the test task has worked 10 days and is projecting another 13 workdays. The ambitious task estimate for test was 10 days, so it is already causing additional project buffer penetration. Test's total duration is estimated to be 23 days, using another 13 days of buffer. Considering that each of the three tasks is taking longer than its ambitious times, the cumulative buffer usage is now projected at 33 (5 + 15 + 13) (see Figure 31.6).

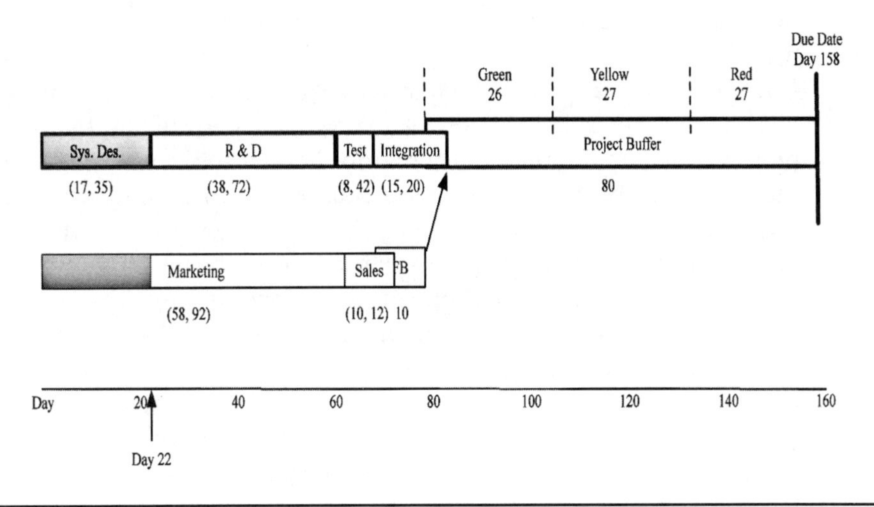

Figure 31.6 Day 93, during test

Project buffer penetration is 33/45.5 or 73%—red zone. Now is the time to act! The project manager should:

- Immediately review and update the buffer recovery plan, consulting with appropriate resource managers as required.
- Implement the buffer recovery plan with the assistance of the appropriate resource managers.
- Monitor the buffer recovery plan to ensure it achieves the desired results.
- Monitor the impact of the remaining tasks on the project buffer since they may incur variability that causes the project buffer to go red again.

Other Ways to Determine Red-Yellow-Green Buffer Status

In the 20-plus years of execution buffer management, additional methods to determine the red, yellow, and green regions of the buffer have been developed:

1. *Percent of critical chain complete to percent project buffer consumed.* As a project executes, we expect to consume the buffer. Our promise date to our customer is at the end of the project buffer. Ideally, we consume the buffer about as fast as we complete critical tasks. So if we completed 25% of the project and we have consumed 25% of the buffer, we would call this a green zone. If we completed 75% of the project and used 75% of the buffer, we are still in a green zone—as expected, no interference or

recovery is necessary. The actual determination of what is green, yellow, or red is according to the relationship between these two percentages over time.

2. *Using trend instead of single points of data.* Variability occurs. A snapshot of data viewed in isolation does not give a good picture of how the entire project (or group of projects) is progressing. Viewing trend data, rather than just single points, can be a good indicator for when to intervene. In this case, we could use the percentage figures as shown above, but view multiple rather than single points. For example, if we have completed 25% of the critical work, but in the process have consumed 50% of the buffer, this may or may not be alarming. Using trend data, we can tell if we are consuming buffer faster over time and this would put us in a red zone. On the other hand, if we are actually completing critical tasks faster than we are consuming buffer over the past few weeks, then we are in a green zone—whatever problems in the past caused us to consume buffer have been corrected.
3. *Changing project buffer.* As each critical task completes, the project buffer size is adjusted based on the amount of variability of the remaining critical tasks. The green/yellow/red region sizes remain at one third each. Currently available software does not calculate the changing project buffer requirements over time, but it is not difficult to determine the needed buffer and region sizes with a spreadsheet.

Conclusions

Every project is different, even though sometimes the tasks may sound similar. The tasks are being performed to a different set of requirements, on potentially different materials, with different vendors, by different people or sometimes by the same people but in a different state of mind, etc. What remains the same is the process for managing the project buffer (and contractual milestone buffer) and for intervention/non-intervention. It is critical that managers at all levels avoid special cause variability (intervening when it's not needed, not intervening when it is needed, and intervening in the wrong area). The rules for managing buffers are as follows:

1. Determine project buffer status according to how much of the buffer was used versus the amount of critical work that was completed.
2. If a non-critical path causes significant penetration to the project buffer, recover immediately, no matter what region the penetration is in.

Recover until the critical chain or critical path is once again determining overall remaining project duration.

3. When the project buffer is in the green region, keep monitoring the task updates. Ensure task updates are current and correct.
4. Yellow region penetration requires action primarily by the project manager to define and evaluate potential options for buffer recovery. Senior management is involved in approving the recovery plans. Recovery plans are not implemented unless and until there is red region penetration.
5. Red region penetration requires activation of the recovery plan developed when the yellow zone was reached. Recognize that variability will continue to occur and additional adjustments to the recovery plan may be needed.

Questions

31-1. Project priorities are only used when?

31-2. What time buffers are managed during project execution?

31-3. Which of the following statements are incorrect?

a. Assume task variability exists.
b. Buffer penetration can only be in one direction.
c. We expect buffer penetration.
d. We do not expect to use all of the project buffer.
e. Time buffers have three regions.
f. Project due date is at the left side of the project buffer.

31-4. True or false? The project buffer stays static (the same size) throughout the project.

31-5. The length of the buffer required is based on what?

31-6. When a non-critical chain of tasks causes the most penetration into the project buffer, what should the project manager do? What if it causes penetration into the green region of the project buffer?

31-7. True or false? The contractual milestone buffer(s), if any, and project buffer are managed the same.

32. Resource Manager Execution Role

The Premise

The old rules of engagement for project work were:

- Keep everyone busy.
- Assign as many tasks to each resource as needed to keep them 100% busy.
- Review tasks when you have time—once a week is plenty.

The new rules of engagement are:

- Assign resources to tasks, not tasks to resources. Put as many resources as practical on a task to ensure the project task is completed as quickly as possible.
- Review tasks daily and update the project data daily.
- Don't worry about keeping everyone busy—that's not why your organization was created.

Accomplishing Project Tasks—The New Rules of Engagement

Resource managers deploy their resources to the correct tasks in the correct order to achieve the task completion criteria to the required quality with good work habits. Resource managers assign their resources to one task at a time and do not move a resource from an in-process task unless, in a rare case, it is part of an approved buffer recovery plan implementation. Resource managers ensure that all resources clearly understand the task completion criteria, their role(s) on each task, and any additional notes provided for a task. Using software, they are responsible for daily updates as follows:

- Marking a task in process
- Gathering and posting task updates according to the designated schedule

- Providing comments on delays, significant findings, and when task completion criteria are achieved
- Marking a task complete

Resource managers also manage their resources' assignments, ensuring that when one task is complete, the resources are assigned to the next highest priority task or to productive non-project work while waiting for another project task to become available.

As discussed in Chapter 31, they are also responsible for working with the project managers to do buffer recovery planning and implement the approved plan when required.

Criteria for Starting a Task

The assumption is that a resource will begin working on a task as soon as assigned. Therefore, a resource manager should not assign resources to a task until it is time to start the task. Certain conditions must be met:

1. The required predecessor task(s) must be complete, if any. If the task is a path start, and not a critical task, it must be started no earlier than the date of the path start. (See Chapter 30, Figure 30.1 for an example of a critical task that is a path start, but not the first task on the critical chain or critical path; in that case, the task [J] cannot start until the predecessor task [H] has been completed.)
2. All necessary conditions to be able to start the task are in place. Materials and equipment needed to start the task are available. Management decisions are made. If a minimum number of resources are mandatory in order to begin work (e.g., the full crew of an aircraft is needed before closing the door of the aircraft and beginning the flight), then the resource manager ensures that is in place. Whenever a task has a delayed start, both the delay and a notation of what the task is waiting for in order to start are captured for future analysis.

What If More Than One Task Is Ready to Start (for the Same Resource Skill)?

There are three possibilities when multiple tasks are ready to start for the same resource skill:

1. The quantity of resources available (not already assigned to another task) exactly matches the requirements. When this is the case, the available resources are assigned to the available tasks, in the correct quantities.

2. The quantity of resources available is greater than the required quantity. Resource managers should first look for the possibility of using those available resources productively to speed up existing tasks. Under the old paradigm, it was OK to assign the required quantity of resources and find other, productive, non-project work for the remaining resources. There are all kinds of excuses for this behavior, such as a task needing those resources may be nearing completion and they will be available for that assignment. Resources must be paid for; assigning the additional resources to a project that did not budget for them wastes project budget. Instead, the resource manager must develop a new mindset by constantly asking himself/herself, "Is there a way that we can productively use these available resources to get project tasks done faster?" It does not necessarily mean using those resources to do the task work. The resources may be used to handle other work requests that might have interrupted the resources doing the project work. For example, in one mechanical engineering department, a small pool of resources was used to handle production inquiries on drawings from prior projects, thus insulating the other engineers from interruptions. The resources also might be used to prepare future tasks for execution.

   If the resource manager does not think this way, simply assigning more resources may increase the task time because it puts both a communication burden and a review burden on the existing resources and additional rework may be incurred.
3. The quantity of resources may be less than the required quantity. This situation requires a priority system so that the available resources are assigned where they are needed most. The priority system is NOT based on the project's overall priority to the organization. The priority system IS based on the status of all the project buffers needing the resource. As an example, there are five projects, each with tasks available to start today, each task needing one resource. The resource manager has only three resources available. The resource manager deploys his/her resources based on project buffer penetration! The three resources should go to one or two or all three tasks on the prioritized task availability list, per the discussion above. Notice how the list has been sequenced: first by resource skill, then by the available to start day (today to the future), and finally by project buffer status (descending, meaning most penetrated to least penetrated).

What would happen in the instance of the first task in Table 32.1 if we had planned to do the task with one resource and in fact could put all three available

Table 32.1 Prioritized task availability list (AT = ambitious time)

Project	Task	Resource Skill	Quantity Required	Avail. to Start	AT	Project Buffer Penetration
J57-16	Test 1734	Elec. Eng.	1	Today	9d	59%
K45-87	Circuit 35	Elec. Eng.	1	Today	6d	53%
P34-12	Circuit 23	Elec. Eng.	1	Today	7d	39%
X23-78	Test 1221	Elec. Eng.	1	Today	4d	27%
A92-03	Circuit 35	Elec. Eng.	1	Today	6d	21%
G65-76	Circuit 57	Elec. Eng.	1	Today + 4	5d	55%
P34-12	Test 1734	Elec. Eng.	1	Today + 4	9d	39%
A92-03	Test 1734	Elec. Eng.	1	Today + 7	9d	21%

resources on it? If the nine-day ambitious time could be completed in three days, we've added six days to the project buffer and passed that task on much more quickly to the next resource. Because we only had one task active rather than three tasks, the resource manager was better able to coach and help bring the work back on track. Any support needed or any management decisions needed have a much higher chance of being done more quickly when there is only one task active rather than three tasks active.

What about the two tasks that are ready to start today, but without resources? The resource manager should note the reason for the delayed start (no resources available) and put in an estimated day for the tasks to start (based on the information from the latest task updates indicating when the next two resources predict completing their current tasks).

The projects in the example above did not contain any contractual milestone buffers. Contractual milestone buffers protect dates that are important to the project, could not be negotiated away, and occur before the end of the project. In some cases, if the contractual milestone date is missed, the project itself may be canceled. Therefore, it is important for all managers of a project to understand the priorities between contractual milestone buffers and project buffers. In virtually every case we've seen, contractual milestone buffers are ranked higher than their corresponding project buffer. The ranking of the buffers is as follows:

- Contractual milestone buffer (CMSB) red region
- Project buffer (PB) red region
- Contractual milestone buffer yellow region
- Project buffer yellow region
- Contractual milestone buffer green region
- Project buffer green region

Table 32.2 Prioritized task availability list driven by contractual milestone buffer

Project	Task	Resource Skill	Quantity Required	Avail. to Start	AT	Buffer (PB or CMSB)	Buffer Penetration
B52-14	Test 4247	Elec. Eng.	1	Today	4d	CMSB	53%
M43-85	Test 7563	Elec. Eng.	1	Today	8d	PB	53%

Note the additional column in Table 32.2. In this example, both buffer penetrations are the same amount, but if only one resource is available, it will go to the B52-14, Test 4247 task due to the higher priority of a contractual milestone buffer.

Task Updating

A question that always comes up is "How often should tasks be updated?" Before answering that question, let's make sure both types of task updates—*in-process* and *impact*—are understood; the answer is different for each type.

In-Process Task Updates

At the end of each workday* (see top of next page for an explanation), the resource manager talks with the resources that have been working the task (or to a task manager if there is a more senior, supervisory person assigned to the task). There are at most two questions asked: "How much time (workdays) until you reach the task completion criteria?" and "Are you having any problems with the task?"

That's it. No *percent complete*; no *day* or *date* when the work will be finished. We know when the task was started (because the resource manager marks the task *in process* after assigning the resource[s]), so we know how many workdays have elapsed. Resource managers get the update at the end of the day so that day's progress is accounted for. The remaining duration is the projection of how many more workdays will be needed until the task completion criteria are achieved. Remaining duration may be a different number every day the task is being worked on; it depends on the difficulties or successes that have been achieved that day, as well as the best estimate (consider it the ambitious estimate) of how many days remain from right now based on what the resource and their manager know about the task right now. When this remaining duration is put into the software, it calculates how many projected days of buffer will be used or not used. What we're interested in is the projected buffer status and whether there is a problem for which the resource manager needs to provide help.

Here are some comments about that asterisk after workday on the previous page. What should the in-process task update frequency be? All projects should update at the same time so that buffer status and task priority lists have credibility—it would not make sense to believe any data coming from a system where Project A updated at the end of each day, Project B updated every Friday, and Project C updated every other day! Another key to turning update data into valuable project information is to have those data consistently provided. The longer time lapses between updates, the longer delay there is to find out about a problem and address it. If task reviews are done in the manner suggested above, unless there is a problem they can be done in a minute. We strongly recommend providing task updates at the end of each workday.

Impact Updates

As tasks are completed in the project, knowledge is gained that impacts future tasks. We need to see the impact of this knowledge on the project's buffers. Periodically the project manager and resource managers meet and discuss what has been discovered through tasks already completed that impacts the assumptions and estimates about tasks that have not yet started. Types of findings can include availability of materials, tolerances of test items, preliminary drawings or designs—anything that significantly impacts the task time estimates, resourcing estimates, iteration possibilities, and specific risks to schedule, budget, due date, and scope that need to be addressed. We recommend the impact update be part of a weekly project meeting.

Managing Resource Availability

Planned versus actual resource loading was introduced in Chapter 24. As tasks experience variability, their actual resource histograms change as well. Resource histograms show ambitious load times for tasks not yet started and show actual duration plus remaining duration for in-progress tasks (see Figure 32.1). If a task experiences longer than ambitious time, the load on the resource for that task increases; if the task experiences shorter than ambitious time, the resource loading for that task decreases.

It is important for resource managers to understand what *fully loaded* means for their resources. When using a buffering system, about one third of the time we expect to use to complete the task work is in a buffer and not in the calculated individual task times. Therefore, the term *fully loaded* for resources dedicated 100% to project work means about 66% since the histogram represents

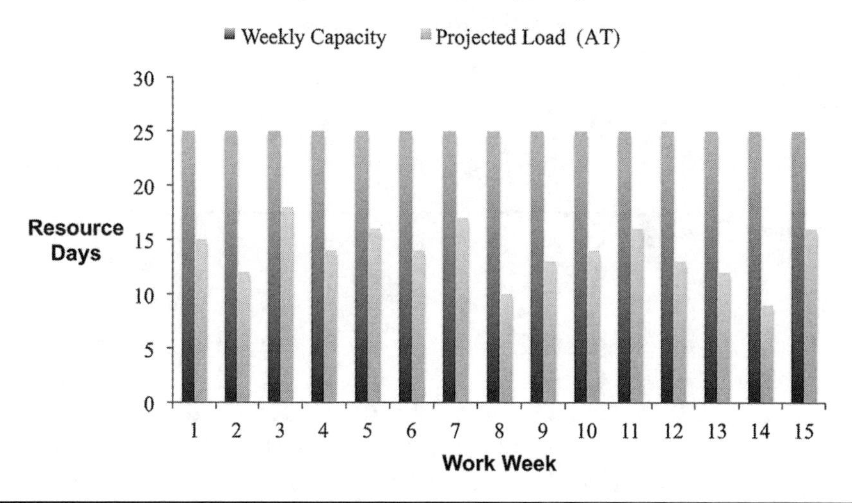

Figure 32.1 Histogram of resource load compared to capacity

ambitious times. For resources that also work non-project tasks, fully loaded for project work may be as low as 40%. We expect peaks and valleys in planned resource loading so that there is room to accommodate variability.

Resource Manager Intervention

When actual resources are fully loaded (i.e., around 67%) for three or more weeks, we call those resources overloaded—there is little or no opportunity to accommodate variability by shifting chunks of work from one week to another. When overloads/projected overloads are indicated for weeks, we are no longer in the world of occasional common cause variation. Without intervention, the risk of many tasks being late is compounded. In this case, the resource manager must notify the project managers immediately and recovery must take place. This is different from buffer recovery for a single project; it is resource recovery for all projects using that resource. The purpose of this recovery action is to prevent problems across all projects due to the looming unavailability of the resources for assignments to many upcoming tasks. In Figure 32.2, the mechanical engineers are shown fully loaded for weeks 11 to 15. There are no valleys to absorb variability. Recovery options can range from overtime to off-loading to other resources, exempting those resources from administrative tasks (e.g., staff

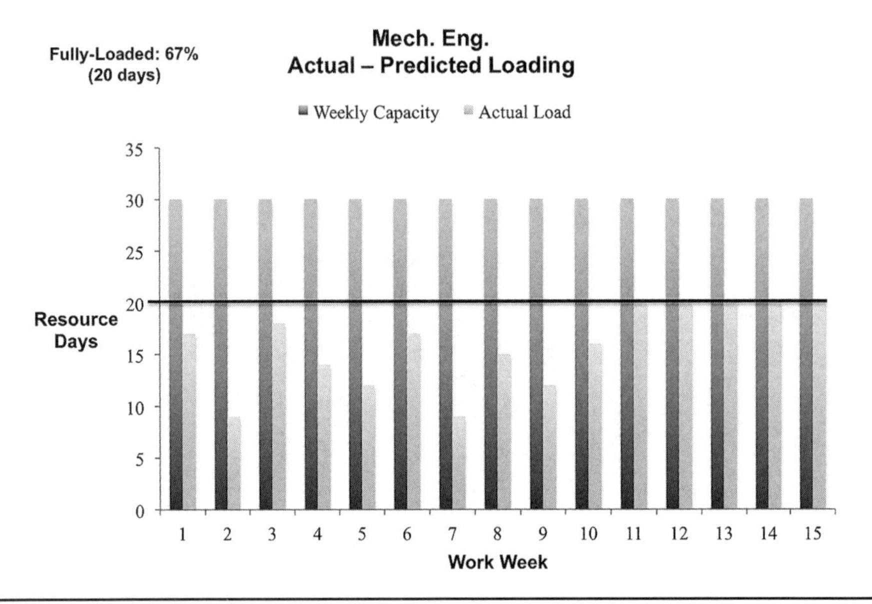

Figure 32.2 Histogram example of an overload, considering ambitious estimates

meetings), subcontracting, etc., which would increase their availability each day to perform project task work.

Conclusions

One of the biggest paradigm shifts in this new model of multi-project execution occurs with resource managers. Instead of worrying about how they will keep everyone busy, their first concern is how to get project tasks completed much more quickly, without compromising quality. Some of the new paradigm includes hard and fast rules; for example, assign only one task to a resource and only when the task is ready and clearly defined. However, some of it includes a challenge to think differently about how to use resources to reduce the duration of tasks. This chapter provided a detailed discussion of these new paradigms and the daily reporting required to drive priorities and actions and make every project's and task's status transparent in real time.

Questions

32-1. Resource managers are responsible for what?

32-2. When should a resource manager assign a resource to a path start task?

32-3. What if all required resources are not currently available to start a *ready to start* task?

32-4. If a task start is delayed, what should the resource manager do?

32-5. True or false? The process for determining task priorities is based on the project's priority to the organization.

32-6. What do contractual milestone buffers protect?

32-7. True or false? A contractual milestone buffer can be found during and at the end of the project.

This book has free material available for download from the Web Added Value™ resource center at *www.jrosspub.com*

33. Senior Management Execution Role—Daily Fast-Track Meetings

The Premise

As projects execute, issues arise that need management resolution or, at least, intervention. Work cannot proceed without the information, decision, and/or guidance that only management can provide. Our goal, once a task starts, is for it to progress as quickly as possible, without compromising quality. Anytime a task stops or slows down, productive time is being lost to the task and project overall.

Currently, tasks can wait for days or weeks for top management attention. Sometimes, it is difficult to have the seniority to even get the required management attention to resolve the issue. Therefore, the daily fast-track issue resolution meeting, run by a member of the senior management team, is the correct, proven process to overcome these blocking delays.

The Daily Process

The daily fast-track issue resolution process is a daily meeting, run by a member of senior management. All project managers attend this meeting to identify and resolve blocking issues. The senior manager in charge of the process is expected to resolve all blocking issues within 24 hours or freeze the project so no additional time or resources are wasted waiting for the issue to be resolved. The consequence of having to freeze a project puts the correct sense of urgency on blocking issues. With the right senior manager running the meeting, often issues are resolved on the spot.

Typically, these meetings are held either at the end of the workday, after update information has been communicated, or first thing in the morning, which gives the project managers overnight to research the issue and prepare recommended solutions.

Issues to Discuss and Not Discuss

Often, when these meetings are first initiated, they are mistaken for review meetings of all projects. This practice must be stopped at the very first meeting. The only purpose of the meeting is to unblock issues that are holding up a project right now. Therefore, general project comments or reviews are out of place and waste precious time of all project managers.

Sometimes, project managers relate issues that need answers, but are really not blocking the project from progressing. They are perfectly able to obtain the answers through the normal course of events (e-mails, meetings, etc.), but because of the convenience of having a senior manager in the room use the opportunity to save themselves time. Again, this is not the purpose of this meeting, and this practice must be stopped right away.

The senior manager is the best judge of what is a blocking issue and what is not. Therefore, the person running the meeting sets the stage for the discussion. The best meetings that we have witnessed take no more than 15 minutes per day, and most issues are resolved on the spot or within an hour of the meeting. As the process unfolds, usually by the second or third week, most project managers no longer have blocking issues and simply pass when they get their turn.

Who Else Should Attend

Senior resource managers find that attending this brief, daily meeting keeps them informed of project and task issues. They also can sometimes help resolve a blocking issue through their vast experience. If the organization has a project management office, a representative of that office should be present.

Other Details about the Process

Someone is designated to take minutes at each meeting, which include the results of the previous day's issues, how the issues were resolved, what if any issues are still outstanding, and what the current action plan is, including any actions on freezing a project. These minutes have proven to be extremely important as documentation for all concerned. For example, in one implementation, the general manager read the minutes of the meetings, which were run by one of his direct reports. For a week, he saw that issues were being carried forward, day after day. He took over the meetings and taught his direct report how to resolve these issues on the spot.

The senior manager may designate someone to resolve the issue, depending on the nature of the challenge. In any case, as soon as there is an answer resolving the issue, it is communicated immediately to the project manager. In other words, there is no waiting until the next day's meeting to communicate the answer. The sense of urgency is maintained and project flow is enhanced by the process.

Conclusions

Almost every organization has some means of resolving project issues. The process outlined in this chapter is different in that:

- A senior executive runs the daily meetings.
- The policy allows a maximum of 24 hours to resolve blocking issues.
- A project is frozen if it remains blocked.

With this sense of urgency, the fast-track issue resolution process drives project flow much faster and prevents unnecessary rework by getting senior management focus to provide correct answers to tough issues sooner than would otherwise happen.

Questions

33-1. Once a task starts, what is the goal?

33-2. What is lost anytime a task stops or slows down?

33-3. What is a daily fast-track issue resolution meeting?

33-4. Who should attend these daily fast-track issue resolution meetings?

33-5. Who is expected to resolve all blocking issues?

33-6. If a blocking issue cannot be resolved in 24 hours, what should happen?

33-7. What is a benefit to holding daily fast-track issue resolution meetings first thing in the morning?

34. Senior Management Execution Role—Full-Kitting Projects

The Premise

In a multi-project environment, projects and tasks are often activated before they are ready to be worked on. We see huge pressure to start project phases before specifications are complete, before *customers* have signed off, and before internal feedback has been given and internal approvals obtained. When such pressure exists, projects repeatedly suffer from the same kind of rework or the same kinds of delays. In such cases, management will find the concept of *full kitting* of projects to be extremely valuable.

There are four main concepts behind a full kit:

1. A senior manager is assigned to be the *full kit manager*. Note that this is not a full-time position. It is one of the essential roles in a multi-project organization.
2. The full kit is a list that specifies what is needed to begin a phase of a project. If all of the necessary items are not present and signed off by the right people, then the project is frozen.
3. There are a maximum of two (preferably one) full kit points in a project family. In other words, do not pile on endless bureaucracy into this project process. Focus the full kit process on the one or two major pain points, based on known problems. The full kit points typically represent the beginning of a major phase of a project, but not necessarily the first phase; for example, when finished with the overall design/architecture of a system and before beginning the detailed design, when starting the construction of a new facility, or when commissioning a site.
4. Full kit meetings are held before the beginning of the phase to validate that all necessary items and sign-offs exist and if not to take urgent action to make them available before the phase begins.

Note that not all projects necessarily need this full kit process. However, since a great deal of damage is done by delaying projects or enduring rework, almost every major project can benefit from such a process. Everyone involved in full kit preparations must have the same mindset—to do everything possible to have all the items in the full kit ready by the time the phase is set to begin. Typically, the full kit manager will escalate a problem to senior management before freezing a project.

For organizations that have implemented this process, they find rework is substantially reduced, for the simple reason that the culture of the organization has changed. Everyone considers the full kit meeting to be the final deadline for having firm specifications. Everyone knows that changes made to design or specifications after the full kit meeting are costly, and therefore no one wants to be embarrassed by such a situation. The sign-offs, necessary to declare that the preparatory work is finalized, are obtained, including those needed from the client.

This chapter goes into detail and provides an example of a full kit process.

Step 1: Appointing a Full Kit Manager

A *full kit* manager is typically a member of the senior management team. Note that this is not a full-time function. Assume that it will require about two hours for each full kit process within a project if everything is normal. He/she has the primary responsibility of ensuring that every project meets its full kit requirements, without delaying or freezing a project. This person has the necessary skills to ensure that internal and external customers understand the relationship between providing final specifications and sign-offs and project commitment dates. They drive the process of creating a full kit template—a master list of requirements and sign-offs for a common type of project. Then, upon project activation, they use the template to create an actual, customized full kit document(s) for each specific project.

Before a full kit meeting, the full kit manager follows up with all responsible participants to anticipate and correct any major blocks to having a full kit complete. Unlike many stage gate processes, where management may use the process to block continuing investment in a project until certain criteria are met, the full kit process is intended to *prevent* blocking or delaying a project.

The full kit manager is often working with people who do not report to him/her directly. Their authority is to be able to freeze a project based on not having the full kit ready. They typically are detail-oriented, knowledgeable about the project processes, and able to analyze reasons behind full kit issues. They also have influence and garner respect for their knowledge and integrity and can get others to take actions, even when they do not hold authority over those other individuals.

The advantage of having such a function in a company goes beyond the positive impact on individual projects. The full kit manager learns what is commonly blocking projects or causing rework, and therefore has important input to the organization's continuous project improvement process. For example, in an engineering firm where the customer decision was often the cause of project rework and/or delays, the firm was able to break the customer decision into several key components. This provided the customer with shorter lead times for some critical decisions. At the same time, the engineering firm gained the contractual commitment from the customer that any delays in these decisions would result in a change in due date of the project. This was a win-win for the customer and the firm.

Step 2: Building the Full Kit Templates/Documents

Figure 34.1 shows an example of a full kit document. It is a simple, fill-in-the-blanks approach, where each resource group's responsibility is clearly shown. Since many projects are similar in nature in a multi-project environment, master full kit templates can be developed for like project families.

When customizing a template or developing a new one, the full kit manager should ask what the minimum requirements are to proceed with the project, without major risk of rework or delay. In other words, this document's purpose is not to simply have a list of everything that would be nice to have on *judgment day*. Aware that anything missing from this list is cause to freeze the project, the full kit manager ensures the team's focus on those few things that are absolutely necessary.

This document is circulated for each project phase where a full kit is required. The full kit manager may circulate the document one to several weeks ahead of when he/she is planning the full kit meeting. This gives everyone a chance to ask questions, prepare, and do whatever it takes to achieve the completion of their part of the full kit.

In the engineer-to-order example in Figure 34.1, you see that many of the requirements are specifications, which are needed for mechanical and other engineers to proceed with sourcing of materials, drawings, etc. Similarly, in an IT project, there would also be a requirement for final specifications on hardware, software, and user requirements before proceeding with detail work.

Full Kit

Completed and signed off Date	FK Manager

Build a Conveying System — Project Name

12345 — Project Number

Time Line

Start Date	Review	Review	Review	Review	Review	Finish Date
11/20/2012						4/12/2013

Full Kit Resource Requirements		Remarks
PM	*System's Arch (SA)*	
Technology (TECH)	*Design Eng. (ENG)*	
Software Eng (SE)		
Mech. Engineering (ME)		
Elec. Engineering (EE)		

#	List of Documents/Information	Resources	Completion Date
1	P&I	TECH, ENG	
2	Basic Equipment List Structure	PM	
3	Main Equipment and Process Equipment data	TECH, SE	
4	Pipe sizing, Compressed Air requirements, PV sizing, valve sizing	ENG	
5	PV criteria sheet i.e. cycles, relevant pressure etc.	TECH	
6	Dust filter/fan sizing	TECH	
7	Design criteria	PM, TECH	
8	Preliminary Functional Description of System Operation (FDS)	ENG	
9	Schedule of drawings	PM, ME	
10	GA with Silo data	TECH, ENG	
11	Electrical main data	EE	
12	List of Instrumentation suppliers/types, deviation requests	EE	

Figure 34.1 Example of a full kit document

The document also shows the resources responsible for each line item and the completion date, which would also be initialed by the head of that resource group or department. When this document is used correctly, the full kit meeting is often completed within an hour and only held once. In cases where the full kit manager suspects that there will be issues, he/she may well hold a preliminary meeting, conduct a review, and then schedule a final meeting if the issues/questions are straightforward.

We have seen some cases where a full kit also includes preliminary specifications for long-lead-time items. This is intended to provide procurement with enough information to source and price the long-lead-time items, even though the final drawings or specifications may be a few weeks away.

Full kits can also include legal sign-offs, for example, immediately prior to a new product launch or a major policy change. Each organization will have its own version of such a document, based on its specific experiences with the rework and delay issues it has encountered in its project work.

Full Kit Points in a Project

Having full kit points in a project is extra work for all involved, since it demands an extra level of scrutiny of specific requirements by a group of people and at least one meeting. Although many people who have experience with projects can become paranoid about having all necessary critical preparatory work done, there is another extreme—hysteria!

We recommend starting with one full kit point in a family of like projects. Get the process initiated and working. Get the senior manager in charge of the process comfortable with doing the work and driving the process. Get the major benefits out of the one place, out of all the project phases, likely to cause rework or delays.

Such an approach brings major focus of the entire team of project and program managers and other resources to the importance of preparing work properly for projects. Remember that there is a learning curve and major cultural change required to stop reacting to pressure to move forward with an ill-prepared project. In the past, each project sponsor, in isolation, saw only the benefits of moving forward with tentative specifications. Yet today, everyone lives with the price tag of 25% or more of resource time wasted by rework.

This does not suggest that it is impossible for projects to have more than one full kit point. If a second such point is required, we are only suggesting that you wait to get the first full kit process working before introducing a second full kit point in a project.

Be careful not to duplicate processes that may already be in place. For example, a marketing department may already have the equivalent of a full kit process for launching new products. At the same time, don't confuse a look-alike process and its intent with full kit. The organization may be using a stage gate process that may have some components of the full kit process (without the sense of urgency to proceed).

On very long projects (e.g., greater than two years) such as pharmaceutical development or nuclear energy plants, there may be more than two full kit points. The reason that we declared a maximum of two such points within a project is for focus. When you overburden people with too much checking, the process can become meaningless. In pharmaceutical development, the 10-year development life cycle of a new drug is often viewed not as one project but as several projects, each with a defined deliverable. Therefore, from our point of view, the caution of a maximum of two such points per project family is valid.

Step 3: The Full Kit Meetings

The full kit meeting is held before all the necessary specifications and final approvals are needed. The intent of the meeting is to ensure continuous project flow. Therefore, the people who need to attend such a meeting are those with the authority and knowledge to provide the final answers needed to proceed without delay and without rework.

Prior to the meeting, everyone should have received the full kit document(s) and a call or e-mail from the full kit manager to confirm understanding of the requirements. Issues should not come up as surprises during the meeting.

A full kit meeting could be intentionally preliminary, to discuss issues that different resource groups have in common, and lays the groundwork for further investigation before the final meeting. In such a case, it is vital that the full kit manager understand the typical lead times that the organization has encountered in the past in dealing with such issues. That is another reason why a senior manager is typically given this responsibility.

It is common for the project manager and, in large project companies (companies that earn their income by doing projects), the salesperson or head of sales to attend this meeting. The full kit meeting is a turning point in the project. It is the final confirmation of readiness to proceed.

The meeting should review each line item in the full kit document, getting final confirmation of the status and noting any issues. Often, a second page is used to capture notes relative to each individual line item.

The full kit process does not expect perfection. The name of the game is to significantly reduce rework and delays. A multi-project organization can live with rare occurrences.

As preparation for this meeting, anyone who has an issue should document it before the meeting, giving all participants the chance to think about it, ask questions that may require research in advance of the meeting, and contribute their thoughts and experience to possibly dealing with the issue.

We have seen some organizations that ask all project managers to attend full kit meetings during the first few months. It is a great way for them to learn the process and to contribute their own ideas to deal with issues as they arise.

With a senior manager in charge of such meetings, they are focused and driven to conclude quickly and with the needed results and decisions. It also drives much better cross-functional communication, with the senior manager reporting back to the executive team on the major roadblocks encountered and how they were overcome.

Conclusions

The full kit process is designed to minimize rework and delays in projects, especially in transitioning from one major phase of a project to another. The process consists of the use of customized full kit templates, indicating the minimum, critical required preparatory work and authorizations needed to proceed with that phase. It includes the appointment of a senior manager to drive the process and full kit meetings (preferably one per full kit point in a project) to ensure continuous project flow.

It is possible for a project to have more than one logical full kit point. However, to ensure that the process is working correctly, we encourage organizations to start with only one point. Get the process and senior management focused first on the most dangerous, critical point in the project where pressure to proceed causes rework or where the biggest delays in preparations are found.

A well-run process saves enormous time by getting all parties to the project on the same page about critical specifications and customer approvals. When executed correctly, it is like the operating theater for major multiple-transplant surgery, involving multiple surgeons and support teams. Such a process, when executed well, can save the project's life.

Questions

34-1. Describe the four major components of the full kit process.

34-2. Explain the difference between a stage gate process and a full kit process.

34-3. Why do the authors insist that a senior manager be appointed as the full kit manager? What do you think would happen if a more junior person were to hold this responsibility?

34-4. The authors indicated that full kits were not needed for every type of project. Describe one type of project that would likely *not* be a good candidate for this process.

34-5. If a full kit template has been designed for major, new, engineered-to-order products, how long do you think it should take to customize it for a specific project—hours, days, or weeks?

34-6. Why do the authors claim that full kits are needed? Explain the current situation without full kits and the underlying causes.

34-7. Why would an organization ever need more than one full kit meeting before entering a major new phase of a project?

35. Senior Management in Stage Gate—How to Avoid the Huge Damage

The Premise

A stage gate process assumes that from the time an idea (typically a new product, service, or major change) develops until it is finally implemented, an organization invests a great deal of money and resources. The second assumption is that as the organization moves from an idea through research, design, initial budgeting, project planning, development, testing, and launch, the quality of information about the likely future costs and benefits improves. Therefore, a management review at each major phase of a project is performed to determine the efficacy of continuing the project, freezing the project until further information is available, or killing the project. In some projects, at certain phases, alternative investments become a better choice than the current project investment, because over the lifetime of the project many things have changed. Market potential has changed. Customer tastes may be different. Competitors may have already launched competing projects.

Therefore, the stage gate process (and there are several different versions with different gates and specific processes) requires a management/steering committee review at each gate, to either allow the project and additional investments to continue to the next gate or be killed or frozen pending further analysis. It is a logical and sometimes effective process, except for a few major negative side effects:

- Stage gate steering committee meetings are often held monthly or infrequently, when a batch of projects at various stages can be reviewed at the same time. What is the cost of delaying a project by up to a month if you've just missed a review meeting date? For some new products, such as an iPad, Kindle, or Intel chip, it can be a *million to several million dollars, per week*. Compare that lost revenue to the cost of continuing the project for a month.

- No matter what stage you are at, and how much research your organization conducts, there is often little more discovered beyond the original research about how well the market will accept a new product or service. After a project is started, much of the important discovery is during trials and beta testing, when customers have their hands on the new product. Therefore, the greatest risk might be the risk of delaying the project. Often, there is a false sense of security with a burdensome analysis process. It is easy to create fantasies on paper.
- We have seen project management offices that try to impose too much rigor on project management. There is a delicate tipping point between focusing on process versus focusing on results. Too much process can discourage good people from bringing ideas forward. "It will never pass the first gate" is a common mantra. Although major investment in any project should be subject to scrutiny, an organization also needs a supportive mentality of experimentation with new ideas without the same level of scrutiny.
- Stage gate processes are often slow, suffering unnecessarily high overhead.
- Stage gate processes often stifle innovation.

Given this brief discussion, the authors take the position that there is some good to be derived from a stage gate process that keeps an organization from wasting money and a lot of good in keeping projects flowing continuously without interruption. This chapter explains how to accomplish both.

Using Stage Gate Wisely

According to Wikipedia,[1] the most common stage gate process descriptions include the following gates:

- Ideation (or sometimes called *discovery*)
- Preliminary analysis/scoping
- Business case
- Development
- Testing
- Launch

There are stage gate companies that sell their methodologies and have other definitions. Some companies have a stage gate process for large projects and a different process for small- or medium-sized projects. The number of gates ranges upward from five.

We are going to use the above definitions, not because they are necessarily the *best* (whatever that means). Rather, we do not want to waste time on silly arguments. The principles remain the same.

Ideation

From our experience, some limited risk taking is essential for the survival of any organization, including non-profits. If a company wants to generate an additional $100 million over the next three years, it better have the $1+ million ideas going through its discovery process. Some of those ideas need to have potential for real breakthroughs for the customers. If an organization's track record of success in ideation is 50%, it will need 200 $1+ million ideas or at least 100 $2+ million ideas or 50 $4+ million ideas. Most organizations have much less than a 50% success rate with new ideas. The organization cannot afford to waste a month waiting for a steering committee review on this number of ideas, or it will never get far enough out of the gate (pardon the pun) to reach its goals.

We have worked with several companies recently that had far too few ideas at the beginning stage—ideation. Some stage gate organizations will tell you that this is not really the first gate; rather, they claim, it is preliminary to the first gate. We disagree and also point out that this is symptomatic of focusing on the wrong issue. The biggest challenge in multi-project management is getting management attention. For an organization that does not have enough of the right projects in the ideation stage, this is likely far more worthy of management attention than other stages.

When you consider an organization's situation over the next six months, what is the biggest single leverage point for improvement? It will typically be in one of three categories:

1. *In the market.* This is true if the organization has the internal capacity to handle more work but lacks the customers. If another customer came to your organization today and wanted to do business with your company, do you have the capacity to accept the order and deliver what they want within acceptable lead times to the customer?
2. *Internally, inside the organization.* This is true if customers are either being turned away due to lack of internal capacity or are going away because the lead time your organization is quoting to them is longer than your competitor's. With such an issue, it is never the case that your organization has limited capacity everywhere. It is almost always within one functional area or department. It might be within engineering, within IT, within one or two departments in a manufacturing operation, in

skilled service personnel, etc. This concept applies equally well to a non-profit organization; for example, a hospital that has more patients coming to its emergency room than it can safely handle, or a government that cannot safely conduct enough agricultural inspections to ensure a safe food supply.

3. *With suppliers.* You have enough internal capacity and you have customers ready to buy. You simply cannot get sufficient raw materials from one or more suppliers. If you are a service organization and you use subcontractors to provide the service, you cannot find enough subcontractors with the necessary skills.

Management must look carefully at the ideation stage and ensure that the majority of ideas are focused on the biggest leverage point. They must ensure that the ideas are of a magnitude ($1 million, $2 million, $5 million, $100 million) to have a chance of meeting their goals. Finally, they must ensure that there are enough ideas at this stage to translate, based on their typical success rate, to benefits coming out the end of the project pipeline.

All Other Stage Gates

If a $1+ million idea has passed the *ideation* test above (is in the category of addressing the biggest leverage point of the organization), it should not be held up by a stage gate steering committee unless a major investment is at stake. There are three key problems that cause the work in this stage to progress far too slowly:

1. Multitasking of the resources doing the analysis/scoping work
2. Management attention—not getting direction or decisions when needed to progress the work
3. Doing more analysis than is necessary

We have addressed the damage of multitasking several times; for example, see Chapters 2 and 8. It is as damaging when conducting analysis for stage gate reviews as it is in doing project tasks.

We have addressed the issue of management attention in Part I of this text, and particularly in Chapter 4. When management delays decisions or even suspends a project pending a stage gate steering committee review, the organization suffers immense damage from delaying the benefits of the projects.

How much analysis is needed for this stage? If the major leverage point is with suppliers (our experience is that it is not with all suppliers) and if you rank supplier issues, usually there are one or two at the top of the list that account for the biggest leverage point for improvement. This already significantly limits the scope and therefore the amount of analysis necessary for this stage gate review. The preliminary analysis should document who those suppliers are that are willing to work with your organization. It must quantify their impact on your organization's results. (How much in sales are you losing because you don't have the materials/subcontractors or because the quality of the materials is bad?) It must lay out the scope (deliverables, success criteria) of the effort (e.g., Six Sigma training and implementation with two major suppliers, requiring two of our improvement teams for six weeks each) and therefore the estimated cost of the work to be performed.

If the major leverage point is in the market, the impact of the proposed idea can be evaluated by asking:

- What are the undesirable effects of the market that this idea will overcome? Or what are the new benefits that the idea will provide?
- How much tangible and other damage does the market experience today that this idea will overcome? Or how much more tangible and intangible benefit will the market attain from implementation of this idea?
- How is the market coping today without this idea implemented? (This provides insight into how much change your organization might need to drive with the new idea in order to have customers adopt it.)
- How easy or difficult will it be to market and sell the idea?

Provide detailed meeting summaries of five actual customer or prospect visits conducted to answer the above questions.

This preliminary information answers the question of whether the market today acknowledges the problem or benefits addressed by the idea. Assuming this is true, further analysis must indicate the size of the potential market (whether it is big enough to attain the goals), your organization's market share before and after this effort (to ensure you don't end up with more than 70% market share, a dangerous situation for future growth and options), and the overall expected costs and benefits of implementing the idea, including cost of any new equipment, resources to build or support new products and services, etc.

By keeping the market analysis to the above items, the organization can often avoid costly, multimonth research studies, which typically do not provide any better answers to the above questions and have many, many rabbit holes that the organization can go down.

Lastly, if the idea is dealing with internal capacity issues, the analysis/scoping must explain why this internal area of the organization is a bottleneck, how it will be improved, what it will cost to improve it, and what the expected benefits will be. The biggest problem with stage gate reviews that we have seen is that people confuse doing the stage gate analysis with doing the actual project work.

For example, if our company is looking at the idea of setting up fabrication or machining to replace some work that our customers are now doing, how long should it take to perform an analysis suitable for a stage gate review? We may want our analyst to visit several current clients to see the nature of the fabrication work, to check out the cost and manning requirements for such an operation, and to explore the obstacles that we might have to overcome to get clients to be willing to give up their own fabrication; that is, we need to understand our customers' issues and how this would benefit them.

We've seen several cases where this exact work was done, and it took two months or more to complete. If the idea was a $12 million idea (worth ultimately $12 million in annual revenue), the two-month analysis cost the company $2 million in delayed revenue, plus potentially giving up a competitive advantage by being second or third to market with the new idea. Within two to three weeks, the analyst already knew that the cost to set up the operation would be over a million dollars, require more than 20 people, and customers would be extremely reluctant to give up their own fabrication. This doesn't necessarily mean that the steering committee would have killed the idea. It just means that within a much shorter time there was enough information already known to justify having a steering committee meeting.

In summary, the problem is not just the amount of analysis that is being done, but that it is done too early. Bad ideas should be killed much more quickly. More good ideas need to be brought to the table and experimented with. The key is to avoid having a stage gate process that prolongs the project cycle. Below are four ideas to achieve this outcome.

Idea 1 for Fast Stage Gate Flow—Virtual Steering Committee Meetings

Why do stage gate steering committees meet infrequently (e.g., once per month)? The answer we typically hear is that the people on the committee (or senior management team) are very busy. For the sake of their efficiency, and recognizing the difficulty of getting such a group together, steering committee meeting dates are set well in advance, so that everyone's schedule can be accommodated. Does it make sense that, for the sake of efficiency of organizing these meetings, an organization lets millions of dollars go?

We suggest that when any project is ready to enter the next stage, a virtual team meeting is called. With web-based facilities, there is simply no good reason to batch stage gate reviews. If most of the parties can meet within 48 hours, hold the meeting. Have the people who cannot attend delegate their authority to someone else.

The target should be that no project is delayed more than 48 hours waiting for a stage gate review. If you see obstacles to doing this, document every obstacle and ask yourself, "What condition would have to be in place to overcome this obstacle?" For example, an obstacle might be that "current policy dictates that the CFO and the senior VP are the only ones who can authorize a project through a stage gate." The real obstacle might be that these two individuals are booked several weeks in advance. Another aspect of the real obstacle might be that steering committee meetings typically require a half day, because of batching of stage gate reviews. In this example, we might need two conditions to overcome the obstacle. One condition is that "stage gate review meetings are not batched and therefore require a maximum of half an hour." It is probably much easier to get half an hour of an executive's time than half a day. The second condition is that "the policy is that the authority of the CFO and senior VP must be represented at steering committee meetings and available on 48 hours maximum notice." Such a policy allows the executives to delegate authority when appropriate, but makes the quick availability of a stage gate review much more likely.

Idea 2 for Fast Stage Gate Flow—Projects Are Not Delayed

This idea is that projects are not delayed, even though they are waiting for a stage gate approval. The project work proceeds, barring any major capital investment. Combined with Idea 1 above, this means that the maximum damage the organization encounters, should the stage gate review result in freezing or killing a project, is the additional investment of a few days of resource time. However, in a well-run stage gate process, most projects are not killed or frozen—they continue. Therefore, the damage is negligible compared to the benefits of speed to market and fast project flow.

The implementation of this idea also puts some degree of pressure on the steering committee to not accept excuses from members about not being able to attend. In this paradigm, steering committee members either subordinate their time to this work or delegate their authority so that the damage is minimized and project flow is not interrupted.

Idea 3 for Fast Stage Gate Flow—Minimize Analysis and Reporting Requirements

Stage gate is a risk mitigation process, not a substitute for sponsor authority or intelligence. When used correctly, it brings alignment throughout the organization, melding financial, marketing, sales, engineering, supply chain, and other operations considerations with the execution of phases of a project. Don't confuse or mix project work with stage gate work.

According to *Business Week*, Larry Keeley, president and cofounder of Doblin, Inc., created a controversy when he delivered the keynote address at The Management Roundtable's Product Portfolio & Pipeline Management Conference in 2006. Keeley said, based on exhaustive research and more than $7 million worth of data behind the assertion, "the Stage-Gate model as we know it today is . . . going to guarantee total performance mediocrity for your businesses."[2]

There are now many advocates for eliminating or drastically reducing the stage gate process requirements. At the very least, look at the existing documentation and analysis requirements and assign a senior manager to cut them in half.

Idea 4 for Fast Stage Gate Flow—Allow Only Two Gates

Consider having only two gates. One gate is heavily loaded at the front end of the project, with sufficient analysis to determine if the project is the best choice to achieve the organization's goals and is sufficiently well scoped to avoid major scope creep during its life. The second gate should be at the back end, post trials and testing, to validate that sufficient and correct effort will be put into launching the product successfully. Many organizations think that the project is complete when a new product is developed but, in fact, the biggest and most important learning time for the organization is post-development, post-beta trials, but pre-launch.

Conclusions

A parent who exercises absolutely no supervision or control over his/her children during the formative years will likely experience major problems. A parent who exercises too much control often ends up with rebellious or apathetic children. It probably sounds *corny*, but stage gate processes are like this. Most of the ones we have experienced are far too cumbersome and slow and therefore doing damage to project flow, speed to market, and realization of benefits. In multi-project environments, the damage is not additive—it is exponential. This is because the amount of batching, given the number of stage gate reviews required, is high. Meetings are long because there are always more than one or two projects ready for review. The longer the meetings, the less frequently they tend to be held, since the people attending have to plan their schedules far in advance to accommodate such long meetings.

The solution, as this chapter suggests, is not just streamlining the process. There are fundamental changes required to avoid the massive damage from stage gate processes, while still retaining the risk mitigation and other benefits. Ideas discussed in this chapter for speeding up the process include virtual steering committee meetings within 48 hours of readiness, allowing projects to continue work while waiting for stage gate review approval, minimizing analysis and reporting requirements, and cutting back to only two gates.

Organizations that must be responsive to customer, market, and competitive changes, especially with the ever-smaller world and international considerations, cannot afford a cumbersome, slow, high-overhead process. Risk mitigation is necessary, but must be accomplished quickly without all of the current negative side effects.

Endnotes

1. See http://en.wikipedia.org/wiki/Stage-gate_model.
2. Copyright Management Roundtable Inc., 2006, from the web-based article: http://www.pd-advantage.com/images/RethinkingtheStage-Gate_Process_AReplytotheCritics.pdf.

Questions

35-1. What are the benefits to having a stage gate process?

35-2. What negative side effects can be caused by a stage gate process?

35-3. What did the authors mean when they insisted that you must not confuse project work with stage gate work?

35-4. Describe four ideas the authors suggested for improving the stage gate process or eliminating the current negative side effects.

35-5. Why should an executive or senior manager make himself/herself available within 48 hours for a stage gate meeting?

35-6. In many stage gate systems, the front-end ideation or discovery phase is not considered part of the stage gate process. Explain why not and why the authors consider it so important to include.

35-7. What are the three main reasons that stage gate processes take so long, and what do the authors suggest be done about it?

36. Senior Management Execution Role—Portfolio Review Process

The Premise

In a multi-project environment, senior management has the dual role of:

- *Leadership:* driving the organization to pursue the right projects without wasting precious resources and
- *Auditing:* ensuring that the part of the overall goals related to projects is being achieved and results are attained quickly enough

Leaders carefully monitor that the right number of projects, with the correct scope, are moving quickly through execution and delivering the necessary results. Great multi-project leaders know what the capacity of their organization is to perform project work and ensure that projects are not bottlenecked due to scarce resources. This responsibility is discussed in depth in Chapter 7. Chapter 36 focuses on the review process for choosing and monitoring projects.

A good project portfolio review process for senior management requires about two hours per month and consists of the following major steps:

- Review of the active project portfolios by exception (projects/programs/portfolios at risk)
- Review of actual results and result trends of completed projects
- Governance: review and decisions on new project requests, requests to freeze or kill projects, requests to activate an approved project, and stage gate review issues
- Review of the process of continuous improvement for projects and results
- If the organization did not get expected results, determine necessary changes going forward

Each of these topics is further discussed below.

Portfolio Review by Exception

If the entire multi-project management system is working correctly, there should rarely be more than 10% of the projects/programs/portfolios that are in a red zone (in danger of missing either due date, budget, or scope, which includes the danger of missing original project objectives). Looking only at the red zone issues, senior management should already have, before a review meeting, the information about what task(s) or issue is currently holding up the project, what action has been or is about to be taken, and whether any further help from the management team is requested.

Senior management has the right to exercise due diligence on the exceptions—to probe the situation to determine if actions are likely to be sufficient to bring the project back under control. If senior management perceives that the market situation has changed, they may want to review the agreed upon scope of a project or portfolio to reassess the project sufficiency to reach the original goals.

Given that all other avenues of escalation were tried before a senior management review, the expectation is that almost all red zone issues have already been dealt with. However, the depth of senior management experience, combined with the cross-functional presence, may bring new light and therefore new solutions to a difficult problem.

Review of Actual Results and Result Trends

A study of over 100 companies by IAG Consulting[1] found the following: Sixty-eight percent of companies are more likely to have a marginal project or outright failure than a success due to the way they approach business analysis. In fact, 50% of this group's projects were *runaways* that had any two of:

- Taking over 180% of target time to deliver
- Consuming in excess of 160% of estimated budget
- Delivering under 70% of the target required functionality

Although the study focused on IT projects, we have found similar results across all projects. The senior management team must have a process to audit results, not just at the end of the project but for 12 months following the completion date, to learn firsthand about bad assumptions that are often made in project planning. No other level in the organization can have such a 50,000-foot view of what is going on with projects in the company, and even more importantly, no other level can fix these types of problems.

In reviewing results, there are four types of results to audit:

1. Did the project finish on time? We are not concerned about a four-month project taking two weeks longer than planned to finish (for most projects). We are concerned about more than 10% of projects being late and any project going more than 10% beyond the expected completion date. Senior management should seek to understand the major underlying cause and to fix it.
2. Did the project finish on budget? We have the same comments as above.
3. Did the project finish within scope, including meeting all of the original objectives, design criteria, and tangible deliverables? If scope was cut, why?
4. Did the project get the tangible, desired results in terms of organization goals—monetary and other? If not, it is worth senior management's time to investigate and try to understand. When senior management sees common problems across some or many projects, they will do the investigation and most often draw the right conclusions.

Between the time a project completes and the time that actual expected results are generated, there is often a significant time lag. During that time lag, there are leading indicators that give senior management a crystal ball into the likely future effects. For example, when a new product or service is launched, is there an increasing trend of early adopters? For a major product or service, are there more and more sales cycles started? Are there more and more presentations to key decision makers? By monitoring the leading indicators, we find that senior management gets a much earlier indication of the likely project results. Also, they often see issues that can be overcome. When recognized earlier rather than later, the return on the project investment is achieved sooner and with a greater magnitude.

Governance

We define governance as decision making with all of the appropriate due diligence that goes with it. In a multi-project world, there are two dangers: activation of too much project work, creating unnecessary delays in project execution, and slow governance, creating again unnecessary reduction in project flow.

For project activation, senior management must first have a good, in-depth understanding of the organization's multi-project capacity. Most projects today spend more time waiting than they do having tasks executing. A lot of the wait time is for decisions or for support group work, neither of which is modeled in project plans. This is discussed in Chapter 7.

Given the approach suggested in Chapter 7, the governance for project activation is straightforward. Senior management must perform due diligence to determine if too many projects are in a red zone. If so, is that likely to change within the next week or two? If not, it probably means that there is too much project work activated, and one or more projects must be frozen and possibly rescheduled to allow the system to return to normal.

In the event too many projects are in the red zone more than once in a year, it is a good indication that the rules that were established for determining the number of projects that could be activated were too optimistic and need to be changed. This is also a governance decision. Otherwise, senior management should follow the established rules for activation. Exceptions should be rare. If senior management grants an exception to the activation rules, it is incumbent upon them to explain the logic behind the exception (why they are making it and why it will not throw the multi-project system out of control) to all key managers (project, resource, and functional managers). This is vital to ensure ongoing support of the system processes and to avoid anarchy and chaos within the system.

Earlier, we explained that the second major governance issue is slow governance—taking too long, agonizing too much over decisions. Good governance allows projects to move quickly and to encompass some degree of experimentation in the real world with minimal risk.

For example, we worked with a company that needed a major enhancement to a product from a supplier. The product prototype had to be in their hands by a certain date or the entire project would slide by weeks (this company had their customers lined up for beta testing and committed to not go to competitors, but that commitment would only last so long). The supplier had cash issues and therefore much different priorities for where they put their limited resources. It was obvious, eight weeks before the prototypes were due, that this supplier was not going to deliver on time. Good governance meant taking action to get a prototype from a non-preferred supplier simultaneously with having the CEO of the company meet with the CEO of the supplier company to determine what else was needed to prioritize their order.

In this model of governance, the role of senior management goes beyond due diligence and decision making. It is also to drive and facilitate faster project flow using their authority and know-how. This is a major multi-project responsibility of senior management to shareholders /owners, customers, and all other stakeholders.

Continuous Improvement Process and Results

When we consider the difference in success between Apple and Research in Motion (Blackberry), we see that Apple continuously improved its speed to market, reliability in delivering new products, and the alignment of projects between market research, development, production, supply chain, and product launch. This is not to say that Apple was perfect—only that in one of the most challenging environments of rapidly evolving products and worldwide supply chain, where Apple started from behind, its continuous improvement was observable. In contrast, Research in Motion, the undisputed leader in at least the cell phone technology at one point, had newsworthy problems of delivering projects on time and within scope. When this was compounded by poorly chosen projects (e.g., trying to compete with iPad), it turned a bad situation worse.

The value of continuous improvement in multi-project management can be witnessed in the stock price of public companies. Research in Motion went from over $130 in 2008 to barely sustaining a stock price around $13 in 2012. Apple went from a stock price of $100 in 2008 to $600 in 2012.

We understand that continuous improvement is not the only factor and that it is not needed just in project management. The problem is that so many organizations today, which believe strongly in project management, are willing to settle for mediocrity in their continuous improvement process and focus. As a result, they see 1–5% improvement after a year of struggling with intensive, complex processes, maturity models, and stage gate systems. We suggest that this is not the right focus for improvement.

Multi-project environments provide a wealth of statistics about project tasks that are waiting for something. The more often they wait for the same thing, the more obvious it is where the improvement is needed. The longer they wait for the same thing, the more obvious it is where the improvement is needed.

Of course, before starting any continuous improvement effort, as Dr. W. Edwards Deming taught millions of people in the last century, you must first have a system under control. In projects, this means consistently delivering projects over 95% on time (according to the original due date commitment), on budget, and within original scope. Once this is attained, start collecting the statistics.

Statistics need to be collected for three different types of events:

1. When we are in a yellow or red zone, what are we waiting for?
2. When a task is not started on a planned start date, what are we waiting for?
3. When a task is stuck for more than two days with no work on the task, what are we waiting for?

If all of the potential things that a project could be waiting for are pre-documented in a list, then all the project or task manager needs to do when the event occurs is select an item from a list and note how long of a delay is being driven. In a multi-project system, this kind of information can be easily lost, if the collection of the data is not driven by project software or by a diligent project management office. Once every two to four weeks, a continuous process improvement team must analyze these data. Pareto analysis is usually the most effective tool, assuming that there is no cause-and-effect relationship between the different things we are waiting for (i.e., that the causes of waiting are independent of each other). Otherwise, a root cause analysis approach is best.

The job of senior management is to ensure that the continuous project process improvement effort is focused on the right things and targeted to yield at least 20% improvement each year in project flow. This means that senior management must think about what this means for the organization. For example, in pharmaceutical development, there should be a result in terms of the number of new products brought to market. Since projects run over many years before a new drug is approved, the initial measurement on continuous improvement would be the duration of those phases that are within the organization's control (i.e., not tied to government approval cycles). In an engineering company, the number of different types (small or large) of projects completed per year was one metric, whereas the throughput dollars per week generated from billable engineering was another measure.

When the metrics are correct, understood by everyone, and helpful in driving behavior, then senior management can ask the right questions:

- What impact will this proposed change to our multi-project system have on revenue (or goal units in a non-profit)?
- What will the impact be on return on investment?
- Why will this change make projects flow faster?
- Why will this change reduce rework?
- If an investment is recommended, for example, in additional resources, model the investment as if it had been made a year ago, and model the change in results. Return on investment for almost any investment in project management improvement should be returned in less than a year.

When Projects Do Not Deliver Results

A healthy organization depends upon understanding the cause-and-effect relationships that govern its business, its industry, and its markets. When a project does not deliver the expected result, it is vital to understand what the wrong assumption(s) was that led to the unexpected result. This is important, even if the results were *better* than expected. Remember that when a company launches a new product and ends up with far more orders than expected, it has a backlog, which extends lead times to supply the product and can make customers upset.

With a cross-functional team, senior management must look at results in the year following every major project completion and examine assumptions when results are significantly alarming. When this is done from the point of view of scientific curiosity, rather than finger-pointing, both senior management and other key players throughout the organization learn a great deal. Dive into the history of any great organization, and you will find it fraught with mistakes and catastrophes. This is normal. This is good, but only when the organization, and not just individuals, learns from it.

It may be necessary to launch a project to really learn why results are different than expected. For example, we worked for two years with a custom kitchen cabinet company to improve reliability in the lead times to deliver the product. At the same time, the logistics allowed the company to deliver in a quarter to half of the standard lead time, which they offered for a premium. Standard lead time was six weeks. They offered to deliver in four weeks for a 25% premium and two weeks for a 50% premium.

This kind of offer had received high acceptance rates from customers in other industries. However, with this company, although it did get orders for two- and four-week delivery, the number of orders was much smaller than expected. The assumption behind the premium percentages came from other industries, where a $400 product, for example, was going into a $100,000 machine or a million dollar airplane. In the case of a custom kitchen, the $15,000 (wholesale price) kitchen was going into a $100,000 renovation. The relationship between the premium pricing and the presumed benefits of faster delivery is different.

In this case, the learning process would require visits to actual dealers, with a predesigned questionnaire or approach to discover perceptions of kitchen designers and their customers. It would require more experimentation with different premium levels. For sure, there were many more opportunities to gain premiums on orders, but not at the percentage premiums that the company had planned. By maintaining a process of monitoring project results after completion, management will provide key input into improving the multi-project execution.

Conclusions

Within two hours per month, the challenge to any project portfolio review process is to have at least a 15% impact on bottom-line results within each year. The team conducting the review must divide their time between auditing, decision making, and increasing project flow. Therefore, with a small amount of time devoted to each part of the process, there is no time to review all of the projects in each portfolio. Rather, the focus is on exceptions (projects or portfolios in a red zone) and on the 50,000-foot view of project data from across the horizon of all projects, programs, and portfolios.

The governing team conducting the review must have a deep understanding of the capacity of the organization to do project work. When too much work is in the system, they must make the tough decisions quickly to either freeze some existing projects or invest in more resources.

The process also demands a look at completed projects with a bright shiny mirror and the willingness to face it when results go astray. An effective process allows for investigation, discussion, and learning from bad assumptions of the past, without finger-pointing. A good process looks not just at project tasks, but at those things that project tasks wait for that were not modeled in projects (management and support group attention). At the end of the day, any team can analyze project data and speculate on possible improvements. Few teams can actually focus their organization on actions that yield a 15% or more measurable improvement in organization results. This chapter provides the approach and suggests where to look to have such an effect.

Endnote

1. IAG Consulting, *Business Analysis Benchmark*, 30-page report, research conducted in association with Info-Tech Research Group (2008), Keith Ellis, download available at http://www.iag.biz/resources/library/business-analysis-benchmark.html.

Questions

36-1. What is wrong with reviewing all of the projects in a multi-project portfolio? Why do the authors insist on reviewing only exceptions?

36-2. The chapter cites a study highlighting a high failure rate of projects to achieve their goals. What actions do the authors suggest an organization take to overcome this situation?

36-3. If an organization already has achieved an excellent success rate with projects and is at or near the top of its industry, should it forgo the review process covered in this chapter?

36-4. Describe the five minimal components of a project portfolio review process.

36-5. Should this project review process be incorporated into a general senior management review of the organization? Explain your answer.

36-6. What should the team conducting the review process do when a project does not deliver expected results in a marketing/new product project? In an internal improvement project? For how long a period of time should the team monitor the project results after project completion?

36-7. Why do you think that many project improvement processes yield minimal (<5% impact) results? Explain why the continuous improvement process suggested in this chapter is different.

PART VII

ENTERPRISE PROJECT RESOURCE PLANNING

Until now, the six engines of multi-project management were discussed separately. Yet resources had a major interaction in every previous part. Part VII brings together all previous discussions and provides some new highlights on the biggest leverage points in dealing with multi-project resource challenges. A summary of the key points is:

- Understanding resource loads and knowing when to elevate capacity
- Dealing with supervisor and management workloads correctly
- Understanding how more and more project implementations affect the operations of the organization and avoiding major mistakes
- Short-, medium-, and long-term resource challenges

Part VII is about the strategy for dealing with the multi-project resource challenge, the non-intuitive problems that can cause projects to come to a grinding halt, and the approaches to deal with these issues pragmatically.

37. Distinguishing between Temporary Bottlenecks and Need to Hire/Contract

The Premise

Much of the information you will find in this chapter has been discussed previously. However, it was presented under a variety of headings and chapters, as related to the specific challenges focused on by those chapters. This chapter gathers it under one roof, for a laser beam focus on resources.

When you implement this book's approach to multi-project management, it changes the way that project resources are managed. This is because:

- By reducing the amount of active project work, many resources that were bottlenecks before are no longer blocking project progress (see Part V).
- By preparing tasks properly for execution (full kit, entry and exit criteria), rework on tasks is reduced (see Part VI).
- By doing daily task management and fast-track issue resolution, resources are better utilized and receive appropriate and faster help with tasks when needed (see Part VI).
- By ensuring that resource managers are *not* doing project tasks, and instead are more available to coach resources and transfer skill sets, the organization's flexibility with resource skill sets is increased (see Chapter 32).
- By focusing on the resource dependencies that really block project progress, project planning only needs to be practical and realistic, NOT DETAILED. This means that you don't need to model every resource and every task to its lowest level of detail. In fact, this becomes counterproductive (see Part III).

Given the above changes that this new approach brings to projects, an organization really has no idea which resource skills are blocking its ability to get projects done until this new way of managing projects is implemented and stable for a few weeks. Then, by following a few simple rules, the organization gains short- and long-term control over enterprise project resources. These simple rules are:

1. Plan all projects using the same standardized skill sets, but do not attempt to model every skill set in an organization.
2. Plan authorized projects and put them into a pipeline, so that resource managers can look several months ahead to see expected workload. This is much easier to do when you make use of project templates to at least have a rough idea of the resource demand. Use resource histograms, which show trends over time, to detect both temporary and permanent overload time frames.
3. Determine a resource pool's real capacity by ensuring that the time required for operational and other responsibilities is realistically taken into account.
4. Use aggressive task times in project plans, but then consider 67% utilization of a resource skill set as fully loaded. This accounts for project buffers that are the safety nets for project task variability.
5. Use a capacity elevation team to proactively plan how to deal with resource overloads with enough lead time to prevent a resource crisis.

Many organizations wonder if it is better to have project management resources centralized in a project management office (PMO) type of organization versus decentralized in a matrix organization. Although how to organize an effective PMO was dealt with in another book by one of the authors,[1] the assumption here is that the considerations discussed below apply to either type of project management structure.

Modeling Resources in Projects

Appendix C has examples of resource skill sets from many different types of organizations. However, before attempting to define all of the skill sets in your organization that might be used within projects, take note that the most successful project organizations we know model only some resource skill sets. In fact, one of the most successful engineering organizations modeled only five. Think this way: have 30 in mind as an absolute maximum number of resource pool definitions and you are more likely to be successful with this new paradigm. Which of the resources have the greatest impact on your organization's ability to flow projects quickly?

For example, consider an organization launching a new product set in the market. In this case, the product requires customers to sign a standard set of contract documents. In the old way of doing things, you might have defined in the project plan the separate tasks and resources as:

- Marketing analyst: develop draft contract documents
- Legal: review drafts and comment
- Marketing analyst: revise drafts
- Sales management: review second draft for customer acceptability and salability
- Finance: review contract for financial risk/implications
- Marketing management: propose final draft
- Legal: review and prepare final contracts

Under the original approach, each of these tasks would have had times and dependencies. Imagine if you did this with all of the project work; a project plan could easily grow to hundreds or thousands of tasks, with a lot of complication in trying to manage it.

Instead, in the new approach, all of the above would be defined as one task under one resource skill set:

- Finalize contract documents—Marketing analyst

The involvement of all other resources would be noted as a list of work to be done to complete that one task in the project plan. However, the task would be managed as one task in the project plan, with one task duration. Remember, if the marketing analyst or project manager runs into problems with this task, they now have a fast-track issue resolution process, run by a senior manager, who will fight to have blocking issues resolved within 24 hours.

The key assumption behind this approach is that there are very few resource skills that actually determine how fast projects flow within an organization. Therefore, we should be very selective about which resources we model in an organization. The vast majority of resource skill sets are not capacity issues that would seriously block project work. Once the organization agrees on which skill sets it will model, then every project must use the same master resource pool to define project work.

A second but also important assumption is that projects and resource tasks are planned in far too great detail. Rather than giving better control, this type of too detailed planning actually causes organizations to lose control. As the expression goes, they can't see the forest for the trees. The level of detail of resource modeling is good if it covers key resource interdependencies within those resource skill sets that are most critical to the organization.

For support groups, for example, such as legal, finance, and even some IT groups within non-IT project portfolios, the amount of actual task work they do is a very small percentage of the overall project work content. However, they can easily hold up projects for days or weeks if the organization either has too much work in the system or puts priority on non-project work. The way to address this is by reducing the amount of project work in process, by having a fast-track resolution process to expedite when project work is being blocked, and by getting agreement from top management and support groups that project work is the #1 priority, with rare exceptions.

Using Project Pipelines to Predict Resource Bottlenecks

There are two extremes: One is trying to plan every project that our organization might do over the next five years. This is about as useful as trying to predict where the next tornado might touch down or how much rain will fall in London over the next few years. The other extreme is not pipelining any future projects (i.e., only working with project data from those projects currently active).

As a general rule, we use the assumption that the further out that projects will be activated, the less accurate the data. However, since some resource skills are very difficult to recruit, and may take a long time to develop to the point that they are productive within your organization, the project pipeline is one tool that shows possible upcoming issues. For short-term bottlenecks in a project system that is updated daily or at least frequently, the data are very useful.

Before assuming that a specific resource skill is becoming a bottleneck, you must be able to view all of the tasks by project coming up for that resource. Ask yourself: Can any of these tasks be done by other resource skill sets? Can parts of these tasks be assigned to other resource skill sets? Can other resources better prepare these tasks, so that the planned task duration for critical resources can be reduced?

Another point that is not so obvious about project pipelines and the implications for resources is the increasing workload for operational support on some of these resources. For example, with new IT systems being implemented, the workload/demand for support often increases, unless the system is replacing a support-intensive older system. For each new product developed, customer service and support demands increase. Therefore, the pipeline provides important data with implications for both modeled and non-modeled project resources.

Project pipelines are not a substitute for good communication between senior management and the people managing the multi-project environment. One senior management initiative can have a dramatic and drastic impact on specific resource skill demand. However, the use of pipeline software within project management technology provides a great tool for *what if* analysis to test assumptions and ensure that you have a reasonable and realistic view of future project demand.

Capacity of Resource Pools

Given the horrible effects of multitasking on productivity, we would like to see resource pools that are 100% dedicated to projects. Typically, organizations are not set up this way. So how should resource pools be set up to increase their overall productivity? How much capacity does a resource pool really have to do project work?

One common misperception is that if about a third of a resource pool's time is spent doing operational and all other responsibilities, two thirds of their capacity is left for project work. The reason why this is incorrect is that when a resource begins to do project work, every interruption robs him/her of much more than just the interrupted time lapse.

When people are interrupted, they have to set down what they were doing. Sometimes, this can be significant. For example, a department in a plant setting up machines to produce a prototype of a new product could lose hours if interrupted to focus on an operational emergency.

When the resources return to continue their project work, they have to put their minds and any physical setups back where they left off. For engineers or IT people doing complex work, this could be many minutes or even hours.

The more frequently people are interrupted, the more time they lose. Every environment is different. We find that often half of the assumed available time of some resource pools is lost due to these multitasking effects. We also find that many department managers are working with outdated assumptions about the amount of project time available, due to increasing complexity of work, more systems being implemented that need support or questions answered, etc.

The preferred way to set up a resource pool to maximize productivity is to split it between project work and other work. The bigger the pool of people, the easier this is to accomplish. This is a decision that many managers have avoided until now because either they didn't have the time to cross-train some of their people or they wanted the flexibility of being able to take anyone out of their total resources available to respond to urgent needs.

Our observation is that a serious evaluation of how to change this paradigm is a must to move forward in the new world of drastically increased project velocity. In Zurich, Switzerland, when a mechanical engineering department split a staff of 25 into a project pool of 22 with, on average, 3 engineers available to deal with questions from past work, *emergencies*, sales proposals, procurement questions, etc., the productivity noticeably increased. In Manitoba, Canada, when a customer service department dedicated 2 of their 10 people to project work, a task that would have otherwise taken a month (working a couple of hours per day with interruptions) was accomplished in three days. In Virginia, a product development team took five years to bring a new product to market, when there was actually about one year of real work involved (i.e., the opposite of what was desired, at a cost of four years of lost product revenue!).

In some resource pools, this requires some careful planning, cross-training, buy-in, and commitment of the top resource manager. In others, such as the customer service example above, it simply required a brief talk between a vice president of the company and the customer service manager. The talk went something like this:

> **Customer service manager:** "There's no way I can give up two people for three days."
>
> **VP:** "Why not?"
>
> **Customer service manager:** "Because each customer service rep has certain customers that only call them. They'll be upset if they can't reach their rep if they call."
>
> **VP** (somewhat sarcastically): "Does that mean those reps never get sick or take vacations?" (Note that the sarcasm was uncalled for!)
>
> **Customer service manager:** "No, but . . ."
>
> **VP:** "If one of your reps is sick or on vacation, do you normally have someone else substitute, or do you hold your customers' inquiries until they're back?"

The VP went on to explain the importance of the dedicated time of these customer service reps. One very important piece of information he used was the value, per day, of delaying the project in question. Since this was a sales project, every day's delay meant $25,000 to the company's bottom line. This was based directly on the expected benefits of the project. Once the customer service manager understood this, making projects the #1 priority for those two reps was much easier to stomach.

What about the capacity issues in the above examples? In all cases, there is less capacity required when you eliminate or drastically reduce the bad multitasking that is inherent in today's resource practices. In the customer service example, minimal overtime was required from a few of the remaining eight reps for three days, allowing the two reps to do the project work much faster than they would have otherwise. In other words, overall resource capacity issues diminish significantly when we do project work the right way.

Capacity Elevation Team

Project resource capacity elevation is a skill set that we rarely find in organizations. Most organizations seem to take a tactical approach to project resources—each resource manager adds capacity according to annual head count budgets, in isolation from other departments. Although every organization has some justification process for adding head count, what is missing is a *strategic* look at the project portfolio.

Our assumption is that an organization will never have sufficient resources to do every project that is formally desirable or justifiable in some tangible way. Therefore, if resources are limited, it makes more sense to add precious resources where the organization will gain the biggest benefits. By modeling proposed projects in a pipeline against available resources, and knowing what the ROI or benefits are from the proposed projects, the organization is much better able to put a value on adding resources in one skill set versus another, given that choices often have to be made.

Choices are not obvious, since there is much more to the decisions than what you find in a histogram. For example, a big law firm (1,000 lawyers) has a large IT infrastructure and support group. This group does many projects per year. Some projects make the lawyers more productive in their work. Some projects allow lawyers to do more and better research for clients. Some projects allow lawyers to manage large amounts of information to provide better answers for clients, better defenses in litigation, save money, reduce client risks, etc. Which of these various types of projects are the most lucrative for the law firm?

By having a capacity elevation team, which is cross-functional in composition, the organization builds a strategic view of project resources, in addition to the still necessary tactical view of "we're running out of capacity." Within the strategic view, the capacity elevation team looks at the goals of the organization, and the histograms, and makes strategic recommendations about where to add. With the tactical view, they look at gaps in capacity that are likely to block project on-time completions and make tactical recommendations to add. Both of these views are proactive; that is, recommendations are made well in advance of when the capacity is needed.

This team may also be responsible for non-human resources. For example, in one company that makes large forgings, a new forging press might require an investment of tens of millions of dollars and require a lead time of two years before it is available. To the extent that equipment or even new buildings, opening new geographic facilities, or similar issues are part of an organization's project world, the capacity elevation team plays a major role in keeping the organization always ready for the next level of performance.

Conclusions

Software will not suddenly make multi-project resource management easier. Before an organization knows which resources are really an issue, they must bring the multi-project system under control. Then the organization can build a much better, deeper knowledge of the tactical need to add resources where projects are really blocked from getting done quickly enough. More importantly, the organization can add resources strategically, where the investment of both money and time to recruit, train, and use the resources brings the biggest benefits to the organization overall. This skill—capacity elevation of project resources across an entire organization—is best held within a *capacity elevation team*. Enterprise project resource management, and especially capacity elevation, is a learning process that connects the senior management needs to accomplish change with project planning and execution.

Endnote

1. See Gerald I. Kendall and Steve C. Rollins, *Advanced Project Portfolio Management and the PMO* (Boca Raton, FL: J. Ross Publishing, 2003).

Questions

37-1. The authors claim that until you change the way that project work is planned and executed, an organization cannot really know what to do about its resources. Explain what you believe the authors' logic to be.

37-2. If you are going to create a resource pool (skills description and quantities of people available), the authors suggest you limit the number of different skill sets modeled in projects. Why shouldn't you create a resource pool for the entire organization (assuming that the time it takes to create such a definition is not the issue)?

37-3. Assume you are talking to a resource manager. Explain why that manager, looking at a histogram produced by software, should consider 67% to indicate a fully utilized resource skill set.

37-4. Resource pools often have less capacity to do project work than their managers assume they have, even taking into account all of their other responsibilities. Why is that?

37-5. What process addresses the issue of support groups not responding quickly enough to project needs or to holding up project progress?

What one change is required in the way that support groups respond today that would make this process effective?

37-6. Explain the role of a capacity elevation team. Given that role, what types of people should be on the team? Who (what job function/level in the company) should chair the team?

37-7. Based on this chapter's discussion of project pipelines, how far into the future would you like to see project work in the pipeline—three months, six months, a year, longer than a year? Explain your answer.

This book has free material available for download from the Web Added Value™ resource center at *www.jrosspub.com*

38. Supervisor and Management Loads

The Premise

When supervisors spend much of their time doing tasks instead of supervising and coaching, project work often takes longer to complete. When managers do not have sufficient time to think, problems linger and often worsen. Consider the following example:

> The company is a leader in the implementation of radio and wireless systems on the U.S. east coast. It has three types of work—unscheduled (some of which are true client emergencies and all of which are urgent in the clients' eyes), scheduled short term (typically less than two weeks, and the work is of a highly repetitive nature), and scheduled long term (more than two weeks and often several months). There are no resources dedicated to the unscheduled work, including no dedicated project managers. In order to accommodate this work, resources are pulled from short- and long-term scheduled work. The supervisor responsible for scheduling is spending a lot of his time playing musical chairs with the employees. He devotes almost zero time to coaching, training, or following up with these resources. The first time we visited to start a redesign process, he had come in at 5:00 a.m. to do time cards and payroll for the 19 people for whom he is responsible.
>
> This scenario is like visiting an emergency room that had no dedicated staff. When you walk in with your broken leg, you find a phone instead of an emergency room greeter. You pick up the phone and beg for help, and the operator tells you that the physician who sets legs is doing rounds at another hospital, and he should be with you within a few hours. The physician eventually arrives, but at the expense of the hospital rounds he was supposed to complete. Oh well, hopefully those patients are OK for now. However, those who were due to be released will have to wait another day.
>
> Back to the original story. The manager of this services group fights fires and is in meetings every day, many of them resulting from pulling employees from scheduled work. When you pull an employee

from a longer term project to work on a shorter term project, that resource might be away from the project for two weeks. Typically, the person being pulled has a unique skill set. This means that the longer term project is now delayed by two weeks. If this happens several times during the course of the project, the client gets upset, the resource who was pulled gets upset, the project manager is furious, and the salesperson who sold the project is demoralized. No wonder so much time is spent in meetings.

As the expression goes, "When you find yourself in a hole, the first thing to do is to stop digging." Management and supervisors will never be in a position to do what their job needs them to do if they are constantly fighting fires. For managers and supervisors, the steps are:

1. Bring the system under control, so that firefighting/expediting occurs less than 10% of the time, and preferably less than 5%.
2. Free up at least 20% of management's time to think. This is not a vague wish—it is mandatory to have even the remotest chance of improving multi-project management.
3. Forbid supervisors from doing project tasks.
4. Every time the organization adds project resources, consider the implications for supervisors and managers.
5. Monitor the number of times a project is in a red zone, waiting for the same manager to resolve an issue or make a decision. This is an excellent leading indicator of the need to address management capacity as an issue.

Bring the System under Control—Stop the Excessive Firefighting

There are several symptoms that the multi-project system is not in control:

- Frequent priority changes in projects and/or tasks
- Too many meetings related to project schedules, scope creep, juggling of resources, fights over specifications, etc.
- Too many projects that are either late, over budget, or out of scope
- Too often, during a project's active life, the project is in serious danger of being late, over budget, or not within scope
- Multitasking of resources and/or project managers, where they frequently stop/start tasks
- No gating mechanism exists for activating new projects

- No escalation mechanism exists for resolving blocking issues quickly

Although this book presents the processes to resolve all of the above issues, sometimes a more drastic action is needed up front when initiating this new approach. To bring the system under control, and give management and supervisors the capacity to do their jobs properly, we sometimes freeze a significant portion of active project work.

By freezing, for example, 50% of the active projects, the number of meetings decreases drastically—by more than 50%. Projects and tasks suddenly get the needed attention and start to move much more quickly. Priorities no longer, or rarely, need to change.

The counterintuitive aspect of freezing project work is that all projects, including the frozen projects, will complete much more quickly. The same process is used on some busy highways, for example, in California, where only so many cars are allowed to enter the highway per minute. *When designed properly*, the system keeps the highway traffic flowing fast, and at the same time the queues of cars waiting to get on the highway remain short. Of course, with highways you don't have supervisors and managers with each driver on the highway to coach them to become better, faster drivers, as you would on projects using our system. You also can't increase highway capacity (add another lane) as quickly as you can by adding resources for projects.

When projects are frozen, the resources that had been assigned to those projects are either reassigned to existing projects or are assigned to properly prepare tasks on the frozen projects to ensure they can be worked on when released to a resource. Now a supervisor has time to think about how to assign the work, so that more resources can work on fewer tasks and move the work more quickly. In many cases, this freezing mechanism has allowed a department to reorganize its resources so that some are dedicated to handling operational responsibilities and emergencies, whereas others are dedicated to project tasks.

Management should take this breather time to put in place the fast-track issue resolution process, so that blocking issues are addressed daily with all project managers in a 15-minute meeting. With senior management driving this process, managers and supervisors can focus on the coaching necessary to get the tasks done.

The second element that will prevent a lot of future firefighting is the proper definition of project scope and networks for all new or recently activated projects. Once again, the approach for this is outlined in detail in Part III of this text.

Free Up 20% of Management's Time to Think

It's easier than most managers think. This is one day per week of quiet time. How do you get it? When we've asked managers to document their last week's time, and to note every interruption they received when trying to do this kind of *thinking* work, the result is something amazing but not at all surprising.

The first thing that is amazing is what percentage of time managers are spending on firefighting. The 20% or more might already be delivered by completing the first step above. However, the other amazing thing is the extent to which managers tolerate interruptions that are not emergencies. E-mail systems provide multiple interruptions per hour. As if that weren't bad enough, now we have tweets and twitters, keeks, and cell phone applications. What we don't seem to have any longer is that two hours a day or one day per week of totally uninterrupted think time.

Once the majority of the fires have been put out, the manager needs only to make the decision to turn off the e-mail, cell phone, and other sources of interruption. If in an office, the manager can put a sign on the door: "Thinking—Please do not disturb until . . . (time)."

However, for many managers that we have worked with, there is another fundamental issue blocking this dedicated time: it is the inability to properly delegate. This reminds us of a meeting where we were reviewing manager interruptions. Some of the issues were so trivial in nature, we asked, "Why on earth are YOU dealing with this?" For many (not all) of these types of issues, it was simply that this had become a habit over the last years or decades.

Delegating is a very simple thing to do, once you have made up your mind to stop those kinds of interruptions. The next time someone comes to you with such an issue, deal with the issue, but ask the person to stop by again as soon as the issue has been dealt with. Then ask four questions:

1. What policy or rule prevented that person from dealing with the issue himself/herself?
2. What is the purpose of that policy or rule and is that clearly understood by the person?
3. What action could that person take that would meet the objective of the policy, even though the action might be an exception to the policy?
4. What authority would you like to grant this person, so that they never need to interrupt you again when such an issue occurs?

For example, project managers were frequently interrupting the service department manager to get permission to buy parts immediately that either were not shipped to a site or were broken or unsuitable. The policy was that all parts were either bought by their procurement manager or had to be approved by the service department manager in advance. The purpose of the policy was to ensure that their projects/jobs completed within or as close as possible to budget. However, when the project manager had to wait for either the service manager or procurement to get low-cost parts that they could have bought from any hardware store, the company was tying up other labor on a job site. The policy, in these cases, was actually costing, not saving, money.

The service department manager concluded that he and the procurement manager weren't the only ones in the company who were smart enough to make such decisions. In discussing this with all of the project managers, he set the allowable exceptions to the policy: "For all parts under $500 per job, you, the project manager, now have the authority to purchase these parts in any case where you have labor or a site waiting for the parts to proceed with work." By empowering and delegating such authority to the project managers, he gained a half hour a day.

On average, managers have several (we guess around five) such empowerment/delegation issues. This means that some managers can gain much more than an hour per day by following this simple model.

Once managers have freed up this time, and are committed to using it to improve the multi-project system, the question becomes: "What is the best use of this time?" The answer depends on whether there are still systemic root problems which have a major negative impact on the system or whether there are many independent causes of variation in completing projects on time, on budget, and within scope.

An example of a systemic root cause is a shortage of a key resource that is needed on many or almost all projects. With the time to think, the manager only needs the root cause analysis skills in order to properly analyze the situation. Sorry—teaching those skills is outside the scope of this book, but if you need such training, we do offer powerful workshops.[1]

Examples of independent causes of variation include the following:

- Waiting for a resource to finish a task on another project
- Vendor hasn't provided answers to questions
- Customer has not given a decision on a specification
- Legal department hasn't approved a contract
- Software is taking longer than expected to install/test
- Equipment is not yet delivered

For these independent causes of variation in the multi-project system, the manager needs a system to capture and report the reasons why projects end up late or in the red zone. If you don't have such a system, this is an excellent use of the manager's time—to set it up and ensure the reporting is implemented. Once implemented, the manager does a Pareto analysis (80/20) on the reported data. Which of all of these sources of variation is the most frequent or does the most damage to our multi-project environment? Now the manager finally has the time to work on this *one* issue and fix it permanently.

Forbid Supervisors from Doing Project Tasks

Forbid sounds like such an unreasonable word. We can already hear the reaction: "That would never work here. Our supervisors have to be able to do work sometimes." True—if you have a small department (e.g., two people and a supervisor), it may be appropriate. What is the priority of the supervisor then? Is it to do the work or to supervise?

The supervisor's project job is to coach, train, encourage, hold people accountable, track, facilitate, and escalate. Only when all of those are done would a supervisor have time to do tasks. Supervisors are the leverage point for the productivity of all of the resources who report to them. Often, supervisors already split their time between operations work and project work. How much time do they really have left to do project tasks? The answer, in reality, even in a very small department, is none.

If a supervisor has only two people reporting to him/her, and the very reason that person is the supervisor is that he/she knows how to do the work 25% better and faster than the subordinates, the best use of the supervisor's time is to help those two subordinates become as productive as the supervisor.

Supervisors are often much more comfortable doing the work than supervising the work. This is one of the primary reasons why they resort back to doing tasks when they don't see an immediate fire that needs to be put out. Most people, when they are in their first management/supervisory role, are uncomfortable giving direction. In many cases, the resources they are supervising make it even more uncomfortable.

To leverage supervisors in a project environment, two things are essential. The first is to forbid them from doing project tasks themselves. They are welcome to help any resource that needs help to complete a project task. This rule should be formally announced to the department, emphasizing the new role of the supervisor and the expected benefits for everyone. When implemented properly, the benefits must be:

- Removal of obstacles that any resource has in completing their task or completing it faster

- Skill transfer, to allow resources to learn, grow, and work in a way that is more productive for the organization
- Clearer entrance and exit criteria for tasks
- Less rework

There is a second essential condition to support this framework. Supervisors must be trained in the skills to supervise and encourage people without micro-managing. People need recognition and accountability to perform project tasks better and better.

The supervisory work is not only for a person with the title of supervisor. As pointed out in the book *Influencer: The Power to Change Anything,*[2] peer accountability is a major force in workplace performance.

There is another element of supervision that is often overlooked when supervisors spend too much time doing tasks. That element is cross-training. Too often, we see resource pools that consist of one or two people with a given skill set. Too often, when these people are needed on a project, they are either too busy somewhere else or out on vacation, sick, training, etc. When supervisors are forbidden from working on project tasks, they can be cross-training resources where it makes sense, to add flexibility and speed to completion of project work.

Elevating Resources—Implications for Supervisors, Managers, and Other Resource Pools

All that is required to increase resource capacity is some cause-and-effect thinking. We are just a tiny bit sarcastic about the use of the word *all.* Although it is not difficult to do, enterprise mentality seems to elude the process of increasing resources. Some examples best illustrate the problem.

A high-technology company seemed to be constantly short of software engineers for development. The company added dozens of engineers, but lagged behind in the hiring of expert managers, so for years the productivity of the resources got worse and worse. Finally, one new top manager was hired who implemented an *Agile* methodology. That was followed up with an overall critical chain approach. And then, before they knew it, the engineers were out of work.

To keep the engineers busy, the company needed the marketing/*ideation* group to come up with new ideas that could turn into products and services that customers would buy. But the marketing group had been so used to waiting forever for their ideas to be implemented, they never added capacity to their team. For almost an entire year, dozens of engineers were unproductive, waiting for the next good idea to be properly specified and vetted with the market.

A different example comes from a large law firm, where most of the projects were delivered by the Information Technology and Services group. They never seemed to have enough project managers to complete all of the projects that the company needed. In one year, the number of project managers tripled from 4 to 12. The next year, all of the project managers were fighting over precious IT resources—systems architects—who held up some projects for months at a time.

A third example is actually quite exciting for its implications. A San Francisco-based multibillion dollar services company became so adept at delivering projects on time that it was implementing change faster than its users could absorb it. The company had to slow down the rate of change to avoid impacting a user department more than once in a quarter.

The implication of these stories is quite basic and simple. Before you elevate any single resource pool, think through the cause and effect on other departments in the company and on the span of control of existing supervisors and managers. Every change in one department has cause and effect in other departments.

That is why any capacity elevation is best considered at both an enterprise and local level. The local level may first recognize the increased demand for its resources and its inability to respond within current capacity. However, the local level often does not see all of the implications beyond its area.

An Australian company set a goal of advertising major new products every week. It achieved that goal by contracting a marketing company and increasing operational capability to handle customer phone inquiries. However, the company failed to look at the capabilities of its retail stores and distribution system to handle the increased load. As a result, hundreds of customers each week went to their local stores to ask about the product only to find that the product was not in stock.

See the previous chapter (in case you skipped it) to learn about or refresh your memory on the role of the capacity elevation team.

What Resource Are You Waiting on the Most?

Every time a critical project task waits on a resource (human or other), by definition we are delaying the benefits that the project will bring to the company. The first thing we want to understand is who or what we are waiting on when a project is in the red zone. The reason is that now we have management spending time expediting.

By accumulating simple statistics on who/what we are waiting on every time we enter a red zone, and addressing the resource that comes up most often, by definition we are almost guaranteed to reduce the duration of future projects.

Therefore, this information must be highly visible to senior management. The visibility should remove any hubris involved in any resource not being responsive. But more importantly, it should focus a team approach on figuring out how this resource can become more responsive to project tasks.

A case study cited by the Oxford Radcliffe Hospitals of the United Kingdom[3] describes this exact approach in achieving the target time frame for emergency room treatment of over 1,000 visits per week. Starting with less than 70% of visits achieving complete service within four hours, they moved these miniprojects to over 95% of visits completed within four hours, whereas the number of visits per week increased and staff remained at the same level.

You can certainly become more sophisticated with the data collected. For example, you could collect not just the number of times you are waiting for a resource, but also how long the wait was. Then you could act on the resource that you are waiting for the longest, rather than the one you wait for most often. You could also collect data on what resource you are waiting for at any time, not just in a red zone. We recommend that you try the simpler approach described initially above before becoming more sophisticated.

Our experience is that there is a pretty good correlation between the resource that holds up a project most often and the one that holds it up for the longest time period. If that is not the case, then the offending resource is usually so obvious that you don't even need the statistics to identify it.

The problem today is not typically in the quality of the statistics. It is that management does not take the time to gather information and think about how to use it to increase multi-project flow. Today, there are too many band-aids, in the form of frequent priority changes and frequent reallocations of resources. One of the worst examples is a true story from a customer visit, pre-implementation of this new system. A resource was seen hanging around the building after closing time. A fellow worker asked him why he was still there, and he replied, "I've gotten five changes to where I'm supposed to go tomorrow morning and which task I'm supposed to work on. I'm not leaving until I get the final answer!"

Conclusions

In a multi-project world, resources change frequently. Every such change has implications for management. Managers and supervisors must have the time to devote to the project environment in order to adequately help their resources and, in turn, help their organization to become much more productive in delivering project work.

Therefore, the organization must first work to reduce the level of firefighting that often consumes so much of a manager's and supervisor's capacity. Although the entire process covered in this book is designed to do exactly that, we often find the need to do one more step at the beginning of implementing these processes, which is to freeze a significant percentage of existing project work. This chapter also describes the approach to then free up at least 20% of management's time to devote to improving the multi-project flow. Managers must deal with both deeply rooted, systemic issues and common cause variation in projects in order to have a lasting impact. Statistics on what projects are waiting for when they are in a red zone are useful to gather and analyze, but this only happens when managers have sufficient time to do so.

For supervisors, the needed transition is from doing project tasks to coaching, mentoring, transferring skills, unblocking obstacles, and properly preparing and tracking tasks. This requires both a policy forbidding supervisors from doing project tasks and the training to be able to help their resources without micromanaging.

Although the above changes make a huge difference, the icing on the cake is to see management thinking through any resource changes and the implications across the organization. When managers consider, in advance, how elevating one resource might affect the needs in other areas, and how managers with the right span of control can help increase project flow, then the organization has achieved a level of multi-project maturity rarely seen today.

Endnotes

1. See www.tocinternational.com for services and workshops. The catalog of programs includes a Thinking Process workshop that includes root cause analysis and solution in five Thinking Processes.
2. Kerry Patterson et al., *Influencer: The Power to Change Anything* (New York: McGraw Hill, 2008).
3. See Oxford Radcliffe Hospitals Case Study (Edgware, Middlesex, UK: Goldratt Consulting Europe Ltd., 2003).

Questions

38-1. Why do you think supervisors and managers in many organizations spend a large percentage (e.g., over 25%) of their time firefighting?

38-2. How might an organization implement a freeze of some projects in its environment? That is, how might an organization decide which projects to freeze and which ones to keep active? Who would need to be involved? Who would need to buy into freezing some projects, and why?

38-3. What are the different ways that managers could free up 20% of their time?

38-4. Assuming that managers are able to free up time, how do the authors suggest that time be used?

38-5. If supervisors are forbidden from doing project tasks, won't there be negative effects? If you believe there would be negative effects, how would you prevent them from happening?

38-6. The year is 2011. A company that supplies products to the housing industry has several major projects lined up to improve the productivity of its plant production facilities around the world. Currently, due to the ongoing recession in the housing industry, the plants have excess capacity. To accomplish these projects, the company has hired five project managers to work with its 15 plants over the next six months. Explain the possible implications of these projects and the hiring of these new project managers on other functions in the company. Provide at least two recommendations for the company to avoid possible negative consequences from improving the plants.

38-7. What kind of statistics do the authors recommend gathering? Provide an example of what those statistics might tell a senior manager and what changes could result that would improve project flow.

39. Increasing Load on Operations from Project Completion

The Premise

Every organization has some kind of operations—loosely defined as the work required to deliver a product or service to a customer. Almost every type of project has some impact on operations. For example:

- New product/service development projects require both prototyping, which is usually done within production functions, and, in the end, modifying operations schedules and processes to accommodate the new products or services.
- A project to improve sales, either directly or through better marketing, results in more orders to the company, which means more work for operations to accommodate.
- A change in internal technology or systems often impacts some aspect of operations. For example, a new bar-coding system for tracking inventory in Malaysia was intended to cause operations to do their work with half the inventory they had been carrying previously. This required major changes in operational policies and procedures. A new enterprise resource planning system required retraining of all the operations people, but, more dramatically, meant a change in how distribution centers interacted with ordering and fulfillment, affecting every transaction they executed.

Although there are many other types of projects, the ones described above are examples of the major projects that most organizations engage in to remain competitive or to meet customer needs. Often, when one of these new systems is implemented, the load on operations increases. This increased load can be in the form of additional work to be done, or it can be in the form of increased complexity. Consider the following example:

A successful Canadian custom kitchen cabinet manufacturer fought off the great housing recession of 2008 by delivering new products to the market. Not only did they provide new designs and colors with existing materials, but they added new types of materials, new styles, and metal oven hoods to their vast product line. At the same time, the average order size (number of cabinet boxes ordered per customer) declined. The result was that they were able to maintain their top line (sales) but with huge pressure on the bottom line. Operations had to deliver the work, but with many more production changes, less efficiency due to having to work with different materials in smaller quantities, and a much steeper learning curve for their people.

In such a situation, the increased load on operations from successfully completing new product projects created a huge demand for a different type of project in operations—a project that would dramatically increase plant productivity in bottlenecked areas with a much faster learning curve for new people. It was 2011 before this need was realized, driven by a now unprofitable company that was no longer able to deliver orders on time to customers.

The point of this chapter is to highlight a simple process to examine the impact of implementing new projects on the existing operation. This process urges you to:

1. Ensure that operational capacity exists to do both operations and support and project work.
2. Examine the need for *sister* projects when a new project is implemented that impacts operations.
3. Periodically review the need for an operations flow and productivity project as a direct result of the changes in operations brought by other projects. These projects must be planned into the organization's future project workload.

Ensuring Sufficient Operations Capacity for Operations, Support, and Project Work

Today's silo approach to multi-project management ignores the impact of implementing new projects on operations. Today's silo approach to operations ignores the need to have explicit additional capacity for doing project work. Some of that capacity must exist within people and some must exist within equipment, IT, and other support resources.

In order to do project tasks quickly, without disrupting operations, management must have the ability to:

- Free up 100% of operations personnel time to work on a project task. Squeezing someone from operations for an hour or two a day to work on a project task whenever they have a spare few minutes is the wrong approach. It will prolong the project work and likely be done poorly, based on the authors' vast experience with multitasking.
- Execute project tasks without disrupting operations. If by doing project tasks operations work gets repeatedly delayed, this is a symptom that the organization is caught in a horrible conflict between operations and projects that remains unresolved. To avoid disruption, operations management must have advance visibility to upcoming project task work.
- Execute project tasks continuously until done—not stop-and-start tasks.

For this approach to work, operations management must understand and accept the new world of faster project flow. To support this world, management often must think differently about how project work gets done. In the past, where operations said, "I can let Joe and Sue work on the project, but only for two hours per day, because they are the only skilled operations people I have on a given process (or piece of equipment or for a customer)," now we seek a different mindset. The thinking must be, "If Joe and Sue were both sick for a week, we'd still have to get our operations work done. So surely, I can spare Joe and Sue for a dedicated week to complete a project task."

This often is within the realm of current possibility. It may be that operations needs to schedule some overtime during that week when some of its resources are doing projects or may even need to schedule less production work, if possible. If ongoing project work is a fact of life in operations, this may mean that operations has a need for 11, not 10, people, for example, to be able to satisfy both operations and project demands without compromise.

At the same time, the senior management area responsible for the multi-project environment (e.g., CEO, CIO, and PMO) must consider the impact of each new project implementation on operations demand, in advance of implementing the new project. At a company in Zurich, each new ship unloader that the company commissions generates a requirement for spare parts inventory. There are always some and sometimes many new parts that must be stocked. This requires space. At some point, the volume of operations transactions (ordering parts, physical inventory counts, fulfilling customer requests, transportation logistics) increases to a point where it cannot be handled by the existing operations staff.

Often, the overriding assumption with the implementation of new projects is that existing operations can handle it. That is a great assumption for keeping cost of operations down, but unfortunately it is not always correct.

In the original planning of a project network, the tasks required (if necessary) to allow operations to absorb the change that the project will bring is the correct, proactive approach to ensuring customer and employee satisfaction.

Need for Sister Projects

Often, one project is not sufficient to bring the total or even partial benefit to the organization. Here are two examples.

Example 1: Bar-Coding Project

> A project to implement a new bar-coding system for inventory control in plants worldwide was sponsored by the corporate IT department. The intention was that by having accurate raw material inventory, the plants would be able to cut their inventories in half. Since the inventories were perishable and also subject to bug infestations, it was envisioned that the company's investment in inventory would be reduced significantly and waste (in the form of inventory write-offs) would also be drastically reduced. However, the corporate IT department did not plan the sister project that would have saved all of this money.
>
> You see, in all of these plants, the operating procedures had built in the extra inventory to protect production—to ensure that plants never ran out of raw materials. The plants had no project activated to immediately follow the bar-coding project that would change procedures or reduce inventories. Given that each plant maintained over 100 different unique raw materials in varying quantities and in multiple warehouses, this sister project was not trivial.

Example 2: Major New Broadband Communications Capability

> A California high-technology company launches major new suites of products several times per year. The project plan includes the design, development, and testing portions of the product, including the beta testing of products on customer sites. Then what happens? The answer is almost always a totally disappointing first-quarter sales number, followed by urgent actions, followed by either success (once every three years), redesign of the product (almost always), or abandonment of the product (often after years of redesign). This approach resulted in fewer and fewer customers willing to be beta test sites for this company's new products, since they too often found the products lacking the basic capabilities.
>
> Two sister projects are missing from this case. A front-end sister

project is needed to do the market research to validate the need for the new products in advance of building them. This project would also determine the design features needed to have a major impact on the market, avoiding the need to redesign after the fact. This project would identify the target markets and sufficient beta test customers so that the product would have a likely sales impact in its first quarter.

The other sister project is the product launch through marketing and sales, to the point that the product is generating sufficient sales to self-sustain. This requires proper marketing support, lead generation, sales training, and sales hand-holding until the product is able to be sold without any special sales support. Many product development projects ignore the marketing and sales tasks.

The way to examine the need for *sister* projects is to ask a simple question: "How much tangible benefit must this project deliver in order for senior management to call it 'successful'?" Tangible benefit implies a measurable, numerical impact on increased sales, reduced investment, and/or reduced operating expenses. Once we know these numbers, then we ask the question: "Are the tasks defining this project sufficient to deliver the needed benefits?" Often, when we ask this question, we get answers from the technical side of the house: "No, but that's not our problem!" Correct, but it is the problem and challenge of the project manager, and senior management, to build in the time and tasks required for the sister projects.

As you can judge from these examples, *sister* projects are simply the collection of subprojects that must go hand in hand with the major project in order to get the desired results. In a holistic approach, these subprojects are part of original planning and expectations. That is one good sign of a mature multi-project organization.

Periodically Review Operations Flow and Productivity

The changes brought by projects will have a life-threatening impact on operations eventually. The question that we don't know the exact answer to is "how fast this will happen."

Just look at any industry to validate this. How is any aspect of banking done today versus even 20 years ago? The implementation of ATMs was just one precursor to online banking and its implications for operations. Even the issuance of new mortgages is largely done online today. As one Florida credit union discovered much too late, customers even in the late 1990s were no longer willing to wait six weeks to find out if they qualify when they could get an answer online in 15 minutes. It was no longer acceptable for the capacity of the underwriters to govern operations response time.

In the year 2000, most people were willing to go to a bookstore, browse, and even order a book and wait a few weeks for its arrival. Today, half of books are sold with only seconds of wait time to download to a device.

You don't need to be a fortune teller. Simply conduct a frequent review of operations flow and productivity to determine if the changes from the recently implemented projects are driving demand for another project to improve operations. How frequently to do this depends on the industry and the extent of change it is experiencing. In general, there is enough change in any industry to warrant an annual review.

We have implemented many projects that involved improving operations. These are difficult, challenging projects with the potential to have a serious negative impact on customers if not conducted carefully.

However, more often we see operations neglected, especially over the past few years, when global economic challenges have driven some interesting behaviors. Operations *improvement* over the recent past often meant closing plants or downsizing workforces. These changes did not put the organization in a better position to succeed in the future. All they did was allow the organization to survive. But to be sustainable, organizations must not just survive, and operations must continually evolve to support new models of doing business.

Henry Ford was the genius behind the mass production system, with lots of batching and efficiency in producing the same products over and over. Taiichi Ohno, of Toyota fame, was the genius behind changing this type of operation to mass customization with quick changeovers in production.

The periodic review is conducted to answer four questions:

1. Is the operations flow quick enough to match or beat our significant competitors?
2. Is the operation efficiency good enough to be price competitive?
3. Is the operations quality sufficient to be acceptable to most customers?
4. Is the operation still scalable to grow to meet the coming year's market demand?

Without the periodic reviews, these issues creep up on operations and hit at the worst possible time—when the market demand is growing and the company has all of its project resources tied up in other major efforts. The whole point of enterprise project resource planning is to be proactive about those things that make an organization's success sustainable. This chapter guides you in aligning operations continually, by proactively seeking those projects that overcome the effects of other improvement projects.

Conclusions

Many of the projects and changes that an organization implements have an impact on the organization's operations. When the project sponsor is from an area other than operations (e.g., engineering, product development, marketing, IT), the implications of the new project on operations are often ignored or downplayed. Over the course of astonishingly short time periods (e.g., often less than three years), the entire operations infrastructure can become cumbersome, difficult to manage, or worse—unable to deliver what customers want when they want it.

Further, operations is often involved in performing tasks on projects. The entire premise of this book is to focus on getting more projects done faster. This means that the demand on operations to participate in projects increases over time. This means that operations needs to find a way to provide dedicated resources to project tasks, which often requires a change in mindset.

A proactive approach to managing the multi-project impact on operations is to ensure that operations departments have the capacity to dedicate resources to project tasks. Further, such an approach ensures that projects include *all* of the necessary operations subprojects to achieve the full, tangible organizational benefit desired. Finally, being proactive demands a periodic review of operations flow and productivity, to assess the potential damage unintentionally caused by the implementation of new products and services, changes to systems, etc. Four questions are provided within the chapter to provide the foundation of such a review.

Operations and projects interact with each other. This chapter guides the management of both projects and operations to interact with synergy and to remove otherwise destructive forces that are a way of life today for many organizations.

Questions

39-1. Explain, through an example, how a *non-operations* project could have a significant impact on operations.

39-2. The chapter highlights three steps to bring synergy between operations and projects. Explain how each step is a win-win for the managers within operations and the managers of projects.

39-3. What makes it so difficult for operations managers to dedicate resources to projects?

39-4. The chapter emphasizes the need for *sister* projects that take operations considerations into account. What is the concept of a *sister* project, and how do you identify whether or not such a subproject is needed?

39-5. Why is a periodic review of operations flow and productivity necessary as a result of project implementations?

39-6. Pick one company in one industry and speculate on what your answers (as a senior manager) might be to the four questions asked during a periodic review.

39-7. Why do the authors single out operations as needing special attention in that function's alignment to the multi-project world?

40. Short-, Medium-, and Long-Term Challenges

The Premise

As the project management office (PMO) or the manager responsible for ensuring the continued, expected progress of all projects, you need to see, at a glance, where your resource challenges are:

- In the short term (e.g., the next one to four weeks)
- In the medium term (the next one to two months)
- In the longer term (the next three to twelve months)

From a resource management perspective, a portfolio of projects equates to the collection of projects that uses his/her resources. From a program or product management point of view, a portfolio of projects equates to the projects necessary to achieve his/her program or product goals. From a functional executive perspective, a portfolio of projects equates to those projects necessary to achieve his/her functional objectives. In other words, the term *portfolio* can mean different things to different people.

No matter how your organization defines *portfolio*, you still need to be able to look across all projects (active and planned) and determine the upcoming resource constraints that require intervention (the one or two areas maximum). For the short term, you don't have time to hire people, so your choices are limited. For the medium term, you might be able to hire and train people, but their ability to actually resolve a serious resource constraint within that time frame is usually not the answer to such a constraint. For the longer term, resource issues are best dealt with strategically.

This chapter suggests a generic approach to dealing with the short-, medium-, and long-term resource issues in a way that is both practical and most beneficial to the organization. In a multi-project environment, resource issues cross functional and level boundaries. When an organization buys into and uses a common approach across these boundaries, there is peer pressure to comply. At the same time, there is genuine help from one functional manager to another, in terms of having common goals and ways of attacking the project resource issues.

Short- and Medium-Term (One-Week to Two-Month) Resource Issues

Most short-term resource issues, within the multi-project management system described in this text, can be dealt with by local managers and supervisors without special intervention. The only short-term resource issues that we want to focus on are those that look like they will delay a project to the extent of missing a due date or critical milestone.

We often find that when you narrow down the short-term resource issues to only those resources working on tasks in a project red zone, there is often misunderstanding of the real underlying issue(s) and whether there is any need for further management action. Here are examples of such issues and implied possible actions. In all cases below, the project(s) are assumed to be in red zones:

- The project entered into a red zone due to previous tasks taking longer than planned. Current tasks are being handled diligently. The resources are already prepared to work hard and fast to help recover some project buffer and ensure the project completes on time. All that management has to do is to get out of the way and clear the track so that the relay runners can run the race without obstacles.
- There is an overload on a critical resource (one who is required on one or several tasks for projects in red zones). The amount of estimated project work is well beyond the capacity of this resource. The types of management intervention that we have seen be successful in such a case are:
  - Freeze operational/other responsibilities and commitments until the resource workload normalizes.
  - Examine the project for unapproved scope creep; if found, remove the unauthorized scope creep.
  - Off-load some project tasks to less experienced people or to subcontractors. This often puts a significant extra burden on immediate supervisors/managers to do such off-loading so that the critical resource does not get bogged down in helping others do the delegated work.
  - *Extreme overtime* for the short term. For example, it may require 80 hours a week to catch up. This can be an excellent solution if and only if this is an infrequent occurrence (e.g., once or twice a year). Too often, it becomes the norm and the predicted effect is that resources burn out.

    - Off-load some project tasks to more senior people (e.g., managers). Although the policy is that managers/supervisors do not do project tasks, this exception to the policy can be helpful in very short-term situations. If this becomes the norm, then it is a sign that the system is no longer working.
    - Provide the best management help possible to speed up the task completion. Sometimes the resource is estimating a long time to finish a task due to inexperience or special problems they are encountering. We have seen frequent examples where the organization has someone with vast experience who has moved onward and upward or even retired. When such a person is willing to help, the resource pool and active tasks get a boost that recovers buffer for the project.
- Although the issue is showing up as a people resource overload issue, it is actually something else that is responsible for tasks requiring long durations to complete. It may be another physical, non-human resource (e.g., computer equipment, access to a lab or prototype resource, etc.) or it may be, for example, waiting for decisions in order to do further work on the task. In that case, the short-term action is to find more of the other resource.
- The overloaded resource may be spending a good deal of time doing rework, rather than original project task work. In this case, the short-term approach is to attack the underlying cause of the rework. You may need a large bandage to stop the bleeding and then a project to prevent future rework.

Another different type of short-term situation occurs when there is a major overload on a given resource pool where the tasks they are working on are not yet *red*. However, if management does nothing, it is predictable that one or more projects will be red within the short-term horizon. For example, a company with limited IT resources had an internal systems crisis. Its order entry system, which interfaced to all of its customers, went down, and IT worked on it day and night for an entire week before recovering the data and solving the problem. By the end of the week, the resources were exhausted.

Generally, in cases where we have not yet reached the red zone of a project, the only action recommended is to put a recovery plan in place. Make sure that such a plan is agreed to by the resource manager(s), the project manager(s), and senior management where necessary. However, there is no need to execute the plan until projects actually enter a red zone.

In rare cases, where the actions above do not bring the system and resource workload back under control, it is necessary to freeze one or more projects.

When a project is unfrozen, it may need to be rescheduled. If this is required more than once or twice a year, once again it is a symptom of the system not working properly.

In a medium-term view, the above actions are still valid. A resource pool that looks overloaded in one week out of a four- to eight-week period but has ample capacity the rest of the time typically does not require management attention. Properly sized project buffers easily absorb the up and down demands. Often, some project work can be shifted by a week and project deadlines can still be met.

However, if a resource is overloaded for two weeks or more out of the four- to eight-week view, and seems to be quite fully loaded for the remaining weeks, then the above actions are appropriate for resources working tasks in the red zone.

Some companies we have worked with do maintain subcontractor resource pools that have people familiar with the company and its work environment. We would add that in some cases, companies would be doing themselves a service if they paid a retainer fee to a subcontractor who agreed to make their people available on reasonably short notice when needed. Many companies do not take advantage of such an approach because they look only at the increased cost of the retainer and not at the benefits of keeping their projects on schedule or even finishing early. This behavior is common in organizations that fail to put tangible values on their projects.

Long-Term Resource Issues

The advantage of having different portfolios of projects mapped out with resource demands is that the organization can make both tactical and strategic resource decisions. It may look like there is an overload of a certain resource skill set. However, that resource skill set may not be strategic for the organization going forward. For example, a marketing department may have project overloads for web developers over the next six months, but after that the skill that will be needed is lead generation through social networking.

For example, one organization we worked with had a very poor track record of bringing new products to market on time. As the VP commented, "It took us five years to bring the last product to market, and it should have taken a year." After implementing the multi-project management approach in this text, the company found a resource skill set lacking as it began to map out and execute projects. The scope on R&D projects and new product development projects was not clear and not well understood. The company was in the process of bringing on new product managers, which could fix this issue, but also realized that the new product managers lacked some market analysis skills. These are the kinds of issues that take months to fix.

The strategic view asks what resources we must hire or develop to ensure better results from projects, without wasting project investments and not blocking the company from executing the number of projects with the speed needed to meet company goals. The tactical view asks which resources most block project progress.

Although multi-project management software helps to answer the tactical issues very well, the strategic resource questions are better answered by quarterly review meetings with senior resource managers and executives. The challenge we have seen for many organizations is that traditional software has been difficult for many people to use. As a result, we see many organizations, even very large ones, operating without formal project plans or having plans but no detailed updates during execution of projects. Therefore, even though the software has the capability, many organizations do not even have the tactical data with which to drive proactive resource decisions in the medium to long term.

To get some useful longer term project resource data within a relatively short period of time, consider the following actions:

1. Use project templates for types of projects; for example, new product development, new IT system implementation, upgrade project.
2. Model only those resources that are strategic or those that are likely to be a problem for completing projects on time.
3. Don't force everyone to use a complex, fully functional project management software product. There are simpler products on the market that are perfectly suitable for basic modeling and tracking of projects, which can feed an enterprise system.
4. When you are part of a central multi-project management function that is asking others for data, provide two things in return. One thing can be as simple as showing people the report(s) you are producing to guide senior management resource decisions or to show where project demand is creating real bottlenecks in the organization's ability to support and deliver projects on time. Another is the hand-holding required to build the initial data. Templates only work if people know how to use them. If someone has to learn a whole process or, even worse, a new software product in order to provide data, many people will resist or simply not do it. With hand-holding, something that might otherwise require hours or days of work can be done within an hour or two.

The key point to remember in long-term project resource planning is to not get bogged down in a large, bureaucratic exercise of trying to predict the demand for all project resources or to do a plan for much longer than you can reasonably predict demand. No matter what industry or size company we have worked with, we have never seen more than two resource skill sets that really blocked the company from doing more projects faster.

Conclusions

In reality, there are few resources that govern how many major projects an organization can accomplish in any given time period. When projects are organized into portfolios (e.g., groups of projects for products or programs, for functional areas), an organization can strategically look at its one or two precious resource skill sets and make a decision as to where it prefers to invest that resource's time. The organization can also make investment decisions when it wishes to add resource capacity.

Once this strategic planning for project resources is done, the organization must deal with the ongoing resource loading issues during execution of multiple projects. From an execution standpoint, it really doesn't matter how the organization groups projects—it still must deal with resource overload issues for the short, medium, and long term.

The chapter outlines different approaches for dealing with overloads for different time frames. The key is to be proactive and watchful and to get the entire organization using the same process to identify and deal with resource constraints. In the worst case scenario, when resource issues are getting worse and worse, one or more projects may need to be frozen to allow resources and remaining projects to get back on track. When such a frozen project is unfrozen, it may need to be rescheduled.

If the organization does not have sufficient project data to determine resource loading over the medium or long term, the suggestion is to use project templates to model future projects and to only model those resource pools and tasks or project phases that are critical to meeting the goals of the company. The chapter provides examples and insights into this highly focused approach.

Questions

40-1. In the way that the authors define short-, medium-, and long-term project resource planning horizons, what are the key differences between short and medium term? What are the key differences between short and long term?

40-2. Why do the authors claim that an organization only needs to do enterprise-wide planning for a few resource skill sets and not every skill set?

40-3. Many organizations have few or no alternatives to having people work extra hours when projects fall behind. Explain why you think this is true and how to bring an organization to consider other alternatives.

40-4. When project tasks are given to managers and supervisors, as an *emergency* measure to recover from falling behind, what are the possible negative consequences? How would you prevent such negative consequences from occurring?

40-5. If an organization does not have the project resource data for the medium to long term available, but wants to do some proactive modeling to see if it might have issues, explain how you would do this and have some reports available within a week.

40-6. What are the pros and cons of modeling plans for project resources beyond the one-year time horizon?

40-7. If you were a director of a PMO or a senior manager responsible for enterprise resource loading and planning, explain how you would get data from functional areas that have historically not been cooperative in providing such data.

This book has free material available for download from the Web Added Value™ resource center at *www.jrosspub.com*

PART VIII

MULTI-PROJECT SOFTWARE REQUIREMENTS

One of the most powerful ways to get quick improvement in the execution of all of an organization's projects is to align the projects with the capacity of the organization to do the work. This is relatively simple conceptually, yet most software does not account for it, either in planning or in execution. Instead, many project management software *solutions* approach this problem by trying to balance workload across all resources. Such approaches cost organizations millions of dollars (not just in software, but ultimately in major project delays) and often fail miserably. To be successful, software must:

- In planning, allow for the use of buffers, with global resource definitions and with alignment to the organization's capacity to do projects
- In execution, allow for buffer monitoring, easy task updating, and a single priority system
- Provide executive and other role-based views to drive consistent understanding, decisions, and actions across all projects

Part VIII brings these major software requirements into focus.

41. Software Planning Requirements—Buffers, Global Resources, and Alignment

The Premise

Beware of sophistication! In our opinion, the more sophisticated features a project management software product has, the less likely it is to be used or understood across organizational levels and functions.

A project management software product must provide, in project planning, the ability to:

- Learn and use the basics within a couple of hours
- Buffer projects holistically (at a project or subproject level, not at a task level)
- View resource demands globally (across all projects and portfolios)
- Use a common resource pool definition
- Use and save templates
- Work together on projects globally (in today's delivery mechanisms, this implies cloud and/or web-based capabilities for viewing and constructing project plans)
- Align and gate projects according to the capacity of the organization to do project work
- Organize projects into portfolios (in larger organizations)

Basic project planning skill and recognition of the major damage that results from activating too much work (multitasking and the resultant delays in accomplishing objectives) are lacking in many organizations. Software can help to bridge the knowledge gap, but only if the software is generally usable and not so complicated as to require experts or specialists for the basics.

Today, without such skills, many supervisors and managers plan projects as lists of *to-dos*. The dependency between tasks is not recognized. The required sequence is therefore not recognized. The resource skill sets required are not recognized. The overlapping demands on some critical resources are not recognized.

When projects are planned as *to-do* lists within functional areas, you can often witness review meetings where conversations are regularly repeated and negative:

> **Functional head:** "How come you didn't get this done, John? It was on your 'to-do' list to be complete by last week."
>
> **John:** "So were three other 'to-dos' from other lists, and I also had two corporate 'to-dos' from George [VP of another function]!"
>
> **Functional head:** "This is simply not acceptable. We need this done ASAP. When can you commit to having this done?"
>
> **John:** "I can do it this week, but that will mean NOT working on the other five 'to-dos.' Will you talk to George and the other managers?"

We must stop wasting hours per week in such meetings. The ability to properly plan work and align it with the capacity of critical resources is as basic a management skill as using word processing or spreadsheets.

To bring project management skill to the masses of managers, we need to step up the hand-holding of managers through the first use of such tools and have the accountability supported by senior management to make it happen. Providing this skill set to multiple managers is a project that will leverage the organization's capacity and capability to get more projects completed faster.

Ability to Learn and Use the Basics within Two Hours

Think of some of the applications now available on iPhone and other such products. People who download the applications generally receive no formal training. Many of the applications have advanced functions, but do not require the users to become knowledgeable experts on the first try.

The tricky parts of learning project management software to plan a project are:

- Creating a task with the essential elements (task described properly, time estimate, resource[s] required)
- Determining how to specify a resource for a task
- Creating dependencies
- Knowing how to buffer a project
- Finding the critical chain of dependent events—either task or resource dependencies

To achieve a rapid learning curve within two hours, visual management is key. Readily accessible videos (preferably web-based or available on the organization's server) showing the step-by-step approach within the software are vital. Of course, an online help index and search engine are also important. But many users are easily frustrated by not knowing where to start.

When you think about the iPhone model, ask yourself what makes these applications so successful and broadly used. You don't need to wait for a software engineer to install the application. The options are available by point and click. The data use a fill-in-the-blanks approach. Data from multiple sources (e.g., between the iPhone and computer) are automatically synchronized. Plus, the applications are cheap or free.

A new user of such a product should not have to think about defining resource skill sets. These are best chosen from a drop-down menu, with an individual's selections already filled in. This ensures a good level of consistency in modeling an organization's project resources.

Most project management software today provides some easy way to create task dependencies (e.g., by clicking on one task and dragging a line or connector to another task). However, in many organizations, resource dependencies within a project can determine what the most critical tasks are. There are many project management software products that do not recognize resource dependencies across a project's different paths. Ideally, to know which series of tasks will likely determine how long the project will take, it would be nice to be able to press a magic button and see these tasks highlighted.

Projects must be protected from variability to have a projected finish date that is reliable and also that meets top management needs. Traditional project management software does not recognize the need for inserting buffers, so project managers often insert their own buffers manually. This leads to a lot of disparity from one project manager to another. In many organizations, project resources providing estimates to a project also insert their own buffer to protect their part of the project plan.

In the new, simpler world of multi-project management, the software should be inserting buffers consistently and automatically. Many organizations have tried very sophisticated algorithms to determine how much protection a project should have. Most of these are impossible to explain easily and lead to distortions in behavior (e.g., product development knows that it takes three years to bring a new product to market and buffers accordingly when, in fact, there is a year of work and a half year of variability, with the remaining year and a half wasted in multitasking and long decision lead times). A commonly used, statistically valid approach is to take half the length of the critical chain of tasks (those dependent tasks that most likely determine the project's actual duration) and use that as a project buffer.

With minimal hand-holding, the average manager should have a comprehension of all of the above and be able to use the software to plan the first project within a couple of hours.

Buffer Projects Holistically

Where will variability occur within a project? The truth is nobody knows in advance. All that we have are speculations based on the different experiences of people involved in the project planning. In shipbuilding, for example, one of the most difficult trades to recruit is the shipfitter: this is the craft that shapes the rounded metal of the hull. Normally, one could predict difficulty in recruiting enough of these skilled people to build a large ship. However, when the U.S. Navy has a lull in shipbuilding, more of these people are available and therefore variability decreases. When you offer these people premium overtime (more than other shipyards), your recruiting success increases. Can you predict what your competitors will be offering this year? The answer is no! Therefore, in the same way, you can't predict how much variability you will encounter in the recruiting process for shipfitters.

Some tasks will have positive variability (take longer than expected) whereas others should have negative variability (take less time than planned). Trying to protect each task individually, by estimating a little or a lot more time, is comparable to an insurance company having one house in its portfolio. However, if we use the principle of reasonable insurance through aggregation of the risks of many houses, we achieve a reasonable protection for each house by spreading the risk across many houses. When we use the same principle of aggregation to buffer a project, we also get four different benefits of such an approach:

1. Statistics work in our favor. Whereas some tasks may greatly exceed estimates, others will do better than estimated. Overall, it is statistically improbable that the risk for a project will exceed more than 50% of the entire estimated time duration for the entire project.
2. We can plan projects comfortably using aggressive time estimates, knowing that we have protection for the overall project. In our experience, by changing normal project time estimates, which today include the effects of multitasking and insufficient support systems, to aggressive estimates, the overall time saving, even when adding back a 50% buffer, is greater. Therefore, the overall project duration is much shorter than before.

3. By planning aggressive times, managers are encouraged to stop the practice of multitasking resources. There is no way they have a chance of meeting estimated times if they continue the bad practices of the past.
4. Project durations are reduced, which in turn reduces rework due to changing times and changing designs. The organization receives the benefits much sooner.

Software must be able to automatically insert a buffer at the end of a project based on the expected duration of the project. Remember, project durations are governed not just by task dependencies (critical path) but also by resource dependencies (critical chain). Since the determination of the critical chain of a large project with many paths is a mechanical process, as is the calculation of the proper buffer size to insulate the critical chain from variation, this should automatically be done by the software, with little or no manual effort by the user.

View Resource Demands Globally (across All Projects and Portfolios)

In a multi-project environment, each week resources experience some level of variation from the task times that were estimated, which impacts next week's workload. A resource manager must be able to quickly and easily see the planned short-, medium-, and long-term demands on resources, based on current estimated workloads. A project manager must be able to see the availability of resources needed for his/her project to progress. If a resource that was supposed to start on his/her project this week had a delay on another project, the project manager wants to be aware of such impacts. Some senior managers want to check the general pulse of demand across all project resources to ensure that there are no systemic issues blocking several or many resources from progressing.

There are many different ways for software to present these views. However, each organizational role described in the above paragraph must be able to dive deeper into their analysis, based on what they find from the 40,000-foot-level view. For example, the resource manager, seeing an overload in a given week for a given skill set, may want to view the status of the projects that these resources will be working on. Depending on status, and the duration of the overload situation, the resource manager may choose to do nothing. The project manager may want to look at what other tasks will be impacted by a resource arriving late to the project and see if there is any way to make up the time lost. A senior manager may want to look at reasons for delays to determine underlying causes.

Using the iPhone model, software should allow any of these people to click and select other levels of detail to investigate an issue. The user should be able to also detect normality (nothing is wrong and therefore nothing needs attention) within five minutes or less. The same is true for abnormality, including getting to further details.

The key aspect that makes such data useful is the currency of the data. In other words, if the software is easy to use but the data are not kept up-to-date, then the solution is not sufficient to bring major value to the organization. The software must make it easy to update status frequently (e.g., daily). The organization's management must hold task managers accountable for such updates. These topics are addressed in Chapter 42 on execution.

Use a Common Resource Pool Definition

Every manager in the company must be able to plan projects using the same common resource pool definition. A functional manager in marketing may not know who Frank, the senior engineer, is, but knows that a senior engineer is needed to test a new product before it is released in beta form to customers. This implies that not only do we need commonly understood skill set definitions, but we must never use people's names in planning projects.

All that the software must do for everyone is provide the ability to store these resource pool definitions and select from a list. Some users must be given the ability to update the definition list. Since skill set definitions can be unclear, it is also useful for the software to provide an extended definition capability for any resource; for example, the ability to attach notes, an organization chart, or other such additional information needed to provide clarity.

Use and Save Templates

Project management software can save a lot of time by providing the ability to save a project plan as a template. Many projects look alike in terms of tasks, task dependencies, and even the skill sets required. For example, when the corporate IT department rolls out an upgrade of the enterprise resource planning system, the tasks and resources are similar, especially if there are templates for the different subapplications. When marketing rolls out a new product, many of the tasks are alike. When engineering works on developing and testing something new, they can benefit from the framework used during the last development.

Software needs the ability to easily store templates and reuse templates, preferably by different categories such as functional areas, type of project, etc. The principle is the same as with standard word processing software. Tasks, resource skill sets assigned, and task dependencies are part of a template. Generally, time estimates are different for every project and therefore would not be part of a template. The number of resources assigned may also vary greatly from project to project. Often, this depends on the due date of the project and the resource pool capacity at time of project activation. Therefore, the number of resources assigned is generally *not* part of a template.

A template is merely a starting point for a project plan. However, in the best cases, we have seen the planning go from days to hours with the use of templates. The software must make it easy to modify/customize a template to suit the current project plan's needs. Therefore, the ability to insert tasks anywhere in the project, to input estimated times and numbers of resources, and to do *what if* analysis with different parameters are all software requirements.

Work Together on Projects Globally

In almost all of the companies we work with, the people involved in projects are located in different geographic areas. Travel is expensive and time-consuming. Software should mitigate these conditions by allowing people in different locations to construct a project plan working together, viewing the same project plan at the same time. Each person should be able to add tasks or dependencies, with everyone seeing the immediate results.

This software architecture has to house the project data somewhere that is accessible to all involved in the project plan development. It must give program access to all parties, no matter where they are located or what interface they are using. Today's cloud-based architecture fulfills these requirements. The old style of collaboration forced organizations to buy expensive copies of software and predetermine on what physical computers those copies were installed. The client-server environment made this a little easier, but still often required client software to be physically installed, although at a lower cost per client and with fewer restrictions. Cloud architecture is more like the iPhone model. For a few dollars or potentially for no additional cost, project participants can begin accessing the software and collaborating almost immediately.

Align and Gate Projects

We accept as a fact of life that every organization has limited capacity to execute projects. Rarely do we encounter executives who do not accept that the multi-project system is overloaded. Although it is only an assumption that the system is overloaded, software can easily help an organization test the assumption by providing an alignment and project gating mechanism. If the system is overloaded and we align project work to have much less project work active than is currently the case, within days to weeks we will see the projects moving much faster and should quickly be meeting or beating expectations. If the system is not overloaded, but we believe it is and align project work accordingly, fewer tasks in progress means more resources assigned to existing tasks. The tasks still move faster and projects get completed earlier.

We know of two major ways to align a collection of projects:

1. By the spacing of projects according to the capacity of a resource pool. This should only be done with one resource pool per portfolio. Assume that the resource pool that is currently most multitasked or most in demand across all projects is, for example, IT architects. Assume that we have nine of them, and the most we can assign to any single project is three. That would give us a range of three to nine active projects, depending on how we assign them.
2. By the spacing of projects according to a phased approach. For example, assume that the most critical phase of all projects our organization does is the integration phase at the end of a long product development cycle. In the integration phase, we must have certain resources from engineering design (mechanical and electrical), overall design, development, and testing. Some of these same resources are the only resources available for all other project integration phases, as well as other phases of projects. We set a rule: no more than two projects can be active in integration at any time. This becomes our mechanism for alignment of multiple projects. Further, the integration phase has priority over all other phases when all previous paths have been completed.

Software must provide a simple, straightforward way to align projects according to either of these criteria, with *what if* capability to test different resource allocations and number of active projects and quickly see the effects. To do this, the software must allow the person responsible for controlling the multi-project environment to define the alignment mechanism.

A gating ability in software requires the capability to put projects into the system without activating them. Further, the software must put the security and control of gating into one person's hands, so that multiple projects are not activated unless intended.

Although such alignment and gating functions are mandatory for the overall system, managers should have the ability to create and activate projects that are small and contained within a single functional area, provided that they do not block the organization's major projects from progressing. This implies that the same software is scalable in both features and numbers of users across an organization.

Organize Projects into Portfolios

In large organizations, there is often a need to view different collections of projects. For example, in a tobacco company operating globally, there are corporate projects that often affect or require projects to be completed in different countries. Each country has its own improvement projects, some for operations (plants) and others for marketing and sales. Other functional areas, such as marketing/product management, have global brand responsibility, with improvement projects for their brands. Some of those improvement projects are on the cost side, requiring changes in each plant's operations. Some are on the marketing or sales or supply chain side.

The software needs the ability to group projects into different portfolio collections, so that each of the above views is easily seen. The person responsible for a corporate initiative that requires changes worldwide wants to see that status of all subprojects for the initiative(s) by region and all together. Similar views are needed by country, by region, and by functional area. As noted previously, the ability to dive into greater detail to identify the source of any problems is also critical.

Conclusions

Software can be a great facilitator for bringing a multi-project management culture to an organization. To do so, it first must be easy to use, or the organization will have an insurmountable job trying to collect project plans and execution data. It must make it easy for people to collaborate on all aspects of projects, from initial learning through use of common resource definitions, through development of project plans.

Older generations of project management software were not designed for the masses. In fact, for a long time, project management software has been used by relatively few people in organizations and often only those with IT, engineering, or other highly technical skills. This must change if an organization wants to get to the next level in moving projects much faster.

Although this chapter does not delve into the detail of specifications, it outlines what we have seen in software used in the fastest implementations of drastic change in multi-project management. With a little help and hand-holding, and the right software, an organization can finally embed project management skills into all managers within a couple of hours. They can move from *to-do* lists which never get done or take much longer to accomplish to rapid multi-project completions. They can move from narrow local views to global collaboration. To do this, beware of software sophistication. This is what exists today, and although it may have helped us get to where we are, at the same time, it is blocking us from moving to the next level of performance.

Questions

41-1. When you compare the number of iPhone application users and the number of, for example, word processing users in an organization with the number of project management software users, how do you explain that there is typically such a small number of project management software users?

41-2. Why is it vital for project management software to be learnable within two hours?

41-3. Since many project tasks do not execute as planned (i.e., in the same estimated time frame or within the same dates), what is the value of software providing a resource management view across all projects?

41-4. What data does a project template contain, and what data should it not contain?

41-5. What are the two ways of aligning projects within a multi-project management system? Given these two ways, is it better to align by portfolio of projects or across all portfolios?

41-6. Today, even if project management software does not have *cloud*-like capabilities, people can collaborate in planning projects by using web-based meeting facilities. What is the difference between that mode of collaboration and the description of *cloud*-like facilities?

41-7. Why is portfolio management capability helpful in project management software? Based on your answer, for what type(s) of organization would it be mandatory?

42. Software Execution Requirements—Buffer Penetration, Project, and Resource Trends

The Premise

The tsunami that hit Japan in 2011 caused meltdowns at three reactors in the Fukushima Daiichi Nuclear Power Plant complex, and the associated evacuation affected hundreds of thousands of residents. No one had time to read the thousands of pages of power plant operating procedures. Even if the disaster had happened in very slow motion, the manuals still wouldn't have helped. History simply did not illuminate how to deal with such an event.

When project execution starts to go astray, it is like the beginning of a tsunami. When the earthquake hits, don't run to get the *PMBOK® Guide*—it's too late for that! The earthquake has struck, and your software signals must be swift to recognize the problem and very visual in providing the warning. Adjustments in priorities may need to be made to more than one project task.

Most of the organizations we have worked with have out-of-date project execution data. Either projects are not tracked formally during execution (i.e., not updated frequently against a plan) or the execution data are at least several days to several weeks old. How much good would it do you to know that the tsunami happened several days ago and the nuclear meltdown occurred next door to your home last week? Oh, but you claim projects are different. NO, they are not!

Project resources are much too precious to waste for days or weeks without being aware of an issue. Human behaviors are much too latent when it comes to projects. The chain of cause and effect from not dealing quickly with a project earthquake can be enormous. For example, on Monday the purchasing manager decided that since the order entry system was being revised, this was the perfect opportunity to squeeze in the new procurement and inventory management changes that he had already discussed with the IT department. By Tuesday, the IT architect, who was already overdue with design work for three other projects, was spending her time drafting a rough design for the purchasing manager in order to provide a revised estimate for the order entry project. The requirements were complicated, and it took her through Thursday afternoon before she could let everyone know that this project would take six weeks longer than originally planned. The new products, which needed to be available to the order entry system, could not be released for six additional weeks, at a cost of $200,000 to the company and a disastrous reputation with customers. By the following Monday, when the project manager did the weekly review, there were 12 resources already working on the revised order entry/purchasing system to accommodate the major changes that had never been approved by top management.

Can you think of one good reason why you would want to allow such a bad situation to linger for days or weeks without intervening? We are astounded when we talk with managers who claim that updating execution data on projects once a week is good enough or that they don't need formal project tracking—they have *regular* review meetings with their resources. The problem is not simply the bad practice of infrequent updating—it is just as likely to be complex software updating and reporting mechanisms that block daily updates.

To be effective, software needs just a few execution capabilities:

- Ability to recognize an earthquake and impending tsunami
- Visual management
- Constantly updated resource assignments and trends
- Single, up-to-date, task priority system reflecting daily changes

This chapter provides an overview of these software capabilities and how they are used today in organizations worldwide.

Recognizing Earthquakes and Impending Tsunamis

Here are the six loud signals the software must warn about:

1. *Sudden scope creep.* Yesterday, the system architect predicted four days left to finish the design task. Today, after working on the task for a day, the prediction is 10 days left to finish the task. There may be reasons other than scope creep for the execution issue, as outlined below. However, if it is scope creep, then senior management must curtail it immediately, or it will fester and continue to push the project off track. Alternatively, senior management must accept freezing the project and rescheduling it, since the assumptions under which it was planned and synchronized originally are no longer valid.

2. *Unexpected and damaging variability.* The first tremors of the earthquake show up as task completion estimations that are longer than planned. However, the trend of time left to complete the task gets worse and worse, as the resources learn more and more about the task and the difficulties they are facing. Software gives an early warning, but reviews by task managers determine whether the variability is abnormal or not.
3. *Bad multitasking of resources.* The software must make it easy to discover that the same resources are assigned to multiple tasks/projects at the same time. Another way of discovering the tremors is by looking for tasks that are assigned before they need to start. In the past, starting a project task early was mistakenly thought to be a good thing, allowing a head start on the work. In reality, it is proven to be generally a very bad practice since it leads to multitasking of resources, causing tasks to take much longer than planned and priorities to be masked and unclear. It also leads to rework, since tasks started much earlier than necessary are often subject to task definition changes resulting from learning from completion of other tasks.
4. *Buffer consumption at a faster rate than project completion.* If the safety allocated to a project is being eaten away at a faster rate than critical tasks are being completed, a tsunami will occur soon. This is analogous to a company, government, or family spending money at a faster rate than money is being earned.
5. *Increasingly late starts on tasks.* When a software trend shows more and more tasks are starting later than planned, there is a cascade effect going on. It's only a matter of time before the tsunami hits shore.
6. *Frequent priority changes.* If resources must be frequently moved or pulled off tasks that have already been started, it is a sign that the entire system is out of control.

Visual Management

For the single project, the relationship between critical work completed and buffer used during that timescale tells a compelling story. In this weekly report in Figure 42.1, you can see that after the first week, for two time periods, it appeared that no progress was made. This could be scope creep (e.g., last week there were 10 days to complete the task, but after working on it for five days there are still 10 days of work left to complete the task), or the same reporting could be due to variability or the resource being unavailable. While this visual

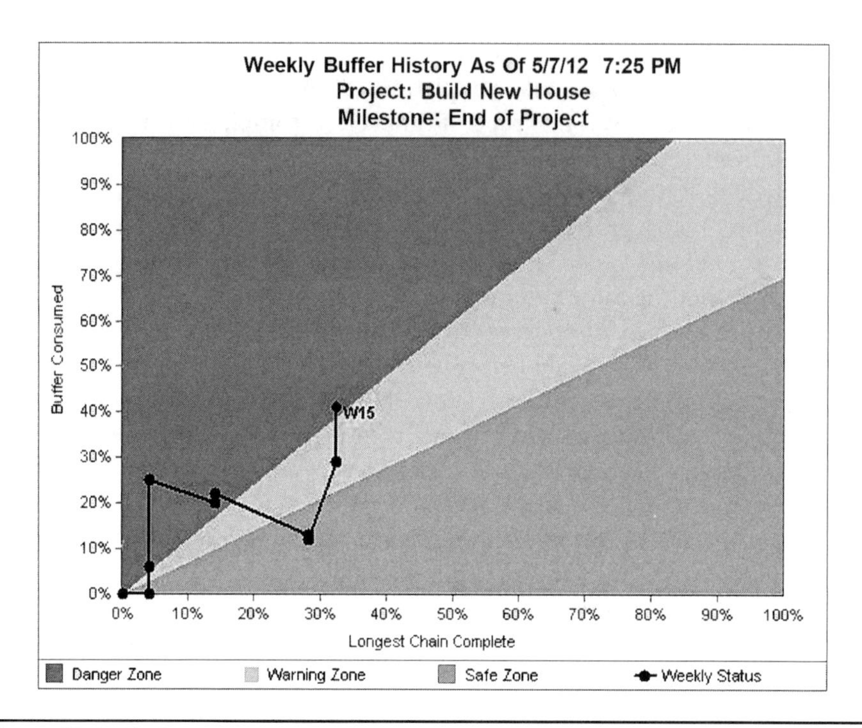

Figure 42.1 Project progress trend

does not tell the entire story, it at least highlights when there is a problem and shows trends over time.

On which tasks should the project manager focus? Out of all the tasks in the project plan, at any point in time, there are only a few that are currently penetrating buffers. Visually, the project manager should be able to find those within seconds. Look back at Table 32.1 for an example.

Pictures are telltale for time-phased resource loading. These pictures, such as the one in Figure 32.1, should be provided for all resources. Based on the picture, a resource manager must be able to drill down to determine which projects are most in jeopardy.

At a glance, we want to see the status of all projects in execution, as in the example in Figure 42.2. For those that are in a red zone or at risk, we want to be able to dive more deeply into each project, as shown in the single project view. When too many projects are in a green zone and remain in that zone through multiple reporting periods, it shows that planning was not aggressive enough. We expect some projects to be in the red or yellow zones from time to time.

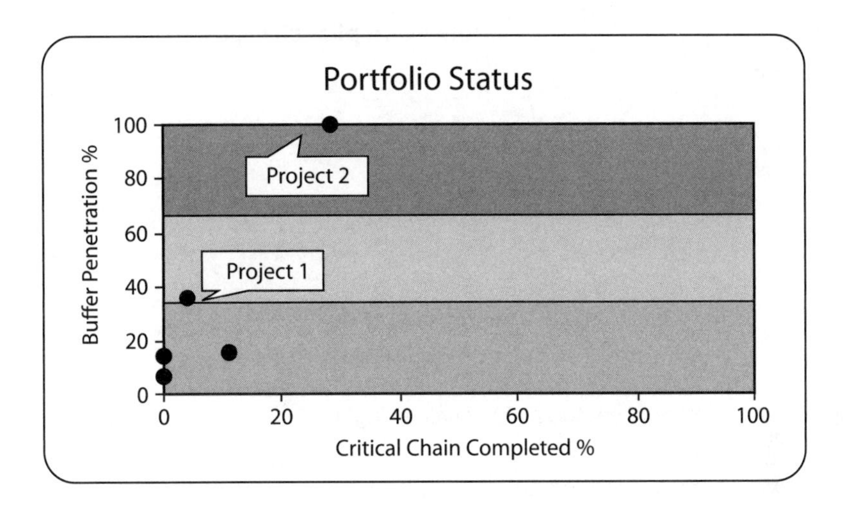

Figure 42.2 Portfolio status of all projects

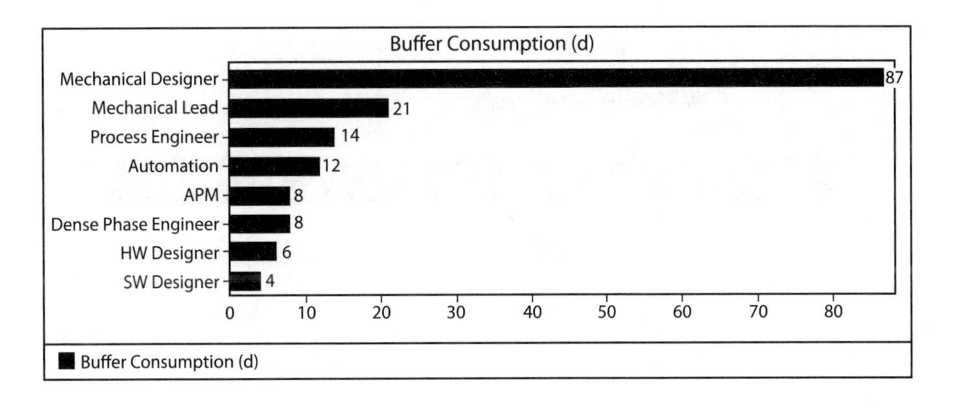

Figure 42.3 Buffer consumption

When a project is consuming buffer at an alarming rate, for which resource are we typically waiting? Having this information at a glance (see Figure 42.3) tells the resource manager where either more resources need to be hired or better coaching or task definition is required.

Is the organization starting tasks too early? The indicator in Figure 42.4 shows the number of tasks started before the planned start date. While it's OK to

Figure 42.4 Starting work too early (multitasking?)

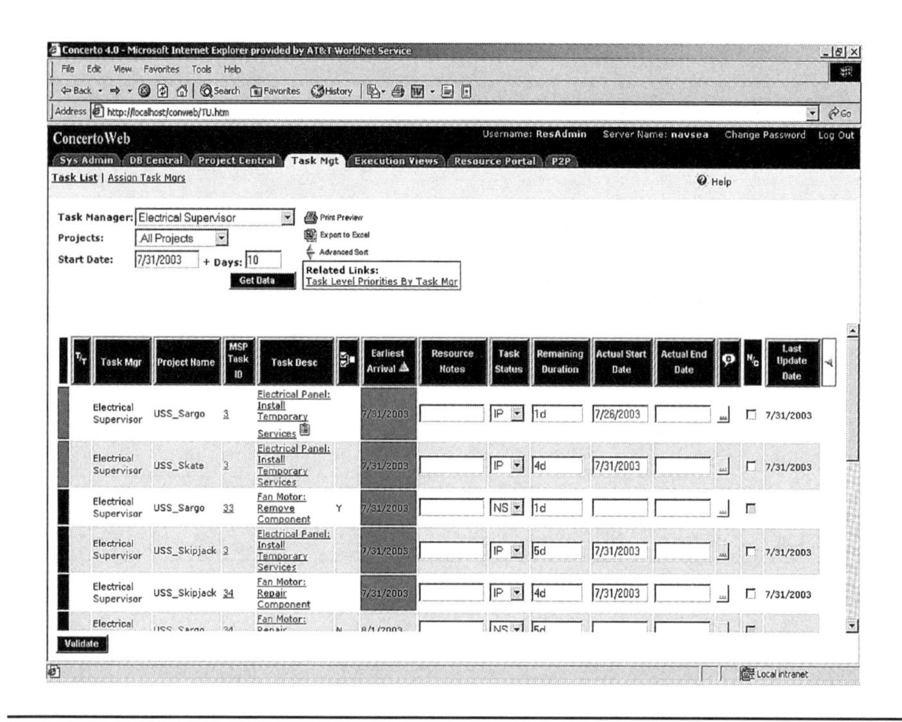

Figure 42.5 When are tasks available to start?

start a few tasks a little earlier than planned, this chart, in a few seconds, shows a trend over time.

A resource manager would want to see when the earliest availability of a task is likely to be, based on current progress on prior tasks. For easy reporting, he/

she would want to have one column to fill in for each task with the number of days predicted to finish the task (see example in Figure 42.5).

Note: By showing only a few very critical examples of visual management, we are not implying that this is all that you want a software package to provide for execution. We do not believe that showing you 100 pages of screen shots would be very helpful. The key is that the software visual aids must allow you to quickly detect earthquakes and tsunamis, find out where they are coming from, and give you the supporting data to determine likely impact and repercussions of any actions you take.

Diagrams such as Gantt and PERT charts are common to all project management software. We have focused instead on those visual aids to manage multi-project execution from the perspective of different roles and responsibilities.

Constantly Updated Resource Assignments and Trends

If we depend too much on individual skill sets, rather than the capabilities of an entire pool of people, we tend to get into trouble, frequently without a logical way of recovering. Over the past two decades, complexity in most organizations has grown exponentially. Departments have had to learn new skills, new software, and new products, while still maintaining support and knowledge for all of the old skills, software, and products. With the practice of having too many projects active within the organization, resource managers tended to have specialists rather than generalists. They generally failed to cross-train people to develop a broader array of duplicated skill sets. We often hear resource managers say, "We don't have the time to cross-train."

Therefore, when a project has a task that needs to be worked on now and a certain skill set (say systems engineer) is needed, the resource manager often cannot use any available resource (e.g., only Joe can do this work). This, in turn, leads to organizations and resource managers trying to use project management software as a personnel scheduling system, with individual calendars, modeling of many non-project tasks such as training, etc.

From our experience, this is entirely counterproductive. Project management software should allow an organization to look at its ocean of projects, quickly spot tsunamis, and prevent damage. The software serves the main purpose of facilitating project flow, keeping things moving quickly toward a successful conclusion across the entire portfolio of projects.

These observations do not negate the need for a staff scheduling system if a resource manager has too many things to keep track of with individuals. Our strong recommendation is that you do this outside of the project management system. The only calendaring that we believe is important in project management software is that which is appropriate to an entire department or organization.

Therefore, the software must make it easy to update assignments at a resource pool level and to report on the pool utilizations and trends. Examples are provided above in the visual management section. When assigning a resource to a task within the project management software, you want to show that you've taken a marketing subject matter expert out of the pool, not that you've taken a specific person out of the pool. When you look at a resource utilization trend, you want it to be for that pool of resources, not for individuals. While this is as much a function of how you use the software as opposed to the software capabilities, the ease of updating the software often drives how much it is used.

One Task Priority System with Daily Updates

Resource managers must be able to view current and upcoming tasks across all projects. Generally, to avoid multitasking we should not stop a task once it is started. The exception is when the same resource is needed for another task for a project that is in deep trouble, and then only if there is no other alternative.

For tasks that are available to be assigned, the task priority should be shown by the software and calculated by the associated project's status. Red project tasks must be done before yellow and those before green. If there are two red tasks available for the same resource pool and only one resource to assign, the two tasks should be prioritized according to the level of buffer penetration. If the system is working correctly, rarely should any resource manager feel the need to override what the software is showing as a priority.

If the task status is updated daily, with the number of days left to finish the task, then the system can take this information and recalculate priorities based on the very latest task updates. We do not claim that the system can be run by robots. However, the energy of management should be put on the value-added work of project managing—how to flow work faster through the system, how to recover when Murphy strikes a really bad blow, and how to recruit better and better people.

The software must provide the ability to assign a resource to a task at the time the task becomes available. Resource managers should always be thinking about the maximum number of resources that they can assign to a task to impact the speed at which the task gets done. Therefore, it is really helpful if the software can show all of the tasks available to be worked on for a given resource pool, the status of each task, and the available resources this week.

Conclusions

To facilitate good multi-project execution practices, software must make it easy for different people with different responsibilities to understand what is going on. Resource managers must know, within seconds, what tasks are in trouble, what tasks are available to assign, what resources are available, and any short- or long-term congestion. Project managers must be able to see, at a glance, if their project is in trouble and if so, what task(s) is holding up the project right now. Program managers and functional and senior managers must be able to see the relevant portfolio of projects, with summary status of each project, and dive down for greater detail.

While meaningful, easy-to-understand visual display is extremely important, the display is truly meaningful if the data are current. Even week-old data can mask a huge problem or show a project status as bad when, in fact, recovery actions have already been taken and are working.

Finally, good software facilitates a single priority system during execution. The software makes it easy to assign the right tasks. It should show clearly what the basis is for resource assignment, even though a project manager may not like it. As long as there is a single priority system based on and designed around getting ALL projects completed on time, it will make sense to all parties involved. The priority system should facilitate faster flow of project work by preventing the constant juggling of priorities and resources through bad multitasking.

Questions

42-1. Who are the key users of multi-project software during execution?

42-2. Give two examples of questions each type of user might have during project execution and what the software would need to provide to answer those questions.

42-3. How is visual management different from traditional project reporting?

42-4. One multi-project organization has 37 projects active, with an average of 200 tasks for each project. Projects span 20 weeks in average duration. There are 25 resource pools and each has an average share of the project work. If you were a manager of one resource pool, how many of those tasks would you expect to look at in any given week, in order to update work being done and prepare for upcoming tasks?

42-5. How should a software package prioritize the project tasks across all projects?

42-6. How might project management software show scope creep or variability during execution in a Gantt chart? Based on your answer, do you think that a Gantt chart is useful for quickly grasping these kinds of issues?

42-7. What makes multi-project management software valuable to an organization during execution?

43. Role-Based Software Views

The Premise

We strongly believe that software should enable, not enslave! Whereas Chapter 42 focused on the few execution capabilities effective software must have, this chapter focuses on what the effective software should present in order to enable the senior managers, project managers, and resource managers to more easily perform their multi-project management roles. Some illustrations are repeated here, but now in the context of these roles.

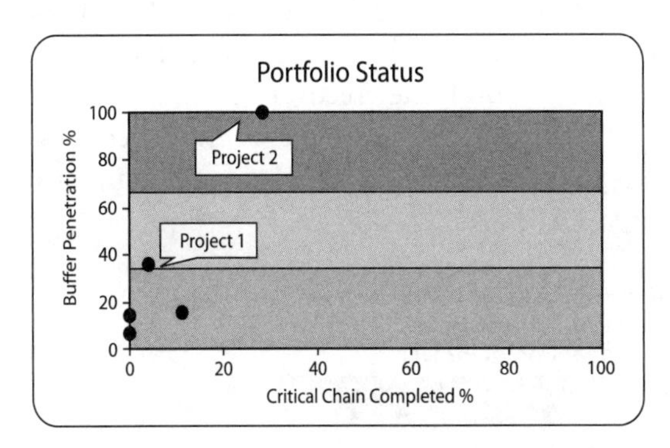

Figure 43.1 Portfolio status

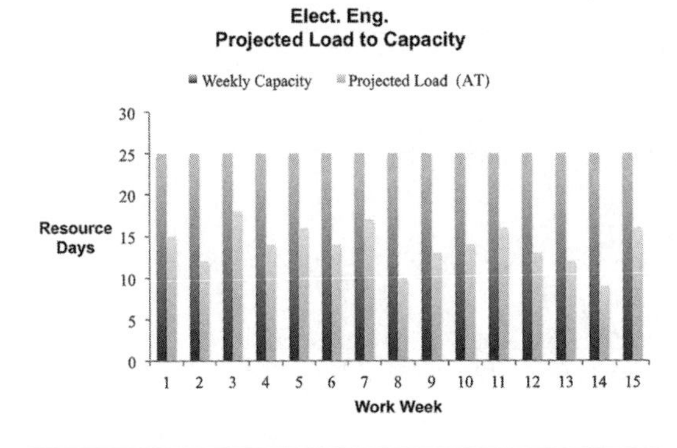

Figure 43.2 Resource load

Senior Managers

As you've seen in earlier chapters, senior managers are concerned about the overall status of the organization's projects. They need to see how they are progressing in context (see Figure 43.1). It should be apparent to them which (if any) projects are currently in jeopardy so they know which project managers should be intervening in their projects and which should not! Fast-track issue resolution meeting notes should be easily available along with portfolio data. Senior managers also have an interest in looking ahead at the workload—whether or not resource overloads are looming (see Figure 43.2).

Figure 43.3 Measure of compliance to rule of not releasing tasks early

Finally, since senior managers are the sponsors of the multi-project management system, they need to understand how well the processes are being institutionalized. Visuals on rules compliance (see Figure 43.3) can indicate where coaching, mentoring, and/or retraining may be needed.

Project Managers

Project managers need to have a daily understanding of the status of their project(s) as well as developing trends in terms of percent critical tasks completes versus percent project (or contractual milestone) buffer consumed (see Figure 43.4). They need drill down access to which chain of tasks is causing the most penetration into the project buffer to be aware of the need to do buffer recovery planning. Notes from task updates are essential for keeping the project manager informed. The capability to attach or link documents to the system enables planning documents,

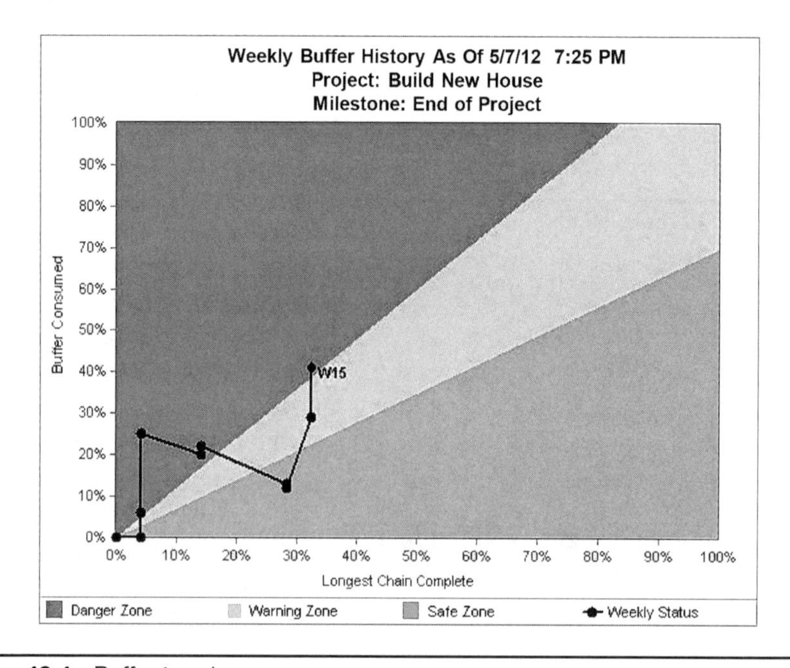

Figure 43.4 Buffer trend

Table 43.1 Prioritized task availability list (AT = ambitious time)

Project	Task	Resource Skill	Quantity Required	Avail. to Start	AT	Project Buffer Penetration
J57-16	Test 1734	Elec. Eng.	1	Today	9d	59%
K45-87	Circuit 35	Elec. Eng.	1	Today	6d	53%
P34-12	Circuit 23	Elec. Eng.	1	Today	7d	39%
X23-78	Test 1221	Elec. Eng.	1	Today	4d	27%
A92-03	Circuit 35	Elec. Eng.	1	Today	6d	21%
G65-76	Circuit 57	Elec. Eng.	1	Today + 4	5d	55%
P34-12	Test 1734	Elec. Eng.	1	Today + 4	9d	39%
A92-03	Test 1734	Elec. Eng.	1	Today + 7	9d	21%

duration reduction assumptions, buffer recovery planning, and fast-track issue resolution minutes to be immediately available.

Resource Managers

Resource managers need access to correctly sorted and easy-to-read prioritized task availability lists (see Table 43.1); it's useful if the look-ahead horizon is changeable.

It's important for resource managers to know which resources have tasks waiting on them the most, when buffers are red (see Figure 43.5).

Resource histograms are the only way to view upcoming overloads of resources (see Figure 43.2).

For task updating, resource managers need one easy-to-use screen to mark tasks in progress, identify by name the resources assigned, perform end-of-day updates of the days remaining on a task, capture significant notes about delays or problems, progress, and mark a task complete (see Figure 43.6).

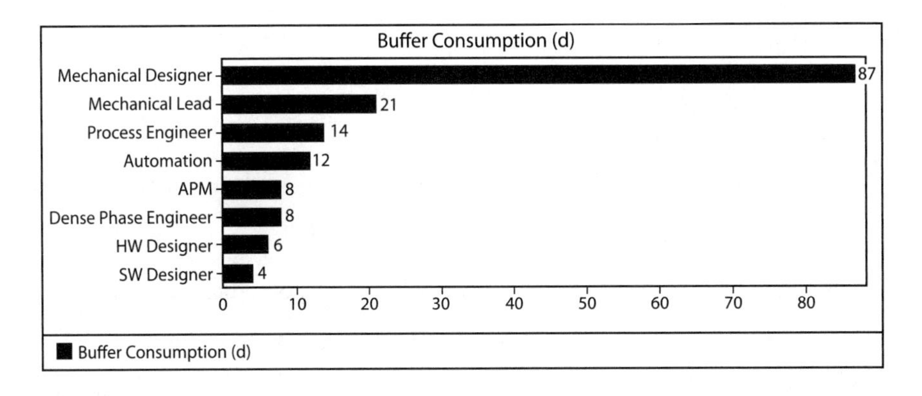

Figure 43.5 Reasons for buffer consumption—which resource is the task waiting for?

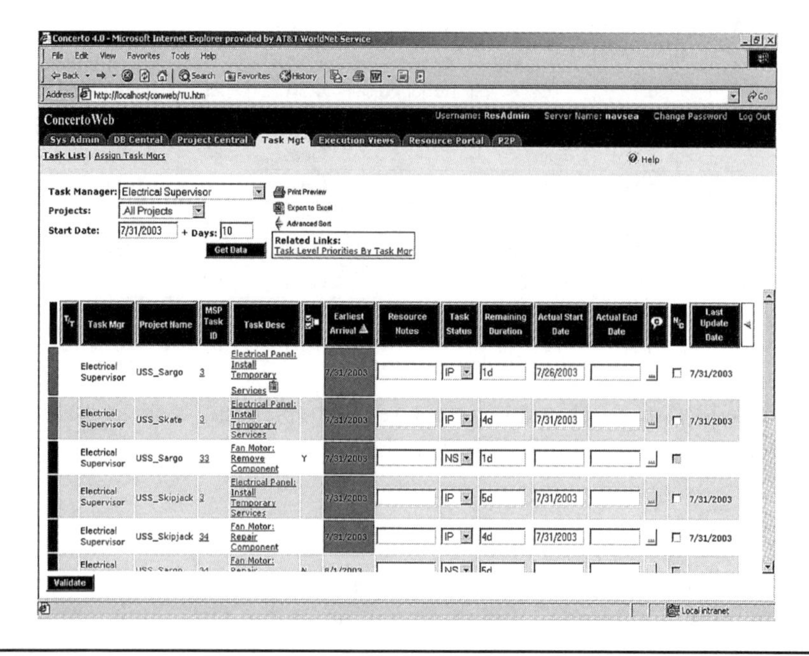

Figure 43.6 Easy task updating

Conclusions

Screens and associated information (project notes, fast-track issue resolution meeting minutes, etc.) customized for senior managers, project managers, and resource managers enable them to perform their multi-project management roles more effectively. Good software makes it much easier for these people to do their project management work.

Questions

43-1. How can software enable those in management to more effectively perform their roles?

43-2. Why not provide all information to all managers on one or two screens?

43-3. What are two key areas where software can help senior managers?

43-4. Why provide visual displays—wouldn't tables of data be better?

43-5. List three areas where software can help project managers.

43-6. Why do resource managers need access to multi-project management software?

PART IX

EXECUTIVE BUY-IN AND CONCLUSIONS

Executives must lead the transformation of the multi-project environment from slow to rapid, from unpredictable to superb, and from inadequate to prolific. Some of the changes described within this text can be made at a tactical level with measurable progress. The real gains are driven strategically, as an absolutely key part of meeting the organization's major goals, now and in the future.

Part IX illustrates some buy-in tools and offers final conclusions on the entire text.

44. Executive Buy-In and Simulations

The Premise

It is difficult, if not impossible, to implement the six *gears of change* that drive the multi-project solution without having senior management buy into the methodology. Without the buy-in, the established paradigms, processes, and measures will continue to operate—in opposition to and overriding the required changes highlighted in the previous chapters.

So many have tried for so long and so hard to make needed changes—the frustration level is extremely high. After these experiences, it's no wonder that no one wants to be known as the evangelist for something that can't possibly succeed! We've seen senior leadership view the six elements almost as a buffet line: "I'll take this one and that one, but not those over there." Hopefully, by now, you are convinced that would be a waste of time and effort. The predictable failure to get results from cherry-picking pieces of the solution will further decrease its credibility. That is the real-life experience we have observed of those choosing the *buffet line* approach to multi-project environments.

In our experience, there is an extremely powerful process for buy-in that when followed generates significant senior management support for the paradigm shift. This chapter introduces you to that process, along with two group activities to aid you. Several of the files used to obtain buy-in are provided as Web Added Value™ files, available as downloads at www.jrosspub.com/wav.

Buy-In Process[1]

Buying into and ultimately approving and leading a major organizational change does not happen instantly. It has taken you most of the book to understand all that is involved! Senior management must be convinced that this change will move the organization to better and more quickly accomplish its goals. Rather than using the traditional "how wonderful this latest approach is" style of buy-in, we recommend overcoming senior management's five layers of resistance to change in sequence as follows:

1. *Getting senior management agreement with at least one of the three root causes to the problems experienced in multi-project management.* Everyone is used to trying to resolve the symptoms of the problems they face in a multi-project environment. Executives have already seen that when the underlying root causes are not resolved, the symptoms just keep coming back.
2. *Getting senior management agreement on the criteria of a good solution.* You must help them understand the primary engines of successful multi-project management. You must also facilitate their acceptance that all six elements are required to be successful.
3. *Getting senior management agreement that implementing the change will solve the root causes.* They must be able to see that results can come quickly—as early as three months into the implementation, and that the results will continue to grow.
4. *Addressing senior management's concerns about major negative ramifications of the solution*—particularly the possible negatives of freezing some projects for a short time.
5. *Getting senior management's complete support to help overcome implementation obstacles.* Senior leadership's stamp of approval for instituting a change is required, but so is a commitment to help remove any obstacles to putting the new system in place.

Getting Started

What we need is agreement from senior leadership on at least one of the three root causes for the problems they (and we) experience in the multi-project environment. Recall the three root causes (from Chapter 1):

- Project plans incorrectly account for variation (with poorly defined networks and without correct buffers).
- Too much project work is active in execution (beyond the organization's capacity to flow it quickly).
- Project tasks suffer poor execution (through excessive multitasking, conflicting priorities, and long wait times to resolve issues).

Our experience with senior managers is that hands-on exercises are an overwhelmingly better way to enable them to really acknowledge, understand, and agree on the problem than long, boring presentations. Our exercises address root causes 2 and 3 and enable a discussion about root cause 1.

Root Cause—Too Much Project Work Is Active in Execution

Use the Multi-Project Mancala exercise. The purpose is to compare the difference in projects completed and revenue generated when releasing projects as soon as they are won versus tying the release of projects to the organization's capacity to perform projects.

In this simulation, there is a board (see Figure 44.1) with 13 positions at the top. The largest position on the far left is for projects ready for release (ideas). Another large position on the far right is for finished projects. Positions 1–11 are for the months of the year. Flow of projects (designated by coins, wrapped candy, poker chips, etc.) is from the ideas stage through months of execution 1 through 11 until they are done, which represents the 12th month of work and the end of the year.

Each project requires 12 person-months of work. One project is released at a time from the idea position, progressing through each position until it is complete. There are six resources available to work the projects released at any time.

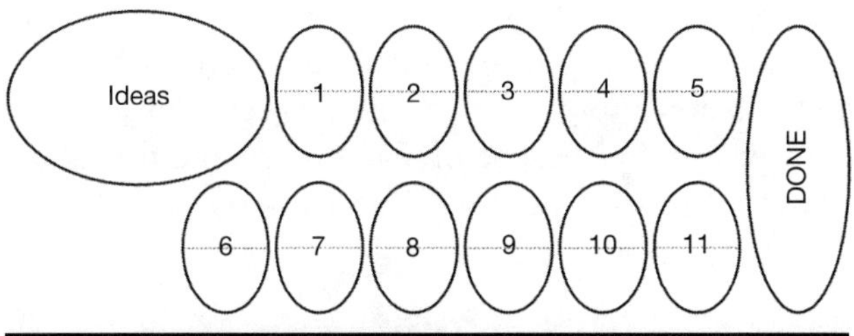

Month	Move	Month	Move
1	6	1	6
2	3	2	3
3	2	3	3
4	1.5	4	3
5	1.5	5	3
6	1	6	3
7	1	7	3
8	1	8	3
9	.5	9	3
10	.5	10	3
11	.5	11	3
12	.5	12	3

Figure 44.1 Multi-Project Mancala simulation board

Resource managers are forced to allocate resources evenly across projects. The table below the positions indicates how the resources are deployed to work projects. There will be two runs; the left two columns of the table are for the first run and the right two columns are for the second run.

Our experience is that most senior managers prefer the hands-on exercise. If your senior managers are not in that category, you can run the simulation by having *players* make the moves and letting the senior managers observe the effect.

Simulation 1—Too Much Project Work in Process

To run the first simulation, in month 1 all six resources are able to work the first project (Project A), so it progresses to position 6. In month 2, when Project B is released, the six resources have to split their time evenly on all active projects (since all project managers are screaming to see progress), so it's three resources for each project, meaning Project A moves from position 6 to position 9 and Project B moves to position 3 (see Figure 44.2).

During month 3, another project (Project C) is released, so the resources are spread even thinner. Now it is two resources per project. The result, as shown in Figure 44.3, is that Project A advances from position 9 to position 11, Project B advances from position 3 to position 5, and Project C advances to position 2.

As soon as any project finishes, be prepared to fill out the financial data (see Table 44.1), allowing $100,000 per month starting the month after the project completes.

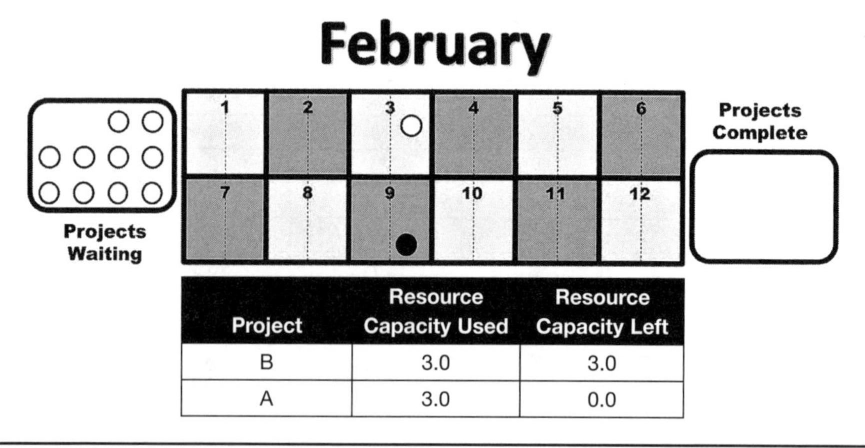

Project	Resource Capacity Used	Resource Capacity Left
B	3.0	3.0
A	3.0	0.0

Figure 44.2 Status as of the end of month 2

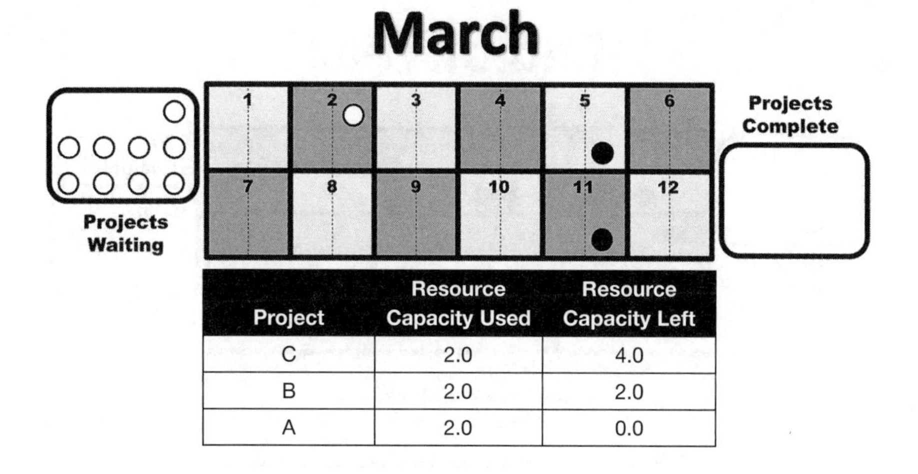

Project	Resource Capacity Used	Resource Capacity Left
C	2.0	4.0
B	2.0	2.0
A	2.0	0.0

Figure 44.3 Status as of the end of month 3

Table 44.1 Multi-Project Mancala simulation financial tracking

Beginning the month after a project delivers, each project returns $100,000 per month for the remainder of that year

Projects	Month										Total
	3	4	5	6	7	8	9	10	11	12	
1											
2											
3											
4											
5											
6											
Total Value $											

Projects	Month										Total
	3	4	5	6	7	8	9	10	11	12	
1											
2											
3											
4											
5											
6											
Total Value $											

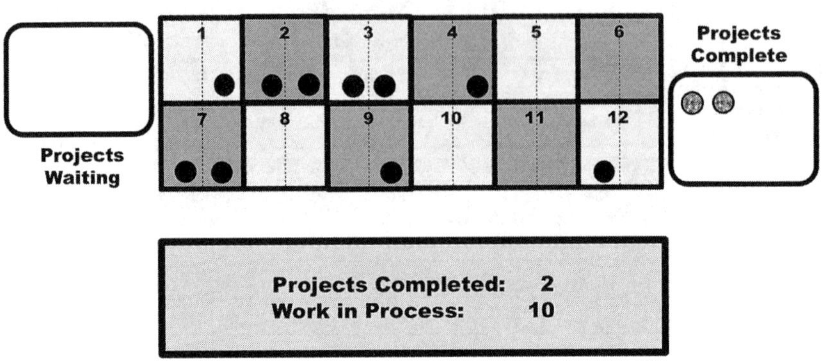

Figure 44.4 Status as of the end of month 12

The process continues month after month, with the number of resources available per project dropping as additional projects are released (see the table at the bottom of Figure 44.1 on page 355). By the end of the year (month 12), the status is as shown in Figure 44.4.

In spite of all of the investment in the projects, only two projects completed. Senior management also sees the weak financial performance. By tracking when the organization starts seeing money coming in from released projects (using the financial tracking chart in Table 44.1), senior management sees that project investments keep increasing and the wait is longer and longer for the financial return.

Simulation 2—Controlling the Amount of Project Work

In the second run, a new rule is in place to align the release of projects with the organization's capacity to quickly flow projects to completion: No more than two projects are allowed to be active at a time. When one of the two projects finishes, a new project can be released.

In month 1, one project (Project A) is released, is able to use all six resources, and progresses to position 6. In month 2, one project (Project B) is released; each project now has three resources, so Project A advances to position 9 and Project B advances to position 3.

Beginning in month 3, we see a huge change from simulation 1 because of the new synchronization rule. That means each project will always have at least three resources available. Figure 44.5 shows the end of month 3. Since the first project released has now finished, the *player* may claim nine months of revenue from that project on the financial tracking sheet.

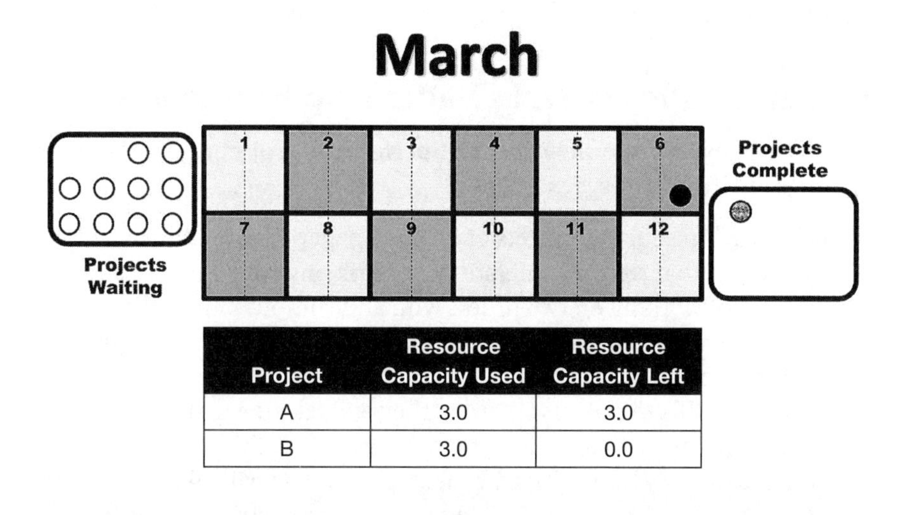

Project	Resource Capacity Used	Resource Capacity Left
A	3.0	3.0
B	3.0	0.0

Figure 44.5 Status as of the end of month 3 when synchronized on only two projects active at a time

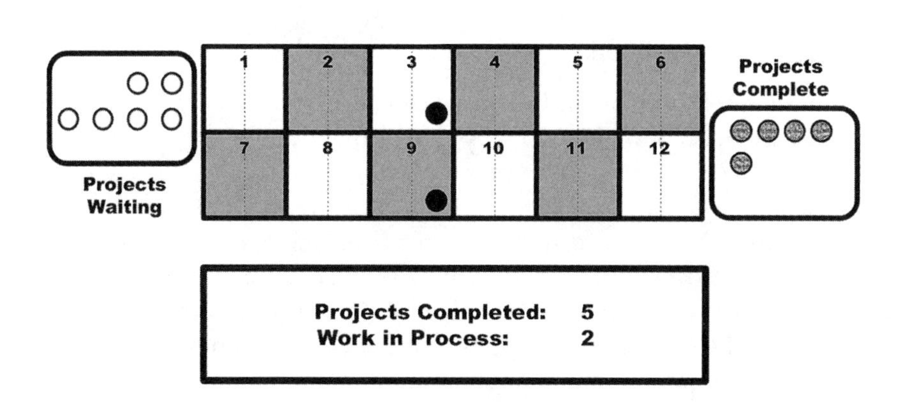

Figure 44.6 Year-end status when synchronized on only two projects active at a time

As the table below the game board in Figure 44.5 indicates, each project (A and B) has three resources assigned to each active project every month for the remainder of the one year simulation. The contrasting results (from simulation 1) at the end of the year are illustrated in Figure 44.6.

Filling out the financial tracking sheet for simulation 2 helps to point out how much earlier the organization sees the benefits and the quantity of benefits in one approach versus the other.

Root Cause—Project Tasks Suffer Poor Execution

In this exercise, have senior management perform as project resources required to multitask. Instructions are as follows:

1. Give each person two sheets of 8.5 × 11 paper of two different colors.
2. Tell them that we will simulate their work environment to examine the impact of working on two orders with and without multitasking. We will measure both time duration to complete both orders and quality (we will describe how in a minute).
3. Tell them that to process an order, they will take the first colored sheet of paper and make five vertical tears of approximately the same width, giving six strips (demonstrate for them). Then they will take each of the six strips and make four tears, giving five pieces per strip. For the first sheet, that would make a count of 30 if they did this perfectly (quality perfect). Follow a similar process for the second sheet, but make six vertical tears, giving seven strips. Take each of the seven strips and make five tears, giving six pieces per strip. Perfect quality would mean a count of 42 on the second sheet.

Simulation 1—Multitasking

Start a clock, preferably on an LCD projector so participants can see the time. Simulate the effects of multitasking by having them do four operations (tears) on one color sheet, then switch to four operations on the other color sheet, and switch back and forth every four tears between the two tasks until finished. Make sure that they don't tear multiple strips in one operation. Ask them to yell out their time when finished and have a recorder note the time. When they are finished, have them count the number of pieces in each order. Both orders correct = two check marks for quality, one order correct = one check mark, and neither order correct = no check marks.

For scorekeeping, use a three-column matrix as shown in Table 44.2. In the middle column, record the number of people finished in each time interval

Table 44.2 Multitasking tracking sheet

Time	First Exercise	Second Exercise
1:00		
1:15		
1:30		
1:45		
2:00		
2:15		
2:30		
2:45		
3:00		

for this exercise, and use the last column for the number of people finished in that time interval for the second exercise (no multitasking). The time intervals should start at one minute and progress in 15-second intervals.

Also record quality count and the participants know the quality percent compared to total potential. For example, if 10 people participated, a perfect quality count would be 20 for both projects with the correct number of pieces, which would be 100%. If the actual quality count was 3, then quality was 3 out of 20 or 15%.

Simulation 2—No Multitasking

The second exercise is the same as the first except *no* multitasking is allowed. Do all operations on the one sheet, then do all operations on the second sheet. We often ask participants to predict the outcome; that is, they typically expect an improvement by not multitasking, but we ask how much of an improvement they expect. The answer is often in the 10–40% range in timing. The actual results are typically much better, but the other eye-opener is in the quality results. Even with a very simple exercise such as this, quality suffers badly from multitasking. In real life, it is far worse.

These exercises are powerful eye-openers that take care of a major portion of buy-in steps 1–3. Senior management still needs to understand the benefits to the organization, the steps to implement the solution, the cost-benefit analysis, and what is expected of them to make it work. These elements are largely facilitated through the use of the *Strategy and Tactics Tree* outlined in Appendix A and available in PowerPoint format through the J. Ross Publishing Web Added Value™ website (www.jrosspub.com/wav).

In project companies, we take senior management through the entire Strategy and Tactics Tree, usually one or two days at a time, with a total investment of about five days of their time. However, in the buy-in session, we would at least cover the first two levels of the strategy and tactics. This explains the overall benefits targeted by the change and the four major steps required to implement the change.

Prior to conducting this type of buy-in session with senior management, we strongly recommend practicing the simulations and the strategy and tactics presentation with peers and other groups, especially with some groups who are not familiar with this text. Invite questions and skepticism, and even ask some of the audience to role-play senior management. This is excellent preparation for a winning session.

Conclusions

Senior management does not have the same perspective on multi-project management that you do, now that you've made it through all of these chapters and have worked the exercises. It is unrealistic to expect that you can walk into your boss's office and immediately get approval to start changing the way the organization plans, schedules, releases, executes, resources, and responds to multi-projects. Buy-in is required, often multiple times with multiple levels of the organization! The process and simulations described here work! We recommend you use them.

Endnote

1. See http://en.wikipedia.org/wiki/Theory_of_constraints.

Questions

44-1. Why is senior management buy-in important?

44-2. What are the six engines (gears) in our multi-project management system?

44-3. Senior management is used to presentations. Why not give them a 15- to 30-minute presentation on the benefits of changing the way multi-projects are managed?

44-4. Why is there such a difference in the results of the second run of the Multi-Project Mancala exercise?

44-5. People used to be highly valued for their ability to multitask. Is this still important for project resources?

44-6. Why is there such a difference in quality and duration in the second run of the multitasking exercise?

45. Conclusions

A Mammoth Improvement in Three to Six Months

It's time for a major change in the way we manage projects. Executives are tired of the disappointments and constant surprises. Project managers are fed up with the constant battles over resources and priorities. Resource managers and resources don't have time to think and hate the constant pressure and overtime. Stakeholders have been burned too many times. Based on so much bad experience, including endless efforts to overcome the problems, it is hard for people to be enthusiastic about any new approach. That is why we all face enormous resistance in making a major change.

In looking at the horrible statistics of project management success, we find only one plausible explanation for perpetual failure to achieve at least 95% on time, on budget, and within scope projects. It must be that we have been focusing our improvement efforts on symptoms of problems rather than root causes. You may recall that we state at the beginning of the book that we see three major root problems:

1. Project plans incorrectly account for variation (with poorly defined networks and without correct buffers).
2. Too much project work is active in execution (beyond the organization's capacity to flow it quickly).
3. Project tasks suffer poor execution (through excessive multitasking, conflicting priorities, and long wait times to resolve issues).

The six gears (see Figure 45.1) provide the way to permanently address these three root problems. It is vital to be patient and take key stakeholders through the six essential gears and the changes required to implement them. The necessity for all of the gears to mesh spells out a warning in how the change must be made. From our experience, most pilot approaches do not work. You have to jump in and swim on day one, or you will surely drown. We have seen organizations try to implement the approach on one or two projects, only to have their resources stolen halfway through the effort by a crisis. The need to make the

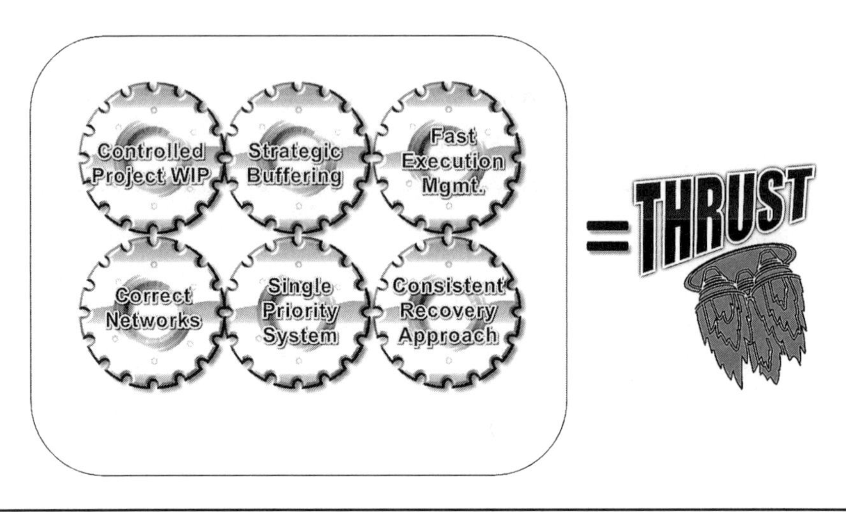

Figure 45.1 Six gears of multi-project management

total transformation, rather than sticking one foot in the water and yelling, "It's too cold to jump in," is important for the stakeholders to understand.

There are many encouraging elements today to help you make the change. For example, we can certainly remember multiyear efforts to accomplish the results we've described: 30% faster projects with double the number of projects per year completed without adding any significant resources. Now, using the strategy and tactics approach outlined in Appendix A, there is a consistent, noticeable impact within three months and a major improvement within six months.

Another helpful element is the vast and diverse array of organizations that have spoken publicly about their results, some of which are referenced in Appendix B. And certainly, the major software solution providers have made a huge contribution, not just by making it easier to implement this approach, but also by ensuring that their clients get the results.

Today, every organization involved with multiple projects faces a choice: continue on an evolutionary improvement approach (status quo with minor improvement) or take a revolutionary approach. We are not so arrogant as to claim that ours is the ONLY revolutionary way, but we do claim it has proven, time and time again, through experience to yield breakthrough results.

In our opinion, the biggest challenge most organizations face in implementing a paradigm shift of this nature is in getting and holding top management attention. That is the major reason why it is vital to take time on the front end to build buy-in, to design the changes carefully, to educate project and resource and program managers thoroughly, and then to implement at lightning speed.

In conclusion, it is so exciting for us to finally share what we have learned, developed, and implemented over the past 20+ years of multi-project management. We hope that this book has helped you to both understand the full process and build buy-in for the change. In your reading, we expect that you have some nagging questions and perhaps even disagreement with some of the concepts. Please help us change the world of multi-project management. Send us an e-mail[1] and let us know what you think, so that we may further clarify and evolve this process. We wish you success.

Endnote

1. E-mail Gerry Kendall at gerryikendall@tocinternational.com. E-mail Kathy Austin at kaustin@aptconcepts.com.

This book has free material available for download from the Web Added Value™ resource center at *www.jrosspub.com*

Appendix A

Strategy and Tactics Approach for Multi-Project Management

Over the past 20 years, some remarkable leaders have shared a wealth of knowledge on strategy. If you have read best-sellers such as Bossidy and Charan's *Execution*, Collins's *Good to Great*, or Kotter's *Leading Change*,[1] you may wonder what the difference is in this strategy and tactics for multi-project management. What makes the difference, in one word, is *focus*.

This strategy is as much about choosing to *not* do many things as it is about *focusing* on the single biggest leverage point for improving project results. It assumes that within every complex system, there is *inherent simplicity*. This implies that there are *very few* constraints (leverage points) that determine project results, both in terms of quality of results and speed of execution.

The key to driving success is to keep a project management improvement team focused on one single biggest leverage point at a time, long enough to sustain results. This strategy is designed to drive exciting, measurable results starting within a few weeks. Without such an effect, it is easy for any team to lose energy and readily choose diversions.

Appendix A illustrates a format of strategy called a *Strategy and Tactics Tree* or *S&T* for short. The S&T knowledge shared in the diagrams were implemented and used successfully to generate outstanding results. This Appendix is available as a PowerPoint file, complete with built-in navigation, and is downloadable from the WAV (Web Added Value™) portion of the publisher's website at www.jrosspub.com/wav.

Overview of the Structure of an S&T

What information should be contained in a strategy description?

1. There must be enough detail so that all implementers and executives, at any level and function, can understand what they must do in order to meet the improvement goals. This has major implications for anyone tasked with creating a strategy for improving project management within an organization. Simply listing objectives and actions or ideas is only a start to providing the clarity of direction for all executives and team members.
2. There must be an answer to the question "Why is this necessary to achieve the goal or the next higher level strategy?" In this knowledge-worker age, most people don't want to just be told *what* to do. Their commitment requires them to understand *why* they need to do it.
3. The strategy must spell out what components will be sufficient to achieve the desired intermediate results and the overall goal. By forcing ourselves to try to understand the full context of what is required to achieve a major goal, we often discover missing pieces in advance. This alone can significantly speed up an improvement process and prevent painful mistakes.

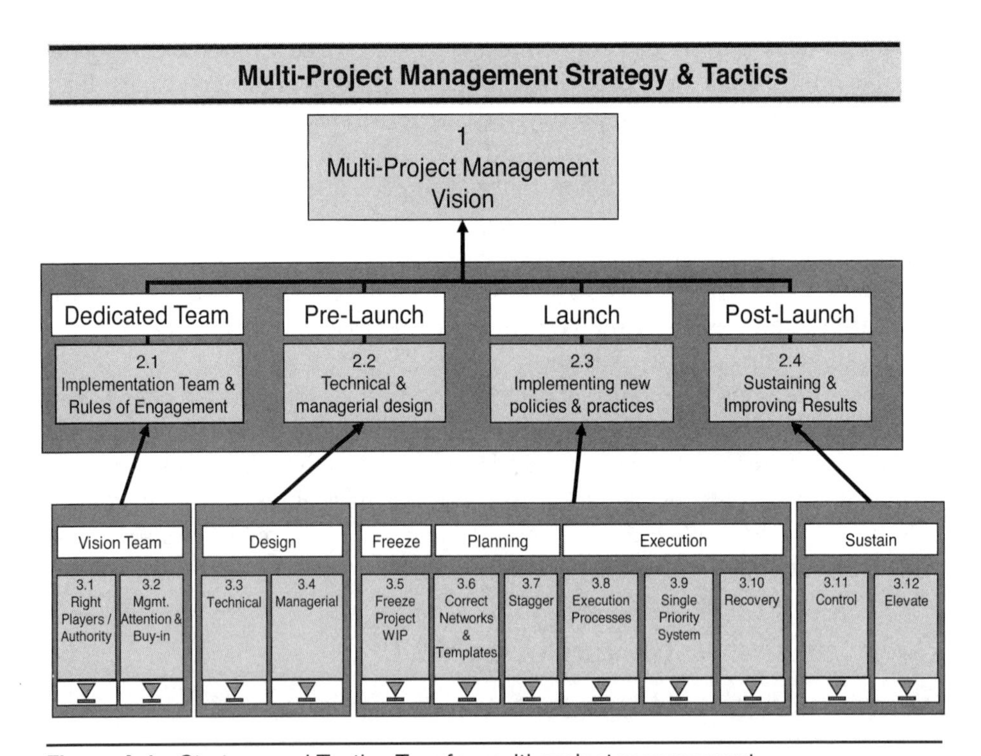

Figure A.1 Strategy and Tactics Tree for multi-project management

Generic Content of S&T Structures

The S&T consists of a structure (see Figure A.1) and corresponding text containing strategy, tactics, and assumptions (see Figures A.2–A.18).

The structure is hierarchical. Each lower level in the diagram contains strategies and tactics necessary to achieve strategy represented in the level above. A correct structure means that implementing the tactics at the lowest level is sufficient to achieve the entire strategy. Therefore, you may ask why we need anything but the lowest level. There are three reasons:

1. To communicate the relationship between the lowest level of the tactics and how that is linked to achieving the ultimate organization goals.
2. For each level of an organization to understand their responsibility and necessary outcomes in managing it to meet the organization goals.
3. Finally, as you will see by the example below, to idenitfy assumptions at each level so that they can be shared and tested with other people. If the assumptions in the S&T are correct, the strategy should work. If not, it is better if we find out before we attempt to implement it.

1	Multi-Project Management Vision
Assumptions Behind Strategy	The time it takes to complete many projects is endangering the organization's ability to meet and continue to meet its goals.
Strategy	Within three months of implementation, the organization is completing projects at least 20% faster than before, with a capacity to complete more project work with the same resources.
Assumptions Behind Tactics	➢Getting the magnitude of results requires a paradigm shift, which cannot occur without dedication and executive support. ➢Two types of skills are mandatory–technical and managerial. ➢To get the results, we must drive major behavior changes in the way we manage all projects. This requires changes in policies and practices that are deeply embedded in our PM culture. ➢One of the biggest dangers after implementing a major change is slipping backwards.
Tactics	➢Empower a team to drive major improvements in multi-project management with 100% executive support. ➢Mandate the team to design both technical and managerial changes in policies and practices. ➢Launch the changes in policies and practices within one day after training all personnel. ➢Do whatever it takes to make the changes stick.
Take Note!	Designing and implementing a paradigm shift is NOT a part time effort.

Figure A.2 Overall strategy for a multi-project implementation

In every S&T, the strategy is shown in the box labeled *Strategy*. At the very top level, the strategy should be a statement of measurable performance well beyond what the organization is currently targeting. For example, in Figure A.2, it is to reduce project durations by at least 20% while simultaneously increasing the amount of project work completed within three months without adding any resources. The organization would need to have before and after metrics to gauge if it is meeting this goal, and the rationale behind it, since it does not have the opportunity to re-execute the identical projects. Anyone reading this goal statement can legitimately ask many questions, such as "how do you measure that project durations are reduced." The beauty of the S&T structure is that the meaning becomes more and more clear as you move down through the levels of the S&T.

Assumptions behind tactics shown in Figures A.2–A.18 provide insight into why the tactics make sense as a means to achieve the strategy. The assumptions may indicate facts or warnings you must take into account in coming up with tactics or facts that will make it possible or easier to achieve the strategy. Since we are at the very top level of the strategy, Figure A.2 assumptions are for the top executives. The assumptions in this case contain four warnings:

- *First warning:* This is not one person's part-time job. A team must be prepared to spend the better part of three months implementing this change. Without the full support of every member of top management, the effort risks failure.
- *Second warning:* Two very different types of skills are needed in a functional team.
- *Third warning:* Be prepared to slaughter some sacred cows in policies and practices.
- *Fourth warning:* After implementation, the organization is in intensive care. Make sure that the changes do not die a slow death of backsliding.

Tactics explain how to achieve the strategy. At this high level in the S&T tree, the statements are very general conditions that must be implemented. At lower levels in the tree, the tactics represent actions that individuals or small teams will take. In the four tactics statements shown in Figure A.2, the organization is told to:

1. *Empower a team to drive major improvements in multi-project management with 100% executive support.* How? The answer is detailed at lower levels. What is "major improvements"? This is detailed in the strategy statement above.

2. *Mandate the team to design both technical and managerial changes in policies and practices.* Note that at this level, the tactics are not specific about exactly which policies and practices must change. Once again, those items are spelled out in more detail below. The key understanding is that the team is empowered to *design* a new system. Executives retain authority to approve the design before launching it.
3. *Launch the changes in policies and practices within one day after training all personnel.* Once all of the changes have been designed and approved by executives, they are launched literally overnight. In our experience, typically the top level manager holds a general meeting for about one hour, explaining the changes and proclaiming, "Tomorrow, we launch—all these changes are in effect then."
4. *Do whatever it takes to make the changes stick.* This post-launch intensive care is still a responsibility of the implementation team.

Take Note! is the final section of each S&T page, which provides a key requirement for lower levels of the diagram. This note may be in the form of a warning or a reminder of what you must achieve at lower levels. In this case, the warning is for both senior management and the selected team—do not attempt to implement these changes on a part-time basis.

The *direction of implementation of* S&T is from left to right, generally one box at a time. The remaining 16 S&T boxes follow.

Endnotes

1. Larry Bossidy and Ram Charan, *Execution: The Discipline of Getting Things Done* (New York: Crown Business, 2002); Jim Collins, *Good to Great: Why Some Companies Make the Leap . . . and Others Don't* (New York: Harper Business, 2001); and John P. Kotter, *Leading Change* (Boston: Harvard Business School Press, 1996).

2.1	Having the Right Team & Rules of Engagement
Assumptions Behind Strategy	Only a team appointed by top management can change an embedded culture quickly.
Strategy	Top management has the right team candidates with authority to design and implement the changes needed to drive major improvement in multi-project management within three months.
Assumptions Behind Tactics	➢Only key people with technical and managerial skills inside the organization can make the necessary changes. ➢The most likely candidates with the right level of experience, respect, and drive are difficult to release from current responsibilities. ➢Level of Authority is best not left to chance or assumptions.
Tactics	➢The top management team develops two lists of candidates—one with technical skills and one with managerial skills capable of driving major project management change. ➢Top management chooses final candidates and instructs them to delegate all responsibilities for 3 months. ➢Top management delegates full authority to design all necessary technical and organizational changes needed to drive at least a 20% improvement in project durations without adding resources.
Take Note!	There are characteristics of team members that facilitate major change. There are characteristics that block major change. Succeeding is not just a matter of design. It largely depends on buy-in.

Figure A.3 Top management's role in setting up the right team with the right authority

2.2	Pre–launch
Assumptions Behind Strategy	It requires several weeks and significant top management decision-making to do the preparation, training and software work required to launch the multi-project management system changes.
Strategy	The organization has all technical and managerial design work complete, including all organization training, with all requisite decisions approved by top management.
Assumptions Behind Tactics	➢On the technical side, the organization is likely using incorrectly modeled, unbuffered networks, and inconsistent resource definitions, with projects activated without formal synchronization. ➢On the managerial side, the organization suffers from multitasking of resources, inconsistent task management, infrequent task updates, time consuming issue resolution, inconsistent recovery planning, project rework and other symptoms of poor project flow.
Tactics	➢The technical team chooses software needed to address the solution requirements, and completes all technical design, including training of project and resource managers and a synchronization expert in the use of the software. ➢The managerial team writes the new rules of engagement for multi-project synchronization, buffer management, recovery, task updates, fast track issue resolution and full kits, and prepares all training material for roll-out.
Take Note!	There is a lot of crossover between technical and managerial design. The teams can easily work in parallel, but must debrief frequently to avoid designing a solution with inherent conflicts and to avoid rework.

Figure A.4 Technical and managerial design teams

2.3	Launch
Assumptions Behind Strategy	The biggest risk in launching any major change is not getting results quickly. The faster a major change is implemented, the better the results and the less painful the change.
Strategy	The new multi-project paradigm achieves measurable results within the first four weeks of implementation, and is fully implemented within three months.
Assumptions Behind Tactics	➢When there is too much project WIP, resources multitask too much, management support and decisions take too long, and tasks wait for support group attention. It is not effective to reduce WIP gradually. ➢Poorly defined project networks account for a substantial part of the current problem. ➢Projects are activated without tangibly recognizing the organization's capacity to do the work. ➢When too many projects are "in trouble", execution is largely driven by who is screaming the loudest with constantly shifting priorities.
Tactics	➢Execute a freeze process on day 1 of Activation of at least 25% of active project WIP. ➢All Project Managers follow the 10 step process for building all future project networks. ➢The multi-project manager rigorously follows a process to activate (synchronize) new projects ONLY in line with the capacity of the organization to do the work and according to the rules agreed to in the Design Phase. ➢Project and resource managers drive project execution through daily task updating and fast track resolution processes, a single priority system and a consistent recovery approach.
Take Note!	There is a lot of crossover between technical and managerial design. The teams can easily work in parallel, but must debrief frequently to avoid designing a solution with inherent conflicts and to avoid rework.

Figure A.5 Implementing new policies and practices

2.4	Post–Launch
Assumptions Behind Strategy	➢About half the benefits of the multi-project solution are driven after the initial launch. ➢There are two different ways to continue improving. Without a specific strategic choice, it is possible to do damage to project flow.
Strategy	➢The multi-project solution continues to drive benefits post-launch sufficient to meet the goals. ➢Control mechanisms are sustaining and continually improving results without endangering project flow.
Assumptions Behind Tactics	➢Most people revert to old habits unless they are held accountable. ➢A common approach to try to improve project management is to throw more project resources at the problem. With the new solution, this could have negative effects on project flow.
Tactics	➢The implementation teams, in collaboration with top management, perform frequent audits (daily at first, then weekly) to correct wrong or lapsed behaviors. The team relaxes audits only when it is proven that the correct behaviors are sustained week after week. ➢The implementation teams establish and use a mechanism to continually improve project flow. They educate all management about the dangers of increasing capacity through adding resources, especially project managers.
Take Note!	The job of the implementation team is not complete until the organization has achieved the full results. It is easy to succumb to organizational pressure to release members of this team too early.

Figure A.6 Sustaining and improving results

3.1	Forming a Team with the Right Players
Assumptions Behind Strategy	The integrity, drive, and skills of the team will make or break this entire effort.
Strategy	Technical and managerial team members have the right characteristics to lead their peers, subordinates and even their bosses to drive significant business results through accomplishing more projects at least 20% faster.
Assumptions Behind Tactics	➢All candidates must have top-notch buy-in skills and an excellent understanding of the business needs. ➢Technical people sometimes have difficulty getting out of the detail enough to understand the purpose of a technique. At the same time, network building is not a skill that someone can learn for this implementation. Experience makes a huge difference in success. ➢People who get stressed by having to define and then sell major organizational change are not good candidates for the managerial team.
Tactics	➢From a list of potential candidates for a technical team and a managerial team, top management narrows the list down to those candidates with excellent buy-in and business understanding skills. ➢Top management selects a maximum of 3 people for the technical team, at least one of whom has network building skills and one of whom has experience working with multiple projects, either as a Project Manager, Program Manager or similar function. ➢Top management selects a maximum of 3 people for the managerial team, who are at a senior enough level that they are comfortable with leading policy changes, establishing metrics and defining roles and responsibilities.
Take Note!	Technical and Managerial Teams must also be able to work with each other.

Figure A.7 Right players on the vision team

3.2	Ensuring the Team Has Management Attention and Buy-In
Assumptions Behind Strategy	There are too many active internal initiatives which occupy senior management and the implementation team's attention. This will significantly slow down implementation and delay the benefits.
Strategy	This multi-project implementation is the only active initiative by the implementation team and is being given daily priority by senior management.
Assumptions Behind Tactics	➢This initiative will require full time effort of the team over a period of 3 months. If the effort is half time, for example, it will require 6 months to implement, and the team and the organization will grow restless. ➢During this implementation process, there will be frequent discussions with and decisions from senior management. Without daily priority, the accumulation of delays will significantly delay results.
Tactics	➢Each member of the implementation teams makes a list of current responsibilities and initiatives and delegates to the point that they have 8 hours per day totally free to devote to this implementation. ➢The senior management sponsor of this initiative secures the commitment from the entire senior management team to respond daily to team requests for decisions and input.
Take Note!	Senior management teams have much greater buy-in when they experience, through a simulation, the huge negative effects of multitasking and its impact on results.

Figure A.8 Dedicate the team—remove other commitments

3.3	Technical Design
Assumptions Behind Strategy	Technical design is a labor intensive, time consuming effort, requiring many decisions and the interaction of the Technical team with project sponsors, project managers, senior management and subject matter experts.
Strategy	The Technical Design is complete, ready for activation, within 6 weeks.
Assumptions Behind Tactics	To be complete, the technical design must address: • Project Networks & templates • Synchronization • Resource Pools • Schedule analysis/compression • Software • What if Analysis • Buffering • Software updates • Software reporting
Tactics	➢Determine software, procure and install. ➢Build project networks and templates for all projects that will be part of the launch, using the 10 step process. As networks are built, determine the resource pools that will be used for modeling. Analyze schedules and compress, capturing the before and after durations. Ensure all final project plans have 33% buffers. ➢Finalize synchronization mechanism, perform what-if analysis and synchronize all projects. ➢Determine software reporting requirements and build reports. Train users on updates and use of software.
Take Note!	Building proper networks and templates is typically the most time-consuming part of this effort. Projects which are almost finished should not undergo this effort.

Figure A.9 Work of the technical design team

3.4	Managerial Design
Assumptions Behind Strategy	Managerial design is a labor intensive, time consuming effort, requiring many decisions and the interaction of the Managerial team with resource managers, project managers, and senior management.
Strategy	The Managerial Design is complete, ready for activation, within 6 weeks.
Assumptions Behind Tactics	To be complete, the managerial design must document the following policies, processes and organization: • Fast Track Issue Resolution • Daily Updating • Full Kit • Project Recovery • Freeze • Task time estimating • Synchronization control • Training & Audits • Track assignment • Resourcing of projects • Single Priority System • Long term resourcing
Tactics	➢The managerial team documents processes for Fast Track Issue Resolution, daily task updating and project full kit points and gets senior management approval. Senior management determines which member of their team will run the daily fast track issue meetings and who will run the full kit process. ➢The managerial team documents processes and develops training materials for project recovery, task time estimating, task assignment to avoid multitasking, resourcing of projects, use of the single priority system and resource planning/ long term elevation and gets approval from senior management. ➢The managerial team defines policies for synchronization control, initial freezing of projects and gets approval from senior management. ➢The managerial team trains all resources and senior management and sets up audit process.
Take Note!	Getting people to follow the processes and policies requires training, buy-in and follow-up.

Figure A.10 Work of the managerial design team

3.5	Launch Step 1 – Freeze Project WIP
Assumptions Behind Strategy	Past pressure has led to having more projects in execution than the organization has the capacity to flow quickly. This in turn has led to excessive multitasking of resources and long delays in task execution due to lack of support group and management attention.
Strategy	The number of active projects is aligned with the organization's capacity to do project work.
Assumptions Behind Tactics	➢At the outset of the launch, it is vital to get quick, tangible results. The most effective way to do that is to "shock" the system into immediate performance. ➢An overnight freeze of a significant amount of project work in process will drastically reduce bad multitasking, and shorten the wait time for support group and management attention.
Tactics	➢The top management team determines the prioritization of all active projects and freezes at least 25% of the lowest priority projects. ➢Top management informs all stakeholders about the freeze. ➢The process to unfreeze projects is according to the staggering mechanism outlined in 3.7.
Take Note!	Many people will have the wrong assumption that freezing projects will delay their delivery date. In fact, with too much project WIP, the delivery dates would actually be later than by freezing projects, flowing all existing work much faster and unfreezing the projects. Every project benefits, but buy-in is essential.

Figure A.11 The *Freeze* process in launching the solution

3.6	Launch Step 2 – Correct Networks & Templates
Assumptions Behind Strategy	➢Project execution is doomed to managing by the seat of the pants and miscommunication without the use of a correct project network. ➢Most project networks suffer from three major mistakes—full stakeholder needs are not captured, too much detail, and incorrect resource modeling.
Strategy	All active projects have correct, resource-based networks.
Assumptions Behind Tactics	➢A project of any size can be easily managed by a project manager with 200 tasks or fewer. People building networks put in too much detail when they try to use the network as a reminder list, a "how to" manual in performing the task, or breaking the task down into its lowest level of work breakdown structure. Details of how to build a network are spelled out in Chapter 5 and Part III of the Advanced Multi-Project Management text. ➢In most multi-project environments, many projects are variations of the same generic project. Using templates (networks of generic project types) to start constructing the network of actual projects, drastically reduces the required time and eliminates making the same mistakes in constructing networks.
Tactics	➢Project managers learn and use the 10 step network building process to construct all networks. All projects are strategically buffered. ➢Project managers use templates when available, and add to the template library when appropriate.
Take Note!	Most project managers have lived with bad project network habits for a long time. Most project managers have not experienced a consistent network building process that also drives project execution. The implementation teams should expect significant resistance and fully audit new project networks until this process is correctly used by all project managers.

Figure A.12 Launching with resource-based, scrutinized networks

3.7	Launch Staggering Process
Assumptions Behind Strategy	In multi-project environments, some or many key resources work across projects. Competition between projects for certain resources drives either multitasking of those resources or long delays. Also, Management and support groups, who are often not modeled in project plans, cause significant delays in project execution.
Strategy	Project flow is not hindered by too much project work in progress.
Assumptions Behind Tactics	➢Trying to balance the workload of all resources across all projects during a planning process does not work. This is true for two reasons–first, some resources critical to project success, such as management and support groups, are not modeled in the project plans. Secondly, projects do not execute as planned, and therefore the perfectly balanced plan would fall apart on the first day of execution. ➢There are two proven ways to stagger projects effectively. Only one of these is necessary.
Tactics	➢The person designated by senior management as the multi-project manager uses the chosen staggering mechanism to perform what-if analyses of possible ways to stagger upcoming projects. They present the results to top management, who decides which projects to stagger next. ➢The multi-project manager releases projects strictly according to the staggering mechanism to ensure rapid project flow.
Take Note!	The assumptions used to stagger projects are sometimes overly optimistic. In that case, it may be necessary to revisit the assumptions and further reduce project WIP.

Figure A.13 Rules for staggering projects for fast flow

3.8	Launching Execution Processes
Assumptions Behind Strategy	➢Today's common practice in managing project tasks is to intervene when there is a crisis. The problem is that management finds out too late to recover.
Strategy	All projects flow much more quickly in execution.
Assumptions Behind Tactics	➢No one knows, until someone works on a project task, whether or not there are problems. ➢The longer an issue blocking a task exists, the longer the task, and hence the project is delayed. ➢The start of major phases is often delayed due to missing necessary items (other than resources). If work is started without all items, this frequently results in rework.
Tactics	➢The manager responsible for monitoring tasks assigned to resources performs a daily review and update of all active tasks. The reviewer asks how many days are left to complete the task and compares this to the aggressive estimate. Only if the answer suggests a major issue will the reviewer further investigate and take corrective action if necessary. The reviewer NEVER comments negatively about how long the task is taking. ➢Project and resource managers use buffer penetration as a signal for necessary intervention. ➢A senior manager runs a daily, 15 minute fast track issue resolution meeting with all PMs and resolves blocking issues within 24 hours or freezes the project if unable to do so. ➢The senior manager responsible for full kitting projects runs a full kit meeting before the designated major phase starts, with the sole objective of ensuring all major pieces are in place so as NOT to delay the project and not have rework.
Take Note!	Execution processes, when implemented properly are quick, painless and very effective.

Figure A.14 Bringing execution processes to life

3.9	Launching Single Priority System
Assumptions Behind Strategy	In the past, too much project WIP often resulted in conflicting priorities. Managers of resources doing project tasks often faced conflicting priorities and shuffled resources frequently, losing project momentum and resource productivity.
Strategy	All tasks are executed according to a single priority system, with speed of task completion foremost in mind.
Assumptions Behind Tactics	Within a Critical Chain or Critical Path system using holistic buffers, during execution: ➢After daily updates, each task has its priority according to the impact it has on its project completion–percent penetration into the corresponding buffer. ➢Every day, the software provides the resource manager with two lists of tasks: The list of tasks currently being executed and the list of tasks available to assign, both sorted according to their up-to-date priorities. ➢Tasks that the software shows are available to assign have all necessary entry criteria to be able to start them: E.g., approvals, designs, (uninterrupted) resources etc.
Tactics	➢Following the single priority system and according to which resources are NOT currently working on any other tasks, resource managers assign the maximum practical number of resources to tasks. ➢The implementation team audits task assignments to ensure that every resource manager is rigorously following the single priority system, that tasks are not assigned earlier than needed to meet the schedule, and that no resource is multitasked.
Take Note!	The Single Priority System still leaves some discretion to the resource manager when multiple tasks have about the same priority according to buffer penetration. However, there is a big difference between discretion and violating the system.

Figure A.15 Operating according to a single priority system

3.10	Launching Consistent Recovery Approach
Assumptions Behind Strategy	When projects are in danger of missing commitments, recovery efforts often fail because they are started too late or do not consider a good range of options. Options grow more limited when recovery is attempted too late.
Strategy	Projects almost always are able to recover to meet more aggressive due dates.
Assumptions Behind Tactics	➢Buffer management provides the correct signals of when to plan to recover and when to execute a recovery plan. ➢Senior management has visibility into project status, and also can choose to intervene if they are not happy with a PM's recovery plan. ➢The daily fast track issue resolution process highlights blocking issues sooner than they would have been uncovered otherwise, thus reducing the number of instances where recovery plans are needed. With less fires to fight in multi-project management, resource managers, senior managers and support groups are in a much better position to help projects recover when necessary.
Tactics	➢Project Managers make recovery plans when buffers are yellow. They execute when buffers turn red. ➢PMs document recovery plans. Senior management reviews recovery plans and intervenes on the rare occasion that they perceive the plans are insufficient to recover or beyond the PM's span of control.
Take Note!	The implementation teams are in an excellent position to facilitate a better recovery process, with the view of all projects and their experience during this implementation.

Figure A.16 Getting all project managers using one recovery approach

3.11	Sustaining Control
Assumptions Behind Strategy	Sustaining a solution has two challenges–preventing behaviors from reverting back and getting newcomers on board with the solution's required behaviors.
Strategy	Project flow is never endangered by backsliding.
Assumptions Behind Tactics	Most people are good. With peer support, management reinforcement and the proper skills, they will behave correctly.
Tactics	➢Senior management puts someone in charge of training newcomers and continuously auditing all project and resource managers to ensure correct behaviors are maintained. ➢Senior management monitors statistics on project flow monthly to ensure there is no deterioration.
Take Note!	Empirical evidence speaks much louder than people's words. Clear, simple data is effective in reinforcing the right behaviors and pointing out the wrong ones.

Figure A.17 Ensuring permanent rapid project flow

3.12	Sustaining Through Controlled Elevation
Assumptions Behind Strategy	The nature of an organization's projects changes over time. As speed of project execution improves, senior management may want to have more active projects than previously. However, because management and support group attention are not modeled in projects, these actions may lead to the same problems as before–too much WIP, projects slowing down, missing commitments.
Strategy	Project flow is never endangered by increasing the number of projects or resources.
Assumptions Behind Tactics	The assumptions behind the staggering mechanism must be closely examined before making changes. If a change is desired, experimentation through a carefully orchestrated pilot will mitigate risk.
Tactics	➢The senior management team ensures that any changes to the synchronization process are vetted thoroughly and piloted experimentally, monitoring project flow, before implementing a permanent change. ➢Senior management monitors statistics on project flow monthly to ensure there is no deterioration.
Take Note!	Senior management must always examine cause and effect implications when considering adding more projects to the currently active portfolios.

Figure A.18 Understanding implications of adding project capacity

Appendix B

Success Stories and Video References

Industry	Project Type	Company	Results	Reference
Aerospace	Design and assembly	Boeing Space & Intelligence Systems	Doubled throughput and decreased cycle time by 28%.	www.realization.com
Aerospace	IT	Lord Corporation	Found additional 60% capacity without hiring people.	www.vectorstrategies.com
Air	Engineering	Boeing (Military)	Reduced required wing assembly time by 50%.	www.goldratt.com
Air	Engineering	Boeing Wing Assembly	On schedule, under budget. Reduced required wing assembly time by 50% (F-22).	www.golddratt.com
Air	Repair	Delta Air Lines, Inc.	23% increase in engines produced per year; 30% reduction in engine turnaround time.	www.realization.com
Air	Helicopter manufacturing and maintenance	Erickson Air-Crane	Increased projects on time from 33% to 83%.	www.realization.com
Air	Engineering and assembly	Lockheed Martin	Cut aircraft full finish time by 57% without reducing scope.	www.goldratt.com
Air	Engineering	Spirit Aerosystems	Reduced cycle time from 12+ months to 7 months.	www.realization.com
Aluminum	Engineering	Alcan Alesa Technologies	Number of projects completed increased over 30%.	www.realization.com
Automotive	Product development	Chrysler	Cycle time for prototype builds reduced from 10 weeks to 8 weeks.	www.realization.com
Automotive	Engineering	ThyssenKrupp	63% gain in productivity; 15% more projects completed.	www.realization.com
Biotechnology	Engineering	Danisco (Genencor)	Increased from 20% projects on time to 87%.	www.realization.com
Communications	Product development	Airgo Networks (Qualcomm)	Cycle time improved from 19 months to 8 months.	www.realization.com
Communications	Telecom switch design	Alcatel-Lucent	Increased throughput by 45% per person.	www.realization.com
Communications	Customized software development	Amdocs	14% increase in revenue/man-month; 20% reduced cycle time.	www.realization.com

Communications	Network design and installation	elRcom	On-time delivery improved from 75% to 98%+. Average cycle time was reduced from 70 days to 30 days.	www.realization.com
Communications	IT	elRcom	From 40% to 90%+ of projects on time; lead time reduced from 150 days to 30 days.	www.toc-goldratt.com
Construction	Theme park design, install, and commission	Action Park Multiforma Grupo	Increased number of projects complete from 121 to 153.	www.realization.com
Construction	New hospital facility	California Department of Corrections	Built and opened new mental hospital in 6 months that other approaches failed to do in 12 months.	www.vectorstrategies.com
Construction	Manufacturing plant	emcocables	Reduced 11-month average project duration to 7 months. Increased revenue by 55%, received 4 months earlier.	www.realization.com
Construction	TV station	Emesa	€ 5 million penalty avoided.	www.realization.com
Construction	Home building	Shea Homes	Reduced cycle time by 40% from 91 days to 56 days.	www.vectorstrategies.com
Consumer goods	Product development	Heineken, Spain	20% faster time to market. Improved projects on time from 90% to 98%.	
Consumer goods	Product development	HP Digital Camera Group	Improved new products from 6 in 2004 to 15 launched in 2005.	www.realization.com
Consumer goods	Sales	Oregon Freeze Dry	Increased number of sales projects completed per year from 72 to 171.	www.realization.com
Defense manufacturing	Product design and manufacturing	Tecnobit	Reduced project cycle times by 20%.	www.realization.com
Durable goods	Product development	Hamilton Beach Brands, Inc.	Increased from 34 to 52 new products in first year, 70+ in second year with no increase in head count.	www.realization.com
Durable goods	Custom design, manufacturing and installation	TRS Refrigeration	Reduced average project cycle time from 75 days to 46 days, and increased project capacity by 30% with no added manpower.	www.tocca.com.au

Industry	Project Type	Company	Results	Reference
Energy	Cleanup	BP Oil	Saving of over $700 million with accelerated project and production required to meet project needs.	www.pinnacle-strategies.com
Energy	Engineering	FMC Technologies	50% reduction in test and final assembly time.	www.pinnacle-strategies.com
Energy	Design and manufacturing	LeTourneau Technologies Inc.	Reduced design and engineering from 15 months to 9 months, production engineering from 9 months to 5 months.	www.realization.com
Energy	Engineering	Von Ardenne	Cycle time reduced from 17 weeks to 14 weeks, while projects on time increased from 80% to 90%.	www.realization.com
Financial services	Software development	Confluence UK	95% of projects on time.	www.criticalchain.co.uk
Health care	Emergency room and in hospital—patient as a project	Oxford-Radcliffe Hospitals, UK	Increased patients through emergency room from <70% within four hours to 100%, while patient load grew by more than 25%.	www.tocinternational.com
Manufacturing	Engineering and manufacturing	Rex Materials Group	Lead time down from six weeks to 10 days.	www.cmg-toc.com
Manufacturing	Design	Valley Cabinet Works	Went from 200 projects per year to 334 projects in the first nine months of the year measured.	www.realization.com
Medical	Product development	Medtronic	Improved software release intervals from 6 months to 9 months to every 2 months.	www.realization.com
Medical	Product development	Medtronic, Europe	Reduced project cycle time from 18 months to 9 months.	www.realization.com
Military	Repair	French Air Force	Returned two out of five aircraft to Air Force (€ 300 million value).	www.realization.com
Military	Repair, logistics, and testing	U.S. Air Force (multiple bases)	Turnaround time reduced 25–30%, multiple aircraft returned to Air Force.	www.realization.com

Military	Army fleet maintenance	U.S. Army Fleet Support	32% reduction in CH-47 and 52% reduction in UH-60 turnaround time.	www.realization.com
Military	Repair	U.S. Army, Corpus Christi	Throughput increased from 5.4 aircraft per month to 6.3.	www.realization.com
Military	Repair and logistics	U.S. Marine Corps (Multiple bases)	Repair cycle cut by up to 50%, on-time delivery increased to 95%+, product rate increased.	www.realization.com
Pharmaceutical	Product development	Dr. Reddy's Laboratories	83% increase in projects completed in first 12 weeks; 75% increase in new product launches year over year.	www.realization.com
Pharmaceutical	Product development	P&G Pharmaceuticals	Increased projects completed per quarter from five to eight, and on-time rate from 55% to 90%.	www.realization.com
Power	Engineering	ABB AG, Power Tech. Division	Throughput increase over 33% from 300 Bays to 430 Bays per year.	www.realization.com
Power	Engineering	ABB Cordoba	Engineering cycle time reduced from eight months to three months.	www.realization.com
Power	Repair	ABB Halle	Number of projects completed per year increased from 42 to 54, >25%.	www.realization.com
Power	Engineering	C.N. Cotrentes	Increased due date performance from 60% to 95%.	www.realization.com
Power	Engineering	Central Nuclear Almaraz Trillo	Increased number of projects completed from 19 to 24–30 per month.	www.realization.com
Power	Engineering	Siemens Generator Engineering	Went from 110 to 128 projects completed, with 30% increase in throughput.	www.realization.com
Power	Engineering	Skoda Power	30% increase in casings per year. Went from 60% to 90% on-time delivery, with 20%+ faster cyle time.	www.realization.com
Process manu-facturing	Plant engineering	Owens-Illinois	Decreased cycle time from 6 months to 2.5 months.	www.realization.com

Industry	Project Type	Company	Results	Reference
Rail	Repair	Railcare Wolverton, UK	100% on-time delivery. Increased from one project at a time to three.	www.realization.com
Resource	Engineering	BHP Billiton	25% reduction in hours needed to complete project and project finished three weeks early.	www.realization.com
Semiconductor	Design and manufacturing	e2V Semiconductors	Cycle time reduced from 38 months to 23 months.	www.realization.com
Semiconductor	Plant construction	Harris Semiconductor	Began full high-tech production in 13 months, instead of 54-month industry norm.	www.goldratt.com
Semiconductor	Engineering	Ismeca Semiconductor	25% reduction in cycle time, from 84 days to 64 days.	www.realization.com
Semiconductor	Design	LSI Logic	Went from major tool releases were always late to released on time for three years in a row.	www.realization.com
Software	Software development	Alna Software	Cycle time reduced by 25% and project completions increased 17%.	www.realization.com
Software	Flight simulation systems	CAE USA	Reduced cycle times by two to four months, with a $37 million increase in the number of profitable programs.	www.goldratt.com
Software	IT	Celsa Group	Increased completion of SAP projects from 15 to 20 per month.	www.realization.com
Steel	Plant maintenance	Tata Steel	68% faster project time; went from 11-day planned shutdown to 5 days.	www.realization.com
Textile	Design	Skye Group	100% due date performance with 30% reduction in lead times.	www.realization.com

Appendix C

Sample Enterprise Resource Categories

Information Technology

Systems Engineer
Software Engineer
Technical Documentation Specialist
IT Project Manager
User Project Manager
Business Analyst
Technical Analyst
Programmer
Database Analyst
Infrastructure Analyst
IS Architect

Engineering

Electrical Engineer
Mechanical Engineer
Software/Firmware Engineer
Hardware Engineer

Process Engineer
Automation Engineer
Engineering Documentation Specialist
Drafting Engineer–2D
Drafting Engineer–3D
Testing Engineer–Internal
Testing Engineer–External
Engineering Project Manager
Tool Draftsperson
Tool Design Engineer

Marketing

Market Development Analyst
Sales Analyst
New Product Setup Specialist
Retail Store Setup Specialist
Pricing Analyst
Market Research Analyst
Market Materials Specialist
Graphic Artist
Creative Designer

Production

Operations Development Analyst
Process Improvement Specialist
Production Maintenance Specialist
Engineering Data Analysis Specialist
Outside Vendor
Costing Analyst
Packaging Analyst
Finishing Analyst

Production Data Collection/Entry Specialist
Machine Operator Trainee
Machine Operator
Lead Machine Operator
Inventory Management Specialist
Production Scheduler
Tool Fabrication Specialist
Quality Data Collection Specialist
Operator Trainer
Certification Specialist

R&D

R&D Project Manager
R&D Tester–Internal
R&D Tester–External
Prototype Fabrication Analyst
R&D Design Engineer
R&D Development Engineer
Technician
Certification Research Specialist
R&D Documentation Specialist
R&D Data Analyst
Machine Fabrication Specialist
Machine Design Specialist
Formulation Specialist

Finance

Pricing Analyst
Financial Analyst

Appendix D

What about Agile?

We are not intimately familiar with Agile. Yet we have been asked several times what the differences are between our approach and Agile. We are not methodology bigots or fanatics. Typically, every methodology has its strengths and weaknesses. When we dive deeper, we also find methodologies have similarities and differences.

There is a lot that we agree with about the Agile principles, as we understand them. We agree that many traditional approaches have not met the customer's needs, to which we are both committed. We agree that many traditional processes are much too encumbered with documentation and standards that deliver no value and detract from the end result. Where we disagree is over the use of processes and tools—we believe that there are a few (very few!) processes and tools that increase customer satisfaction and help projects meet stakeholder needs. And we believe in following a plan, although we freely admit that most project plans we see are next to useless.

Here is one CIO's perspective that was shared with us, not from an Agile expert but from one who has been exposed to Agile more than we have. We are extremely grateful to Denise M. Hart, CIO, Envision EMI for reading an overview of our book and, through numerous dialogues, providing these insights. Hopefully, those with Agile experience and beliefs will find this useful:

> One of the signature features of an Agile approach to software development is the preparation and use of a product backlog. The product backlog is essentially a list of features and functions that the resulting solution should have, and can be added to or subtracted from at any point in time. The list is codeveloped with the project stakeholders to ensure their full engagement in the effort. During the software design-build-test cycle, the project team, working in close conjunction with the business process owners (ideally colocated), tackles between one and

four weeks' worth of effort from the list of features and functions. At the end of each cycle, known as a sprint, the goal is to have a functional and cohesive piece of software in place. The team then takes up the next sprint, works the next set of features and functions to some semblance of completion, and the cycle continues until the list of features and functions has been exhausted. The advantage of this approach is that it provides opportunities for early feedback from project sponsors on progress to date, puts working software on the table early in the process, and affords all involved an opportunity to make early course corrections in terms, scope, direction, and approach.

Another signature characteristic of an Agile project is the 15-minute daily stand-up meeting where all members of the project team report out on status and issues. This level of daily engagement with the team surfaces issues early so they can be addressed immediately. In addition, the chief user is embedded with the project team so that as questions arise, answers are given, and wait times on decisions are reduced or eliminated.

Within these two constructs, the Agile team is able to achieve a sustainable pace of development without over taxing the team members, who in traditional project management methods often fall victim to scope changes that occur without corresponding schedule accommodations. In Agile, the project proceeds at the pace of the resources and scope changes are simply added to the product backlog list, to be picked up in a future iteration. The stakeholders, since they are witness to the sausage being made, have their scope and schedule expectations managed on a daily basis. This is a real advantage in that it solves the problem of excessive overtime and resource constraints through better pacing of the project.

However, in solving the resource constraint problem, Agile leaves scope and schedule rather loosely defined. For the investors in the project, who are looking for a return on investment and a payback period *prior* to making their investment, an open-ended schedule presents its difficulties. Agile proponents would argue that scope and schedule are unknowable, and perhaps they are right, but it remains a tough sell to investors. To further complicate matters, as the project gets under way the product backlog ebbs and flows. The longer the project takes, the later the returns come in and the more likely the project will be overcome by events. In either case, the return on investment is diminished.

Your approach is refreshing in that it finds a middle ground between traditional project management techniques, which also have their shortcomings, and Agile, which has solved the resource constraint issue, yet introduced other less than desirable side effects. Tackling the resource constraints and wait time head-on and bringing executive attention to the choke points in the organization is much more sensible. It helps solve not just a project management issue but also addresses overall organizational efficiency.

> *Authors' comment*: We are not suggesting an either/or approach between Agile and our methods. Agile has proven very effective for some software development environments. From our minimal understanding of it, we believe that our approach and Agile serve the same goals, albeit through similar tactics yet differing approaches.

Appendix E

Complete Case Study on Project Planning

Case Study Introduction

This case study provides a comprehensive example to test your skills on Part III of this text, the project planning/network building 10-step process. For professors/instructors who wish to use this text, a set of answers to the case study and to all questions from the text chapters is available. Please contact J. Ross Publishing at customerservice@jrosspub.com to obtain this material.

As a reminder, the 10-step network building process is:

1. Define the project's measurable goals, tangible scope, and sponsor criteria.
2. Define the backbone of the network.
3. Expand the skeleton of the network.
4. Define additional dependencies.
5. Check the network against project goals, scope, and deliverables.
6. Resource the project tasks.
7. Scrutinize with subject matter experts.
8. Estimate time durations.
9. Reduce durations without compromise.
10. Perform a final risk assessment.

This integrated case study is broken down into the following sections, with each section followed by questions and exercises relevant to that section:

- Step 1 of the 10-step process: Planning, conducting, and documenting the stakeholders' meeting to determine the project's measurable goals, tangible scope, and stakeholder needs

- Steps 2 through 7: Building the project network
- Steps 8 through 10: Primarily focused on estimating durations and reducing project duration

Case Study for Step 1: The Project's Measurable Goals, Tangible Scope, and Sponsor Criteria

Summary

As an internal improvement project, the Generic Example Company (GENEXCO) is upgrading its current *Absolutely-Essential* software to the most current release. Upgrading to a new software release means that all user machines, conference room machines, training room machines, applicable servers, software training materials, and users must be modified/upgraded. It is important to GENEXCO that the upgrade be completed with all the required support and knowledge in place on a timely basis, that the end product delivered to the users is fully functional (both old and new features), and that the users are satisfied with the new release.

Environment

GENEXCO has users spread across multiple locations, with computers and servers connected via high-speed network. There are currently 700 users of the *Absolutely-Essential* software in various user categories (with more being added almost daily). Senior management in each division as well as in GENEXCO's headquarters access the software over the Internet to see the status of various projects on a daily basis. Users access the software on their computers during planning and while in execution to check status, ensure the correct tasks are being started, view upcoming tasks, and plan for and execute any required recovery plans. Users also access the software to determine where to assign their resources (start tasks), look at resource loading projections, and perform daily updates on in-progress tasks. There are software experts in most locations who provide software support, as well as planning and execution support. GENEXCO has two *Absolutely-Essential* system administrators (IT personnel) who perform the upgrade testing, set up and maintain user accounts, maintain the configuration, monitor server performance, and serve as liaisons from the *Absolutely-Essential* software to the GENEXCO IT personnel.

The *Absolutely-Essential* software uses Oracle[1] on the production server; however, the software training developer uses Access. The *Absolutely-Essential* software also uses Java. Most of the reports are exportable to Excel. The software has multiple modules, most of which are accessible via the Internet; however, some users and all software experts also have specific modules on their desktop computers.

GENEXCO is currently using several servers to support its *Absolutely-Essential* software use. The production server is where the operational database resides. The development server is the backup for the production server except when upgrade testing is in process; during that time, the scenario server becomes the backup for production. Otherwise the scenario server is used on a reservation basis to test different modeling assumptions/scenarios. GENEXCO has access to five training rooms and has the software loaded on the servers in each room. Additionally, the expert in charge of the training materials has an additional computer on their desk configured (using Access) as a server in order to produce and check training materials, as well as to create screen shots for all materials and presentations.

Software Upgrade Overview

The software experts want a guarantee that there will be minimal user disruption and downtime when the software is upgraded. The system administrators need to ensure that the new software functionality is verified prior to release. They are also concerned that any database conversions are done successfully and that there are no major surprises after the new software is deployed to the users. The new software release must not cause any system performance degradation.

Leadership has asked for a *Go Live* point in the project plan. There are multiple reviews and approvals required throughout the upgrade process.

Software Training Materials Overview

The current software training courses include a software Overview (available for all users), a Planning module, and Execution training for senior leadership and users. Leadership has requested that a separate Task Updating module be created.

In addition to the full set of software training materials that reflect the new version, the software training developer must determine the training plan for users of the current version: What does each category of user need to know in order to effectively use the new version, how will it be taught, does it need to be presented in the computer training room, and what materials need to be developed? The software training developer is responsible for preparing these materials and getting leadership review and approval before they are presented as well.

Since GENEXCO is not responsible for training the software experts, there are no training materials to update for them; the software vendor will provide that training as part of an ongoing maintenance contract.

The software training developer does not train the end users, but is responsible for training the software experts who have been approved to deliver software training on the new training materials as well as the upgrade training.

Software Upgrade Testing Overview

GENEXCO IT requires a test plan and test procedures for every software upgrade as well as a test report documenting the results of testing. The test plan summarizes the types of testing that will be performed during the test phase, including testing the overall functionality of the software, testing compatibility with new and existing third-party software, testing scenarios from the updated draft training materials, and testing the proposed configuration settings.

Functional verification cases must be complete before installing the software on the development server and on the computers that will be used for testing in the various user categories. After the upgrade of the development server to the new release, the functional verification cases can proceed according to the written procedures. Once the functional verification has been completed, the results can be incorporated into the test report and the final GENEXCO installation instructions can be written (making any required modifications to the draft instructions that were discovered during testing).

Writing the usability verification cases cannot begin until the draft training materials for all user categories (including software experts) have been created. After the usability verification cases are complete, the system administrators can begin that verification. When complete, the results are incorporated into the test report (which must be submitted for leadership review). Additionally, the results need to be coordinated with the software training developer so that any discrepancies (in configuration and/or training materials) can be fixed and, if necessary, retested.

Software Installation Overview

Software must be installed on the development server (for upgrade testing), on the training servers and computers (but the training rooms do not have to be upgraded simultaneously, depending upon the training plan), on the production server, on the scenario server, on all software experts' computers, on all of the campus conference rooms' computers that use the software, on the web interface users' computers, on the project managers' and network builders' computers, and on the computer used by the GENEXCO headquarters software expert responsible for training materials. The system administrators must also have access to computers to use during testing that can be configured for the various user categories.

With few exceptions, GENEXCO IT is responsible for upgrading the servers and all of the users, including headquarters. Installation on the production server is performed during scheduled IT maintenance weekends (there can be delays of up to six weeks between the time of request and the install date). Whereas all users can be upgraded simultaneously, the preference is to upgrade the software experts, then users who have modules installed on their computers in addition to accessing software on the Internet, and only then the Internet-only users (conference rooms can be updated at any time). Since *Going Live* cannot occur until a significant number and types of installs have been successfully completed, the system administrators must have a process to confirm the successful installations by the various support IT personnel.

Potential Risks/Delays Overview

There are several potential delays during the upgrade process (usually a waiting period after requesting work from GENEXCO support organizations). Scheduling reviews/approvals can also cause delays.

Questions

1. Create a list of meeting invitees.
2. Using Table 13.1 as an example, prepare the pre-stakeholders' meeting checklist.
3. Using Table 13.2 and the case study material above, determine the stakeholders' meeting results. Use no more than two pages, double-spaced with minimum font size of 12.

Case Study for Steps 2 through 7

Summary

As an internal improvement project, the Generic Example Company (GENEXCO) is upgrading its current *Absolutely-Essential* software to the most current release. Upgrading to a new software release means that all user machines, conference room machines, training room machines, applicable servers, software training materials, and users must be modified/upgraded. It's important to GENEXCO that the upgrade be completed with all the required support and knowledge in place on a timely basis, that the end product delivered to the users is fully functional (both old and new features), and that the users are satisfied with the new release.

Environment

GENEXCO has users spread across multiple locations, with computers and servers connected via high-speed network. There are currently 700 users of the *Absolutely-Essential* software in various user categories (with more being added almost daily). Senior management in each division as well as in GENEXCO's headquarters access the software over the Internet to see the status of various projects on a daily basis. Users access the software on their computers during planning and while in execution to check status, ensure the correct tasks are being started, view upcoming tasks, and plan for and execute any required recovery plans. Users also access the software to determine where to assign their resources (start tasks), look at resource loading projections, and perform daily updates on in-progress tasks. There are software experts in most locations who provide software support, as well as planning and execution support. GENEXCO has two *Absolutely-Essential* system administrators (IT personnel) who perform the upgrade testing, set up and maintain user accounts, maintain the configuration, monitor server performance, and serve as liaisons from the *Absolutely-Essential* software to the GENEXCO IT personnel.

The *Absolutely-Essential* software uses Oracle on the production server; however, the software training developer uses Access. The *Absolutely-Essential* software also uses Java. Most of the reports are exportable to Excel. The software has multiple modules, most of which are accessible via the Internet; however, both users and software experts also have specific modules on their desktop computers.

GENEXCO is currently using several servers to support its *Absolutely-Essential* software use. The production server is where the operational database resides. The development server is the backup for the production server except when upgrade testing is in process; during that time, the scenario server becomes the backup for production. Otherwise the scenario server is used on a reservation basis to test different modeling assumptions/scenarios. GENEXCO has access to five training rooms and has the software loaded on the servers in each room. Additionally, the expert in charge of the training materials has an additional computer on their desk configured (using Access) as a server in order to produce and check training materials, as well as to create screen shots for all materials and presentations.

Software Upgrade Process

The software experts want a guarantee that there will be minimal user disruption and downtime when the software is upgraded. The system administrators need to ensure that the new software functionality is verified prior to release. They are also concerned that any database conversions are done successfully and that there are no major surprises after the new software is deployed to the users. The new software release must not cause any system performance degradation. The software training developer needs to understand the changes in the new release before recommending any configuration modifications and before determining which software training materials must be upgraded or modified. The software training materials must be modified before testing can start (the usability verification) because that testing is performed using those modified training materials. GENEXCO IT also wants verification that all of GENEXCO's previously identified bugs and problems have been fixed as promised.

There are many things that must be done to have a successful software upgrade. The system administrators must have an approved test plan before testing can begin. Training material must be reviewed in light of the new release and any required modifications made. Training materials (and methods) for current users on the new version's capabilities must also be developed, approved, reproduced, and presented to the software trainers and, ultimately, the end users in each of the user categories.

Leadership has asked for a *Go Live* point in the project plan. *Going Live* means that the software has been installed on the production and development servers, the users have been trained (the identified key users—approximately 80% of total users), and the new software version will be used from that point on. After *Going Live* there will still be some project tasks to complete, such as monitoring the production server performance and upgrading the scenario server.

Before GENEXCO can *Go Live*, there needs to be confirmation that all the users' computers have been upgraded (user computers include all categories of users) including the computer training rooms and all conference rooms that access the *Absolutely-Essential* software.

Before any of the users' computers can be upgraded, the production server must first be upgraded. Since the scenario server is the backup for the production server (during the upgrade testing period), the scenario server can't be upgraded until after the production server is upgraded and performance has been monitored for a month (20 working days). The production server upgrade may be delayed until after IT has been notified and there has been time to schedule the upgrade during a monthly IT maintenance weekend.

Also, before upgrading the users' computers, requests for upgrade must be submitted to IT (along with the user names, upgrade specifics, and installation instructions). GENEXCO's IT managers must be notified in advance that there will be requests coming for upgrades of users' machines. The system administrators must get a list of software users, categorized and prioritized, before they can submit the user names and installation requirements to IT.

Reviews and Approvals

There are multiple reviews and approvals required throughout the upgrade process.

The initial approval is required to begin evaluating the upgraded software. Before getting this approval from senior leadership, the software vendor must provide, at a minimum, notification of upgrade and provide the version-specific *Release Notes* (which contain their installation instructions, bug fixes, enhancements, features, and other comments).

Another approval is required after the high-level test plan is prepared, the GENEXCO preliminary configuration has been determined, the draft GENEXCO installation instructions have been prepared, the software has been received, and the relevance or non-relevance of the new software features has been determined. This senior leadership approval is to load the software and begin testing on the development server, the test computers, and the software training materials person's computer.

The final training materials must be approved before any train-the-trainer materials can be produced. To get to this review/approval, the final version of all training materials must be complete (both upgrade training and full training materials), and the final configuration must have been determined.

After the final GENEXCO installation instructions are complete and a sufficient number of users (typically 80% of the total, all of the high-priority users) have been trained on the upgraded software, it is time for leadership to review and approve deploying the new upgrade to the production server and users. After this approval, the system administrators can request the prioritized user install list and can also begin notifying IT personnel of the coming upgrade, request downtime for upgrade of the production server, and provide IT with the software and the approved installation instructions.

The final review and project closeout approval for the upgrade comes after the upgrade of the scenario server and the confirmation of the successful install and upgrade of all server and user machines.

Software Training Materials

The current software training courses include a software Overview (available for all users), a Planning module, and Execution training for senior leadership and users. Leadership has requested that a separate Task Updating module be created. For each training module, the software training developer must keep in mind the course design: What should the student be able to accomplish after completing the training, how will it be conducted, how many exercises, and what exercises are needed to reinforce the material? The general format used is to *show what*, *show where*, and *show how*, and then reinforce with exercises. After that has been determined, the software training developer can determine the need for screen shots and then build the exercises and materials, including any updates to the instructor notes.

In addition to the full set of software training materials that reflect the new version, the software training developer must determine the training plan for users of the current version: What does each category of user need to know in order to effectively use the new version, how will it be taught, does it need to be presented in the computer training room, and what materials need to be developed? The software training developer is responsible for preparing these materials and getting leadership review and approval before they are presented as well.

Since GENEXCO is not responsible for training the software experts, there are no training materials to update for them; the software vendor will provide that training as part of an ongoing maintenance contract.

The software training developer does not train the end users but is responsible for training the software experts who have been approved to deliver software training on the new training materials as well as the upgrade training.

Before the software training developer can begin drafting the updated materials, they must first understand what is contained in the new release and determine what changes, if any, are required to the configuration. Then they present the findings/recommendations to GENEXCO's senior leadership for review and approval. After approval to proceed, the actual work can begin on drafting the proposed changes. When complete, they are given to the system administrators to incorporate into the usability verification test procedures.

After the system administrators have completed the usability verification, the results must be provided to the software training developer so any required changes to the software training materials and configurations can be incorporated (retested if necessary) and compiled into the final documents to be presented to leadership for approval.

When the final version of the software training materials has been completed, the software training developer can begin practicing and preparing to deliver the train-the-trainer class and the upgrade class for the software experts. When the final version of the configuration has been determined, the computer training rooms can be upgraded to the new version.

Leadership approval of the final training materials kicks off ordering the reproduction of the train-the-trainer set of materials. After the materials are received, the training room is upgraded and training of the software experts can begin. This needs to include upgrading the software experts to the new version (for them as users as well as all the other user functions impacted by the upgrade), training them to deliver the upgrade training materials, training them to deliver the full training materials upgraded to the new version, and teaching them how to load, use, and remove the training databases.

When training the software trainers is complete, the end user training materials can be reproduced, and the end user training can begin. After a sufficient number of each of the user categories has trained on the new version (typically 80%), and the final installation instructions have been completed, it's time for leadership to review and approve deploying the software to the production server and installing the software on all of the different categories of user machines.

Software Upgrade Testing Process

GENEXCO IT requires a test plan and test procedures for every software upgrade as well as a test report documenting the results of testing. The high-level test plan is based on templates received from GENEXCO's testing personnel as well as the IT procedure information section. It summarizes the types of testing that will be performed during the test phase, testing the overall functionality of the software, testing compatibility with new and existing third-party software, testing scenarios from the updated draft training materials, and testing the proposed configuration settings. The high-level test plan must be reviewed and approved by leadership before the software can be loaded onto the development server and the computers that will be used for testing in the various user categories. The system administrators can begin developing the functional verification cases (related to how the software interfaces with the existing software and hardware infrastructure, whether existing functionality is maintained, compatibility with third-party software, verifying the customized written installation instructions, etc.). Note: Also, before the new software can be loaded onto the development server, the system administrators must notify the software experts that the scenario server is no longer available for their use (it must serve as the production server backup during upgrade testing), the scenario server must be verified as being in the production server configuration, and the development server database must be refreshed to match the current production server database.

Functional verification cases must be complete before installing the software on the development server and on the computers that will be used for testing in the various user categories. After the upgrade of the development server to the new release, the functional verification cases can proceed according to the written procedures. Once the functional verification has been completed, the results can be incorporated into the test report and the final GENEXCO installation instructions can be written (making any required modifications to the draft instructions that were discovered during testing).

Writing the usability verification cases cannot begin until the draft training materials for all user categories (including software experts) have been created. After the usability verification cases are complete, the system administrators can begin that verification. When complete, the results are incorporated into the test report (which must be submitted for leadership review). Additionally, the results need to be coordinated with the software training developer so that any discrepancies (in configuration and/or training materials) can be fixed and, if necessary, retested.

Software Installations

Software must be installed on the development server (for upgrade testing), on the training servers and computers (but the training rooms do not have to be upgraded simultaneously, depending upon the training plan), on the production server, on the scenario server, on all software experts' computers, on all of the campus conference rooms' computers that use the software, on the web interface users' computers, on the project managers' and network builders' computers, and on the computer used by the GENEXCO headquarters software expert responsible for training materials. The system administrators must also have access to computers to use during testing that can be configured for the various user categories.

GENEXCO IT is responsible for upgrading the servers and all of the users including at headquarters, except as noted below. Installation on the production server is performed during scheduled IT maintenance weekends; this means the system administrators must request the install and IT must approve and schedule the upgrade for a regular IT maintenance weekend (there can be delays of up to six weeks between the time of request and the install date). Software administrators coordinate the scheduling of all installations and must provide customized installation instructions for each category of user and machine. The system administrators must notify IT management of the impending upgrade before they (the system administrators) can submit and queue the user upgrade requests (these must be in place before IT upgrades the production server). Separate sets of user upgrade requests are required; these include upgrading the software experts (although the system administrators will do these upgrades), upgrading the project managers and network builders, upgrading the Internet-only users, upgrading the conference rooms, and upgrading any remaining computer training rooms. Whereas all users can be upgraded simultaneously, the preference is to upgrade the software experts, then project managers and network builders, and only then the Internet-only users (conference rooms can be updated at any time). Since *Going Live* cannot occur until a significant number and types of installs have been successfully completed, the system administrators must have a process to confirm the successful installations by the various support IT personnel.

The system administrators use the software vendor's version-specific *Release Notes* and the vendor's *Installation and Configuration Guide* as well as campus installation instructions and guidelines to compile the required installation instructions. These draft installation instructions must be verified during testing, and then the final campus installation are instructions prepared and distributed to IT for all of the different types of user and server installations. The required installation instructions include those for server installation, software experts' computers, project managers' and network builders' computers, Internet-based users' computers, as well as secondary instructions for upgrade only of both the software experts' computers and the project managers' and network builders' computers.

Potential Project Risks/Delays

There are several potential delays during the upgrade process (usually a waiting period after requesting work from GENEXCO support organizations). Scheduling reviews/approvals can also cause delays.

Questions

4. Using the steps in Chapter 14 and the expanded case study above, create the backbone of the project.
5. Using the steps in Chapter 15, the expanded case study above, and the backbone created above, complete the skeleton of the project.
6. Using Chapter 16 and the expanded case study above, complete the forward pass on the skeleton created above.
7. Using the outputs from Steps 1 and 4, check the case study project network against the results of the stakeholders' meeting. Make any required adjustments.
8. Using the output of Step 5 and the expanded case study, identify the critical resource skill levels and quantities and resource continuity, if any.

Case Study for Steps 8 through 10

Summary

As an internal improvement project, the Generic Example Company (GENEXCO) is upgrading its current *Absolutely-Essential* software to the most current release. Upgrading to a new software release means that all user machines, conference room machines, training room machines, applicable servers, software training materials, and users must be modified/upgraded. It's important to GENEXCO that the upgrade be completed with all the required support and knowledge in place on a timely basis, that the end product delivered to the users is fully functional (both old and new features), and that the users are satisfied with the new release.

Environment

GENEXCO has users spread across multiple locations, with computers and servers connected via high-speed network. There are currently 700 users of the *Absolutely-Essential* software in various user categories (with more being added almost daily). Senior management in each division as well as in GENEXCO's headquarters access the software over the Internet to see the status of various projects on a daily basis. Users access the software on their computers during planning and while in execution to check status, ensure the correct tasks are being started, view upcoming tasks, and plan for and execute any required recovery plans. Users also access the software to determine where to assign their resources (start tasks), look at resource loading projections, and perform daily updates on in-progress tasks. There are software experts in most locations who provide software support, as well as planning and execution support. GENEXCO has two *Absolutely-Essential* system administrators (IT personnel) who perform the upgrade testing, set up and maintain user accounts, maintain the configuration, monitor server performance, and serve as liaisons from the *Absolutely-Essential* software to the GENEXCO IT personnel.

The *Absolutely-Essential* software uses Oracle on the production server; however, the software training developer uses Access. The *Absolutely-Essential* software also uses Java. Most of the reports are exportable to Excel. The software has multiple modules, most of which are accessible via the Internet; however, both users and software experts also have specific modules on their desktop computers.

GENEXCO is currently using several servers to support its *Absolutely-Essential* software use. The production server is where the operational database resides. The development server is the backup for the production server except when upgrade testing is in process; during that time, the scenario server becomes the backup for production. Otherwise the scenario server is used on a reservation basis to test different modeling assumptions/scenarios. GENEXCO has access to five training rooms and has the software loaded on the servers in each room. Additionally, the expert in charge of the training materials has an additional computer on their desk configured (using Access) as a server in order to produce and check training materials, as well as to create screen shots for all materials and presentations.

Software Upgrade Process

The software experts want a guarantee that there will be minimal user disruption and downtime when the software is upgraded. The system administrators need to ensure that the new software functionality is verified prior to release. They are also concerned that any database conversions are done successfully and that there are no major surprises after the new software is deployed to the users. The new software release must not cause any system performance degradation. The software training developer needs to understand the changes in the new release before recommending any configuration modifications and before determining which software training materials must be upgraded or modified. The software training materials must be modified before testing can start (the usability verification) because that testing is performed using those modified training materials. GENEXCO IT also wants verification that all of GENEXCO's previously identified bugs and problems have been fixed as promised.

There are many things that must be done to have a successful software upgrade. The system administrators must have an approved test plan before testing can begin. Training material must be reviewed in light of the new release and any required modifications made. Training materials (and methods) for current users on the new version's capabilities must also be developed, approved, reproduced, and presented to the software trainers and, ultimately, the end users in each of the user categories.

Leadership has asked for a *Go Live* point in the project plan. *Going Live* means that the software has been installed on the production and development servers, the users have been trained (the identified key users—approximately 80% of total users), and the new software version will be used from that point on. After *Going Live* there will still be some project tasks to complete, such as monitoring the production server performance and upgrading the scenario server.

Before GENEXCO can *Go Live*, there needs to be confirmation that all the users' computers have been upgraded (user computers include all categories of users) including the computer training rooms and all conference rooms that access the *Absolutely-Essential* software.

Before any of the users' computers can be upgraded, the production server must first be upgraded. Since the scenario server is the backup for the production server (during the upgrade testing period), the scenario server can't be upgraded until after the production server is upgraded and performance has been monitored for a month (20 working days). The production server upgrade may be delayed until after IT has been notified and there has been time to schedule the upgrade during a monthly IT maintenance weekend.

Also, before upgrading the users' computers, requests for upgrade must be submitted to IT (along with the user names, upgrade specifics, and installation instructions). GENEXCO's IT managers must be notified in advance that there will be requests coming for upgrades of users' machines. The system administrators must get a list of software users, categorized and prioritized, before they can submit the user names and installation requirements to IT.

Reviews and Approvals

There are multiple reviews and approvals required throughout the upgrade process.

The initial approval is required to begin evaluating the upgraded software (2d, 6d). Note that the task time convention shown here represents (ambitious time, standard time) with "d" representing days and "h" representing hours. Before getting this approval from senior leadership, the software vendor must provide, at a minimum, notification of upgrade and provide the version-specific *Release Notes* (which contain their installation instructions, bug fixes, enhancements, features, and other comments).

Another approval (2d, 6d) is required after the high-level test plan is prepared (10d, 22d), the GENEXCO preliminary configuration has been determined (6d, 16d), the draft GENEXCO installation instructions have been prepared (7d, 24d), the software has been received, and the relevance or non-relevance of the new software features has been determined (3d, 9d). This senior leadership approval is to load the software and begin testing on the development server, the test computers, and the software training materials person's computer.

The final training materials must be approved (2d, 6d) before any train-the-trainer materials can be produced (2d, 8d). To get to this review/approval, the final version of all training materials must be complete (both upgrade training and full training materials [6d, 17d]), and the final configuration must have been determined (1d, 3d).

After the final GENEXCO installation instructions are complete (1d, 4d) and a sufficient number of users (typically 80% of the total, all of the high-priority users) have been trained on the upgraded software (9d, 24d), it is time for leadership to review and approve deploying the new upgrade to the production server and users (1d, 4d). After this approval, the system administrators can request the prioritized user install list (0.2d, 0.5d) and can also begin notifying IT personnel of the coming upgrade (0.5d, 1d), request downtime for upgrade of the production server, and provide IT with the software and the approved installation instructions ([1.5d, 5d] for sending requests, providing software, and installation instructions).

The final review and project closeout approval for the upgrade (1d, 3d) comes after the upgrade of the scenario server (2d, 5d) and the confirmation of the successful install and upgrade of all server and user machines ([0.1d, 2d] each to confirm upgrades of servers, users, training rooms, and conference rooms).

Software Training Materials

The current software training courses include a software Overview (available for all users), a Planning module, and Execution training for senior leadership and users. Leadership has requested that a separate Task Updating module be created. For each training module, the software training developer must keep in mind the course design: What should the student be able to accomplish after completing the training, how will it be conducted, how many exercises, and what exercises are needed to reinforce the material? The general format used is to *show what*, *show where*, and *show how*, and then reinforce with exercises. After that has been determined, the software training developer can determine the need for screen shots and then build the exercises and materials, including any updates to the instructor notes.

In addition to the full set of software training materials that reflect the new version, the software training developer must determine the training plan for users of the current version: What does each category of user need to know in order to effectively use the new version, how will it be taught, does it need to be presented in the computer training room, and what materials need to be developed? The software training developer is responsible for preparing these materials and getting leadership review and approval before they are presented as well.

Since GENEXCO is not responsible for training the software experts, there are no training materials to update for them; the software vendor will provide that training as part of an ongoing maintenance contract.

The software training developer does not train the end users, but is responsible for training the software experts who have been approved to deliver software training on the new training materials as well as the upgrade training.

Before the software training developer can begin drafting the updated materials, they must first understand what is contained in the new release and determine what changes, if any, are required to the configuration (6d, 17d). Then they present the findings/recommendations to GENEXCO's senior leadership for review and approval. After approval to proceed, the actual work can begin on drafting the proposed changes (Draft software training materials [28d, 91d] broken down as follows: Overview [3d, 5d], Planning [10d, 35d], Senior leadership execution [3d, 8d], Users' execution [9d, 38d], and Task updating [3d, 5d]). When complete, they are given to the system administrators to incorporate into the usability verification test procedures.

After the system administrators have completed the usability verification, the results must be provided to the software training developer so any required changes to the software training materials (5d, 20d) and configurations (1d, 3d) can be incorporated (retested if necessary) and compiled into the final documents to be presented to leadership for approval.

When the final version of the software training materials has been completed, the software training developer can begin practicing and preparing to deliver the train-the-trainer class and the upgrade class for the software experts (4d, 14d). When the final version of the configuration has been determined, the computer training rooms can be upgraded to the new version (3d, 7d).

Leadership approval of the final training materials kicks off ordering the reproduction of the train-the-trainer set of materials (0.1d, 0.5d). After the materials are received, and the training room has been upgraded, training of the software experts can begin. This needs to include upgrading the software experts to the new version (for them as users as well as all the other user functions impacted by the upgrade), training them to deliver the upgrade training materials, training them to deliver the full training materials upgraded to the new version, and teaching them how to load, use, and remove the training databases (3d, 4d).

When training the software trainers is complete, the end user training materials can be reproduced (4d, 12d), and the end user training can begin (10d, 20d). After a sufficient number of each of the user categories has trained on the new version (typically 80%), and the final installation instructions have been completed, it's time for leadership to review and approve deploying the software to the production server and installing the software on all of the different categories of user machines (3d, 10d).

Software Upgrade Testing Process

GENEXCO IT requires a test plan and test procedures for every software upgrade as well as a test report documenting the results of testing. The high-level test plan (8d, 15d) is based on templates received from GENEXCO's testing personnel as well as the IT procedure information section. It summarizes the types of testing that will be performed during the test phase, testing the overall functionality of the software, testing compatibility with new and existing third-party software, testing scenarios from the updated draft training materials, and testing the proposed configuration settings. The high-level test plan must be reviewed and approved by leadership (1d, 3d) before the software can be loaded onto the development server and the computers that will be used for testing in the various user categories (3d, 14d). The system administrators can begin developing the functional verification cases (related to how the software interfaces with the existing software and hardware infrastructure, whether existing functionality is maintained, compatibility with third-party software, verifying the customized written installation instructions, etc.) (10d, 25d). Note: Also, before the new software can be loaded onto the development server, the system administrators must notify the software experts that the scenario server is no longer available for their use (0.1d, 0.5d) (it must serve as the production server backup during upgrade testing), the scenario server must be verified as being in the production server configuration (1d, 3d), and the development server database must be refreshed to match the current production server database (1d, 3d).

Functional verification cases must be complete (10d, 25d) before installing the software on the development server and on the computers that will be used for testing in the various user categories (3d, 12d). After the upgrade of the development server to the new release, the functional verification cases can proceed according to the written procedures (10d, 20d). Once the functional verification has been completed, the results can be incorporated into the test report and the final GENEXCO installation instructions can be written (making any required modifications to the draft instructions that were discovered during testing).

Writing the usability verification cases cannot begin until the draft training materials for all user categories (including software experts) have been created. After the usability verification cases are complete (10d, 18d), the system administrators can begin that verification (10d, 35d). When complete, the results are incorporated into the test report (which must be submitted for leadership review). Additionally, the results need to be coordinated with the software training developer so that any discrepancies (in configuration and/or training materials) can be fixed and, if necessary, retested.

Software Installations

Software must be installed on the development server (for upgrade testing), on the training servers and computers (but the training rooms do not have to be upgraded simultaneously, depending upon the training plan), on the production server, on the scenario server, on all software experts' computers, on all of the campus conference rooms' computers that use the software, on the web interface users' computers, on the project managers' and network builders' computers, and on the computer used by the GENEXCO headquarters software expert responsible for training materials. The system administrators must also have access to computers to use during testing that can be configured for the various user categories.

GENEXCO IT is responsible for upgrading the servers and all of the users including at headquarters, except as noted below. Installation on the production server (1.5d, 2.5d) is performed during scheduled IT maintenance weekends; this means the system administrators must request the install and IT must approve and schedule the upgrade for a regular IT maintenance weekend (there can be delays of up to six weeks between the time of request and the install date). Software administrators coordinate the scheduling of all installations and must provide customized installation instructions for each category of user and machine. The system administrators must notify IT management of the impending upgrade (0.5d, 1d) before they (the system administrators) can submit and queue the user upgrade requests (these must be in place before IT upgrades the production server) (1d, 4d). Separate sets of user upgrade requests are required; these include upgrading the software experts (although the system administrators will do these upgrades), upgrading the project managers and network builders, upgrading the Internet-only users, upgrading the conference rooms, and upgrading any remaining computer training rooms. Whereas all users can be upgraded simultaneously, the preference is to upgrade the software experts (7d, 20d), then project managers and network builders (2d, 5d), and only then the Internet-only users (2d, 6d) (conference rooms can be updated at any time [2d, 6d]). Since *Going Live* cannot occur until a significant number and types of installs have been successfully completed, the system administrators must have a process to confirm the successful installations by the various support IT personnel ([0.1d, 1d] each to confirm upgrade of project managers' and network builders' machines, conference room machines, and Internet-only user machines).

The system administrators use the software vendor's version-specific *Release Notes* and the vendor's *Installation and Configuration Guide* as well as campus installation instructions and guidelines to compile the required installation instructions (10d, 20d). These draft installation instructions must be verified during testing and then the final campus installation instructions are prepared (1d, 3d) and distributed to IT for all of the different types of user and server installations. The required installation instructions include those for server installation, software experts' computers, project managers' and network builders' computers, Internet-based users' computers, as well as secondary instructions for upgrade only of both the software experts' computers and the project managers' and network builders' computers.

Potential Project Risks/Delays

There are several potential delays during the upgrade process (usually a waiting period after requesting work from GENEXCO support organizations). These include a one- to three-day delay for a refresh of the development server database from the production database (the system administrators must request the refresh from the database administrator [0.1d, 0.5d]), who coordinates it with IT to agree on a time, and then both IT and the database administrator perform the refresh and notify the system administrators that it's complete ([1d, 4d] to perform refresh and notification).

Expect a month-long (20-day) delay after upgrading the production server to allow the system administrator to monitor system performance with all users (20d, 20d). Once the month has passed, the scenario server can be upgraded; the development server will once again perform as backup server for the production server.

Expect it to take about three to ten days to get training materials reproduced—one delay to get the train-the-trainer materials (3d, 10d) and another delay to get the user training materials (3d, 10d).

The estimate is two to six weeks from the time the request is submitted to have the production server upgraded (during a regularly scheduled IT maintenance weekend) until the upgrade occurs (10d, 30d); if the schedule is already full, the upgrade could be pushed to the next month.

Endnote

1. Trademarks: Oracle is a registered trademark of Oracle Corporation. Excel and Access are trademarks or registered trademarks of Microsoft Corporation. Java is a registered trademark of Sun Microsystems, Inc.

Questions

9. Using Chapter 20 and the information in this section of the case, update (and modify if necessary) the project network.
10. Using the updated project network above, identify the paths and tasks, in priority order, for duration reduction reviews.

Bibliography

Collins, J., and M. T. Hansen. *Great by Choice*. New York: HarperCollins, 2011.

Dinsmore, P. C., and J. Cabanis-Brewin. *AMA Handbook of Project Management*. 2nd ed. New York: AMACOM Books, 2006.

Goldratt, E. M. *Critical Chain*. Great Barrington, MA: North River Press, 1997.

Goldratt, E. M. *Necessary but Not Sufficient*. Great Barrington, MA: North River Press, 2000.

Kendall, G. I. *Viable Vision*. Boca Raton, FL: J. Ross Publishing, 2004.

Kendall, G. I., and S. C. Rollins. *Advanced Project Portfolio Management and the PMO*. Boca Raton, FL: J. Ross Publishing, 2003.

Newbold, R. C. *Billion Dollar Solution*. Lake Ridge, VA: ProChain Press, 2008.

Newbold, R. C. *Project Management in the Fast Lane*. Boca Raton, FL: CRC Press, 1998.

Scherer, A. *Be Fast or Be Gone*. Lake Ridge, VA: ProChain Press, 2011.

Wheeler, D. *Understanding Variation: The Key to Managing Chaos*. 2nd ed. Knoxville, TN: SPC Press, 2000.

Index

ABB 95
activate new projects 69, 211
activation 56, 82, 92, 225–226, 234, 258, 277–278, 333
additional dependencies 44, 107
Advanced Project Portfolio Management and the PMO 92, 209, 294
aggregated buffers 189
Alcan-Rio Tinto 95–97
aligning multiple projects 197
alignment strategy 222
ambitious load times 248
ambitious time 159–163, 168, 182–187, 192, 197, 202, 232–238, 246–249
Apple 90, 278–279
arrows 107, 121–126, 131, 134, 139, 172
auditing 275, 281

backbone 43, 107, 119, 122–129, 130, 134
backward pass 144
bank account 184–185
Be Fast or Be Gone 92
Billion Dollar Solution 92
Blackberry 278
blocking issues 10, 32–36, 65–66, 159, 253–255, 289–299
Boeing 95
bottleneck 6, 19, 199, 269, 275, 287, 290, 310, 321
boxes 107, 121–123, 181, 310
budget 66–67, 82, 98, 100, 112–116, 170, 175, 191, 207–208, 211, 245, 248, 265, 276–279, 293, 301
buffer 9–14, 27–29, 33–36, 43–46, 49–54, 59, 64–66, 69, 82–83, 86–87, 92, 181–190, 197, 199, 202–204, 214–223, 231–241, 245–249, 327–331, 337–349
buffer management 92, 239
buffer penetration 65, 232–238, 245–247, 344
buffer recovery plan 234, 238, 243–244, 348
buffer status 86–87, 208, 233, 235, 240, 245–248
Business Week 272
buy-in 13, 192, 292, 351–354, 361–365

capacity elevation 74, 293–294, 304
capacity elevation team 74–79, 288, 293–294, 304
cloud computing 90–92, 327, 333
common cause 53, 179, 201–204, 249, 306

completion criteria 134, 147–151, 160–168, 170, 175, 183, 203, 234–237, 243–247
continuous improvement 275, 279–280
Contractual milestone (CMS) 115, 187–189, 222, 231–233, 246
Contractual milestone buffer (CMSB) 187, 231–232, 238–240, 246–247, 348
critical chain 8, 75, 86, 167–173, 181, 187, 225–226, 231–244, 303, 328–331
critical equipment 149
critical path 8, 51, 75, 167–172, 181, 187–188, 225, 231, 238, 240, 244, 331
critical resource 4, 21–22, 57, 67, 82, 147–151, 155, 211–219, 225, 234–238, 290, 318, 328

daily task management 51, 287
daily task review 35–36, 53, 232
daily task update 159, 234
delay 19–22, 31–36, 41–42, 55, 148–152, 163, 171–176, 194–199, 229–237, 244–248, 257–277, 325, 327, 331, 349
delayed start 244–246
deliverables 26, 107–108, 113–116, 120–126, 143–144, 156, 167, 175, 189, 203, 211, 262, 269–277
Deming, Dr. W. Edwards 53, 279

entry point 124, 126
Erickson 95
execution 8–14, 25–34, 39–43, 50–70, 77–79, 103, 137–148, 150–151, 160–168, 179–257, 275–287, 321–325, 337–347, 354–355, 360
Exepron 82–83, 90–92
exit criteria (see also completion criteria) 51, 65, 105, 144, 235, 287, 303
expected workload 288
expert scrutiny 155–156, 175, 203

fast-track issue resolution 14, 22, 34, 51, 65, 66, 70, 159, 253–255, 287–299, 347–349
feeding buffer (FB) 183–187, 216, 222–225, 231–238
feeding path 169, 183–186, 203, 238
finish to start 126
firefighting 17, 98
Ford, Henry 314
forward pass 137–140, 203
freeze projects 5, 8, 32–33, 56, 66, 82–84, 212, 253–259, 275, 282, 299, 306, 318–320
Fukushima Daiichi Nuclear Power Plant 337
full kit 69, 91, 159, 170, 229, 257–263, 287
full kit manager 257–262
full kit meeting 257–263
full kit process 12, 257–263
full kit template 258–263
fully loaded 192–193, 248–249, 288, 320

Gantt 14, 25, 343
gating 299, 333–334
Goldratt, Dr. Eliyahu 167
governance 82–84, 275–278
green region (see also green zone) 233–240, 246
green zone (see also green region) 64–65, 239, 340

Harvard Business Review 192, 195
holistic 82–86, 92, 99, 175–179, 313, 327, 330

IAG Consulting 276–277
ideation 266–268, 303
incorrect input 138
incorrect intervention 201–202
increase multi-project flow 305
independent causes of variation 301
Influencer: The Power to Change Anything 303–306
insulation 25–28, 52, 181–184, 188–204, 214, 231–235
iPhone 328–333
iteration variability 163–166, 176, 187–188

Johnson, Jim 49

Keeley, Larry 272
Kendall, Gerald 92, 294

leadership 44, 119, 183, 213, 275, 353–354
level of detail 9, 41–42, 105–108, 125, 287, 289
leverage point 1, 33, 73, 81, 183, 267–269, 285, 302
Lohr, Steve 195
long lead 114, 151–152, 163, 172, 261
longer term 36, 74, 298, 317–321

management capacity 298
management review 265–276, 289
Management Roundtable 272–273
managing project buffers 232
master resource pool 289
measurable goals 43, 107–108
medium term 317–320
metrics 12, 13, 95–100, 280
Microsoft 91
Microsoft Project Server 91
missed dependency 42
missing inputs 138
missing task 139–141
Multi-Project Mancala 355–358
multi-project software 6, 39, 81–82, 226
multitasking 13–14, 21–22, 32–36, 58–60, 78–82, 99, 148, 170, 191–193, 198–204, 212, 234, 268, 291–298, 327–331, 339, 342–345, 360–363
Murphy 33, 63, 344
must have 120–122, 172

named resources 26, 41, 147
network 8–9, 12–14, 25–29, 33, 39–46, 63–69, 103–108, 114–167, 170–203, 221, 299, 311, 354, 363
Newbold, Robert 91–92
New York Times 192–195
non-intervention 203
non-project work 153, 183, 191–192, 244–245, 290

Ohno, Dr. Taiichi 314
on budget 7–8, 42, 49–54, 63, 79, 98, 100–103, 140, 208, 222, 277–279, 301, 363
on time 7–8, 32, 42, 49–54, 63–69, 79, 86, 97–103, 113, 140, 163, 199, 205–208, 222, 277–279, 293, 301–304, 310, 318–321, 345, 363
operational capacity 310
operational data 99–100
operations 63, 69, 88, 179, 193–195, 204, 272, 285, 302, 309–315, 335, 360–361

operations demand 311
operations management 310–311
origin 186
Oxford Radcliffe Hospitals 305–306

path start 43, 124–126, 131–138, 150–153, 162, 225–226, 235, 244
path start date 225–226
Patterson, Kerry 306
periodic review 314–315
PERT 12–14, 25, 343
Peschke, Dr. Richard 204
placement 181–184
planned start date 73, 279, 341
PMBOK 337
portfolio 56, 60, 67–70, 82, 149, 208, 275–282, 289–293, 317–335, 341–347
portfolio of projects 67, 149, 317, 343–345
Post-It® 120–122, 130
prioritized task availability list 245–247, 349
priority list 194–198, 208, 248
ProChain Solutions 56, 91, 92
Proctor & Gamble 95
project activation 226, 258, 277–278, 333
project assessment 44
project backlog 97
project buffer (PB) 54, 64–69, 82–92, 182–189, 202–203, 216, 222–225, 231–240, 245–246, 288, 318–320, 330, 348–349
project cycle time 96
project due date 114, 181, 202–209, 214–218, 225
project duration 7, 10, 22, 34–36, 44, 50, 64, 74, 79–86, 92–100, 122, 166–172, 191, 240, 330–331
project duration reduction 95–97, 168
project flow 14, 17, 22, 77–79, 89, 98, 205, 229, 255, 262–263, 271–272, 277–281, 305–311, 343
project management 7, 14, 33, 45–49, 77–79, 84–92, 96, 100, 152, 165, 280, 288–290, 325–329, 335, 363
Project Management in the Fast Lane 92
project management software 77–79, 88–96, 152, 222, 321–335, 343–344
project manager 6, 9, 12, 14, 27–34, 41–46, 52, 65–70, 82–92, 103, 119, 169, 182, 194, 202–203, 231–249, 253–255, 262–263, 289, 297–304, 313, 319, 329–331, 338–340, 345–349, 356, 363
project metrics 96
project network (see network)
project outcomes 53, 111
project pipeline 268, 290
project plan (see also network) 8, 12–14, 20–25, 33–34, 41–46, 54, 66, 73–79, 83, 91, 103–106, 116, 148–149, 156–159, 175–179, 187, 199, 222, 277, 288–289, 312, 321, 327–333, 340, 354, 363
project portfolio review process 275, 281
project priorities 66, 85, 198, 205–209, 222, 231
project sponsor 67–70, 86, 90, 261, 314
project status 86–87, 235, 345
project WIP 56, 212
proper synchronization 212, 217, 222

quarterly review meetings 321

Realization 56, 91
receivable 152

recovery options 168, 234–237, 249
recovery plan 52, 65–67, 234–240, 243–244, 319, 348
red region (see also red zone) 233–240, 246
red zone (see also red region) 59, 65–66, 74–80, 85–88, 99, 238–239, 276–282, 298–306, 318–320, 340
red zone statistics 76
relay runner 19, 225–226, 318
remaining duration 165, 247–248
Research in Motion 278–279
resource availability 28, 58, 248
resource capacity elevation 293
resource constraints 79, 84, 168, 317–322, 392
resource continuity 149
resource dependencies 8, 9, 167, 181, 287, 328–331
resource histograms 192, 248, 288, 349
resource insulation 191–193
resource issues 79, 92, 159, 317, 318–322
resource leveling 84, 148
resource loading 19, 35, 43, 73–79, 84, 105, 192–193, 248–249, 322, 340
resource management 77–80, 82, 89–91, 294, 317
resource manager 9–10, 19, 26, 31–35, 52, 59, 70–78, 85–89, 103, 137–141, 149–169, 191, 207, 234–238, 243–251, 254, 287–293, 319–321, 331, 340–363
resource overload 74, 249, 288, 319–322, 347
resource pools 13, 60, 67, 73–79, 148–153, 160, 170, 195, 288–292, 303–304, 319–320, 327–334, 344
resource skill set 22–26, 45, 57, 74–79, 84, 89, 119, 162, 192, 212, 287–290, 320, 322, 327–329, 332
resource utilization trend 344
review of operations flow and productivity 314–315
rework 6, 12, 20, 29, 31–36, 65–68, 89, 140, 148, 159, 170–177, 192, 211, 245, 255–263, 280, 287, 303, 319, 331, 339
risk assessment 107, 108
risk avoidance 44–46, 125, 137, 143, 177
risk mitigation 45, 125, 165, 175–177, 271–273
risks 10, 29, 35, 43–46, 51, 65–66, 103, 107–108, 113–116, 121–125, 137, 141–144, 165–168, 175–177, 183–185, 201–204, 221–225, 248–249, 259, 266–278, 289–293, 330, 340
Rollins, Steven 92, 209, 294

SaaS (Software as a Service) 90–92
Scherer, Andreas 92
Schwartz, Tony 195
scientific curiosity 281
Sciforma 91
Scitor 91
scope change 6, 26–27, 50, 68
scope creep 9, 25–27, 67–68, 87, 111–116, 143, 272, 298, 318, 338–339
scrutinize 9, 27, 44, 107–108, 156
senior management 11, 19–22, 32, 52, 56, 66, 69, 70, 77–82, 87–90, 98, 100, 159, 205, 214, 237, 240, 253–258, 263, 270, 275–281, 290, 294, 299, 305, 311–313, 319–321, 328, 338, 353–362
shared resources 197–198, 208
shock absorber 9, 179, 184, 202

short term 43, 89, 211, 290, 297, 317–319
Siemens 95
silo approach 310
single priority system 66, 82–85, 92–96, 99, 159, 199, 345
sister project 310–313
sizing 50, 184–188, 189, 204
skeleton 44, 107, 129, 130–134
SNET (start no earlier than) 152, 163
software solutions 6, 90, 325
span of control 304–306
special cause 53, 179, 201–204, 240
spine (see also backbone) 119, 129
sponsor criteria 43–44, 107–116, 121, 143
stage gate 14, 188, 229, 258–279
stage gate process 14, 258–273
staggering mechanism 57–60, 218
stagger projects 56–60, 82–85
stakeholder needs 9, 12–14, 25, 42–45, 106–107, 111, 119–126, 134, 143, 155–156, 171–175
stakeholders 9, 42–45, 67, 106, 112–114, 120–126, 132, 143, 167–175, 199, 226, 278, 363
standard time 160–168, 181–186, 192
statistics 26, 50, 74–76, 160, 167, 279, 304–306, 363
strategic planning for project resources 322
strategic view 293, 321
strategy and tactics 13, 361–364
subject matter expert 28, 42, 65, 74, 107–108, 149–156, 162, 344
success criteria 26, 269
supervisors 297–306, 318–319, 327
synchronization 212–214, 217–218, 221–226, 231, 358
synchronization buffer 214–217, 222–226, 231
synchronizer 212–218
system under control 279, 294–299

tactical view 293, 321
tangible benefit 68, 269, 313
tangible deliverables 26, 113–116, 120–125, 143–144, 167, 203, 211, 277
tangible scope 43, 107–108, 395–396
task completion criteria (see also completion criteria and exit criteria) 147–151, 160–164, 168–170, 175, 183, 234–237, 243–247
task content 28
task dependencies 45, 137–141, 167–170, 188–189, 329–332
task estimate 9, 25–28, 155–169, 183, 238
task execution 14, 150, 201
task format 122, 130
task interdependency diagram (see also network) 143
task manager 53–55, 65, 70, 88, 247, 279, 332, 339
task note 108, 134, 143, 148–156, 162–164, 175
task priority 66, 205–208, 234, 248, 338, 344
task status 51, 82–86, 344
task update 87, 159–165, 194, 203, 234, 240–248, 344–348
Tata Steel 95
template 44–46, 107–108, 143, 258–259, 288, 321–322, 327–333
theme 155–156
throughput 33, 95–100

time descriptor 162
time durations 45, 97, 107–108, 168, 360
time estimates (see also task estimates) 44–45, 79, 121, 156, 159–175, 181–189, 202–203, 248, 330
timeline 67, 106, 112, 175, 225–226, 234
tsunami 337–343

U.S. Air Force 95–98
uncertainty 10, 28
utilization trends 74–75

variability factor 182–188, 217
visual management 329, 338–344

wait task 152
WBS (work breakdown structure) 106–109
what if analysis 70, 82–85, 205, 221–222, 290, 333
Wikipedia 92, 109, 167–173, 266–273
within scope 7–8, 42, 49, 54, 79, 98–103, 116, 140–144, 208, 222, 277–279, 298–301, 363
wrong action 203–204

yellow region (see also yellow zone) 233, 240, 246
yellow zone (see also yellow region) 64–65, 240, 340